Genesis ROGERS' RANGERS

The First Green Berets

The Corps & The Revivals

April 6, 1758–December 24, 1783

WITH MAPS AND UNIFORM PLATE BY THE AUTHOR

BURT GARFIELD LOESCHER

HERITAGE BOOKS
2008

TO THAT OTHER SEQUEL
MY SON
GILBURT DAMIAN LOESCHER
THIS BOOK IS AFFECTIONATELY DEDICATED

HERITAGE BOOKS
AN IMPRINT OF HERITAGE BOOKS, INC.

Books, CDs, and more—Worldwide

For our listing of thousands of titles see our website at
www.HeritageBooks.com

A Facsimile Reprint with Additional Illustrations
Published 2008 by
HERITAGE BOOKS, INC.
Publishing Division
100 Railroad Ave. #104
Westminster, Maryland 21157

Copyright © 1969, 2000 Burt Garfield Loescher

Other books by the author:

The History of Rogers' Rangers, Volume I:
The Beginnings, January 1755-April 6, 1758

The History of Rogers' Rangers, Volume III:
Officers and Non-Commissioned Officers

The History of Rogers' Rangers, Volume IV: The St. Francis Raid

Library of Congress Catalog Card Number: 46:-20688

All rights reserved. No part of this book may be reproduced or transmitted in any form or by any means, electronic or mechanical, including photocopying, recording or by any information storage and retrieval system without written permission from the author, except for the inclusion of brief quotations in a review.

International Standard Book Numbers
Paperbound: 978-0-7884-4752-5
Clothbound: 978-0-7884-1575-3

PREFACE TO THE SECOND EDITION

I want to thank all of my friends (and all Rogers' Rangerists are my friends). They are, as I have always been, devotees to Rogers' Rangers and to Major Robert Rogers, who justifiably earned the never ending admiration of his followers.

As the time of our existence quickens, it prompts one—who since 1946 has created over 800,000 words in eight books on the hypnotic appeal of Rogers' Rangers—to recognize this widespread fascination in "Rangerana."

An awareness of our desire to be part of the Rangers' history is most rewarding. The expression of this desire is really an effort to be a part of our early Americana, and this is most commendable.

As my vast collection was created to be enjoyed by many, I am happy to present this reprint of my Volume II by Heritage Books, Inc., encouraged by the the enthusiam of President Leslie Towle and Senior Editor Roxanne Carlson.

Volume II, *Genesis: Rogers' Rangers - The First Green Berets*, is my best work on the *complete* history of Rogers' Rangers and Rogers. It starts immediately after their crushing defeat at Rogers' Rock and continues through their various formations and actions and to the end of our American Revolution. The appendices provide copious details of unlimited value to the dedicated Rangerist.

If time permits others of my unpublished books will follow, which go into even greater detail on specific events connected with Rogers' Rangers.

Burt Loescher
July, 2000

— Publisher's Notice —
Frequent references in this book
direct the reader to contact the author regarding his other works.
The author now asks that all queries be directed to:
Heritage Books, Inc.
1540E Pointer Ridge Place, Bowie, MD 20716

ACKNOWLEDGMENTS

For their generous assistance in furnishing material for this History and for their words of advice and encouragement - the author is most deeply grateful to the following living or deceased :

Fred M. Caswell, Manchester, New Hampshire.
Reverend Thomas M. Charland, O.P., Historian of Les Abenakis, Montreal.
Buchanan Charles, President, Grand Manan Historical Society.
William C. Copper, Dundalk, Maryland.
Robert C. Davis, Madison, Wisconsin. For help on Tute and Atherton.
Genevieve N. Dougine, N.Y. Geneological & Biographical Society.
R. S. Embleton, England. For inspirational paintings of the Rangers.
Colonel William A. Foote, San Diego, California.
F. Dwight Foster, Brooklyn, New York.
Mae Gilman, Librarian, Maine Historical Society.
Colonel Edward P. Hamilton, Director, Fort Ticonderoga.
Helen M. Harriss & Emma Melvin, McClung Historical Society.
W. S. Herrington, Napanee, Ontario, Canada.
Elizabeth H. Jervey, Secretary, S. C. Historical Society.
Joseph Henry Jackson, Book Review Editor, The San Francisco Chronicle.
Edna L. Jacobsen, Head, Manuscripts, N.Y. State Library, Albany, N.Y.
Librarian & Staff, Huntington Library, San Marino, California.
David A. Loescher, Editor, The Mountain View Eagle (The Editor).
Helene S. Loescher, Casa Laguna, San Mateo, California.
Edward Franklin Loescher, Loescher Farms, Conejo, California.
Howard Parker Moore, an inspirational friend. Biographer of J. Stark.
Eleanor M. Murray, Librarian, Fort Ticonderoga.
Stanley M. Pargellis, Librarian, Newberry Library.
S. H. P. Pell, President, Fort Ticonderoga Association.
Stanley R. Putnam, Jr., Albany, New York.
Kenneth Roberts, Kennebunkport, Maine.
Enzo Serafini, The Homestead, Sugar Hill, N. H. A continuing friend.
H. A. Sherlock, Canton, Ohio.
Colton Storm, William L. Clements Library.
Melvin C. Tucker, Laconia, N. H. For unstinting help and inspiration.
R. W. G. Vail, Director, N.Y. Historical Soc. For unfailing encourage.
Mason Wade, Cornish. Biographer of Parkman.
Ross M. A. Wilson, Toronto, Canada. A most helpful friend.

CONTENTS

	Page
Books By The Author	ii
Introduction	ix

THE CORPS OF ROGERS RANGERS Apr 1758-1762

I	1758-Abercrombie's Eyes	1
II	1758-Louisbourg Front	27
III	1759-Amherst's Advance Guard for Conquest...	36
IV	1759-Wolfe's Scouting Arm	72
V	1760-Conquest of Canada-Lake Champlain Front	83
VI	1760-Conquest of Canada-Quebec Front	112
VII	1760-Conquest of Canada-Great Lakes Front...	123
VIII	1760-Disbandment and Winter Service	135
IX	1761-1762-Conquest of the French West Indies	142
X	1761-The Cherokee-English War	146

THE REVIVALS OF ROGERS RANGERS

XI	1763-Pontiac's War	153
XII	Interlude-Major Rogers Character Extraordinary	160
XIII	American Revolution-Rogers' Queen's Rangers	167
XIV	American Revolution-Rogers' King's Rangers..	179

ILLUSTRATIONS AND MAPS

Rogers Rangers Uniforms 1758-1783, by the author	6
'On Party,' Maj. Rogers, by Embleton, owned by author	71
Battle of Ticonderoga River, June 15, 1758	10
Battle of Ticonderoga Falls, July 6, 1758	10
Stations & Actions of Rogers Rangers-Siege of Louisbourg	19
Marin's Defeat, August 8, 1758	19
The Three Battles, March 7, 1759	97
Battle of Pointe au Fer, June 6, 1760	97
Action at Old Lorette, March, 1760	116
The Last Battle, August 31, 1760	116
Second Battle of Etchoe Pass, June 10, 1761	121

APPENDICES

I - Battle Honours of Rogers Rangers	202
II - Sources for Actions, Expeditions May 1758-Jan 1783	203
III - Sources for Every Recorded Scout, Apr 1758-1783	233
IV - Uniforms of Rogers Rangers 1758-1783	248
Historical Notes (Footnotes)	251
Bibliography of Principal Sources	284
Index	302

INTRODUCTION

The Green Berets, America's elite force in South Vietnam, claim Rogers Rangers of two centuries past on their family tree. If not by direct unbroken descent at least by an affinity of method and tactics and certain aspects of dress, particularly their headgear and uniform color.

Rogers Rangers, the falcons of the Champlain Valley lakes in the old French and Indian War, swooped down upon their opponents. Like their counterparts The Green Berets, they differed only by the contemporary method of the times. Rogers' famous and definite Ranging Rules for bush fighting have been the Rangers' link, or badge, which have been handed down and adapted by Darby's Rangers in World War II and The Green Berets repelling communism in Vietnam. No other body of American fighting men has piqued the interest of the Americans, British and Canadians, nor maintained their curiosity during the many decades since Rogers Rangers flowed and ebbed from their various encampments to harry the enemy and form a vital role in the formulative period of our early history.

This continuing interest in Rogers Rangers and lack of a complete chronicle of their history has stimulated this genesis or history of the corps from their shady beginnings[1] in the French and Indian War through their revivals and final exile after the American Revolution. If this story of Rogers Rangers appears monumental, it was intended so. Many documentary sources heretofore unknown, were consulted to create this definitive monument to the Rangers. Although, it has taken two decades for the unveiling of the completion, it was never intended so.

Rogers Rangers were a synonym for the free spirit stirring throughout the American colonies in the mid 18th century increasing in intensity to the storm of the American Revolution two decades later. As a body of men they, as one of their discerning officers wrote, personified the new breed of free men that so startled the English officers with their Yankee independence. There was a camaraderie with the men that evoked the best from them. They shared the equality of freedom of expression and left a legacy of great men. The John Stark, Moses Hazen, the Brewers, Jonathan and David, Joseph Wait, great Ranger captains, were but a few of the Rangers to lead the fight to independence in the Revolution.

A fraternity of men, whether a regiment, or a nation, must have its heroes and they become a symbol. The Rangers' devotion gave Major Rogers his stature and by so doing he gave it back because his renown became theirs. Unfortunately their hero was only mortal and he faded, a few ill chosen trails and he was surpassed by his Rangers as the saga will tell.

Chapter I
1758

ABERCROMBIE'S EYES

The Spring of 1758 on the Lake George front brought forth the unparalleled splendor of northern New York's green campaign dress. In harmony with the grandeur of this predominate color could be seen patches of green moving ever northward, slowly, warily. Then, like a falling star to break the tranquil expanse of an unbroken sky, pin-points of red would shatter the green tranquility and the same green patches could be seen ebbing or flowing with accented speed as grey-white and brown patterns entered the panorama.

These preying scouts of Rogers Rangers prior to Abercrombie's advance on Ticonderoga were particularly successful during the months of April and May. They were daring in nature for the Corps strived to retaliate for their crushing defeat at Rogers' Rock.

Returning to Rogers' Island the Rangers' base at Fort Edward with his coveted Major's commission which he had literally wrested from Abercrombie, the new English Commander-in-Chief, [1a] Rogers hurled the above scouts at Ticonderoga and Crown Point. They consisted of five different thrusts: Captain John Stark scouted Ticonderoga on the west side of Lake George. The Stockbridge Indian Company under Captain Jacob Naunauphtaunk was now enlisted for the campaign and Jacob was sent down the east side of the lake with a detachment of his Rogers Rangers Indians. Captain Shepherd was dispatched into the 'drowned lands' of South Bay. III-49 Captain Burbank also moved forward with a party of Rangers. III-50 All of these scouts were sent primarily to bring in prisoners from the French forts who might reveal the strength and movements at the forts, which was so necessary to the British-Colonial invasion army. Major Rogers departed at the same time with 18 men to Crown Point and ambushed a working party three miles above the fort, took three prisoners and one scalp. On the very same day (May 5) Captain Stark executed a bit of audacity by taking two prisoners at Ticonderoga and gathering up four French escaped prisoners who were making their laborious way north from their confinement on Long Island. III-52

Captain Jacob's scout was probably the most successful. His party consisted of 18 Stockbridges and one white Ranger. Lying opposite to Ticonderoga they ambushed a wood-cutting party, in all 45 men, crossing the lake in three batteaus to cut wood for the storehouse. Allowing the first batteau to land, Jacob surrounded the 17 occupants, took ten prisoners and killed and scalped the seven who resisted. The other batteaus fled. II-23

A few days later, in the middle of May, all offensive scouting was halted while Lieutenant Simon Stevens of Stark's Company was sent to Ticonderoga under a flag of truce to negotiate for the exchange of Colonel Schuyler. [2]

No sooner had Stevens returned than the game of ambuscade was renewed with Rogers Rangers losing this round. Ensign Etowaukaum of Jacob's Company was returning from a Ticonderoga scout with his party of 21 Stockbridges and four white Rangers. His back trail had been picked up by the French Canadian Outetat and 30 Algonquins who were returning from a Wood Creek scout. They set an ambuscade six miles from Ticonderoga and completely enveloped Etowaukaum's men. The Ensign and 12 Stockbridges fought their way free and managed to reach Fort Edward. Of the remainder of his party, two white Rangers and two Stockbridges were killed, and two white Rangers and seven Stockbridges were taken prisoners. Two of the Indians were sold and shipped to France as slaves but after many hardships they escaped and made their way to a neutral port where they found passage to America in 1759. II-24

On May 28th Rogers Rangers were given notice that Abercrombie's invasion was taking shape for Major Rogers received "positive orders" from Abercrombie to order all Ranger officers who were on furlough or recruiting to join their respective Companies as soon as possible and to be at the Lake George front before June 10th.[3]

While the Ranger recruiting officers endeavored to replenish the Corps' weakened sinews from their terrific loss of 124 officers and men at the bloody Battle of Rogers' Rock on March 13, Rogers and his men continued their deadly forest duel. Again the Corps suffered a rebuff but managed to execute a brilliant retreat. Rogers' self-appointed pupil, Lord Howe,[4] arrived at Fort Edward on June 8 with half the army and immediately ordered his colleague, Rogers, to make an accurate map of the landing spot at the north end of Lake George and the present roads, terrain and fortifications of Ticonderoga valley. This was in preparation for the landing of Abercrombie's army and its subsequent march on Ticonderoga.

Rogers' force of 50 men including Ensign Downing of the 55th who went as a volunteer and Lieutenant Porter with a detachment of Rogers Mohegan-Rangers From Brewer's Company, and Captain Jacob with some of his Stockbridge Rangers. The balance were white Rangers.

They left Fort Edward on June 12, and arrived at the site of Fort William Henry and embarked the next day in whaleboats brought up in wagons. Arriving near the abandoned French advanced post of Coutre Coeur, Rogers landed on the east side of Ticonderoga River and left Captain Jacob with 35 of his party while Lieutenant Porter was sent forward to reconnoitre Ticonderoga and Rogers took three men and proceeded to Rattlesnake Mountain and made the map that Howe desired. Rogers was returning to his main body and was within 300 yards of them when Jacob was attacked on three sides by Leiutenant Wolfe and 30 to 50 French and Indians. Caught by surprise Jacob overestimated Wolfe's force and thought it best to immediately retire after the first volley with all the Mohegan-Rangers who seemed only too glad to follow his example. Ordinarily this would have been the wisest thing to do. Jacob probably had visions of being completely surrounded as was his Ensign Etowaukaun a short time ago. However, in this instance Wolfe's encirclement was broken by Ticonderoga River at the Rangers' rear. Here lay their whaleboats and although Captain Jacob called to the white Rangers "to run likewise," these veterans, well trained in Rogers' Ranging Rules for extricating themselves from a difficult position, spread out fanwise and maintained a steady fire while they retired in order to their boats. Rogers skirted Wolfe's flank and rallied his Rangers at the river bank. The loading and embarking of the whaleboats was a difficult operation under the focused fire of attackers. Fortunately the French Indians were not all sober and their fire was not as accurate as it could have been. This factor enabled Rogers Rangers to withdraw from their disadvantageous field of action with a loss of only five men killed and three taken prisoners. Among the latter was Ensign Downing, the volunteer from the 55th Regiment. The hardy Rogers was among those wounded. He received a flesh wound in his leg while bravely covering the embarkation of his men to the whaleboats. Wolfe lost three men killed including one of his best Indians.

Lieutenant Porter with his Ticonderoga scout was returning to rejoin Jacob, when, hearing the intensity of the action, he thought it prudent to bypass the battle and return to Fort Edward. It is unfortunate that Porter was unaware of Wolfe's exact numbers for if he had he might have thrown his 10 or 11 Rangers on Wolfe's rear and effected a surprise that could have altered the battle in favour of Rogers Rangers. Unfortunately the bulk of Porter's detail were Mohegan-Rangers and their refusal to throw their weight into an unequal contest influenced Porter's decision. Returning to Half-Way Brook, Porter and Jacob had found Lord Howe advanced with 3,000 men who they informed that "Rogers must be either killed or taken." But Rogers, the 'Wobi Madaondo' (White Devil) of the French Indians, led a charmed existence, for he returned on the 17th, much "to the joy and surprise of all." Lieutenant Wolfe followed Rogers in the next night under a flag of truce to discuss Schuyler's exchange. His interview with Abercrombie proved detrimental to Rogers' accurate report of the battle. Abercrombie was exceedingly annoyed because three prisoners had been taken, particularly Ensign Downing. In a letter to Prime Minister Pitt he blamed Rogers for being "out of Zeal for the service" when, "He, contrary to his Instructions, proceeded with his Whale Boats too far down the Lake." Abercrombie feared that the three prisoners taken would reveal too much about his advance and when Wolfe informed him of the true strength of his attacking party and implied that Rogers Rangers had made a cowardly retreat, Abercrombie turned to Rogers who was present and (according to Wolfe's report to French officers) scolded him "very severly and reproached him with having run away the moment his troops were engaged."

Consequently Rogers, who was not even present at the beginning of the action, received the blame for Jacob's illtimed flight. Abercrombie's obtuseness in even considering the truth of a French report against that of Rogers without at least weighing the two, portrays the character of the Commander-in-Chief who was soon to send so many men to their untimely death. II-28

Rogers was now ordered to join Lord Howe with all his Rangers and together they proceeded to the ruins of Fort William Henry and encamped on the 22nd of June. Rogers Rangers formed their encampment 400 yards in advance of the army on the west side of the lake and this location served as the base for the Corps for the rest of the campaign.[5] The Ranger companies under Rogers' immediate command were led by Captains John Stark, John Shepherd, Jonathan Burbank (who succeeded Charles Bulkeley—killed at Rogers' Rock), Rogers' own, the two Jacobs (of fifty each) and Moses Brewer. The last three captained Stockbridge and Mohegan Indian Companies.[6]

Over 1,000 Rangers had been raised in New England during the Winter and Spring for Rogers' various companies for service in different theaters of action. The Ranger recruiting officers were sent into New Hampshire and Massachusetts (the two principal New England Provinces for recruiting Rangers) to replenish the losses sustained by the four veteran Companies (Major Robers' own, John Stark's, John Shepherd's and Burbank's) in the battle of Rogers' Rock found these provinces

ROGERS KINGS RANGERS
Ranger 1779-1783

ROGERS RANGERS
Ranger 1758-1761

ROGERS QUEENS RANGERS
Ranger 1776-1777

ROGERS RANGERS
1758 - 1783
SEE PAGES 248-250

drained of likely Rangers. Therefore, three of these four companies mustered almost the same number on June 25, as they did after Rogers' Rock. Only the recruiters for Major Rogers' own company were successful. This model Company showed a strength of 106 privates against 71 for Shepherd's, 54 for Stark's and only 43 for Bulkeley's, now Burbanks.

When Abercrombie arrived at Lake George on June 28, and learned the numbers of the above companies he ordered Rogers to beat up the Provincial Regiments for volunteers to be 'drafted' into Rogers Rangers to serve the campaign. Five officers, five Sergeants and 164 Privates responded (of these, one Ensign, one Sergeant and 24 Privates served in Moses Brewer's Company) and swelled thé Companies to their authorized strength of 100 men.[7]

While Abercrombie's army gathered in strength, Rogers Rangers were employed as usual in protecting the camp from surprise attacks. On June 16, "Orders were given for daily Scouts and Patrols being sent round the Camp, through the woods..."[8] This service was effectively executed and the army suffered no losses but unfortunately the Rangers did, and at the hands of the very men they were protecting:

On June 20, Sergeant Hartwell came into Fort Edward with his patrol. They were challenged by a British picket, but it being a windy night, they did not hear the guard's voice. He fired and killed Hartwell and the same hungry bullet passed through the stomach of the next Ranger. It was taken out near his back. One accident like this was disquieting, but two of the same nature within four days of each other was as tragic as being twice scalped by the same Indian.[III-56]

Sergeant David Kerr of Major Rogers' Company was returning to camp with his patrol on the evening of June 24th. He was likewise fired at and killed by a Regular sentry and the bullet also passed through another Ranger who recovered.[III-57]

The Rangers were surprised and overjoyed on June 25, when they read a "Placecard" posted in camp stating that the capitulation of Fort William Henry was broken, due to the massacre which followed after the capitulation had been signed. This was good news to the members of Richard Rogers' Company who were in the capitulation, for this meant that they could take up arms again.[9]

In preparation for Abercrombie's invasion Rogers threw out four scouts on June 23rd—three of them were small parties (one to the narrows of South Bay, one to the west side of Lake George and the other to Ticonderoga) sent out by land.[III-58] Unfortunately the fourth party traveled by whaleboats and were spotted by the enemy. Lieutenants Simon Stevens and Nathan Stone commanded 17 picked Rangers to make "discoveries." They were surrounded by a superior body of the enemy at the Second Narrows on the 25th and all were taken prisoners. Their captors were well led by Ensign de Langy-Montegron, the Rangers' most daring rival.[II-29] He had also been so instrumental in defeating Rogers Rangers at Rogers' Rock. In less than two weeks though, the Corps more than balanced their accounts with this worthy Canadian and also retaliated for all their other accumulative losses since the turn of the year.[10]

Abercrombie's grand invasion Army embarked on Lake George the 5th of July. Rogers Rangers were posted on the left and comprised the advance guard. Rogers' 50 whaleboats had not proceeded far in the early dawn when they saw 150 French and Indians in boats lying near Sloop Island evidently waiting to renew old acquaintances. But their commander, Langy, had no desire to renew their deadly forest duel when he saw 600 Rangers bearing down on him. He hastily withdrew and lost himself among the islands of the First Narrows before the sun rose.[11]

Abercrombie's army of 15,400 men reached Sabbath Day Point at dusk and rested until 10 that night. Rogers, Howe and Bradstreet headed the army and Ranger Lieutenant Robert Holmes, was sent forward by Howe to obtain intelligence on the French strength at Montcalm's Landing.[III-59] Holmes returned to the above threesome[12] about daybreak and reported seeing fires at the landing place. After daybreak, a confirming reconnaissance by the three chiefs substantiated Holmes' report and the army landed at noon.[13] Rogers Rangers landed first and found the enemy too weak to oppose them for Montcalm had no intention of bringing on an engagement here when he had concentrated his force in entrenchments before Ticonderoga. Rogers threw out bush-fighters who drove the landing guard before them as they made an hour march to rising ground within a quarter of a mile where Montcalm was encamped with 1,500 men.^{II-33} Here, in accordance with the bumptious orders of Abercrombie's aid, Captain Abercrombie, Rogers posted his Corps. They were joined shortly by the Provincial Regiments of Fitch and Lyman.[14]

Rogers sent out small reconnoitering parties who informed him of Montcalm's location. One of these scouts, consisting of four men, had a harrowing encounter with the French Indians. Led by Sergeant Paige, the party consisted of two other Provincial drafts into Rogers Rangers (Corporal Wright, Private Thompson Maxwell) and one veteran Ranger Private, Morris O'Brian of Burbank's company. In an attack and pursuit, the Corporal was killed and O'Brian wounded and captured. In a grim race Private Maxwell outdistanced all but two savages. He shot one dead and escaped the other when he hurdled a fallen hemlock. His pursuer lost the race when he failed to clear the obstacle and fell upon it with a grunt. Rejoining Sergeant Paige at Ticonderoga River it appeared that they would still lose the race; for safety lay across the stream and Maxwell could not swim. The stalwart Sergeant solved their difficulties when he swam the river with Maxwell and their two muskets on his back. Provincial recruits such as Paige and Maxwell were worthy additions to Rogers Rangers and enhanced the Corps' fame.^{II-34}

The hour of reckoning with Langy was soon at hand. The French advance party of 350 Regulars and Canadians under Captain Trepezac and Ensign Langy had been watching the advance of the army down the lake from atop Rogers' Rock, but they had been slow in retiring and were now cut off from Montcalm. In working their way back to Ticonderoga they were approaching the first rapids (from Lake George) when Lord Howe fell upon them as he was marching towards Rogers with a strong advance guard of his brigade. Rogers, Lyman and Fitch, hearing the firing hastened forward and hurled their Corps from above upon the trapped French. Rogers with 450 of his Rangers was in the center of the circle that now encircled Trepezac and Langy. Captain Burbank and 150 Rangers were the only Rangers in the expedition that did not share in Langy's defeat.

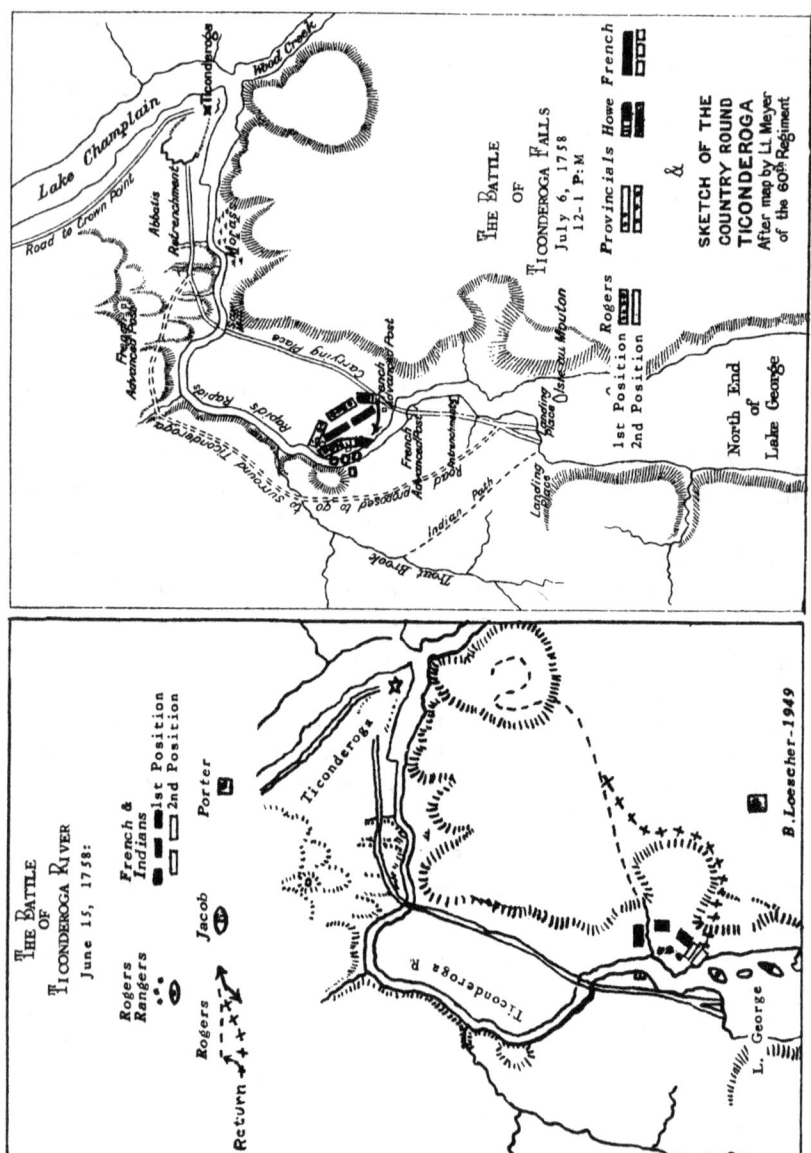

Rogers left them behind to keep an eye on Montcalm at the Sawmill. The only penetrable part of the circle was the cascades and waterfall of Ticonderoga River on the right end of the French line. Toward this doubtful exit the French tried to escape. They fought desperately and eventually about 50 of them managed to cross the rapids and escape. Among them was Langy, who, for the first time in his career, was almost caught in a trap similar to so many that he had prepared for the English. This was a crushing defeat for the French but the only victory of Abercrombie's invasion army. Of the original French force of 350, 151 were captured, 50 escaped and the remaining 150 were killed or drowned in trying to cross the rapids. Red water flowed into Lake George on July 6, and much of the human dye came from the bodies of Rogers' Rock participants who had massacred captive Rangers. As Langy's Defeat ended Rogers Rangers knew that the battle of Roger's Rock had been avenged. II-35

Unfortunately Lord Howe was killed while exhorting his men and Abercrombie lost his valuable leadership and counsel. Instead of relying on the experience and judgment of more practical minds, even though they might be mere Ranger officers, he listened to the suicidal recommendation of his glory-seeking nephew and aide-de-camp, Captain James Abercrombie. Ordered a general assault on Montcalm's entrenchment instead of first levelling it with his artillery which had not come up yet.

An interesting factor presents itself (relative to the history of Rogers Rangers) which might have contributed to Captain Abercrombie's determination to recommend a general assault:

The morning after Langy's Defeat, Rogers, with 250 Rangers, moved back to his advanced position of the previous day. Captain John Stark with 200 Rangers guided Captain Abercrombie and Matthew Clarke, the Chief Engineer, to the top of Rattlesnake Mountain (Mt. Defiance) to look in on Montcalm's fortifications. [15] Rogers undoubtedly sent Stark because he was well versed in the best route to ascend the mountain but it would have been wiser if he had sent some other officer for there was a strained relation between Stark and Captain Abercrombie. Rogers may not have been aware of all the details of a scout in

1757 which the above two made together. Stark, disliking the peremptory orders of Abercrombie had deliberately opposed him and made game of his ignorance of South Bay. Engineer Clarke had served in this scout and had also been indirectly opposed by Stark.[16] Consequently, they turned a deaf ear on Stark's sound advice when he pointed out from the summit of Rattlesnake Mountain the strategy of cutting behind Ticonderoga and severing Montcalm's retreat. He also advised them to drag cannon to where they were standing and shell Ticonderoga. It is incredible that Stark's judgment was not offered to General Abercrombie. But then maybe these two ambitious British officers were afraid Stark would obtain the credit or at least part of it and that would not do at all. Rather than that possibility, they made the rash proposal to attack Montcalm's strong position. The bewildered Abercrombie, groping in the dark since the death of Howe, accepted it as the best method of offense.

The die was now cast, and although a party of Rogers Rangers captured a courier sent to Crown Point for help, Montcalm had nothing to fear. III-60 At 7 A.M. on July 8, Rogers received orders to move his Rangers forward to form the advance guard of the attack. Lieutenant James Clark of Stark's Company preceded him with 50 Rangers. Clark was within 300 yards of Montcalm's entrenchments when he was fired upon by a party of 200 French in ambush. Rogers immediately formed a front of his Corps and marched up to the support of his vanguard who held their ground until he arrived and then the enemy were driven in. Gage's Light Infantry now moved up to the right of Rogers Rangers and Bradstreet's armed Batteaumen to the left and continued to skirmish with the advanced parties of the enemy. For the first time in the war Rogers Rangers had the opportunity to enact the part that Rangers should in a major battle involving thousands of men; that is, of deploying as skirmishers and breaking the way for the advance of the main army.[17]

While Rogers Rangers were thus employed, the main body of the army was forming. At 10 A.M. the Rangers were ordered to drive in the advanced parties of the enemy in preparation for the general assault. This service was vigorously performed and then Rogers Rangers, obedient to orders, fell to the ground at intervals and allowed the British Grenadiers and battalion companies to march through and proceed to the attack. The Rangers had reached, and held throughout the contest several large trees that had been cut down by the French for their breastwork and which had been abandoned. From this scant cover the bulk of the Corps was able to protect itself and give the Regulars a covering fire when they were hurled repeatedly back from the breastwork. Montcalm's entrenchment consisted of a breastwork of large trees felled and piled together to the height of eight feet, presenting a front of sharpened branches and interwoven limbs. It was practically impregnable to an advancing foe, but susceptible to cannon fire which Abercrombie had foolishly not bothered to wait for. Six impetuous attempts were made to carry it by storm and many of Rogers Rangers "were carried right up to the breastworks" in these desperate waves "but were stopped by the bristling mass of sharpened branches." The Rangers suffered six privates killed; two Lieutenants missing; one Ensign, two Sergeants and 15 privates wounded on this bloody day of battle. This was nothing compared to the total English loss of 1,944 officers and men. The Rangers minimal loss points out their vastly superior ability to wage the necessary 'brush warfare' so necessary to win in North America. As the day ended Abercrombie ordered a precipitous retreat to the south end of Lake George even though they outnumbered the French two to one in spite of their huge losses. As always, Rogers Rangers were at the post of danger, whether in opening an attack or safely covering a broken and retreating army. They were now busily employed in the late summer twilight in bringing up the rear. From 6-7 P.M. the Rangers posted themselves in the outskirts of the woods and maintained a covering fire which enabled the army to gather the wounded and retreat to the boats at Montcalm's Landing. Before the merciful darkness finally descended, Rogers Rangers were the last of the army to see the French fleur-de-lis mocking them from Montcalm's entrenchment. They finally melted into the night and embarked behind Abercrombie's army. II-36

Events following this disheartening expedition were decidedly an anti-climax but the army had to be protected against the constant forays of the French and Indians who were now overbold. They managed to inflict two depredations before Rogers stumbled upon them and dampened their ardour. A week after their return to their base at the south end of Lake George Rogers Rangers renewed their old routine of preying northward and eastward for prisoners and discoveries. Captain Jacob was sent to Ticonderoga[III-62] and Rogers made a scout to South Bay[III-61] where he discovered the tracks of a strong enemy party who the next day ambushed a Provincial detachment at Half-Way Brook.* Among them was a detail from Major Rogers' Company consisting of a Sergeant and 13 men.[II-40] Captains Burbank and Brewer had been posted at Half-Way Brook with their Companies of Rogers Rangers and when Captain Wrightson, the Commandant, heard the alarm gun at Ford Edward, he immediately dispatched Captain Burbank and his 45 Rangers then present at the post. Three miles down the road, Burbank met Colonel Hart and 400 Provincials sent out from Fort Edward. They picked up La Corne's trail and came up with his 300 Canadians and Indians staggering half drunk through a nearby swamp. Hart, fearing a trap, ordered his 400 men back to the ravaged wagon train half a mile back where they proceeded to indulge in the same wine that had so intoxicated La Corne's party. Burbank was left stranded in a precarious position where he was outnumbered seven to one. The drunken Indians laughed scornfully at his meager force, but Burbank bravely maintained his position for he realized that he could execute a coup de grace if the cowardly Hart could be persuaded to rejoin him. He sent Lieutenant Andrew McMullen to Hart but the Colonel told him that Burbank was firing at his own men and that he had sent an officer to order Burbank to withdraw. McMullen, never reticent to express himself, angrily swore that he would break his gun to pieces if the Rangers could have no assistance. Burbank now sent Ensign Archibald Campbell Jr. to Hart but he received the same answer. The timid Colonel finally broke down and sent McMullen and

---

*On the 28th the Canadian partisan, La Corne, massacred a convoy of 116 men and women between Ford Edward and Half-Way Brook.

Campbell back to Burbank with 100 provincials. They had hardly gone one-fourth of a mile before all but eight of them ran back to Hart. Soon after a message arrived from Hart ordering the two Ranger officers back to him but they ignored the message and reported the Colonel's disgraceful actions to Captain Burbank. The Rangers could do no more now than maintain a distant fire-at-will upon the Indians until they retired out of range and returned to Ticonderoga.

Ensign Campbell was sent to Abercrombie with a report of Hart's conduct. Abercrombie sent Rogers and Putnam with 700 men to intercept La Corne and ordered Hart to be courtmartialed. Campbell had reported to Abercrombie at 9 P.M. on the 28th and by 2 A.M. the General personally saw Rogers off. They hurried to Rogers' "secret water passage" near Sabbath Day Point and crossed the mountains to "Two Rocks" on the narrows of lower Lake Champlain, an ideal location to form an ambuscade. They were half an hour too late. The only good effects of the scout were the rescue of a starving British regular who had escaped from the French.[III-64] In the meantime, Abercrombie's army had received an alarming report as a result of the imagination of the Provincial guard Rogers had left with his boats. Three of Rogers' batteaus had gone adrift and they were seen on the lake by Captain Davis and his boatmen who amplified their numbers in the dark to 200. Davis abandoned all of Rogers' boats and retired to Captain Champion's advanced breastwork on Sloop Island. Davis sent the bulk of his men to Abercrombie with the news while he made a 'scout' to confirm his alarm. Colonels Haviland and Lyman were sent with 1,000 men to intercept the reported French. At 6 A.M. they arrived at Sunday Island opposite Sabbath Day Point where they found most of Rogers' abandoned batteaus. Haviland sent Lieutenant James Tute of Shepherd's Company along the west shore and islands where he found three batteaus. One of them contained a cask of biscuits similar to those in Rogers' batteaus, thus identifying them as the same and not the 200 that Davis and his men saw. For his bad state of nerves Davis was courtmartialed along with Hart, another neurosis sufferer.

The French Indians continued to make unannounced visits via the Wood Creek approach. On July 31, a Fort Anne scout of 11 Rogers Rangers sent out from Half-Way Brook came on the fresh tracks of 50 Indians. Following them for four miles the Rangers sat down to eat when they were surrounded and attacked by the 50 Indians. In the desperate melee 17 Indians and eight Rangers were killed. Two Rangers were taken alive and Sergeant Hackett alone escaped. In his flight he saw a fresh enemy track leading towards Fort Edward. [II-41] Abercrombie had learned from Haviland on the 30th acquainting him of Rogers' return to Sunday Island from his late pursuit of La Corne. Since Rogers was still in the field, Abercrombie realized that there was a probability of intercepting the above Indians on their return. He sent a dispatch to Colonel Haviland directing him "to detach Rogers and Putnam, from whence they were, with 700 chosen men and ten Days' Provisions, to sweep all that back Country" of South Bay and Wood Creek and come in by Fort Edward. Rogers and Putnam were encamped on Sloop Island the night of July 31 (where their 700 men overran the island, much to the discomfort of Captain Champion, the Commandant there) when they received orders to rejoin Haviland which they did the next morning and spent the day outfitting the expedition. As several of their men were fatigued from their forced march of July 29th, Rogers and Putnam had their choice of fresh Volunteers from Haviland's 1,000 regulars, provincials and (70) Rogers Rangers. Rogers and Putnam (both Majors) seemed to have had a joint command with Rogers the senior officer. There was jealousy between the two and the presence of Colonel Haviland who had instigated it last winter at Fort Edward started the expedition off under a shadow.

On August 2, they repeated their march of the 29th, but avoided Two Rocks, instead, an ambuscade was formed by Putnam at South Bay and Rogers at the junction of Wood Creek and East Bay. Rogers was rewarded on August 6, when a canoe with six Indians cruised into their trap. Before it came within musket fire one of the provincials in Rogers' party made an obtuse challenge: "Pray what Boat may you be?" Upon which the canoe veered off and escaped. About the same time two boats escaped from Putnam by a similar challenge.

Rogers and Putnam now rejoined forces and marched the next day to the ruins of Fort Anne where they encamped on August 7th. The expedition now numbered only 530 for 170 had been sent on to Fort Edward during the day. At 7 A.M. the next morning Rogers and Putnam started their march west towards Fort Edward. It has been said that Rogers waived his customary caution when he and Ensign William Irwin of Gage's got into a friendly argument on their ability as marksmen and before marching shot at marks on a wager. British volunteer present state that members of the party were taking pot-shots at pigeons on the march. Regardless of whom is to blame, three shots reached the ears of Marin, the famous French Canadian Colonial officer and his partisan band of 500 Canadians and Indians. Marin was very close and he quietly rushed his men forward and deployed them in a crescent shape at the edge of the clearing in front of Putnam's line of march. Major Putnam was in the van with his 300 Connecticuts. Captain Dalyell followed with the detachments from the 80th and 44th Regiments. Rogers brought up the rear with his Rangers and rest of the Provincials. They had to march about three-quarters of a mile on a narrow Indian path across the bush-choked clearing before they entered the forest where Marin was waiting for them. Putnam, Lieutenant Tracy and three Connecticuts at the head of the column were overwhelmed and dragged into the thickets. Then the firing began. Marin had the advantage of position and surprise. The Connecticuts fell back in disorder behind Dalyell's advancing Regulars. The battle centered around a huge fallen tree and the Regulars wavered under four volleys from Marin on the other side before they managed to flank the tree and engage the enemy with their musket butts. By this time Rogers had arrived from the rear with his Rangers and Provincials. He hastily formed his line of battle by posting Captain Giddings with his Massachusetts provincials on the left of the Regulars to support Lieutenant Durkee who was rallying the Connecticuts there. Rogers covered Dalyell's right flank with his Rangers and Partridge's detachment of Provincial Light Infantry. Both sides were evenly matched and the action raged for over an hour. Because of the heavy brushwood in the clearing at the forest's edge, every man was more or less forced to fight for himself although assistance was rendered when possible. A gigantic Indian Chief "behaved in a very extraordinary manner." He jumped upon the fallen tree, killed two Regulars opposing him and shouted defiance to all. A British officer attempted to dispatch him with blows from his firelock but he only enraged the giant when he caused his head to bleed. He was about to kill the officer with his tomahawk when Major Rogers proved his prowess as a marksman and shot the Indian. The 'giant' was the largest Indian Rogers had ever seen. He measured over six feet four inches which for the period was exceptionally tall.

The weight of the conflict now shifted to Rogers Rangers on the right of the line. Here Marin made four different attacks which were repeatedly repulsed by the immovable Rangers. Rogers extended the Rangers' flanks and finally some of the Canadians gave way. Rogers Rangers now took the offensive and charged, firing half at a time while the other half reloaded. Thus, a constant fire was maintained and the rest of Marin's party broke. Rogers' whole force, Rangers, provincials and regulars now vigorously advanced and drove Marin from the field of battle. Marin saved his defeat from a rout and eluded pursuit by adopting Rogers' own methods of retreat. He divided his surviving force into small parties and reuniting towards evening, they made their bivouac on a spot surrounded by impervious swamps. Remaining on the field of battle, Rogers' force buried their dead, about 40 in number; and after scalping 52 of the 77 enemy killed (25 were not discovered until August 15, when a Ranger Lieutenant made a post mortem of the unscalped French and Indians which his scouting party discovered on and near the field of action)[III-66] they continued their march to Fort Edward carrying their 40 wounded on litters made of branches with a blanket strung over them. The French report their wounded at 12 but there were probably more. Rogers took two prisoners but lost five Connecticuts. The same day Rogers met Major Munster with a relief party of 400, including 40 Rangers and surgeons with dressings for the wounded. Upon being joined by Munster, Rogers encamped for the night and Marin's prowling Indians who had returned to scalp the dead found the victors drinking and singing in honour of their victory over them.

Rogers received the credit he deserved for turning an

SIEGE OF LOUISBOURG
1758
STATIONS & ACTIVITIES OF ROGERS RANGERS

1. Rogers
2. McCurdy
3. Brewer
4. W. Stark

Fifty Guineas Scout – 23

Landing at Freshwater Cove – 1234

Landing Feint June 5

June 11th Bloodhound Scout

English Camp

Crofton's Sortie

Blockhouse Ambuscade – 3

Ranger Sharpshooters

Siege Works

Cape Noir Sortie

Gallows Hill Louisbourg Patrol Fight

Barachois Bridge Sortie

English Batteries

Road to Mire

Repulse of Boishebert

Construction of Lighthouse Battery

Ranger Patrols

Ranger Posts

CABARUS BAY

LOUISBOURG HARBOUR

B. Loescher - 1949

See pages 27-35

MARIN'S DEFEAT
Aug. 7-9, 1758 a.m.

- Rogers Rangers
- Marin's Corps
- Regulars & Provincials

1st Position
2nd Position
Rangers Flank Move.
Marin in Retreat.
Bushes & Saplings in the Clearing at Fort Anne.
Forest Bordering the Clearing.
Ruins of Ft Anne

See pages 16-20

ambuscade into a skillfully manouevered victory. Dalyell informed Abercrombie that Rogers "acted the whole time with great Calmness and Officerlike." General Abercrombie when writing of the action to Prime Minister Pitt said: "Rogers deserved much to be commended" and the fame of Rogers and his Rangers increased in Europe as well as America. II-42

Rogers, the indefatigable, did not rest on his laurels. He arrived at Fort Edward on the ninth of August and two days later launched forth with 300 Rangers and provincials towards Fort Miller to intercept Indians reported there. III-65 The report was groundless and Rogers returned to Abercrombie's encampment at Lake George arriving on August 13, to find the army alarmed at the sound of Rangers down the lake firing at a deer. [18] Rogers was hailed in camp as a hero for his defeat of Marin in spite of the discrediting stories by Connecticut provincials who had preceded him to camp, and told of his firing at marks with Ensign Irwin (in an effort to minimize the blame which they had been carrying for retreating after Marin's first fire).

They made another discrediting story when they spread the tale that Rogers had boasted of killing Marin, then scalping him and skinning his chest after first writing Marin's name upon it. This story was discredited the same day it was repeated in camp for a flag of truce informed the army that Putnam's life had been saved by none other than Marin himself. [19]

In spite of the above tales Rogers was lauded by both regulars and provincials. His first few days back in camp were one continuous round of toasts and suppers in his honour. [20]

During Rogers'absence from his base at Lake George, various detachments of his Corps had been active in scouts towards the enemy continuing their duties as the eyes of Abercrombie's army. Before these started the routine varied on August 1, for two Rangers staggered into camp. One of them was a rare captive-survivor of Rogers' Rock. The other was a Stockbridge captive of Etowaukaum's Defeat. They had escaped from Canada 14 days before and were almost dead from hunger. A provincial who escaped with them was so weak that men had to fetch him in. [21]

From August 16 to October 6, the Rangers' calendar was

full. There was hardly a day went by when scouts were either setting out or returning to their three bases (Abercrombie's Camp, Fort Edward[III-67] or Half Way Brook.) None of them was on a large scale but several of them resulted in fierce little skirmishes or brazen abductions. Lieutenant David Brewer and six Rangers returned to camp on August 18, with a Frenchman they had abducted while he was harvesting oats three miles south of Crown Point. When Brewer and two other scouts set out on August 7, there was a rumor that Abercrombie had offered 60 guineas for a prisoner. Whether Brewer's part received this reward or the customary five pounds sterling is not known.[III-63] There were several of Johnson's Mohawks encamped with Rogers Rangers and they caused no end of trouble. They would have killed Brewer's prisoner if the Rangers had left him unguarded. By September 25, there were only 10 Mohawks remaining and six of them left that day to go running home to Johnson complaining that they had been beaten up by the Rangers. In spite of Abercrombie's orders forbidding liquor being given to the Indians, they managed to obtain it and one day while drinking with the Rangers a brawl ensued and the Rangers beat the Mohawks up with their fists.[22] Rogers endeavored to modify the causes of this and similar occurrences by keeping all the Rangers in camp actively employed. Alternate parties were constantly employed in patrolling the environs of Abercrombie's camp and details were sent into the woods to cut logs for the entrenchments.[23] Frequent reviews were held: on August 17, Rogers "exercised his men in Bush fiteing which drew a great Number out of ye Camp to view them;" and on September 1, "The Rangers exercised in Scout marches & Bush fighting which made a very pritty figure."[24]

At least one Courtmartial was held during the campaign for "miscrepeant" Rangers for Sergeant-Major Edmund Munroe of the Corps recorded one on September 4, with Captain Neale presiding.[25]

There were exceptional occasions when even Rogers encouraged liquid celebrations. On August 28, when news arrived of the capture of Louisbourg he ordered the Corps under arms at 6 P.M. "to illuminate the rejoicing" and he gave his own Company "a barrel of Wine treat to congratulate this good news to them, and the good behaviour of the four Companies of Rangers at Louisborg."[26]

Returning to the ebbing and flowing scouts recorded by Provincial Diaries at Lake George and an evident Ranger chronicler at Rogers' Island they record that a nine-day scout to Crown Point returned to Abercrombie's camp on the 30th to relate their attempted ambuscade of a party of French pigeon hunters who were warned in time by their barking dogs.[III-68] A Sergeant and five Rangers had a collision with a French party near Ticonderoga. Neither party was aware of the other until they were within three rods of each other. A brief skirmish ensued and after exchanging a few volleys both sides parted.[II-45] On September 3, the Rangers formed an ambuscade at the lake and caught alive several deer who swam across the lake. They were brought into camp and presented to Abercrombie and other chief officers.[27] September 2 saw 100 Rangers in a party under Dalyell returning to the neighborhood of Marin's Defeat on a scout which netted nothing.[III-70] Captain Shepherd returned at night on September 2, from a reconnaissance of Ticonderoga.[III-69] He reported a gathering of batteaus there which alarmed the nervous Abercrombie and Rogers embarked the next night with five men to see if they were advancing. He returned on the 7th to report that a French patrol in batteaus advanced at night to the First Narrows and returned to Ticonderoga in the morning.[III-71] Rogers, the trapper of French and Indians, determined to snare this daring patrol. He embarked on the 9th and set his trap but the wary French had increased the strength of their patrol and Rogers was forced to retire. Unfortunately he had sent two parties of five men each on shore. One he had sent to Crown Point for a prisoner but the other was for a local reconnaissance and they were now cut off from Rogers' boats. There was considerable anxiety over them until they returned to Abercrombie's camp nine days later (September 18th) to give a harrowing account of how they "miraculously escaped ye enemy."[II-48] A Ticonderoga Scout of Lieutenant Holmes and seven Rangers returned on September 6th. After a close reconnaissance of the Fort they crossed over to the eastern shore and ambushed a canoe contining two Indians that came within musket range. The wounded Indians tumbled into the lake and a Ranger swam out in plain sight of Ticonderoga and got the canoe. Drums were beating to arms. Upon which Holmes "tho't it prudent to retire as fast as possible" with his Rangers who "came in all well."[II-47] The game of ambuscade was played close to home on the 9th with Rogers Rangers losing this hand. A sergeant of Lovewell's provincial Rangers and four Rangers of Neale's Company of Rogers Rangers were in a convoy of Regulars sent to escort the teams from Half-Way Brook. Two miles from camp the British Commander unwisely dispatched the five Rangers to inform the teams of their coming. The Rangers had gone less than a mile when they were ambushed by Indians who killed and scalped the Sergeant and wounded a Ranger Private who escaped with the other three. A party of Rangers was sent in pursuit but found the Indians had too great a lead on them.[II-49] The scout of five men that Rogers had dispatched to Crown Point from the First Narrows of Lake George on the ninth returned to camp on the 26th having "made no remarkable discovery."[III-72] Other recorded scouts consisted of three reconnoitres from Fort Edward to Fort Anne,[III-73] Wood Creek[III-74] and Number Four.[III-77] Major Rogers made one last scout of the year on September 24th. His 150 Rangers cut across to South Bay from their secret Lake George passage.[III-76]

Meanwhile a French deserter came into Abercrombie's camp and told of a scout of twenty who had left their two canoes at South Bay under his charge while they prowled southward. The deserter guided a party of Rangers to the canoes where they met Rogers and lay in wait. But traps set in this neutral territory seemed predestined to remain empty for the Indians became aware of Rogers' presence and escaped him. Rogers returned to camp on the 29th with the bulk of his party and the rest followed on October 1.

It seems that the traps set within sight of the French forts were the most successful: The veteran Ranger, Lieutenant William Morris, and nine Rangers lay in ambush opposite to Crown Point in plain view of the fort. Their quarry appeared in the form of two boats loaded with 36 men. Allowing them to come within 20 yards the Rangers poured seven or eight volleys into them. Since there was no response from the boats (the occupants had fallen flat in the boats), Lieutenant Morris and a Ranger stripped in order to swim to the boats and bring them ashore for it was apparent that the 36 occupants were either all dead or wounded. As they were about to dive in, they saw a number of boats setting out from Crown Point to pursue them, upon which Morris wisely returned to Fort Edward posthaste with the enemy on their trail for the first day.[II-50]

The Corps made one more notable scout on the Lake George front in 1758. Lieutenant James Tute was hunting with seven Rangers between Half-Way Brook and Lake George. Tute and one Ranger were a half-mile from the road when they came upon human game in the form of 20 Indians sleeping in a hollow. Fearing that the Indians might be gone before he could collect his other six Ranger hunters, Tute deployed his one Ranger and they made a daring two-man attack by firing and shouting the Ranger war-whoop from two sides. The Indians, believing a superior force was upon them, fled. Tute and the Ranger boldly "tracked them by their Blood two or three Miles, but they could not come up with them."[II-51]

These last two offensive exploits of Morris' and Tute's were exemplary deeds to end the Corps' history at Lake George for the year. Although the Corps suffered minor losses by closing swoops of Indian raiders (a Ranger Sergeant was scalped within two miles of Lake George the end of October;[III-78] Private Timothy Blake was taken at Half-Way Brook on November 1;[III-79] and Private Gershom Flagg was captured near Fort Edward on December 22),[III-84] no more "engagements" occurred until March 7, 1759.

The two Jacob's Stockbridge Companies had been discharged by Abercrombie on September 11[28] On October 6, General Amherst, who was soon to succeed Abercrombie, arrived. The two reviewed the army (including Rogers Rangers) on this day but due to the lateness of the season, no second advance on Ticonderoga was attempted and plans were made for returning the army to winter quarters.[29] The provincial draftees into Rogers Rangers had returned to their respective regiments on August 24, thus reducing the Corps' strength more than thirty percent.[30]

A general return on October 6 of Rogers' seven Companies at various posts in northern New York showed only 417 privates fit for duty instead of the authorized 700.[31] By October 29, six of the seven skeleton Companies had gone into winter quarters on Rogers' Island at Fort Edward (Rogers, Starks, Burbanks, Shepherds, Brewers and Neils) and their strength had shrunk to less than 200 men.[32] The principal causes were the dischargement of all unfit men and the desertion of most of Brewer's Mohegans.[33] However, most of the officers and sergeants were sent into New England recruiting and by April 1759, the companies took the field at their authorized numbers and enough men had been recruited to raise another Company. Major Rogers had wisely started recruiting as early as November thus grabbing the best men before the Provincial recruiting officers started in the spring. The men were signed up during the winter and carried on the Ranger rolls from February 24, although most of them did not arrive at Rogers' Island until the latter part of March 1759.[34]

One vital non-aggressive service was performed by the Corps before the withdrawal of the army from Lake George. In order that the Rangers' whaleboats might be close at hand for early scouts in the coming spring, Rogers received orders to hide them along the lake. The role of Rogers' boat-hiders was more like that of Easter Rabbits hiding eggs for they sank, buried, or hid 29 whaleboats in the brush of Northwest Bay (after carrying them over the peninsula). Then they crossed over to Long Island and hid several more in an adjacent creek and a cranberry swamp. This took place on October 20, and by the following Easter, enemy raiders were looking for them but to no avail.[35]

A study of Wendell's Company of Rogers Rangers, stationed in the Mohawk Valley at Fort Stanwix, reveals that they figured conspicuously in Bradstreet's capture of Fort Frontenac. Colonel John Bradstreet's repeated petition to attack this key French fort, on the north shore of Lake Ontario, was finally granted by Abercrombie, after his failure at Ticonderoga. Hastening to the Oneida Carrying Place, where General Stanwix was building Fort Stanwix, he borrowed 2,600 Provincials —and Lieutenant William Hair, Sergeants Jacob Sever, Ranal

McDaniel, John Castleman and 57 Ranger Privates from Wendell's Company of 105 officers and men.

With Chief Red Head and forty Onondagos, this detachment of Rogers Rangers formed Bradstreet's scouting arm, under the temporary command of Tom Butler, as Captain of Scouts. In this vital duty, Rogers Rangers served in a dashing and incredibly successful expedition, which resulted in a one-day investment and surrender of Frontenac on August 27th.

Rejoining Wendell at Fort Stanwix, Lieutenant Hair and his detachment were hailed as heroes and even Major Rogers applauded the expedition in his Journals. II-45a

One Private in Wendell's—Phineas Atherton—served so conspicuously against Frontenac, that Abercrombie rewarded him with the Ensigncy of Wendell's Company (left vacant by the resignation of Ensign Jacob Snell).

Chapter II
1758
==========

THE LOUISBOURG FRONT

In spite of the failure at Ticonderoga, the British arms had triumphed elsewhere in North America—Louisbourg had been taken by Amherst—and four Companies of Rogers Rangers, the only Americans in the expedition, had contributed largely to its capture.[36] Rogers might have complained about four of his new Companies being separated from his immediate command, but it is fortunate that they were, for they gathered new laurels for the Corps.

Prime Minister Pitt had been very definite in his instructions to Abercrombie to see that 600 Rangers were assembled at Halifax to sail on Louisbourg. Abercrombie's task was made comparatively easy for Loudoun, his predecessor, had ordered Rogers to raise five new Companies for his Corps in January. These Companies were recruited and on their way to Albany for their March 15 rendezvous when the four white Companies, James Rogers', John McCurdy's, Jonathan Brewer's and William Stark's were re-routed to Boston. Here they were lodged on Castle Island until J. Brewer's tardy Company arrived and transportation was obtained. Abercrombie had underestimated the ability of Rogers' recruiting officers for he had ordered the Captains of these four Companies to swell the Companies to 125 instead of 100 (by this means the needed 600 would be raised when Gorham's 100 at Halifax were included); at the same time he played safe and asked Governor Pownall of Massachusetts to have 300 likely Rangers picked from his Provincials; but he had to countermand this request on March 30, for Rogers' green-uniformed Companies marched into Boston over 100 per Company.[37]

Brigadier Lawrence was entrusted with dispatching the four Companies to Halifax. His was a difficult assignment, for Provincial recruiting officers over-ran Boston and they had no qualms about inducing the Rangers to desert and sign up in their Regiments for the higher bounty and pay. In spite of his precautions, these high pressure salesmen were reaching his charges on Castle Island and Lawrence had visions of half of the Rangers deserting unless he got them out to sea. Consequently he did not wait for a convoy from Halifax but drummed up the Province Vessel, King George, to escort the transports. Lawrence hurriedly embarked Rogers Rangers and they sailed on April 2, arriving at Halifax on the 7th.[38]

Brigadier Hopson now saw to their welfare. First, he protected them from a Halifax smallpox epidemic, by landing and quartering them at Dartmouth, where they would also have more room "to stretch their limbs;" next, he exercised them in their Ranging tasks, by sending alternating parties in a boat to lie within the basin near the blockhouse with orders to land a patrol toward daybreak to scour the woods, to frustrate French partisan forces who had been making daring encroachments nearby.[III-48]

This service as maintained until May, when the four Companies, Gorham's Rangers, and 500 Highlanders and Light Infantrymen were formed into a provisional batallion under the command of Captain George Scott of the 40th Regiment.[39] The four Companies of Rogers Rangers were led by Scott at the landing on Cape Breton Isle, but during the Siege of Louisbourg, the Companies were scattered on various detached commands.

Rogers Rangers sailed with the army on May 28, and sighted Cabarus Bay on June 1st but the sea was so rough that Amherst had to wait six days before it was calm enough to venture a landing in small boats. During the night of June 5, a small party of Rangers made themselves obnoxious to the enemy shore forces when they daringly ventured close enough to fire upon them and alarmed them into believing the British were landing in force. III-53

When day broke on June 8, Amherst's invasion boats pulled for the shore. There were four accessible points to land but they were all strongly fortified. A feint was made at three of them, while Brigadier Wolfe made the real attack against Freshwater Cove. The order of landing for his brigade was: the four eldest Companies of Grenadiers, then Scott with the Light Infantry, Rangers and Highlanders, and lastly the remaining eight Companies of Grenadiers. Everyone considered the landing would be a desperate venture but it would have to be effected sometime if Louisbourg was to be invested. Like the rest of the landing force, the Rangers left all their equipment (haversacks and blankets) on the transports. They carried only their weapons (Firelocks, tomahawks and scalping knives) and two days supply of bread and cheese stuffed into their pockets. When Wolfe approached the beach his boats were raked with a deadly fire from Saint-Julien's artillery and 1,000 French and Indians for they had spare loaded muskets, and thus a continuous fire was poured upon the invaders. It appeared that Wolfe's first venture as a Brigadier would be a bloody failure for his boats could not land without being annihilated; but the daredevil nature of 50 officers and men of Rogers Rangers and the Light Infantry soon made it possible for him to execute his assignment. Wolfe waved his hand as a signal to veer off. To his right were four boats of Scott's command, commanded by Ensign Francis Carruthers of James Rogers' Company and Lieutenants Hopkins, Brown, and Ensign Crant of the Light Infantry. They were little exposed to Saint-Julien's cannon, being sheltered by a small projecting point, but the formidable rocky coast before them did not offer the inviting expanse of beach some rods to the left where Wolfe's Grenadiers had intended to land. The officers and men of these four boats soon earned undying fame, for they mistook or deliberately misconstrued Wolfe's gesture and rowed directly into the rocky teeth. Some of the boats stove against the rocks. A few men were drowned, others dragged their drenched bodies upon the rocks and musketless, whipped out their tomahawks and scalping knives and clambered over the slippery crags to follow the bulk of their comrades who had landed dry and with their firelocks. Surgeon Pudd on H. M. S. Kingston, on viewing the daring landing, jotted down in his Diary that "The Rangers landed first" and "behaved to admiration." They were able to scramble up the crags before being opposed in force, for Saint-Julien had thought his two rocky flanks impenetrable and had posted only weak wings upon them. However, by the time the Rangers and Light Infantry reached the summit they found over 100 French and Indians opposing their 50, and more were approaching. In the fierce fight which followed, the heroic Ranger, Ensign Carruthers, was killed; but the other members of James Rogers' Company and the Light Infantry bravely held their foothold until Scott and Wolfe hastily supported them. This admirable feat must have changed Wolfe's hasty opinion of Rogers Rangers, which was anything but flattering. By the time Wolfe and the balance of the Rangers and Regulars had ascended and formed in a solid body, the Rangers had somewhat retaliated for Carruthers' death by killing and scalping a prominent War Chief who led the Indians opposing them. This factor, and a resolute charge by Wolfe's brigade determined the Indians to retreat (an eyewitness observes that "Ye Rangers Started them first," when "they Ran and Hollow'd and fired on them and they left their Brestwork") thus weakening the French troops and causing them to fall back relinquishing the nearest battery. Brigadier Lawrence landed upon Saint-Julien's other flank while this distraction was occurring. The French were now in grave danger of being cut off from Louisbourg, for Wolfe's brigade was almost between them and the fortress. Saint-Julien now abandoned all of his batteries and made a precipitous retreat, circling through the hills to Louisbourg; but not before 70 of them were captured and 50 or more killed. They were scalped by the Rangers, who, with the Light Infantry and Highlanders pursued the French to within cannon range of Louisbourg. The losses in the four Companies of Rogers Rangers (and Corham's) besides Ensign Francis Carruthers, were 3 Privates killed, 1 wounded and 1 missing (total British loss—100 killed, wounded, and drowned.)

    The landing of Rogers Rangers at Freshwater Cove was one of the most admirable feats ever performed by a detachment of the Corps. It is incredible that historians have not given them the credit which they so courageously earned. Because of Ensign Carruthers' untimely death and the fact that British officers penned most of the account of the landing, the credit heretofore has gone to the Light Infantry officers (Hopkins, Brown, and Grant) who landed with Carruthers. However, there were a few honest accounts (besides Budd's and Knap's mentioned above) which gave Carruthers' men and the Rangers who landed to support them the credit they deserve: Brigadier Lawrence exerted himself to praise them. He wrote Governor Pownall of Massachusetts: "I have partucular pleasure in assuring you that the Companies of Rangers rais'd in New England behaved at Landing so as to do great Honor to themselves and the Country they came from..." The Governor gave the above excerpt to the <u>Boston News-Letter</u> and the Corps were publicly lauded. Another eyewitness account states the Rangers" did great service in landing."II-25

Commensurate with this exemplary deed was the exigent service given by the Rangers while Louisbourg was invested. No more than two days passed when the Rangers were once more in the spotlight. A party was prowling close to Louisbourg when they met a reconnaissance scout of Canadians and French. In the skirmish that ensued they were attacked so resolutely by the Rangers that they were "obliged to retire with the loss of 3 men."II-26

Less gory, but expedient accomplishments were the rounding up of French and horses who had been cut off from Louisbourg after the landing. From their haunts in the hills the Rangers flushed out 7 horses and 20 men on the tenth and eleventh. III-54 Captain William Stark's famous Wolf dog, Sergeant Beaubien, earned nis pay in these bloodhound scouts. 40

Two o'clock the next morning saw Rogers Rangers again leading the advance of a special assignment. Scott preceded Wolfe's advance on the abandoned Lighthouse Point and covered his march by taking post in the woods with three Ranger Companies and one of Light Infantry. After Wolfe's safe arrival, Scott returned to Amherst, leaving two Companies of Rangers with Wolfe who posted one Company at Lorembec, ten at Petit Lorembec, and the other Company at Northeast Harbour. These posts were established as bases for patrols who ranged the woods between them to intercept the expected partisan forces from descending on Wolfe's battery at Lighthouse Point. The Rangers helped the Regulars in fortifying these posts, but Wolfe pithily notes that "they are better for ranging and scouting than either work or vigilance," and when his battery was ready to fire on the 19th, he kept only enough Rangers to maintain the patrols and returned the bulk of them to Amherst.[III-55]

Meanwhile the Rangers with Amherst had a notable skirmish on the 13th: 300 French sallied out beyond Gallows Hill. Rangers and Regulars were ordered against them and an engagement began which continued for an hour and a half. The French retired from hill to hill drawing the Rangers and British within range of the cannon of Louisbourg. They withstood two rounds from the cannon while they drove the French in and then withdrew out of range.[II-27]

Six days later Amherst ordered a detachment of sharpshooters from the Rangers and Light Infantry and posted them in a thicket on a hill to pick off the Artillerymen on the ramparts. At the same time Scott, with the remainder, established a permanent camp on the west side of the Mire road for a threefold purpose: to hinder any relief parties from going into the town, to secure communications with Northeast Harbour, and most important, to "be ready to attack and fall on the flank of any parties that may attempt to land or come out of the town on that side."[41]

On June 16, 50 Indians took 5 seamen below Freshwater Cove and later fired into the Cove at the Marines there. The loss of the seamen so rankled Admiral Boscawen that he posted a standing reward of 50 guineas for an Indian if he were brought in alive.[42] Lieutenant Edward Crofton of Brewer's Company almost won the reward on the 29th. He was posted with a picket of Rangers at a blockhouse near the fortress when the approach of Indians became known. Since it was dark, he formed an ambuscade ten yards from the road, killed two Indians and nearly captured a third, but he squirmed free.[II-31]

The Rangers posted before Barachois Lagoon were in a precarious position until the British batteries were ensconced. The French ships cannonaded the British at work and the Rangers were in their line of fire. On the 21st shots were dropping in their camp, and Scott asked Amherst if he might withdraw the Rangers and Light Infantry out of range, but Amherst would not let him "decamp for it."^{43} Weathering the storm until the British batteries were ready to retort did not prove as suicidal as first believed for the Rangers were scattered out and their losses were meager. As Amherst had hoped, their advanced position proved of infinite value, for they were able to inform him of sorties from Louisbourg, and very often disposed of the encroachment by themselves: On the 26th, at noon, a sortie were about to set fire to Amherst's advance blockhouse then under construction. "They got two men in and had a Barrel of Pitch but Mr. Scott sent a party" of Rangers and Light Infantry "so quick on them that they retreated without effecting it, and he drove them into the Town very fast."$^{II-30}$

The 30th, Amherst records, "Skirmishing: in this section; and the following morning, just at daybreak, the French stole across the Barachois Bridge to get old palisades and wood. They were discovered and Wolfe and Scott, with a detachment of Rangers and Light Infantry"pushed them in with a very brisk fire."$^{II-32}$

The Rangers were in no more frays of consequence until July 9, at one p.m. $^{II-37}$ when a picket of 6 Rangers participated in the fiercest sortie made by the French. Quietly approaching the siege works on the Cap Noir side, 724 French attacked the Ranger picket who were posted in advance with 15 British. The survivors, followed by the French, made their way to the main trench. In the grim action which followed there the Grenadiers and surviving Rangers were driven out but upon the arrival of a body of Grenadiers, they counter-attacked and recovered their work and the French retired to Louisbourg.

At last on July 15, the long-awaited partisan, Boishebert, made his appearance from his base at Mire. He made a predawn attack on Captain Sutherland and Rogers Rangers^{II-38} posted at Northeast Harbour. A smart skirmish ensued "and there was a great deal of firing." Wolfe's Grenadiers and Scott with all the Light Infantry went to sustain them but they arrived too late. Boishebert disappeared so quickly that the pursuing

Scot could not overtake him. From a deserter they learned that 50 Indians were at large, intent on Freshwater Cove. Amherst hurried off 100 chosen Rangers from McCurdey's and Brewer's Companies "to try to find them." The first night out they intercepted at least one Indian for they captured one alive and were thus entitled to the coveted fifty guineas reward. II-39

On July 26, Louisbourg capitulated, and there was rejoicing everywhere. When Major Rogers heard of the valorous deeds of his four overseas Companies he paraded his Lake George Companies in their honour and bought a barrel of wine for his own Company "to illuminate the rejoicing."44

There still remained the subjection of the maritime provinces and ports dependent upon Louisbourg. Thirty of James Rogers' Company served in Major Dalling's bloodless seizure of Spanish Bay. II-43 The balance of the Company accompanied Lord Rollo to the Isle St. Jean for the same purpose, II-44 both detachments returning to Louisbourg upon the completion of these tasks.45

On August 30, McCurdey's, Brewer's and Stark's Companies (and Goreham's Rangers)III-75 sailed with Monckton's force to take Fort St. John at the mouth of the same river in New Brunswick. This had been Boishebert's headquarters prior to the Siege of Louisbourg and the Rangers anticipated renewing their brief acquaintance and catching him. But much to their annoyance they found the fort abandoned; and the expedition ended in a desultory raid up the river in which two abandoned villages were fired by the Rangers.III-80-81

Returning to Fort St. JohnII-46 (now named Fort Frederic), the Rangers were dispatched under Scott up the Peticodiac River to destroy a schooner in two different creeks. Due to the lateness of the season, the schooner was encased in ice but the Rangers were determined to bring her in a prize and they literally cut her loose "with much difficulty."III-82 The settlement of 100 houses and barns was burned. Some of the Acadian occupants lurked in the woods and waylaid Lieutenant Caesar McCormick of William Stark's Company and his detachment of three Rangers and two Light Infantry Privates of the 35th. They were straggling too far from the main body and were all taken prisoners. II-52 When Scott was informed of their fate the next morning he immediately sent Lieutenant Edward Crofton with a party of Rangers "to endeavour to retake Lt. McCormick, " and though he strove throughout that day and night he could not "find anything" of McCormick's party. III-83 The wary Acadians, sons of the forest, as well as the sea, had melted away to Miramichi with their prisoners. McCormick was afterwards removed to Restigouche where he was well treated but forced to write letters stating such and "earnestly begging" that if the bearer "should happen to fall into your hands, to use him, or any of his party, as kind as you can; which will be of great service to me, and all other poor captives in Canada." With these letters on their person as insurance of good treatment should they, or their party be captured, the bearers, usually leaders of marauding partisans, would make winter attacks on small parties of wood-cutters from Fort Cumberland and other posts.

Scott's raiders arrived at Fort Frederic on November 18, with their two prizes, and 30 prisoners. The Ranger Companies now went into winter quarters; James Rogers' Company remained at Louisbourg. Goreham's Rangers wintered at Lunenburgh. Brewer's and William Stark's Companies helped McCurdy's men cut wood for their use at Fort Frederic, then embarked for Halifax for the winter. [46]

Chapter III
1759

AMHERST'S ADVANCE GUARD FOR CONQUEST

If Rogers' six Companies at Fort Edward were compared to a human body, a diagnosis in January 1759 would show an advanced case of anemia. Instead of the authorized 600, they numbered less than 200. This dearth of strength gave Major Rogers the excuse for asking Amherst for permission to go to New England to send up all the men his officers had recruited. In order that he might begin his "acquaintance" with Amherst, his new Commander, Rogers asks that he might travel by way of New York and meet him personally. Rogers, a born entrepreneur, strived to promote Amherst into increasing the number of Companies at Fort Edward, appropriately stating that his command would then be strong enough to prevent the Indians from "playing their old pranks."[47]

Rogers was in Albany on January 28, when he wrote to Amherst. He, and the bulk of his Rangers, had convoyed empty sleighs from Fort Edward to pick up provisions. During his absence, Gage, who commanded the New York Forts for the winter, stymied Rogers' plan for a furlough. He wrote Amherst the day before Rogers did, recommending that the recruiting officers could be notified to send up their Ranger recruits by advertising in the papers;[48] and until they should arrive, he took it upon himself to order Colonel Haldimand, the Commandant at Fort Edward, to have 200 Regulars from the garrison serve with the Rangers.[49] This experiment had been proposed by many British officers in the past, and now that it was tried, it proved a failure. The principal difficulty being the question of rank between the Ranger and British officers, as will be seen when the occasion arose.

Returning to Fort Edward with the sleighs Rogers soon learned that his Corps suffered a slight loss on February 1st. At 2 P.M. 30 Indians ambushed two Rangers returning from a scout. They killed and scalped one, the other was wounded but broke free and reached the fort a mile and a half away. Another Ranger out hunting was reported missing. [II-53]

A most hardy Crown Point scout of 23 days was conducted by the veteran Noah Johnson, who had re-joined the Corps during the winter to succeed Captain James Neale when he left the service. Although no prisoner was taken, Johnson obtained information on the situation at Crown Point. [III-85]

While he was out, Rogers made his third, last, and most successful large scale winter excursion against Ticonderoga. [II-55] General Gage wanted a map drawn of the present condition of Ticonderoga so Amherst might have the proper intelligence when he advanced upon it. He sent Lieutenant Brehme, a competent draughtsman from the Royal Americans to accompany Rogers. This was the prime purpose of the expedition but Rogers had orders to take prisoners or strike a blow against the French after Brehme had completed his mission. This was the largest force that Rogers ever commanded in a winter raid against the enchanted Ticonderoga. There were 90 of his Rangers, 217 Regulars and 50 Mohawks under Captain Lotridge who had just arrived from the Mohawk valley to join the expedition. Since the British Volunteers were in the preponderance, their commander, Captain Williams, thought he should outrank Rogers and "there was some Dispute between Rogers and Captain Williams about rank, which at length, the latter gave up to prevent all impediments towards their moving."

This controversial question finally settled, Rogers marched out of Fort Edward on March 3, and encamped that night at Halfway Brook. One Mohawk had an accident and had to be sent back with another to assist him. Rogers was not taking any chance of a repeat performance of the Rogers' Rock tragedy of almost a year ago. All the marching was done at night so that they might arrive at Ticonderoga valley unobserved by the French lookouts on the hills. The weather was sub-zero, and 23 men were frostbitten the second day out, before they had even reached Lake George. They had to be returned to Fort Edward under the care of a careful Sergeant. The next night they marched to Sabbath Day Point, arriving there at 11 P.M., "almost overcome with the cold." Remaining only three hours they continued on and reached the end of the Lake at 8 A.M.

Rogers dispatched a small reconnaissance party who reported Ticonderoga valley was free of enemy parties but on the west side of Lake Champlain were two wood-cutting details. Now was an excellent opportunity for Brehme to make his observations and he went forward to Rattlesnake Hill accompanied by Rogers and 94 Rangers and Mohawks. When he was ready to return, Rogers left a Ranger and five Mohawks to count the number in the wood-cutting parties when they returned to Ticonderoga, so that he might have intelligence on their strength in order to plan a coup the next morning. At dusk Brehme again went forward, accompanied by Lieutenant Tute and ten men. They examined the entrenchments before the fort from end to end much to the amazement of the French in Ticonderoga who were informed of the tracks by a patrol the next morning. At midnight Brehme and Tute returned to Rogers and since the Regulars were suffering terribly from the weather and not equipped with snow shoes, Rogers did not deem it prudent to hamper his effective force with their care; accordingly, they were ordered back to Sabbath Day Point under Captain Williams, and Tute with 30 Rangers accompanied them to build fires and secure Rogers' return march.

Rogers' attacking force consisted of Lieutenants Robert Holmes, Archibald Stark and David Brewer, and 40 Rangers; 1 Regular, and Captain Lottridge with 46 Mohawks. In all, 92 officers and men. At 3 A.M. (March 7th) they dauntlessly attacked the mountains that separated them from lower Lake Champlain, wending their difficult way through them like blanket-shrouded phantoms intent on some ghastly errand. Crossing the arm of the lake at 6 A.M. they discovered tracks of 50 Indians that had passed by the day before towards Fort Edward.

Continuing on to their objective eight miles north, they arrived at Little Mary River and found forty soldiers chopping wood for Ticonderoga directly across from them. Rogers immediately fanned his men out and after stripping off their blankets, which had served as a cloak while marching, they charged down upon them and greeted the surprised French with a combination Ranger-Mohawk battle shout. Seven prisoners were taken, four were killed, and four more wounded, who managed to escape to Ticonderoga with the others. Rogers' party pursued them to within pistol-shot of the fort.

Meanwhile Hebecourt, the Commandant, was aware of strangers on his premises, for two Iroquois on a morning patrol returned hurriedly to report the discovery of Rogers' tracks at the landing place. The moment he fired the signal gun to warn the woodcutters was the instant of Rogers' attack. As Rogers withdrew across the Lake, Hebecourt sent 80 Canadians and Indians to pursue him until he could outfit 150 Regulars to support them. Rogers employed Ranging Rules XII, XIII and XXIX, and drew his resolute pursuers on until he had reached a hill one mile south of his first scene of action. Since they were marching in a line abreast, Rogers' front was easily formed and they repulsed their attackers. The delayed action was continued by Rogers' enticing the enemy on for another half-mile until a long ridge was reached. Here a second stand was made and a fierce skirmish took place. The Canadians and Indians again broke but this time Rules XIII and XXIX were fulfilled when the Rangers and Mohawks counter-charged and routed them before the slogging French Regulars could come up. The march was resumed without further annoyance and Sabbath-Day Point was reached that night at twelve after an incredible day's march of 50 miles in freezing atmosphere and 4 feet of snow.

In spite of Captain Williams' welcome fires a count of the complete force revealed two-thirds of the men were frostbitten, including Rogers himself. Lieutenant Tute was sent to Fort Edward for sleds which met the crippled raiders at the site of Fort William Henry. Arriving at Fort Edward, Rogers, among the rest, was so fatigued, that he did not compile his <u>Journal</u> until a few days later. Meanwhile Gage forwarded to

Amherst a resume of Rogers' success that he had received from Haldimand at Fort Edward. Other heralds of victory waited upon him in the form of forty Mohawks who gave him a prisoner as a gift to be sent to Amherst. Rogers praised the conduct of Lotridge and recommended that he and his Company of Mohawks be taken into service as Rogers Rangers; but any merits they gained were offset by their drunken conduct on their return to the Mohawk Valley. Near Schenectady they shot a Highland sentry who challenged them, wounding him in both thighs. Although Amherst thought that Williams and his Regulars should have been better employed by Rogers, he was aware of Rogers' brilliant execution of a difficult assignment, and he asked Gage to recommend and suggest ways of rewarding those that were deserving. Gage replied that Rogers and Lotridge distinguished themselves most and suggests that Amherst would have it in his power to some time or other reward Rogers and recommends the reward of Lotridge to be left to Johnson. In spite of Gage's reluctance to give credit where credit was due, Rogers' results spoke for themselves. As Amherst read Rogers' Journal, which excelled any adventure story of the time, he could not help expelling a breath of satisfaction when he realized that he would be having the services of such hardy characters in his advance on Ticonderoga.

No sooner had Rogers returned than he was called upon to play the role of diplomat and negotiate with Jacob junior for the services of two Companies of Stockbridges. Jacob arrived tardily at Albany and refused to proceed to Fort Edward, insisting that Rogers should meet him at Albany. As Rogers was frostbitten and thus incapable of being "on party," Gage, the ever contemptuous, made the expansive gesture of ordering him down. Rogers arrived on a sled and the next day, March 25, Gage writes, the two chiefs held their conference. The pow-wow was successful and the two Jacobs Companies re-entered the Corps.[50]

About 150 Ranger recruits straggled into Albany and it appeared that Rogers Rangers would now resume their more corpulent appearance, but unfortunately an epidemic of measles broke out among many of the recruits and only a portion of them were able to march to Ford Edward.[51]

Before Rogers could arrive at Rogers' Island with his recruits his officers had astounded Commandant Haldimand and roused the wrath of Gage when he was informed that they refused to scout unless they had sufficient numbers to protect them from the Indian parties at large. In Gage's prejudiced mind, this bit of sound determination bordered on mutiny, and following as it did, so close on the heels of the Rogers-Williams rank dispute, it riled him into penning a <u>decree</u> to Haldimand in which he manifested his unbending attitude in regard to the Rangers. He ordered the officers and Rangers who would not march to be confined for mutiny. Any officer who attempted to resign would be tried for desertion. As soon as Rogers arrived with the recruits the Corps was to be paraded by a British officer who was "to see them put in some tolerable order, & the six companys leveled & distinguished from each other..." and the articles of war were to be read to them every week. [52]

This determination of Gage's to break up the Corps as a battalion was high-handed for it was Amherst's duty and not his. In his wrath at the Rangers he worked behind Rogers' back as well as Amherst's. Rogers left Albany with orders to put his Companies in order, but before he could arrive at Rogers' Island and fulfill these orders, Gage sent the above instructions to the Commandant at Fort Edward; at the same time he sent a copy to Amherst asking his approval, and ridiculing Rogers' ability to maintain order in his Corps.[53] Gage was jealous of Rogers' latent capabilities and daring. He hoped to take advantage of Amherst's unfamiliarity of his true sentiments toward Rogers and minimize his fame. But he underestimated Amherst's insight of human nature. He read between the lines, and though his British mind was sometimes reluctant to accept the vaunted merits of the Rangers in general, still he never doubted Rogers' ability, and he repeatedly stood up for him or turned a deaf ear when sly aspersions were made against him. Fortunately this second[54] crisis of the life of the Corps survived the jealous fevour gnawing at its existence. Major Eyre relieved Haldimand at Fort Edward at this critical time and this factor with that of a delayed mail delivery[55] enabled Rogers to arrive during this bustle, and quiet the eloquent voicings of his officers who were only sounding his own sentiments. By the time Gage's proclamation arrived, Eyre was reluctant to carry out his orders without confirmation from Amherst.

Although Gage's drastic actions were not taken, still, Eyre followed Haldimand's insistence in sending out small ill-advised scouts which were catastrophic for the bulk of the participants:

On May 1, Sergeant Daniel Hurlburt and 3 Rangers were sent scouting to an Indian village on the Sacandaga River which flowed into the Hudson. Fourteen miles from Fort Edward they were attacked on the southern shore of the Hudson by Indians. A grim duel followed in which only one Ranger managed to escape to Fort Edward, of the others, one Ranger was killed and Sergeant Hurlburt and Private Robert Hewitt were taken prisoners. They elaborated in the information which they were forced to divulge and confused the French about the true state of Amherst's army and forts.[II-57]

About May 11, while Rogers was in Albany settling Ranger accounts, another blow fell: A Ticonderoga scout were returning on foot when they espied 15 craft pulling away from the site of Fort William Henry.[III-87] Arriving at the site the Rangers found the scalped remains of a fellow Ranger. He was one of 30 commanded by Captain Burbank who had slept the night in a large hut with his party. They were attacked at dawn by a superior force of Indians who drove them from the hut by setting fire to it. Most of the Rangers surrendered with Burbank. Some who resisted were "mangled in a shocking manner..." while others were overpowered and joined with those who surrendered. Private Samuel Shepherd while engaging an Indian in front was overpowered when an Indian from behind grabbed his hair queue and jerked him off balance. His brother George ducked a vicious blow at his head which brought a wounded scream from the Tomahawk wielder when it descended upon his own leg. Captain Burbank was mistaken for Rogers and inhumanely butchered and scalped. When told of their mistake by the other prisoners, they appeared sorry, for some were St. Francis Indians and Burbank had been a captive among them during his youth and had "shown them kindness." The loss of

Burbank's complete party seemed a crushing loss at the time, for only three mangled bodies could be found when a thorough search was later made. Since none escaped, considerable conjecture was made as to their fate, but amazingly enough, 25 of the 28 captured were sold to the French and exchanged on November 15, 1759. The other 3 were retained by the Indians, one of them being delivered up in 1760. Besides these who were unaccounted for, the only permanent loss to the Corps were Captain Burbank and two men killed. Burbank's murder was grieved by all, for he was well liked. [II-59]

Not all of the scouts sent out at this time were worsted. It would seem that the deeper Rogers Rangers penetrated into enemy territory the safer and more successful they were. A penetration to Crown Point bagged a Frenchman hunting nearby in the woods who revealed much needy information. [III-88]

In the meantime Rogers had seen Amherst in Albany and squelched Gage's attempt to dissolve his command into separate distinct Ranging Companies. Amherst assured Rogers that he would retain the Majority over his Corps and have the rank of Major in the army from April 6, 1758, the date of his commission from Abercrombie.[56] Rogers was reassured of his continued command over his farflung Companies. Upon the death of Lieutenant Fossit of James Rogers' Company at Louisbourg, Ensign Stephen Holland was promoted at Major Roberts' recommendation.[57] Rogers was notified of Lieutenant Moses Hazen's ascension to McCurdey's command when he was accidentally killed at Fort Frederic;[58] and when Captain Wendell expressed a desire to resign from the command of the Rangers at Fort Stanwix, [II-58] Amherst, at Rogers' recommendation, promoted Lieutenant Joseph Wait of Rogers' own Company to succeed Wendell on May 11, and Rogers advanced Waite money to purchase uniforms and necessities for his Company.[59] Rogers anxiously queried Amherst about the fate of Lieutenant Caesar McCormick, captured in New Brunswick for he wanted him to serve in his own Company.[60] It was through Rogers' intervention that McCormick was exchanged prior to the Siege of Quebec.

Rogers was continually intervening for his scattered flock. On May 11, he vouched for five veteran Rangers and saved them from being pressed into the navy. Sergeant William Clark arrived in Albany to inform the amazed Rogers that he and four other captive Rangers in 1758 had been carried to Quebec, then exchanged to England, and had finally worked their way to New York on the armed ship Essex. The ship's commander, John Curtin, was reluctant to part with them and he confined them on board when they anchored in New York; but the Ranger-Seamen were determined not to serve a life sentence on the Essex and Clark made his "elopement" on May 4, and a week later he arrived footsore at Albany. Rogers immediately sent a Sergeant with Clark's account to Schomberg of the Diana, who was Curtin's superior. He in turn relayed the Sergeant to Amherst who ordered Curtin to deliver the Rangers to the Sergeant. The grateful Rangers who were returned to the Corps were Sergeants Martin Severance and Joshua Conky of Rogers' own; Privates Morris O'Brian and Aggrippa Wells of Burbank's. Private Conky was a rare captive-survivor of Rogers' Rock.[61]

There were ten Companies of Rogers Rangers on the Lake George front.[62] Three Companies were new or revivals. The new Company was led by Lieutenant David Brewer who had not enlisted enough men as yet to warrant a Captain's commission.[63] The revived Companies were those of the two Jacobs. The younger Jacob marched from Albany to Fort Edward on May 9, with his Company of 58.[64] His father, though, was far behind schedule. He arrived in Albany the latter part of the month. Amherst gathered his scattered Company together to march on the 26th, but rum stopped them and it was not until two days later that they were able to march. They had to leave one of their brethren behind for he was almost dead from the wounds they had given him while brawling under the influence of rum.[65]

While Amherst's army gathered at Lake George for his advance on Ticonderoga and Crown Point, numerous scouts of Rogers Rangers were thrown against these forts and around the army for protection and information.[III-89-90-91-92-93-94-95-96-97-98-101-102-104-106-107-108] Their purpose was varied. Attempts were made by Captain Stark to entice enemy parties into a trap. He, and a boatload of fishing Rangers acted as the decoy, but the enemy were too wary.III-99 Rogers bagged a huge bear and diplomatically presented the skin to Appy, Amherst's secretary.66 Appy was in a position to put in a good word for Rogers and he knew it. Two actions of consequence occurred before the army embarked. Captain Jacob Cheeksaunkun's Company was badly cut up on July 5th. The second day out Jacob grew careless and traveled on the Lake in daylight. He was seen at the Second Narrows by a force twice his size and attacked. He ordered his three boats to make for the shore. Jacob in the third boat covered the landing of the other two, but unfortunately when his boat landed they found a steep bank confronting them and before they could scramble up it the Iroquois were upon them. In the desperate fight which followed, five Stockbridges were killed and Jacob and the other four were captured. In their fury at their own losses, the Iroquois tortured and killed the four Stockbridge Privates. Jacob was prudently spared for the high price which he brought from the French. This was a terrific loss for half of Jacobs' little Company of thirty men were killed or captured. The survivors straggled reluctantly into camp for they knew they would be condemned for being on the lake in broad daylight but far worse was the difficult task of breaking the news of Jacob's capture to his son. There was a strong affection between the two Jacobs. When Jacob Naunauphtaunk learned of his father's capture he was overcome with grief and upon recovering he "menaced vengeance against the enemy."II-65

The other action, a more favorable one for the Corps, took place on July 12, when a ruse was attempted in order to dislodge a partisan force lurking in the First Narrows. Majors Rogers and Campbell led a force of Rangers, Gage's Light Infantry and Grenadiers. They started before dawn and rowed along the east shore until they reached the islands of the Narrows, here Campbell remained with the Regulars and a boat with an 18-pounder, while Rogers went forth with his 100 Rangers to entice the enemy from the islands. Rogers' advance boat was fired upon and a Sergeant was killed and a Stockbridge was wounded. Rogers briskly returned the fire and drove the enemy from the island and down the lake with eight deadly rounds of musketry. Campbell came up to support Rogers with his Regulars and 18-pounder but he revealed and fired the cannon too soon. After this discovery, the enemy, about 200 Indians, made haste to keep their distance while they retreated down the lake. This action, though not as successful as it might have been, cleared the Narrows of any lurking foe in preparation for Amherst's embarkation nine days later.[II-68]

The proportion of whaleboats and batteaus for Rogers Rangers was forty-three and on the 17th Rogers was ordered to paint the name of his Corps upon each of them.[67] Other consequential assignments were frequently mentioned in various General Orders;[68] and a promotional item of importance occurred while the army was encamped at Lake George. Captain John Shepherd wrote Rogers on June 25, asking that he might resign on account of poor health. Rogers was glad to comply for now he might recommend Lieutenant James Tute, his friend, to the vacancy. Amherst accepted Shepherd's resignation on July 12, and promoted Tute.[69]

The unknown fate of Captain Burbank inspired a hopeful claim in his First Lieutenant, Andrew McMullen; but to his chagrin, Rogers took over the helm, compiled the muster rolls and received the pay for the Company. McMullen was a brave officer but he was bestowed with a violent Irish temper and he almost had an internal combustion over his frustration. In an angry discussion with Rogers he was accused of being angry because he could not have the "perquisitts" of the Company. This galled McMullen so that he petitioned Amherst on July 16, stating that Rogers might just as well have called him a rogue and a Sutler to the Company. He implied the same of Rogers and accused him of holding back the billeting money that he and the other officers had laid out while marching their recruits to Albany. McMullen asks that he might have the command of the Company until Burbank's return or else be allowed to resign and serve as a Volunteer in some other Corps.[70] In spite of the strong accusations cast at each other, Rogers and McMullen seem to have become reconciled. Unlike other Corps commanders, Rogers could forgive a fiery nature if there was a capable Ranger behind the flame.

On July 20, a scout of Rangers returned to report that

"Hand to Hand" Illustration by Gary Zaboly

"Action at the First Narrows on Lake George" Illustration by Gary Zaboly

the French advance guard had retired to Ticonderoga valley and the next day Amherst's invasion army embarked.III-109 As usual, Rogers formed the advance guard with his Rangers. They were the first body that landed the next day at Ticonderoga Valley. Pushing vigorously forward Rogers surprised Captain Bournie and 400 French and Indians at the bridge crossing Ticonderoga River. Rogers took possession of the bridge and a short but fierce engagement took place on the north side. Bournie's force broke and retired under Rogers' pressure, taking their wounded with them. Bournie lost 4 men killed, and 1 officer and 2 men taken prisoners. II-70

The passage was now clear for Amherst's advancing columns, and the Army took possession of the heights near the Saw Mills. When the French saw Amherst bringing up his cannon to invest Ticonderoga they abandoned Montcalm's lines without too much resistance. The capture of an entrenchment north of the fortress was assigned to Rogers. He sent Captain Moses Brewer with 200 Rangers and they "happily succeeded."II-72 Brewer remained here with his Company and Amherst repeated his strategy at Louisbourg and posted Rogers with the balance of his Rangers to cover his rear from partisan attacks.71

The day after Brewer's capture, a party of Indians sallied forth and attacked his entrenchment. A spirited fire was exchanged and the attackers were driven off. II-74

Every day of the siege saw Rogers Rangers executing some specialIII-110 or dangerous assignment. The night of the 25th saw sixty Ranger sharpshooters in the trenches "to amuse the besieged...by popping into their" watchtowers and gun-turrets while British artificers were busily at work at another point. III-111 The next night Major Rogers was entrusted with the "secret assignment" of cutting off the boom which had been extended across the lake to prevent British boats from passing. Rogers quietly embarked with sixty Rangers and saws in three boats that had been hauled overland for him. At 9 P.M. they were half-way to the boom's end on the east shore when they heard an explosion from Ticonderoga and saw the French abandoning the fort for their boats. Rogers, though outnumbered, was in an excellent position to attack them and harass their retreat. Rogers' little flotilla alarmed the French into believing their force was much greater. Indeed, Rogers' daring attacks netted the capture of ten boats, 50 barrels of powder, a quantity of French coats, 16 to 20 prisoners, and Commandant Hebecourt's portmanteau containing many valuable letters. A coup which a larger force could have boasted of with pride. [II-77]

Ticonderoga had finally fallen. No more would the bells of Carillon ring for French ears.[72] Possessive eyes were now turned toward Crown Point. While Amherst waited for his batteaus to come up and be portaged to Lake Champlain he posted Rogers Rangers beyond the Sawmills as a buffer between Ticonderoga and the partisan bands expected from Crown Point. The Rangers helped to obstruct the road to the lake to hamper the approach of a large force;[73] but small raiding parties sifted through. On July 28, Ensign Jonas of a Stockbridge Company was peeling bark when he was killed and scalped. [III-113]

Small scouts of Rangers were constantly kept out towards Crown Point and Amherst "had not only daily, but hourly intelligence."[74] They were not lacking in daring for one scout entered the French camp and spirited away a British deserter. This bit of audacity was one of those characteristic feats which made listeners stand with mouth agape when Ranger exploits were related. [III-115]

At noon on August 1, a detail from a scout under Lieutenant Fletcher returned with the amazing news of the evacuation of Crown Point. Fletcher himself arrived the next day to relate on his taking possession of the ruins of the once mighty fortress. The French had blown it up and withdrawn to Isle Au Noix at the northern end of Lake Champlain. Fletcher would have hoisted a flag of some kind but the French had not left so much as the halyards; instead, he wrote his name on the flagstaff and brought Amherst some cucumbers and apples from the garden as a token. [II-79] Fletcher's possession of Crown Point was cemented when Captain Moses Brewer was sent with 200 Rangers to post themselves in a strategic position until Amherst's army arrived the next evening (Augst 4th). [III-116]

Commensurate with the passing of ancient French reign

on Lake George and Champlain was the revealing of Rogers' legendary <u>Secret Water-Passage</u> east of Sabbath Day Point. Rogers and Captain Abercrombie had been sent on August 1 to lay out a road over this famous passage through the mountains separating the two lakes so that a road might be built securing Amherst's communications with Fort George now being built near the site of Fort William Henry.[III-114] Rogers, the <u>Surveyor</u>, returned in time to embark with the army for Crown Point. Upon arriving he was encamped with his Rangers as a buffer in front of the army, and they beached their whaleboats at West Bay on the left of their camp.[75] Thus ensconced in their new home Rogers Rangers shared conspicuously in the bustling activities of camp and field while Amherst built a fleet of vessels to protect his advance on Isle Aux Noix from the four French sloops commanding Lake Champlain.

The day after their arrival 100 of Rogers Rangers turned pioneers and cut a road to Ticonderoga so that fresh meat might be herded down on the hoof.[III-117] The same day Major Rogers was sent with a party to the east side of the lake to discover the best spots to cut timber for the new fort to be built at Crown Point. Rogers' party were given permission to hunt and they shot 3 deer and 7 bears.[III-118] The hunt was repeated on August 8, this time 4 Regular officers and 25 Rangers and Light Infantry accompanied Rogers and their sense of sportsmanship was aroused when they were enjoined not to take any "dropping shots at game."[III-119] A more whimsical hunt was maintained by Ranger Private Stilson Eastman: Amherst, being fond of milk, had a cow in camp, which had liberty to run at large, to find the best feeding ground. After a time the cow wandered off and could not be found; soldiers were sent in various directions but to no avail. At length Eastman was sent out and he found her to the great joy of Amherst, who, as a reward, ordered Eastman's canteen to be filled with rum. Being reluctant to let a good thing pass, Eastman, from time to time, drove the cow to its favorite pasture, where no one could find her but himself, and whenever he brought in the cow he received his reward in his canteen.[76]

It was necessary that Amherst get a message through to Wolfe at Quebec and a Volunteer was asked for from the Rangers on August 5; two days later Ensign Benjamin Hutchings earned fame for himself when he stepped forth to undertake the hazardous mission. He traveled by way of Boston where he took a sloop to Fort Halifax on the Kennebec River. From here, accompanied by a guide and two men, he traveled cross-country to Point Levi and Wolfe. They were 17 days on their march and the last four they were without food and were about to give themselves up from sheer necessity when they managed to capture 3 inhabitants who informed them how close Quebec was. Making another notch in their belts they held on and reached Wolfe on September 3rd. Four days later, accompanied by Captain Stobo, recently escaped from Quebec,[77] Hutchings started his return trip to Amherst on board Captain Haynes' sloop. On September 29, they were off the Cape Sable shore when they were hailed by an English voice. Allowing the sloop to come within range they were aware of her true colours when four swivel guns were fired, and 50 French Privateers swarmed aboard. Hutchings and the other English poured 300 rounds from their small arms into the Pirates before they struck. Hutchings was forced to part with all his uniform but his hat. He was also robbed of his Ensign's commission and over 200 dollars, but fortunately he managed to throw overboard his dispatches from Wolfe to Amherst. They were taken to Beaver Harbour on the Cape Sable shore and two days later the Pirate Captain gave them a small fishing schooner and jammed an accumulation of 50 English prisoners aboard. Happily, they had good weather, but only one day's provisions and they were almost starved when they reached Halifax after a three-day voyage. Notwithstanding, Hutchings and Stobo reembarked the next morning for Boston and then by horseback and boat to Crown Point. III-119-A

The day after Hutchings started out from Crown Point on his adventure-packed mission, Amherst had attempted to get another message through to Wolfe. He sent Captain Kennedy and Lieutenant Hamilton of the Regulars and Captain Jacob Naunauphataunk and 4 Stockbridges of Rogers Rangers to Quebec via St. Francis under the guise of offering the Indians peace terms, their answer to be carried to Wolfe. Amherst underestimated the gullibility of the St. Francis Indians for Hamilton's party were captured by a hunting party from this tribe and though Jacob had an expensive belt of wampum and Amherst's message offering them protection for their neutrality, they turned a deaf ear and took them to Montcalm, and not Wolfe.[II-82]

Other detachments of Rogers Rangers were expressing their versatility of abilities. Captain John Stark with 200 Rangers was given the task of building a road from Crown Point to Number Four on the Connecticut River, a distance of about 80 miles, through an almost pathless wilderness. When it was completed in a month's time, it opened up communication with New England.[III-121]

Exploring parties were sent up the Otter,[III-122] Upper Hudson[III-124] and La Barbue Rivers to determine their true nature. Daring scouts were made to Isle Aux Noix. Ensign Wilson led the first scout of Rangers to the island, but two of his men who were sent forward were discovered while trying to pass through the Indian encampment. Wilson effected a safe retreat.[III-120] The canoe pursuing them contained an officer, 6 Indians and 4 Canadians. They left their canoe at the mouth of Otter River and proceeding by land captured 2 Privates of the 55th on the east side.[III-123-125] Meanwhile Captain Tute, Lieutenants Darcy and Solomon and 40 Rangers who were "on party" attempted to capture French officers reported to have been going ashore from their ships to fish, having given up hope of waylaying any on the west shore had crossed over to the east side and discovered the canoe. Tute's party lay in wait and ambushed the French and Indians when they returned. During the skirmish, 1 French Indian was killed and scalped; 2 more were badly wounded but managed to escape with the rest. Tute's force suffered 2 Rangers wounded. One of the 55th Privates managed to make his escape to Tute during the conflict. There was no time for pursuit, the French fleet were at anchor off the mouth of the river and upon hearing the firing they came up the lake with the wind just as Tute was pulling away from the shore in his whaleboat and captured canoe. A thrilling chase followed. The Breeze was with the three French ships and the Rangers had to row furiously to keep ahead of them. Tute was on the verge of trying for the shore and taking the chance of the fleet sailing ahead and landing parties to cut him off from Crown Point, when one of his Rangers (a former New England fisherman) suggested they rig sails with their blankets. This happy thought was quickly put into effect and they were thus able to hold their own until the ships gave up the chase as they neared Crown Point.[II-86]

Tute's odyssey was followed by an incredible feat which introduced to Ranger Annals one of the most daring members of the Corps. The Ranger who made his debut to fame was Sergeant-Major Joseph Hopkins. Amherst embarked two parties of Rangers on the night of August 22, to undertake a dual scouting operation to St. Johns. Lieutenant Fletcher commanded one party of ten, while Sergeant Hopkins led the other of eight. The parties separated a mile from St. Johns after agreeing on a rendezvous at a certain time. Fletcher scouted inquisitively but dangerously toward La Prairie (across the river from Montreal), while Hopkins continued toward St. Johns. He was discovered by a superior force but adopted Rogers Ranging Rule and ordered his 8 men to separate and retreat in different directions. Some hours later, Hopkins and 4 of his Rangers re-united near Isle aux Noix where he decided to lie in ambush for a prisoner. "At length he observed 3 soldiers go in to Swim in the Lake, close by 4 armed Vessels, he immediately stripped himself, and went into swim likewise, his Party lying concealed. He swam along till he came to the 3 Soldiers, when he entered into a familiar Discourse with them in French, which the Sergeant spoke fluently; among the rest that he told them, he said, that where he enter'd to swim there was such a prodigious Number of Fish that he could hardly get along for them; the 3 Soldiers were extremely anxious to be shown the Place, which the Sergeant undertook, and swam along with them to the Place where his Men lay in Ambush, when they rush'd out into the water about Breast high and made them all 3 Prisoners and brought them off, notwithstanding their Hallowing, which alarmed the Enemy, who were seen very numerous on the Ramparts, they being within Gun-Shot and under the Muzzles of the Guns of the armed vessels and in sight of some hundreds of the Enemy; but they did not fire for fear of killing their own Men. The prisoners informed of Lieutenant Fletcher and his Party being taken who gave intelligence of Hopkins, and that a Party was out in order to Way-lay him, but luckily he did not leave his Whale-Boats where he determined to meet Fletcher, and by that Means escaped; for he scarcely put off before the Enemy appeared and fired upon him, but did no damage..." The other four men of Hopkins' party preceded him into Crown Point and informed Amherst that he was probably captured; consequently when Hopkins arrived the next day there was considerable rejoicing, and "when the Sergeant brought the Prisoners to Amherst, the General was exceedingly pleased with the affair and told Hopkins 'He was obliged to him for catching such Fish, and that he had fished to a good Purpose.'"III-126

Hopkins' feat was shadowed by the fate of Lieutenant Fletcher's party. An overwhelming force of 70 Indians came upon his boat, captured one of the two men left to guard it, and then tracked Fletcher until they came upon him and his 8 men near La Prairie. Though surrounded, Fletcher made a brave stand and "behaved well" in the uneven fight which followed. He was soon "compelled by necessity" to surrender for there were only two men left alive with him, three had been killed while three others had broken out of the trap, however one of these was caught up with and taken to Montreal with Fletcher and the other two. Fortunately, Fletcher was redeemed from the Indians with a great deal of trouble by Saint Luke, a French officer. He was a friend to Ranger and British prisoners but he had an ulterior motive in rescuing Fletcher from the savages, for he made him promise that he would ask Amherst to exchange Captain Marin Dinsantrie for him. This expectancy of a French Captain being exchanged for a Ranger Lieutenant bespoke well of the high regard and bartering value the French held for Ranger officers regardless of their rank. II-87

A brief mention of the homesick members of the Corps will be recorded at this point for it is the purpose of this history to set forth an unbiased account of the questionable, as well as the valorous acts, of certain Rangers. Three Rangers deserted on the night of August 30th; and two more were suspected of doing so when a British officer reported them "lost in the woods" while on his scout. III-127 A Ranger was picked up at Saratoga shortly after Amherst's advance on Ticonderoga. He was one of the detachment of Rangers left with Commandant Montressor at Fort George. Montressor, who was already perturbed at his Rangers' reluctance to work on the new fort, "fettered him" to a ball and chain and made him work on the fort. As Stark's Road neared No. 4, 14 Rangers deserted. One unfortunate deserter fell into Amherst's hands. The General had a forgiving nature except for desertion. He ordered 1000 lashes for the Ranger but since he had only deserted to go home he "forgave him 500" and after receiving the other half he was drummed out of the army.[78]

Three days after his return from Isle aux Noix, Sergeant Hopkins was entrusted with a dangerous assignment. After his last exploit, Amherst had complete confidence in his unusual abilities. When Hopkins reported that a new French sloop had been launched, and was now being fitted out, Amherst sent Hopkins to burn the sloop. Four other expert swimmers were sought to assist him, and two Regulars and two Provincials who had been sailors volunteered and they were all instructed in the use of "fire-darts" and "hand-carcasses." Two Provincial officers volunteered to serve under Hopkins and four Rangers comprised the balance of his commando force. If the enterprise was successful, the men were to be rewarded. As utmost secrecy was of the essence they traveled only by night. On September 11, at ten P.M. Hopkins swam out to the sloop with the four best swimmers of his party. One man carried a dark lanthorn with the lighted match on his head. The others carried fire-darts and carcasses in little boxes attached to their heads in the same manner.

Swimming gently to the stern they discovered a Frenchman fishing in a boat. Luck was with them for the present, for they were not seen, and they swam around the boat to the bow. One man almost had his fire-dart screwed in and another was in preparation when a Frenchman looking over the bow saw them. The hue and cry was immediately sounded and there was a frenzied bustle on board until the magazine of powder was thrown overboard for the French feared that their ship was on fire. Hopkins and his commandos were forced—reluctantly

—to abandon their assignment and dive and swim alternately for their very lives. The guards on Isle aux Noix, as well as those on board, were firing at them. One man was grazed in the thigh and barely escaped a broadaxe thrown at him. Reaching the covering party on shore Hopkins was able to escape in the darkness and bring his party safely into Crown Point. So ended an attempt, which, if it had succeeded, would well have garnished Hopkins' fame as well as that of Rogers Rangers. No second attempt to fire the sloop was planned for the now-wary French kept continuous guards and patrols on, and about their vessels, thus making it impossible. III-129

Amherst now feared the French would reciprocate and try to burn his fleet building on the ways, for enemy tracks and boats were seen on the sixth. Scouts by land and boat were sent after them but to no avail. III-130

Rogers Rangers were again employed on a secret and dangerous assignment. It was imperative that Amherst learn the results of Brigadier Gage's sluggish advance to La Gallete on the St. Lawrence River. Lietuenant Tute was sent with 11 men to go to the Riviere de Sable, go up it in a whaleboat as far as possible then strike overland to the St. Lawrence, taking notes on the nature of the Sable River and plausibility of marching an army overland. Unfortunately Tute only took 25 days' provisions with him and the seventeenth day out he had to send back a Sergeant and four men to obtain food and meet him eight miles up the Sable River where they left their whaleboat. Tute struck the St. Lawrence a few miles below La Gallete on September 20, after 27 days out. Their 25 days' provisions were gone and they were famished, but Tute determined to fulfill his mission. They crept forward and reconnoitered La Gallete and Tute resolved to take a prisoner. Unfortunately they had to abandon the scheme for Corporal Cauley of Gage's 80th was sent forward to scout, and he deserted to the enemy (no doubt hunger drove him to it). Tute penned a quick note to Gage describing the strength and situation of the enemy at La Gallete and also the famished condition of his party; he then retired as fast as his party could in their weakened condition towards their boat and relief party with provisions at the Sable River. Fate was against them, however, for the messenger sent to Gage was captured and the enemy were now fully aware of their route of march. Tute's party were trailed and captured on the same day (the 22nd) and taken to La Corne at Las Gallete and then sent to Montreal. II-88

During Tute's absence, Major Rogers stepped into the limelight to lead an expedition that brought undying fame to himself and his Corps. II-89 On September 10, Amherst learned from a flag of truce that Kennedy and Jacob had been captured by the very Indians that they had been sent to seduce away from the French. This riled Amherst considerably for he had felt confident that his naive ruse would work. As a result of this "ungenerous" attitude of the St. Francis Indians, Rogers' pleas to raid their lair were finally answered when Amherst ordered him forth on the 13th "to chastise those savages with some severity." Rogers was delighted, for four years he had been petitioning the various Commanders-in-Chief for the go signal on this, his pet project. As the conquest of Canada became imminent, Rogers was fretful that his project would remain shelved forever, but now that it was taken down and dusted off and brought to life, he threw himself into preparing his expedition with all of his famous vigor.

September 11 and 12th were busy days at Rogers' camp as 200 Rangers, Provincials and Regulars were picked from the swarm of Volunteers that clambered to join the expedition. For security reasons, the objective was kept a secret, but the fact that a secret expedition led by Rogers himself was ordered out so soon after the news of Kennedy's capture by St. Francis Indians prompted the Rangers and Provincials to hope that the home of their heriditary enemies might be their goal. Consequently, Rogers had enough Volunteers to pick only <u>soldats elite</u> that rivalled the selectiveness of the Rogers' Rock participants. Rogers personally advanced 339 pounds 6 shillings New York currency for the equipment needed for so long a march. He was later reimbursed by the British Government. Each man was equipped with two pairs of moccasins, two pairs of footings and one pair of Indian stockings or leggings (this made one extra pair for the 100 Rangers present for they already wore leggings). Hatchets, cases and belts were supplied to the 102 Provincials and Regulars. Twenty tumplines were also purchased for the expedition.

Rogers started his epic scout on the night of September 13, in 17 whaleboats. For some unexplained reason, Rogers' force only numbered 190 men instead of the authorized 200. Arriving at Buttonmould Bay they laid up there the next day and proceeded on to Otter River the next night where they had to lie by for a dark night to pass the French fleet of three vessels anchored off the mouth of the river. While here, Rogers became aware of the physical incompetence of a large percentage of his party. The first day out he had to send back 1 Stockbridge Indian who was sick; and now, the next day at Otter Creek, 40 officers and men had to be returned to Crown Point. They reluctantly returned in three different parties. The last party brought in 2 Highlanders who were wounded when they tripped over some logs and their muskets went off. One of the men, a 42nd Private, died soon after he was carried into Crown Point. Captain Williams, who returned with the second party on the 18th, was badly powder-burned in this accident. In all, 48 (3 officers and 45 men) of Rogers' 190 St. Francis Raiders had to be returned because of illness or lameness before they reached St. Francis (Lieutenant McMullen and 6 other lame or exhausted men were returned on the 25th)—25 were Rangers and Stockbridges, 16 were Provincials, and 7 were Regulars. This loss of one-fourth of his detachment was disquieting to Rogers, to say the least, but he felt reassured as the continual obstacles of the gruelling expedition were surmounted, and he realized that he had with him 142 officers and men of phenomenal endurance.

Finally the French ships sailed closer to Crown Point and the Raiders were able to embark. Other hazards soon became apparent for the French were aware that Ranger scouting parties traveled by night on the lake and they had planted booby traps in small boats and anchored them at various places on the lake in the hope that Ranger boats would collide with them or at least see them and be inquisitive enough to board them and be blown up.

Fortunately Rogers' party "happily escaped their snares of this kind" and arrived at Missisquoi Bay on September 23, ten days after leaving Crown Point. Here they disembarked and hid their whaleboats in the little southern arm of the bay so that the enemy would be less likely to find them. They marched northward keeping abreast of the lake for two days when two Stockbridges who had been left to bring Rogers any news of the discovery of his boats, caught up with him with the alarming news that the boats were discovered by enemy scouts. Rogers' bridges were now burnt behind him (actually they were, for the French burned his whaleboats), and he realized that a party would now be pursuing him. He was correct in this very natural assumption, for Bourlamaque, the Commandant at Isle aux Noix sent 300 men in pursuit and posted 360 men in ambush near the charred ruins of the whaleboats to await the return of Rogers' party. Aware that he would have to adopt part of his original plan of 1756 and return by way of Lake Memphremagog and the Connecticut River Rogers dispatched Leiutenant McMullen, who had become lame, with six others to travel on foot to Crown Point to ask Amherst to send Lieutenant Samuel Stevens to meet him at the ruins of Fort Wentworth with provisions. Though lame, McMullen and his party marched over 120 miles in nine days to deliver this most urgent message to Amherst.

The nine-day march through the foot-deep Missisquoi swamps was not unlike a nightmare and the Raiders must have had many bad dreams in the uncomfortable hammocks they had to swing among the spruce trees that stuck out of the seemingly endless bog. The only good thing that can be said about the swamps is that they made it impossible for Bourlamacque's pursuit party to trail them. When they lost the trail the French hazarded a guess that Rogers was marching against Wigwam Martinique, an Indian settlement on the Yamaska River, it being considerably closer than St. Francis which was safely ensconced near the St. Lawrence River in the very heart of Canada. Rigaud, who commanded at Sorel, poised 300 French and Indians at the mouth of the St. Francis River and sent 215 men to reenforce Wigwam Martinque.

The twenty-second day from Crown Point the Raiders reached the St. Francis River 15 miles above the town. The town lay on the other side but Rogers could not take the precious time to build rafts. Rogers led a group of the tallest Rangers across the swift current and anchored a strong arm around a tree on the farther bank. They stood fast while the tugging waters tried to dislodge them; by this human rope the rest of the party were able to ford the river and march to within three miles of St. Francis the same day. Sighting the town from a tree, Rogers left his party in the woods and reconnoitered the town that night with Lieutenant Turner, Ensign Avery and Samadagwas, a Stockbridge private who was soon to inform of Rogers' attack. They found the Indians quite drunk in celebration of a wedding. Turner, sent for a closer view of the Council House where the dance was being held, was detained en route to become a captive audience to a love-dance by an Abenaki Aphrodite in the woods nearby. This enabled a large portion of the tribe (those who heeded Samadagwis' warning) to leave the Council House on Turner's side and hide themselves in the Sibosek Pines.

This was unknown to Rogers. He was satisfied at this opportune celebration and returned to his main party confident that the superior number of Indians would be in a stupor by daybreak. He marched at 3 A. M. and attacked the town a half hour before dawn in a semi-circle of three different bodies. The surprise was complete, the Abenakis had no time to recover themselves, or resist with any effect, until they were chiefly destroyed. Several attempts were made to escape by the river, but Rogers had posted Rangers there, expecting such an attempt and the few who did manage to reach their canoes were shot. The Indians who did manage to resist inflicted a slight loss on their attackers—Samadagwis, the betraying Stockbridge, was killed, Captain Ogden was badly wounded in the body but able to march. Six others were wounded but slightly. Rogers would have spared all of the St. Francis Indians who surrendered but many remained hidden in the cellars and attics of the well-built houses and they perished when the town was fired. At least 65 to 140 Indians were killed or perished in the fire. Only 20 women and children were taken prisoners. All were set free except Chief Gill's wife, Marie-Jeanne, her two sons, and 3 girls, who, with 5 English captives, returned with Rogers. At 7 o'clock the affair was completely over and it was now imperative that Rogers retire southward in haste. The harrowing return march is best described by Rogers in his official account and the 'Diary' of an Anonymous Rogers Ranger.

The loot taken by Rogers' party consisted of at least $923, a rare ruby, possibly a Golden Calf or Lamb, a great number of Wampum necklaces, silver broaches, scalps. The mission church was sacked. All the vestments and most of the sacred chalices were carried off along with a solid silver image of the Madonna weighing 10 pounds. Sergeant Benjamin Bradley and the others of his detachment, who perpetrated this sacrilege, suffered horrible deaths as a consequence of their avarice. The corn from 3 of the town warehouses sustained Rogers' party for the first 8 days of their return march via Lake Memphremagog and the Connecticut River.

Near the lake, Rogers divided his detachment into nine parties with proper guides in order that they might have better luck in hunting the scarce game. The Connecticut conflux of the Wells and Lower Ammonoosuc Rivers was the appointed rendezvous; for it was expected that Lieutenant Stevens would be awaiting them there with provisions. Sergeant Bradley led one of the divided parties until they reached the Upper Cohase, when, mistaking the Upper Cohase for the Lower Cohase, which would have brought him out at the Merrimack if he traveled in a southeastern direction, decided to take a short cut to his home in Concord, New Hampshire. Three others of his squadron accompanied him: Robert Pomeroy of Derryfield, Stephen Hoit of Canterbury, and Jacob, a negro Private. Their departure was unknown to Major Rogers who would have refused to allow them to attempt this suicidal trek. Weighted down with the silver Madonna, Bradley and his party stumbled into the White Mountains. Tradition states that they wandered for days through the mountains endeavoring to find a way out. Finally all but Private Hoit were too weak to go on. They crawled under some rocks and perished in the delirium brought on by hunger and despair, blaspheming and hurling horrible imprecations at the silver image on which, in their insanity, they blamed all their sufferings. One of them seized the statue, tottered to the edge of a precipice and, exerting all his remaining strength, dashed it down into the gulf below. The next year a party of hunters found the bones of a man in Jefferson near the White Mountains; before him were three half-burnt brands piled together, and a quantity of silver broaches and wampum lay scattered about; the hair was long and tied with a leather ribbon such as Bradley wore; no arms were with him nor any signs of his companions. A repeated search has been made for the silver Madonna but to this day it has escaped discovery. Private Hoit seems to have reached an island in Lake Winnepessaukee for the next spring some clothes and other things were found there. Among them was a snuff-box marked Stephen Hoit, found by Captain Archelaus Miles of Canterbury.

Rogers was to regret giving in to his officers and allowing his force to be broken into small parties for the enemy, close behind, attacked one of the parties under Ensign Avery and captured seven of them. Two of them escaped that night and rejoined Rogers the next morning where they found Avery safe with the rest of his party. II-92 Another party of 20 men under Lieutenants Dunbar of Gage's and Turner of the Rangers was attacked at a later date and after a grim fight both officers and 10 Privates of Gage's were massacred. The other 8 made their escape and were rescued from starvation by Rogers after he obtained provisions from Number Four. II-93

The other detachments were fortunate enough to evade their pursuers but due to the negligence of Lieutenant Stevens with the needed provisions, more than two-thirds of Rogers' losses can be credited to famine. Seventeen men were lost to the enemy since leaving St. Francis but 32 men died of hunger. Their sufferings are related by the leaders of the various detachments:

Sergeant Evans' party were reduced to eating their leather accoutrements after they had been par-boiled. Then they turned to birch bark. Eventually they came upon the horrible remains of Dunbar and Turner's massacred party and most of them sliced off choice portions for food. Evans' revolted at the thought of eating human flesh and he refused his portion. A night or two later he overcame his reticence and creeping up to one of his Rangers' large knapsack he discovered three human heads and cut off a piece, broiled it in the coals and ate it. He declared it the "sweetest morsel he ever tasted," but that he would die with hunger before he would do it again. Evans admitted that when their hunger was greatest, they hardly deserved the name of human beings.

Lieutenant George Campbell's party stumbled upon the same butchered Rangers and devoured the remnants, some of the Rangers bolting the flesh raw.

Lieutenant Phillips and Sergeant Philip, future king of the Pequawket Indians, and a member of one of the Jacob Companies, led a party of 16 directly to Crown Point via the mouth of the Otter River. At one time they were about to kill and eat one of the 3 Indian prisoners they had with them, when a Ranger was fortunate enough to kill a muskrat, which, divided among the party, relieved them of turning cannibals, and enabled them to arrive in Amherst's camp on November 8th.

Another party owed their survival to the fortunute shooting of an owl which was dissected and distributed by the well-known method of "Who shall have this ?" The informant states that he shared a leg, which he devoured without cooking.

By these desperate methods Rogers' party were able to sustain themselves and survive by sheer will power until they reached the visionary haven at the Connecticut, but to their utter despair they arrived to find that Lieutenant Stevens had left a few hours before, leaving them only the smouldering embers of a fire. Hopes were raised when Stevens' signal guns were heard down the Connecticut River. Although muskets were fired frantically in response, Stevens became alarmed, thinking they were Indians, and hurriedly packed the provisions into canoes and embarked from his unauthorized base five miles south and returned to No. 4. To this cowardly act of Lieutenant Stevens can be laid the blame for the bulk of the losses by starvation for it was ten days before Rogers could return provisions to them from No. 4, and many died before this interval.

Immediately upon his heroic arrival at Number Four Rogers dispatched canoes loaded with provisions to his starving men at Fort Wentworth, and two days later Rogers was sufficiently recovered from his own famished state to accompany other canoes to the relief of Ranger detachments who might yet come in by way of Fort Wentworth. Similarly loaded canoes were sent up the Merrimac River for detachments who went that way. In all, Rogers employed 17 men for 13 days on this rescue service at 8 shillings a day to each man. Rogers omits in his Journals the number of survivors he gathered at Number Four but thanks to an "Account of Expenses by Major Robert Rogers for the Relief of his detachment on their return from St. Francis" tucked away in Amherst's papers, the number can now be established. This Voucher states that Rogers purchased 59 Shirts, and 59 pairs of Stockings and moccasins for his survivors at Number Four. Including the cost for canoemen, Rogers laid out more than 151 pounds New York Currency and was later reimbursed by the British Government.

Notwithstanding the fact that Rogers lost over one-third of his detachment, his raid on St. Francis was a phenomenal military achievement. Naturally the French received the news first. Governor Vaudreuil maintained an anxious correspondence with Commandant Bourlamaque at Isle aux Noix through October and November ending his barrage of letters on November 10, with an exaggerated account of Rogers' losses. Meanwhile Amherst began receiving foreboding implications on the general fate of Rogers Raiders. On October 25, Captain Brewer returned from a scout to look for Rogers' seventeen whaleboats in Missisquoi Bay to report that he had found them all burnt by the enemy, III-136 and five days later Lieutenant Samuel Stevens arrived at Crown Point to state that it was not likely that Rogers would return by way of Number Four. Amherst notes reprovingly in his Journal that Stevens should have waited longer for Rogers. Three days later the tension broke when Captain Cadillac arrived to discuss an exchange of prisoners. From him the results of Rogers' raid were learned and the exaggerated account of Avery and Turner's losses. On November 7, Captain Ogden arrived with the first snow with Rogers' official Journal and first-hand information on the raid. That afternoon one of Rogers' Indians came into the camp with a scalp and several hours later, much to Amherst's annoyance, he stated that he had left sixteen of Rogers' party at the mouth of Otter River. Amherst immediately sent a Ranger officer with fifteen Rangers in three whaleboats loaded with 150 pounds of biscuit and a gallon of rum to refresh the starving Rangers, who turned out to be Sergeant Philip's party who were too weak to go any further. When the emaciated Rangers arrived in camp everyone was amazed at the quantity of wampum and fine things they were loaded with.

Meanwhile Rogers at Number Four had completed the gathering of his scattered flock. All the Rangers were discharged except 21 Volunteers who belonged to Rogers' own Company, as only two Companies of the Corps were left at Crown Point for the winter. With these, Rogers arrived at Crown Point the first part of December; on the way they had encountered homeward-bound Provincial troops who were able to carry home first-hand accounts of Rogers' raid.[79] At Ticonderoga Rogers met Captain Pouchot, the French Engineer, and a member of the French delegation arranging the terms for the exchange of prisoners, who had been detained at Carillon. Seeing only Rogers' 21 gaunt and haggard Rangers, the French officers surmised that they were the only survivors and they eagerly spread this statement when they returned to Canada. Governor Vaudreuil must have nodded happily, although somewhat surprised that his exaggerated accounts were for once (supposedly) confirmed.[80]

At Crown Point Rogers found a congratulatory letter from Amherst with instructions to do duty at Crown Point with his two Companies but permission to take a few weeks leave to Albany; which Rogers quickly snapped up after applying to his Commandant who, he was disgruntled to find, was his old antagonist, Colonel Haviland. Haviland's prolific correspondence with Amherst makes no mention of Rogers' achievement, instead he recommends an officer's berth for Volunteer Wallace of the Inniskillings who was still recovering from his "long scout" to St. Francis.[81]

Rogers' fame was at its height as a result of his St. Francis Raid and his name was before the public in half-inch type in the provincial newspapers,[82] and though he naturally basked in his well-earned praise, still, the fact that he had lost so many men from starvation due to Lieutenant Stevens' negligence, gnawed at him; and he did not rest until he had brought Stevens to a court martial. Rogers truly grieved the loss of so many brave men and his letters to Amherst are full of self-reproach.[83] Stevens was clapped in gaol in Albany until Rogers could gather the necessary evidence and witnesses scattered from Number Four to New York. Rogers did not want Stevens to escape punishment, so he took great pains in collecting his witnesses who were men who had served in the raid and barely escaped starvation. Because of the violence of the winter it took Rogers longer than he had planned to gather his evidence and it was not until the following spring that Stevens was tried at Crown Point and found guilty and dismissed from Rogers Rangers.[84]

While Rogers was conducting his epic raid, the command of his Rangers at Crown Point devolved temporarily upon the next senior officer, Captain John Stark. Under his expert leadership the tedium of camp life was maintained and preying scouts as well as expeditions of exploration were fitted out and sent forth. Ensign Wilson returned on September 15 from exploring the Riviere de la Barbue (La Barbue Creek). His party went up to the Pond at the source of it.[III-131] On October 2, Lieutenant Darcy handed Amherst a map he had drawn of the South Bay-Wood Creek region as a result of his field trip for that purpose. Darcy was an excellent draftsman. His timely maps won him the esteem of Amherst and consequently an appointment to the drawing-room in London.[III-132]

October 6th saw Captain Noah Johnson executing an unexciting but essential duty. He was ordered with a party of Rangers to conduct the 29 batteaus of sick Provincials from Crown Point to the saw mills at Ticonderoga and return with a load of provisions.[III-133]

Amherst's fleet was finally built and he started his advance on Isle aux Noix. Tute's method of rigging blanket sails to escape from the French fleet was tested and adopted and each whaleboat in the army was rigged with two blankets.[85] Two days prior to the advance Amherst launched two scouts of Rangers to obtain a prisoner so that he might have the latest information by the time he approached Isle aux Noix. Sergeant Rossier sailed with six Rangers to Point Aux Fer on the west shore where they landed and proceeded towards St. Johns.[III-134] Sergeant Burbank was to lead six men to Windmill Point on the east shore and land, then travel by foot towards Isle aux Noix. Unfortunately Burbank took the wrong passage on Grand Isle and mistook the approach to Missisquoi Bay for that region of

Point Au Fer. On the night of October 12th his party fell in with "a great hammering and noise" which proved to be M. de Laubara scuttling three sloops of his French fleet. Burbank was discovered, driven off, and pursued by a superior party.^{II-90} The two scouts were to have met Amherst on the lake but after eight days out the army met with such a severe storm at that late season they were forced to retire to Crown Point until the following summer.^{III-135, II-91} Burbank and Rosier rendezvoused and dispatched five Rangers to Amherst with the news of Burbank's brush with Laubara; and the following night the two Sergeants arrived at Crown Point half starved and severely buffeted from their two week scouts in the stormy weather.

On October 27th, a week after Amherst's return to Crown Point he discharged the balance of the two Jacobs' Companies then in camp. Twelve Stockbridges had taken it upon themselves to go over the hill on the nineteenth while the army was advancing. Ordinarily Amherst would have been ruffled by this display of homesickness, but ever since Rogers' absence on his St. Francis Raid they had become noticeably idle and inebriated in camp without Rogers' paternal hand to restrain them while under Amherst's reproving eyes, and the General was only too happy "to save unnecessary expenses to the Government" and his provisions by discharging the remainder of them. Although he could not stand their slovenly attitude in camp, still Amherst realized the invaluable contribution of the Stockbridges and Mohegans when active in the field under Rogers' guidance, and he did not wish to affront them, consequently he phrased their discharge paper in timely words: Addressing Lieutenant Solomon Uhhaunwaumot, who commanded the two Companies since the capture of both of the Jacobs, Amherst appropriately states that since the surviving 42 men of both Companies wish to return home he is to set out the next day with them. However, to make sure that they did not loiter between Crown Point and the south end of Lake George, Amherst detailed Lieutenant Darcy with a Sergeant and twelve Rangers to conduct them.[86] Darcy's duty was two-fold for after bidding adieu to Rogers' Indian Rangers at Fort George he proceeded to Fort Edward and picked up "the Cloathing and other necessaties for the Corps of Rangers..."[87] which had been shipped there from the Clothiers and Contractors Agents in Albany.[88] Amherst was not entirely rid of Rogers' Indians for Sergeant Phillip had eight Stockbridges in his detachment of St. Francis Raiders that staggered heroically into Crown Point on November 8th and they remained and nourished themselves back to health until the other Ranger Companies to be discharged left.[89]

Rogers Rangers added a few more items of interest to their record before the close of their fifth year on the Lake George front. With the evident signs of disbandment in the offing, the army stirred restlessly, particularly the Provincial troops. Rogers Rangers became restless also, for they heard that the bulk of them were to be disbanded for the winter, but they did not hurry their return home as one Ranger had tried it in September and received 500 lashes. However, the Provincials were not as patient and a detachment of Rangers were ordered to reenact their role of bloodhounds on November 3rd and overtake a party of Massachusetts troops which duty was partially effected when the Rangers "fetched 3 of the rogues back..."[III-137]

One last scout of the year to Isle-aux-Noix suffered the capture of five Rangers on November 4, when they penetrated too inquisitively close to the island.[II-94] However, November 15 was a joyful day for the Corps as an exchange of prisoners took place and among them were 52 officers and men of Rogers Rangers including the above five captives. The 52 exchanged captives were a galaxy of Rangers each with a first-hand account of their hairbreadth escapes from the hands of their Indian captors or tales of their weeks, months and even years of captivity among the Indians or imprisonment and periods of hard labor at Montreal. Rare captive survivors of some of the Corps' most famous engagements were returned to the fold. There was a captive of La Barbue Creek, one of Rogers' Rock, one of Fletcher's Fight near La Prairie, two of Tute's Capture near La Gallette, two of the Kennedy-Jacob Mission which incited the raid on St. Francis, fourteen of various minor scouts through the years, and most important 25 of Captain Burbank's May 1759 party rejoined the Corps, thus greatly minimizing this supposed "Massacre." Captain Tute and Lieutenants Fletcher and Stone were the Ranger officers exchanged.[90] Needless to say, none of the five Rangers captured in the St. Francis retreat ever had the opportunity to be exchanged for their captors in their fury refused to sell them to the French but butchered them all.[91]

The first part of November saw the scattered detachments of Moses Brewer's Company at Stillwater and Fort George reunited with the Corps at Crown Point.[92] The Rangers were reviewed on November 22, by Amherst and Captain Stark. Amherst expected to engage two full Companies to serve for the winter and through the next campaign but Stark could prevail on only 157 Rangers to stay on instead of the 200 needed.[93] These men were mostly seasoned veterans from all the Companies and they represented the _soldats elite_ of the Corps. Including 21 St. Francis Raiders who volunteered at Number Four to stay on with Rogers, there were 43 Sergeants and men of Rogers' own Company. Fifty of the other Rangers remaining augmented this Company and the recent French prisoner, Captain Tute, commanded Rogers' own Company for the remainder of the war. This left Rogers more time to fulfill his duties as Major of the Rangers, but the Company was still nominally his "own" and was designated as such. The other 90 men were formed into another Company and since Amherst had ordered senior Ranger officers to command these Companies John Stark would have had this Company if he had wanted it, but he declined, stating that he wanted to retire from the service. Since Moses Brewer also resigned, the berth was open to Noah Johnson, the next senior Captain and he quickly accepted.[94]

In all, there were four Companies of Rogers Rangers in service throughout the winter and they formed the scouting arm for the garrisons of all of England's hard-won fortresses and advanced forts. Major Rogers and Captain Johnson's Companies were at Crown Point and an officer and 25 Rangers were detached from them to be posted at Number Four. Captain Waite's skeleton Company of 30 men were posted at Fort Brewerton at the west end of Lake Onieda. Captain Moses Hazen's Company were with Murray's force at Quebec.[95] All of the officers of the disbanded Companies were kept on full pay until

Amherst decided how many Ranger Companies he would need the next spring.[96]

On November 24, 275 Rangers were mustered out and the next day 175 of them marched home via Stark's Road and Number Four. Amherst heralded their arrival by writing instructions to the Commanding British officer at Number Four ordering him not to give the discharged Rangers anything "they might be free enough to ask for..."[97] The other 100 Rangers marched with Amherst via Albany. On the way the weather froze slowing them down and in their anxiety to get home three Rangers stole a batteau and froze to death at night when it overturned in the ice-choked Hudson.[98] Since Rogers was still at Number Four, Stark handled the disbandment and paying off of the Rangers. He had warrants from Amherst to obtain money for the remaining two Companies at Crown Point but had to apply to General Gage (commanding the New York fornt for the winter) at Albany for the balance due to the discharged Rangers. The usual red tape followed, for Gage had received no authority to pay Stark and the exasperated Captain had to send Lieutenant McMullen to Amherst somewhere on his way to New York with the Muster-Rolls and accounts due. Discharged members of Major Rogers' Company were finally paid off February 15-20, at the Widow Osgood's house in Rumford, New Hampshire by Rogers' clerk, Paul Burbeen.[99]

Rogers was on his furlough in Albany in December when he probably astounded Amherst when he received Roger's proposal to lead another superhuman expedition so soon after his St. Francis raid. On the seventeenth Rogers wrote: "If your Excellency should be under any apprehensions of Quebec being in Danger...this Winter and should have occasion to send Reinforcements there, I would be answerable if ordered by your Excellency to carry 500 men to that place in 20 days from the mouth of Kennebec River, provided they should be well fixed with Snowshoes, Provisions, etc..."[100] Amherst was impressed by Rogers' offer but did nothing about it. If he had the outcome of the Battle of Ste. Foye might well have been different but like all of Rogers' daring proposals, this one was shelved until it was too late and disaster had struck. Once again Rogers' unusual abilities were frustrated. How enhancing it would have been to his brilliant record to record that he marched to the Relief of Quebec or arrived in time to enable Murray to chalk up a victory at Ste. Foye instead of a defeat. If Rogers could have obtained the advancements and honors which the results of his proposals would have won for him he would not have reverted to the shady side of his nature and attempted to salve his frustration by dealing in sharp trading practices and employing confidence-man techniques to obtain preferment.[101]

Rogers Rangers at Crown Point suffered two setbacks in December while their commander was in Albany. Before Christmas two veteran Rangers, Reynolds and Hall, were scouting for stray cattle near the Riverhead Blockhouse when they were taken prisoners by a flying party of the enemy. The fact that they were captured was bad enough but since there was only a little snow on the ground Commandant Haviland quickly jumped to conclusions and wrote Amherst that they had probably deserted. This unsubstantiated assumption riled Rogers considerably when he heard of it but he bided his time until the following May when Sergeant Beverly escaped from Montreal and reported that he had seen Reynolds and Hall in Montreal as captives.[III-139]

The second setback occurred a few days later on Christmas and was of far greater portent to Rogers Rangers, for, due to Haviland's stupidity, close to one-fourth of the two Ranger Companies at Crown Point became incapacitated and many crippled for life. On December 25, a British Captain led 100 grumbling Regulars and Rangers from Crown Point to Ticonderoga to bring back the new clothing. Instead of ordering the party to all wear moccasins and socks which would have minimized the chance of frostbite he allowed the greater part of them to march in regulation shoes. As a consequence all of the Rangers and Privates who wore shoes were frostbitten and the Surgeon at Crown Point had to cut off more than 100 frozen toes as a result of Haviland's ill-planned expedition.[III-140]

Chapter IV
1759

WOLFE'S SCOUTING ARM

Rogers' far-flung Independent Companies in Nova Scotia and Louisbourg served conspicuously in Wolfe's Quebec campaign but prior to the rendezvousing of the army they executed several hardy expeditions from their winter quarters. Captain John McCurdy's Company quartered at the wilderness outpost of Fort Frederic interrupted their monotonous wood cutting forays to make a bloodhound expedition up the St. John River valley for refugee Acadians who had settled there. McCurdy was entrusted with the assignment but unfortunately he was accidentally killed the day before by one of the trees falling on him which his men were cutting; an ignominious end for one who had so many startling interludes with death in daring Ranger warfare.[102] The tragic loss of the veteran McCurdy made it possible for First Lieutenant Moses Hazen to assume command and earn undying fame for himself and his Company. When McCurdy's Ranger Company was formed in 1758 Hazen had at first declined the First Lieutenantcy since it would not have given him preferment over his same rank in the Provincials. Fortunate for him was his later acceptance of the berth, for now, at the helm of a Company of Rogers Rangers he was able to realize his formerly frustrated abilities.[103]

On February 18, Hazen marched out of Fort Frederic with 22 Rangers and made an arduous march of 180 miles up the banks of the St. John River to Saint Anne (now Frederickton, the present capital of New Brunswick) and back. At St. Anne he found that the inhabitants had evacuated the village en masse and retired to Miramichi. It is a wonder that the unfortunate Acadians did not make a more spirited defense of their homes for there must have been over 147 men capable of bearing arms for the Rangers burned that many houses besides all the stable and granaries. Being forewarned as they were and with their knowledge of the country which Rogers Rangers did not possess they could have staged an adequate ambuscade and completely routed Hazen's party; instead they allowed them to burn their village to the ground and retire unmolested back down the river. The raiders were ready to believe that the country was void of human beings until their inquisitiveness brought on an armed conflict. Discovering smoke coming from a large house in the woods they picked up the trail of the occupants who had retired to the woods and were ambushed by ten Acadians. Quickly adopting bush-fighting tactics Hazen's Rangers soon surrounded the brave little band and the action ended after a grim struggle in which six of the Acadians were killed. Returning to Fort Frederic with the surviving Acadians Hazen penned a Journal of his raid and it was sent to Amherst in New York.[II-50] The Commander-in-Chief was delighted with the report and he commended Hazen fully when writing to Prime Minister Pitt, General Gage and others. Fortunately for Hazen's promotion was the presence of the Rangers' old friend Colonel Burton who was superintending the embarkation of troops in this region for Wolfe's rendezvous at Louisbourg. Burton recommended Hazen strongly to Amherst for the Captaincy of McCurdy's Company and he was promoted on the strength of his recommendation and that of Major Scott.[104]

At almost the same time a detachment of James Rogers' Company quartered in Louisbourg made a similar raid to the Lake Labrador region and flushed out 18 armed Acadians and 100 other men, women and children who were all brought in without a struggle.[II-56]

The hunt for guerrillas was continued on March 27, when Engineer Lieutenant James Montressor went deeper into the same region with forty men (mostly Rangers). The goal was the far side of Lake Labrador to the settlement of La Badick, but halfway across the lake they found the ice too thin to continue on and had to return to Louisbourg.[III-86]

In May Rogers' four "overseas Companies" joined the army at Louisbourg[105] and during their brief stay there they had an engagement with the fierce Micmac Indians who had been hovering in the vicinity making depredations upon the outposts. On June 1, the Rangers scoured the woods, met some of the marauders and a hot skirmish took place. The Micmacs broke and Rogers Rangers drove them to their "inaccessible fastnesses."[II-61] This was the last action that the Corps fought on the soil of the newly-won maritime provinces for the last British ship of the Quebec expedition cleared Louisbourg harbor on June 6th.[106]

The very day of their sailing there arrived in the harbor a schooner bearing Lieutenant Simon Stephens of John Stark's Company who had made a most remarkable escape from his imprisonment at Quebec. After his capture on June 25, 1758 at Lake George while leading a scout to Ticonderoga, he and Lieutenant Nathan Stone, the other Ranger officer in his party were taken to Quebec where they contrived with Captain Stobo of the Virginians and Major Putnam who had been captured at Marin's Defeat to escape by way of the Kennebec River to Fort Halifax on the coast of Maine. By the time they were ready Major Putnam had been exchanged and winter had set in. The escape was postponed until the following spring when Lieutenant Stone dropped out when it was decided to go by water down the St. Lawrence and attempt to reach Louisbourg. Their escape was made all the more risky when they had to settle for a canoe to carry them. Stephens' party embarked on the night of May 1, and reached Isle Madame before morning. In all, there were nine in the birch canoe: Stephens, Stobo, Elijah Denbo, Oliver Lakin and a man named Clark with his wife and 3 children. Their daring escape was a series of harrowing and exciting odysseys. The second day they were forced to stay in the river all night for a strong wind prevented them from reaching either shore. Two of the party were kept desperately busy bailing out the water which threatened to fill their precarious craft while the others paddled to keep the canoe in the center of the river so that they would not be dashed upon the rocks on the south shore in the dark. They laid up on the north shore on the 3rd and dried themselves and their meagre supplies. The next day they cruised on and encountered a canoe of Indians which they fortunately eluded by escaping in a thick fog. But the same protective fog forced them to remain in the river once more for fear of dashing on the rocks in the dark. The following afternoon an Indian and his squaw were captured and when they tried to escape were killed and scalped. From their camp they obtained two muskets and a quantity of dried corn, sugar and beaver skins. On the 6th they ran into a whirlpool and battled for their lives for over an hour, being tossed round and round like a top. Finally they fought free and landed exhausted on Green Island. A contrary wind kept them lying ashore under their canoe for the next two days. On the 9th they arose and were mending their canoe when they saw a two-masted cutter coming directly towards them. Grabbing their arms they lay in wait and captured the crew of four when they landed. Stephens' party then set sail in this worthy acquisition, putting their four prisoners to work rowing whenever they were becalmed.

That night they held their breath and their muskets ready while rowing past a strong French advance guard on the Isle of Bic. This feat was accomplished against a contrary tide and their reluctant captive rowers who would have welcomed the chance to cry out for help. However, they ran into an armed sloop opposite the isle, were fired upon, and were only able to escape by a fortunate shift of the wind. At sunrise the following morning they passed the Isle St. Barnaby and a French frigate who fired broadside at them. Arriving at the river Metis ten leagues further, they refreshed themselves and gave their prisoners their freedom. Three days later they bravely rounded the Gaspe Peninsula and sailed into the Baie des Chaleurs, a favorite rendezvous of French pirates. Here they discovered a sloop unmanned near the shore. An attempt was made to board her but a rapid tide shot them past and approaching nightfall forced them to abandon another attempt on the sloop and they sought shelter in a cove. Two attempts were made in the next two days to set out but each time a contrary wind drove them ashore and the second time they were almost scuttled and their arms and provisions soaked. They bailed out the water and ran into a small creek where upon examination they found only two days' provisions left. But the next day they revived their spirits by catching 24 codfish while en route to Port Daniel. The following day a hard rain and contrary winds drove them ashore where they made a tent with the mainsail. The storm increased and drove the boat ashore with such force that it drove in a plank and they lost what little wheat they had and eight cod. The next two days were spent in beaching the boat so that it might be repaired.

With an unseaworthy craft and no provisions their plight was a desperate one and they seriously considered striking out by land to the nearest British post of Fort Cumberland. Lieutenant Stephens and Lakin made a scout in that direction and discovered the snow still four feet deep in some places, which factor dampened their ardour for this plan.

Their problem was solved the next day when a sloop and schooner which they had seen the day before reappeared and in desperation they decided to board them. At the same time a canoe with four of the crew from the sloop landed on the shore and were captured. From them it was learned that there were eight more men on the two ships. This made the odds almost two to one, but notwithstanding the disparity of numbers Stobo and Stephens' detachment had their patched-up boat in the water and were pulling for the schooner by ten o'clock that night. Three of the prisoners were left behind to be guarded by Clark's wife, while the fourth prisoner accompanied them as a pilot.

While Clark and Stephens stood at the helm and bow with grapplings, Captain Stobo, who outranked Stephens, was to be given the honour of boarding first. He was placed in the center of the boat as a juggernaut of destruction with a musket, pistol and cutlass. Denbo and Lakin rowed and bailed alternately until one A.M. when they pulled quietly alongside the schooner. Lieutenant Stephens relates the best account of the boarding in his <u>Journal</u>: "...as soon as I grappled her, I jump'd on Board, and found they were all asleep, I ran to the Companion Doors, upon which I heard somebody coming out of the Steerage; he immediately call'd for Quarters, which I readily granted. Clark was the next Person that came on Deck, who immediately ran and took the Candle out of the Binnacle. It was Capt. Stobo's Misfortune getting upon Deck to get hung in the Shrouds, with the loss of his Cutlass and Pistol; but as he came upon Deck, one of the Enemy was coming out of the Steerage (whom I had given Quarters to) which he immediately shot thro'; Clark ran down into the Cabin, upon which, with Capt. Stobo's Courage in killing the poor Prisoner, the Captain of the Vessel call'd for Quarters. I hope the Reader will excuse my being so particular in this Affair, as Capt. Stobo has reported he was the first that boarded the Schooner, and the only Instrument in taking her. After we had secur'd our Prisoners, we weigh'd Anchor and sail'd along Side of the Sloop, and ordered them to come on Board; they refus'd, upon which we fir'd about twenty Small Arms at her; they then call'd for Quarters, and came on board: we confin'd them all in the Hold, except the two Masters. I took the Master of the Sloop, Clark and Denbo, and went on board; we found six Small Arms, one Swivel Gun, and five Days provisions for five Men: I took out the above Articles and then set her on Fire; I then return'd on board the Schooner. We then sail'd to our old Camp, sent the Board on Shore, and bro't off our Women and Prisoners, and what small Quantity of Provisions we had left. We set sail, and after we had sail'd about five Leagues, we put on shore six of our Prisoners: We gave them three Days Provisions, one Gun, and some Ammunition. We kept on board the two Masters with three Prisoners more, whom we ordered to carry the Vessel to St. John's Island, where we all safe arrived (thank GOD) May 27th, 1759.[II-60] The Commandant at St. John's treated us very courteously, and when we departed, he ordered a Serjeant and twelve Privates to guard us in our Schooner to Louisbourg, where we arrived the Sixth Day of June. The Governor treated us with very great complasance as did all the Gentlemen of the Place and upon the General's [Whitmore] Order, I immediately [the same day] went up the River, and Join'd the Army under General Wolfe..."

Stephens was attached to one of Rogers Ranger Companies and served until the Companies were disbanded at the end of the campaign.

The four Companies of Rogers Rangers, viz, James Rogers', Moses Hazen's, William Stark's and Jonathan Brewer's Companies served in at least twenty-two different recorded scouts and actions prior to the fall of Quebec. The two most popular Captains were James Rogers and Moses Hazen with Hazen having the edge. While James Rogers was accepted as the senior officer with "the greatest share of merit as a Ranging officer" still Hazen "met with universal approbation, both on account of his conduct as well as his gallantry,"[107] and he was the shining light of the provisional Ranger battalion placed under the command of Major George Scott. Two of Hazen's Rangers kept Journals of the exploits of their Company and Private Perry proudly describes his Captain:[108] "Our Captain was a bold man. I have seen him cock his piece, and walk promptly up to the enemy, face to face; and our men would never shrink from following such an officer, and they seldom followed him without success."

Hazen was a counterpart of his far-distant commander, Major Rogers, and his deeds were so numerous and bold that even General Wolfe made frequent entries of his achievements in his daily <u>Journal</u>. Hazen's Company started the campaign ignominiously by being the cowboys of the army when they were entrusted with the care of the army's beef on the hoof.[109]

Rogers Ranger Companies first saw action on June 30th when they fought in two minor actions at Beaumont and St. Joseph when the shore opposite to Quebec was taken possession of.[II-62, 63] The following afternoon the Rangers prepared an ambush for a guerrilla force of Indians who were firing on Monckton's Brigade entrenching themselves at Pt. Levi. At 3 P.M. when the Indians reappeared the Rangers surprised them with a withering fire, completely routed them, and, imitating their own ferocity, scalped nine of the Indians.[II-64] The next day Hazen, with his Company on the Isle of Orleans, were relieved of their cow-punching duties to ferret out 73 Canadians on the Island.[III-100] Four days later on July 6th, Major Scott with the bulk of the Rangers made an abortive bloodhound scout as far as the River Chaudiere.[III-103] When they returned to Point Levi all but two Companies of Rangers were divided by Companies and posted on the hills which commanded the road to the British batteries then being erected on the Point.[110]

Wolfe next established himself on the east bank of the Montmorenci River opposite to Levis's camp on the Quebec side of the St. Lawrence. In the landing on July 8, at L'Ange Gardien, Hazen's and Danks' Rangers were in the thick of the hot action to gain the heights.[II-66] After the plateau was won the two Ranger Companies were sent into the neighboring woods to protect the parties who were cutting fascines. Danks' Company were sent on in advance to look for a fording place across the Montmorenci. Four hundred Indians under the Partisan Langlade ambushed Danks' Company at the ford and drove them back with heavy loss upon Hazen and a detachment of Regulars. Hazen and his Rangers won the approbation of Wolfe when they vigorously stood their ground and finally repulsed Langlade. In his retreat Langlade was hotly pursued by Hazen's Rangers who managed to take twelve prisoners, but Langlade's Indians recrossed the ford with 36 scalps of Danks' Rangers, and the French fortified the ford, but the British were allowed to establish themselves on the eastern shore of the Montmorenci.[II-67]

Hazen was now established solidly with Wolfe and it is not surprising that his petitions for daring assignments were granted and July 9th saw him paddling up the St. Lawrence with a picked detail of Rangers in canoes to discover and ascertain the size of the French fleet which they found at Cap Route, and returned with a useful prisoner taken on the Quebec shore.[III-105]

If British accounts are to be believed Lieutenant Caesar McCormick indulged in a bit of unnecessary scalping in a scout on the south side of the St. Lawrence.[III-105-A]

Hazen was again in the spotlight on July 15th. His Company posted on the extreme right of the British line on the Montmorenci were attacked by French and Indians at 4 A.M. Hazen's Rangers had established headquarters in a house which they defended determinedly for over an hour, suffering one man killed and two wounded before the superior body of attackers gave up and withdrew back across the Montmorenci.[II-69]

The east shore of the Montmorenci continued to be the battleground of sudden forest actions, with Hazen's Company being the principal defender for the British. On the 22nd, Second Lieutenant John Butler was scouting up the river when his scout was fired upon from ambush and Butler and Private John Miller were wounded.[II-71]

Hazen retaliated two days later when he scouted for prisoners. He had a successful brush with the enemy, had one man wounded, but brought in eight prisoners.[II-73]

A severe skirmish occurred on July 25, when a large body of British Regulars, Light Infantry and Hazen's Rangers were reconnoitering the ford above the Falls of Montmorency. Fifteen hundred of the Canadians and Indians sallied across the ford and fell upon the British. The numbers were about equal and the fierce contest waged in dispute. Hazen's Company which had been sent ahead to reconnoitre above the ford, returned and with the Light Infantry turned the left flank of the Indians and the whole force broke and fled in disorder back across the Montmorenci. Wolfe, in his Journal, gives Hazen's Company the credit for being the deciding factor in the engagement.[II-75]

The same day, in the afternoon, First Lieutenant Patten of Hazen's was scouting with only seven Rangers when they were attacked from ambush about one mile from Hazen's Post. The ambuscaders fled after their first fire but Patten hotly pursued and managed to overtake one and bring him in.[II-76]

Captain Hazen added six more prisoners to the Company's collection the next day.[II-78]

Rogers Rangers at Point Levi entered the Rangers calendar of events when they made a three-day scout of discovery to the mouth of the Chaudiere River.[III-112]

When Wolfe attempted to scale the Heights of Montmorenci on July 31st, Hazen's Company, in the words of Private Perry, "remained on the bank, with our muskets loaded, as a kind of corps de reserve, to follow the detachment, in case it succeeded in making a breach in the enemy's works. General Wolfe stood with us, where we could see the whole maneuver.."

Two days later Hazen, with ninety men, including the remnants of Danks' Company, went forty miles down the St. Lawrence, had a brush with the inhabitants, and returned with a quantity of much-needed fresh beef.[II-80]

On August 8th Rogers Rangers had their first action with French Cavalry. In Brigadier Murray's attempt to land at Pointe-aux-Trembles were the famous Lieutenant Edward Crofton and twenty men representing Rogers Rangers in the hot action with Montcalm's Dragoons who successfully opposed them at their landing. II-81

The same day, Wolfe, exasperated with the incessant warfare waged by French-Canadian guerrillas against his outposts, ordered the village of St. Paul to be fired, with the added hope that Montcalm's militia would desert to defend their homes. Lieutenant Butler and fifty of Hazen's Company represented Rogers Rangers in the raid. They were fired upon by H. M. S. Zephir who mistook them for enemy craft. The mistake was fortunately rectified in time and the voyage continued. An engagement occurred at the landing at St. Paul but the inhabitants were routed and all but the church burned. II-84

Meanwhile, as a consequence of a scouting party of Light Infantry and Rogers Rangers under Major Dalling being fired upon by a small party of Canadians, the village of Ste. Croix on the south bank of the upper St. Lawrence was destroyed. II-83 Other raids were made on the parishes above and below Quebec and at one time Hazen, by a clever ruse, enticed the will-o'-the-wisp guerrillas from their fastnesses and effected a crushing defeat upon them. II-85

On September 3rd, Ensign Hutchings of Rogers Rangers arrived with disptaches from Amherst and Wolfe learned that he could not expect any help from that quarter. In desperation he increased the intensity of the parish raids by ordering Major Scott with 1,600 men, including all of the Rangers, on a large scale raid down the southern shore of the St. Lawrence. They left September 1, and were gone until after the Battle of the Plains and the capture of Quebec. III-128

After their return Rogers Rangers were kept busy in patrolling the roads leading to Quebec from Ste. Foy and Sillery to watch for any possible return of the defeated French army. Three hundred and fifty Rangers were sent to Isle Madame on Sept. 26, to cut wood for the Quebec garrison. They received one gill of rum per day each and 5 shillings above their regular pay for every cord that they cut and put on board. In this manner Rogers Rangers were employed until the second week of October when all but Hazen's Company embarked for Boston. Before they embarked, a draft of 25 men from Rogers', Stark's and Brewer's Companies—in all 75 Rangers—were annxed to Hazen's Company, swelling it to 134 Rank and File. By this annexation, Hazen's command comprised a representation of veteran Rangers from four different Companies;[111] and their exploits under their brilliant Captain garnished the annals of Rogers Rangers.

After their return to Boston and upon Amherst's orders, James Rogers', William Stark's and Jonathan Brewer's Companies were disbanded by Major Scott who expressed that "... the Rangers in general were well liked and of much use in their way..." The Companies were disbanded on November 30, 1759 but it was not until May 7, 1760 that the bewildered Scott had the Company accounts settled. Major Rogers sent his Clerk, Paul Burbeen, to Boston to obtain the moneys he advanced the four Companies for advanced pay and uniforms when they were first raised in 1758. Ensign Hazen on furlough was called to Boston in January to pay off the men of Hazen's Company that were discharged in November, their enlistments being expired. The Ranger Captains had endeavoured to obtain passage and billeting money for their Companies en route to Halifax and Quebec but this final point of discussion was settled when it was decided that the Captains were in error for they sailed on King's ships.[112]

Chapter V
1760

CONQUEST OF CANADA—
LAKE CHAMPLAIN FRONT

The year of 1760 started out with a reverse for Rogers Rangers on the Lake Champlain front. Major Rogers was returning to Crown Point from Albany with sixteen Ranger Recruits and a quantity of new Ranger arms and gear when they were ironically attacked at Five Mile Point on February 12th. This scene of so many Ranger Ambuscades in the past now proved a victorious field for a French partisan force of seventy Indians and Canadians under Langy, the Rangers' most daring adversary. Langy had attempted to burn the British shipping at Ticonderoga but found them too well guarded. On his return march he decided to play Rogers' old game of lie-and-wait at Five Point. He was rewarded on the morning of the 12th when he espied a Sutler's caravan of fourteen sleighs approaching from Ticonderoga. Rogers' sleigh was a little in advance of those of the Sutlers' and Langy abandoned them for Rogers when he was recognized in the first sleigh. The Sutlers were forewarned the moment Langy fired from ambush and quickly turning about escaped to Ticonderoga. Rogers' party were not all so fortunate. Langy's fire had killed Rogers' sleigh-horses, rendering the sleigh an easy prey for Langy. The most tragic part of the whole affair was the fact that Rogers' 16 recruits, for some unexplainable reason, were unarmed with muskets.

There were 32 new muskets in a wooden chest on Rogers' sleigh but there was no time to break open the chest for Langy's Indians were upon them after their first murderous volley. In the bloody hand-to-hand fighting Rogers' recruits desperately defended themselves with what small arms that they might have, such as knives or tomahawks. Five Rangers were killed and four taken prisoners before Rogers broke through with the seven others to reach Crown Point. In spite of his narrow escape, Rogers would have pursued Langy immediately with a detachment of Rangers but due to the weakened condition of both Rangers and Regulars from scurvy and frostbite, Haviland would allow no pursuit party to go out. In spite of the escape of Rogers, Langy must have exclaimed in amazement and felt duly recompensed when he saw what Rogers' sleigh contained. Besides the case of valuable muskets he found 100 hatchets and 55 pairs of moccasins, and most important, 11,961 pounds of New York currency. Eight thousand and one pounds of this was the payroll for Rogers Rangers at Crown Point; the other 3,961 belonged to Rogers. Langy's Indians could not overlook the opportunity to leave a taunting reminder of their triumph. When Rogers led a scout to the scene of action he found one of his late recruits, an Indian, hanging on a tree with a small mirror before him to watch himself die after he had been scalped alive. Nearby were the mutilated remains of his squaw. [II-95]

The Ranger Recruit Massacre was followed six weeks later by another loss to the Rangers. Winter garrison duty at Crown Point was monotonous to say the least and Commandant Haviland was continually plagued by the more spirited officers to hunt and fish. He finally capitulated on March 30th and allowed Captain James Tute and three Rangers, and Lieutenant Fortescue, Ensign Stuart, and three Regular privates to cross the lake and fish and hunt near the White Rock. The next morning at 10 A.M. they were entries in a thrilling race with the garrison forming the anxious spectators on the ramparts. The party had crossed over in a batteau through an unfrozen passage of the ice-covered lake's shores but the lake end of the passage had frozen again overnight. When a party of French and Indians had interrupted their fishing they leapt into the batteau and hurriedly paddled through the passage. They would have made their escape but for two factors. The enemy surprised them by nimbly running after them on the thin ice. Even so, they would have escaped if the passage had been free of ice, but they had gone 300 yards and had only 200 more to go to reach the open lake when they found the way frozen and their pursuers were able to overtake them without firing a shot. This was the second time that Tute had been captured within a year. He was fortunate enough to be exchanged again in time to join his Company before the advance on Montreal. It was later learned by a Ranger who escaped from Montreal that Langy was the leader of Tute's captors; it was also learned with relief that Langy was drowned in the St. Lawrence River a few days after his return with Tute and the others. III-145

Once again there was no pursuit, due to the sickness of the garrison. However, this was soon remedied, for all of the Ranger officers wintering in New England on full pay, were called back into service and ordered to recruit. Lieutenant John Fletcher, Lieutenant Caesar McCormick (who had joined Rogers after his return from the Quebec front and now served as a Volunteer officer until his friend Rogers could fit him into a Company), and Sergeant Holmes for Rogers' Own and Johnson's Companies at Crown Point.

Now that the Conquest of Canada was swinging into its final act, all of the Ranger officers who had served in 1759 wanted berths in the revived Companies, but there were not enough vacancies to go around. There were four Companies in service throughout the Winter (Major Rogers' Own and Johnson's at Crown Point; Waite's at Fort Brewerton; and Hazen's at Quebec). On March 1, Amherst ordered four more to be raised to join the above for the advance on Montreal. 113 Of the 1759 Captains, Moses Brewer, John Stark and William Stark did not re-enter the Corps. Moses Brewer had no desire to, but the two Starks were greatly chagrined when they were "unprovided for." General Amherst had not intended such a situation, for John Stark had expressed a desire at the close of 1759 not to serve again and Amherst had taken him at his word, but now with the advent of Spring, the call of Ranger life was too strong for this most able veteran, and he busied himself in the recruitment service, acting as the liaison officer between Amherst and the Ranger recruiting officers. Consequently, there were many exclamations of indignation at John Stark's home in Derryfield, New Hampshire on April 6, when John read Amherst's letters to brother William and Lieutenant Andrew McMullen—for none of them were on Amherst's list of Ranger Officers for 1760. Believing that John Stark would not serve again, Amherst had given the Captaincy to James Rogers on March 19, and informed Stark of it after he had done so. Stark penned Amherst an injured letter on April 12, and begged that he might not be forgotten. Brother William wrote a similar letter, and the mortified McMullen personally delivered them to Amherst in New York.[114]

Confronting the irate McMullen, Amherst was faced with an explosive predicament, for the fiery Lieutenant represented three valuable Ranger officers with rightful claims to commands. Probably McMullen was the most disappointed, for he had been in line, and plugging for a Captaincy ever since Captain Burbank had been killed in 1759. Now with Major Rogers' promise of a Company and with forty good men already enlisted for that Company, he naturally expected the command. But Amherst had other plans. After reading John and William Stark's letters he must have mollified McMullen, for he returned to John Stark with a letter stating that McMullen had been ordered to turn over his forty recruits to him as the nucleus for his Ranger Company. John, however, was aware of McMullen's intense desire to command a Company and he would not be an instrument to his disappointment and risk his friendship, even though he yearned to share in the final Conquest of Canada after spending five years of his life as a vital instrument in the successful culmination of British arms in Canada. John Stark declined the Captaincy and asked McMullen if he would step into James Rogers' Company with his recruits, for it was becoming increasingly apparent that James and other Captains would not have enough men to warrant their commissions, as the Provincial officers were offering higher bounty for enlistment in their Regiments.

This was the crowning generous act of this great patriot to be, and was an admirable way to ring down the finale on an enviable carrer as an unexcelled Rogers Ranger officer.

When Stark stepped so graciously from the scene for the good of the service, he instilled a like spirit in the belligerent McMullen who entered James Rogers' Company as a Lieutenant and served the Campaign without once aspiring for a Captaincy, a truly great act for one who aspired so for preferment.[115] William Stark also had a replying letter from Amherst with the consoling statement that it was not through any "dislike or dissatisfaction" of him personally that he was not given a Company. He was assured that if he had been "on the spot" he would have had no objection to offering him a Captaincy. William accepted this in the same good strain as brother John and wrote Amherst on May 31, wishing him "a happy Campaign," not overlooking the opportunity to ask Amherst for delinquent pay for his former Company and putting in an illegal claim for billeting and transportation money from Halifax to Quebec.[116]

Rogers' recruiting officers had to exert themselves to find and induce enough men to fill their complements. Besides the difficult task of inducing likely recruits away from hawking Provincial recruiting officers with their glowing promise of higher enlistment bounty, Rogers' officers could only enlist able men between the ages of 18 and 30 in compliance with a new regulation by Amherst. In the past, age was no barrier, and quite often boys of 16 to old men of 60 had been enlisted. Even though they might have been well versed in Ranging methods prior to their enlistment, still Amherst had been alarmed in 1759 at the sight of so many[117] young and old faces amongst Rogers Rangers. As a consequence of the above barrier, the three new Companies (James Rogers', David Brewer's, and Jonathan Brewer's) raised for the Lake Champlain front arrived at Crown Point mustering only half of their authorized strength. In spite of this disparity of numbers, the personnel of Rogers Rangers were all young, hardy men.[118]

While the new and old Ranger Companies were being recruited, the various Ranger activities and Major Rogers-Commandant Haviland discords were related in newly discovered correspondence between Rogers and Haviland with Amherst.[119]

In January Crown Point was in dire need of fresh provisions for the scurvy-ridden men, and Lieutenant Nathan Stone was dispatched to Number Four for the necessary supplies. He made the difficult trip over John Stark's road and guided the provision train to Crown Point.[III-142]

Several of the oxen had drifted away and bloodhound scouts of Rangers were sent after them. Some times the Ranger-Cowboy round-ups were successful, but often they were not, for the strayed cattle had become wild and were difficult to catch up to. One contrary bullock was finally overtaken, but proved so wild that the Rangers could not bring him in alive. They resourcefully settled the problem by killing him and bringing in the quarters.[III-144]

Other duties consisted of "garrisonning" the outlying blockhouses. Four Rangers were posted in each blockhouse and this alternate duty was not a desirable one for it was intensely cold. There was also the endless task of cutting firewood; and with the budding of spring, work was continued on the moat and the Prince Edward Bastion, not to mention digging a well; repairing lime kilns; and fencing and planting a garden to alleviate scurvy.[120]

Twenty Rangers were so incapacitated as a result of frostbitten toe amputations that they were reluctantly discharged by Haviland after he had personally "secretly" scrutinized each crippled Ranger. Informing Amherst that he was satisfied that they were incapable of service, Haviland writes, that they frequently played tricks to appear unfit. He does not mention that the Rangers were for the greater part, critically "frostbitten" as a result of his ill-advised "100 Toes Expedition" on Christmas Day.[121] To replace these men, Haviland writes Amherst if he might order up the detachment of Rogers Rangers at Number Four, and also asks if he might enlist some of Rogers' Crown Point Rangers into the Regulars, sarcastically adding: "they would be of more service with us than at present." In spite of these innuendoes, Amherst realized the value of leaving the detachment at Number Four for the winter and also the explosion that would be set off if good men were drafted from Major Roger's command. Haviland was informed as much and the Colonel bided his time before riling Rogers further.[122]

The Company of Stockbridge Indians were revived for the campaign under the command of former Lieutenant Solomon, as both of the Jacobs were prisoners of war.[123] The Company was between Albany and Crown Point when Solomon refused to march further until he, his Lieutenant, and Ensign received signed commissions from Amherst. Amherst was furious, for he considered Solomon's distrust an act of Mutiny and wrote him as much. If Rogers had not recommended Solomon and gone to so many pains to raise his Company it is not to be doubted that Amherst would have peremptorily dissolved the Stockbridge Company without further ado. He expressed the same to Rogers on May 30, and enclosed the Indian officers' commission; at the same time sending Solomon a scorching letter via Lieutenant McCormick ordering[124] him and his Company to Crown Point at once.

May proved an active month for Rogers Rangers at Crown Point. The recruits started coming in in small detachments and the tedium of camp life was spiced with the arrival of escaped Ranger captives and a pair of actions. The Rangers posted in the advance Northwest Blockhouse were at first startled, then amazed, when Sergeant Thomas Beverly and Ranger Private, Francis Howgill hailed them and came in exhausted on the night of May 4th. They both had been Ranger captives in Montreal and had escaped on April 27th. Sergeant Beverly had been captured with a number of his recruits on February 12th. Beverly had won the favour of Governor Vaudreuil and had been a guest in his house. Naturally he was in a position to absorb much useful information which he divulged to Major Rogers after his escape and seven-day trek to Crown Point.[125] Haviland sent Beverly down to Amherst with the next mail-patrol from Ticonderoga.

Since the attack on Rogers on February 12, the mail-patrols traveled mostly by night. Embarking in a whaleboat at three in the morning on May 9, the patrol, consisting of a Regular Corporal and six men and Sergeant Beverly, pulled for Ticonderoga, but the wind was too rough and they landed at the southernmost Crown Point Blockhouse, left their boat, and proceeded on foot to Ticonderoga. Evidently enemy Indians had become aware of the night mail-patrols for they ambuscaded them four miles south of the Blockhouse. After a volley of "20 shots" they were all surrounded except Sergeant Beverly who happened to be in the rear of the column. He melted into the night and reached Ticonderoga to give the above account. Fortunately all but the Corporal and an officer's servant also escaped in the darkness to return safely to Crown Point.

The hold-up men were almost all intercepted three days later on their return trip to Isle aux Noir.[II-102] In order to forestall predatory raiding parties, the two sloops and the brig Cumberland, moored at Ticonderoga, were re-commissioned. Rangers with shipwright experience were sent down from Crown Point to make the necessary repairs and the ships were brought up to Crown Point. Lieutenant Alexander Grant commanded them and received orders from Amherst "To give all assistance to Ranging scouting parties...", and offer them succour whenever needed.[126] A new era of scouting now began for Rogers Rangers. With this naval might to convey and support them they could be more bold in their traveling from Crown Point towards Isle aux Noix. Gone were the days of secretive night traveling in whaleboats with muffled oars. Instead, the whaleboats were carried on Grant's ships and Lake Champlain was sailed in daylight if so wished, and the Rangers were able to loll on the decks in comparative ease until their destination was reached. By May one of the sloops and the brig Cumberland were ready; and they were patrolling toward Isle aux Noix on their first cruise of the year when the mail-patrol was captured on the ninth. Haviland dispatched a whaleboat after them with orders for Rogers, who was on board with sixty Rangers and thirty Light Infantrymen, to scour the western shore for the mail-robbers' canoes and waylay them when they returned. However, the message arrived too late for the ambuscaders had regained their four canoes and had paddled to within eight miles of Isle aux Noix when, to their amazement, they saw the Cumberland between them and Nut Island. Grant also espied them and noting that the canoes were gathered in an anxious huddle he hoisted French colours to deceive them, and at the same time ordered strict silence, while hurried preparations were made for an attack.

While his Lieutenant and gunner kept the brigs' guns trained on the canoes, the brig's two boats were ordered lowered and manned by the Rangers armed with hand grenades. Major Rogers was ashore scouting towards Isle aux Noix with two Rangers, and the only other Ranger officer, Lieutenant Archibald Stark, with a whaleboat of Rangers were attending the sloop, posted six miles closer towards Isle aux Noix, to prevent the Cumberland from being surprised, thus leaving the Rangers on the brig without a Ranger officer. Grant remedied this by placing a naval officer in command of the two ship's boats of Rangers.

However, the Rangers did not take favorably to their new commander and when one of the canoes approached these decoy boats to ascertain their nationality, the Rangers fired upon them when the Indians discovered something amiss, and chased the fleeing canoes to the western shore, all this in spite of the naval officer's orders not to pursue until after the ship's guns had fired. It is well that the Rangers had taken matters into their own hands for the ship's powder had become damp and the guns missed fire. Thanks to the Rangers' impetuosity, at least five Indians were killed and wounded, and the Rangers were so close on their heels that all of the canoes and several blankets were taken when the Indians leapt ashore. The Indians were in such hasty flight that they overlooked Major Rogers and his two Rangers who were lying in hiding until they passed. After this close call Rogers continued his reconnaissance of Isle aux Noix and returned to the Cumberland the next day. II-103

In the meantime Sergeant James Hackett (future Master-Ship-Builder of American ships-of-war) with ten other Rangers had completed fitting out the other sloop at Ticonderoga and she was sent to join "Commodore Grant." When she arrived she found that the smallpox had broken out on board the Cumberland, and the expedition had to return to Crown Point before the contagion spread. At Crown Point the victims were lodged with three other suffering Rangers in remote huts, and Haviland asked Rogers not to mention the epidemic for fear that it would frighten the Provincials who were now gathering at Crown Point. Finally a hospital was built on the Point exclusively for smallpox patients.[127] With the sloop arrived a dispatch from Amherst to Rogers ordering him down to Albany "to settle some Ranger and Indian matters."[128] This statement was for the eyes of possible mail-robbers for actually Amherst wished to send Rogers on a dangerous expedition requiring the utmost secrecy.

The squadron arrived at Crown Point on the 19th, and Rogers set out immediately for Albany, arriving, and waiting on Amherst, on May 23rd. This was the first time that Rogers had seen the General since Amherst had dispatched him on the St. Francis Raid from Crown Point on September 13th; and both imposed upon the knowledge and authority of the other. Amherst interrogated Rogers on the Oswego-St. Lawrence route to Montreal, and Rogers took the opportunity to petition Amherst to intervene for him in obtaining the long delinquent pay from the Provincial Governments for his original 1755-1756 winter Company. He also asked that his Clerk, Paul Burbeen, might be appointed Paymaster to Rogers Rangers; it being so necessary, due to the many losses Rogers had sustained by a "Hurry of Business in settling with the Companies himself," and by losses such as the Payroll Massacre in February. Rogers closes by "humbly begging that he may go himself with the acting army" under Amherst from Oswego, hoping thus to be rid of his present immediate superior, Colonel Haviland.[129] But the real crux of the conference was Amherst's orders to Rogers to destroy St. John's, Chambly, and Wigwam Martinique with 300 men, in the hope that this would draw troops away from Levi's army who were besieging Quebec. This was Amherst's only alternative to assist Murray at Quebec, for the slowly arriving Provincial troops made it impossible for him to personally push forward at that time.[130] This vital assignment was probably the most exigent service that Rogers was ordered upon during the war; and though the results were somewhat different than originally ordered, still, Rogers' Richelieu River Valley Campaign was the most successful expedition he and his men ever executed.

Rogers received his orders on the 25th, and after gathering equipment for his raid, he returned to Crown Point arriving on May 30th. Haviland received instructions from Amherst apprising him of the urgency of the raid, and for once in his association with Rogers, Haviland exerted himself to assist him. This was no doubt prompted with an ulterior motive for Haviland was first in line for the command of the Lake Champlain advance on Montreal and this was a good opportunity to feather his nest.[131]

Before Rogers arrived, two Stockbridge Indians who were taken captive in Jacob's defeat in 1759 escaped from Montreal on May 18, arriving at Crown Point on the 28th. They immediately wanted to re-enlist in Rogers Rangers. Lieutenant Joseph Duquipe of the Stockbridge Company was already at Crown Point and recognized the two Indians. He vouched for them, but Haviland suspected their loyalty and sent them to see Amherst first. But the General was regretting the raising of the Stockbridges he already had in service, and he sent them home.[132]

Two days after the Indians' arrival at Crown Point, there came in one "Jonathan", a white man who had been taken captive by the Indians when a child. Although a captive, he had heard of the exploits of Rogers Rangers and now when he was actually among them, he expressed his desire to be a Ranger, eagerly selling himself to Rogers by stating that he knew where to get a prisoner when he wanted one. Haviland, the still ever cautious about escaped captives, sent Jonathan to Amherst who gladly accepted him. A fitting commentary on the comparative dislike that he held for all Indians, that he would readily accapt a total unknown because he was white, and distrust and reject two Stockbridge Rangers because they were Indians.[133]

June 1, was a busy day at Crown Point as Rogers organized his expedition. Captain Solomon's Stockbridge Company were to form part of his 300 men but they were still loitering on their march to Crown Point, and though Haviland sent the following letter to the Commanding Officers of the four posts between Crown Point and Albany:

May 31

As Major Rogers informs me Captain Solomon's Company of Indians are on their way from Albany, That they get drunk at the posts, by which they are rendered incapable of coming here, Agreeable to his Excellency, General Amherst's orders. Therefore it will be for his Majesty's service to prevent their getting Rum, and not let them remain longer at your post than is reasonable for their refreshment. It is also hoped the commanding officer at Fort George will forward them and any Rangers that arrive, by way of the Lake, without Delay.[134]

Rather than wait for them and slow down his exigent service, Rogers left orders for them to follow him as soon as they arrived. The expedition sailed the night of June 1st to avoid detection. Roger's force consisted of 225 Rangers; Ensign Wood, a Sergeant and 12 Light Infantrymen of the 17th Regiment. Solomon was to join him at the end of the lake with 50 Stockbridges as soon as they straggled into Crown Point. The renowned "Bill Phillips" was amongst the participating Ranger officers. Bill had escaped from captivity late in 1758, and found himself without a lieutenantcy, thanks to Abercrombie's contract with Rogers before he gave him his Majority. The call of Ranging life was too strong for the veteran Phillips, and after a winter at home he served the 1759 Campaign and winter with Rogers as a Volunteer. Rogers rewarded the patient Phillips by squeezing him in as an Ensign when the Companies were revived. Phillips replaced Ensign Samuel Stark, for Stark had rendered himself unfit for active service when he fell from a horse, and lay unconscious in the snow through a cold winter's night. This vacancy in Jonathan Brewer's Company was the only possible opening, for all of the lieutenants had been kept on full pay through the winter and there were more than enough of them. Rogers was doing the best that he could for Phillips under the circumstances, and Bill realized it and readily took a lower berth. He was still mentioned as a "Lieutenant' in dispatches, but was actually an "Ensign" on the Rolls.[135]

It was imperative that Amherst get a message through to Murray at Quebec in order to coordinate their advances on Montreal. The message was written on a small piece of paper, and it was at first planned to dispatch "Lieutenant" Bill Phillips across the country via Rogers' St. Francis route. Rogers' expedition had three different missions—he was to lead 250 men against St. Johns and Chambly; Lieutenant Holmes was to take 50 men to destroy Wigwam Martinique, a notorious Indian settlement on the Yamaska River; and a Volunteer party of Rangers were to take Amherst's message to Quebec. It seems that Rogers had adjudged that Phillips would be more valuable serving in Holmes' detachment, for Sergeant Thomas Beverly, lately escaped from Montreal, volunteered, and was accepted for the Message to Murray mission. Rangers were reluctant to step forward for this perilous duty, for they were aware of what would happen to them if they should fall into the hands of any of the surviving St. Francis Indians. Finally, five pounds sterling per man was offered, and three veteran Ranger Privates—Luxford Goodwin, John Shute, and Joseph Eastman—stepped forth with Sergeant Beverly. III-147

Rogers sailed directly to Missisquoi Bay, and on June 3, discharged Sergeant Beverly and his party for Quebec; and Lieutenant Holmes, Stark, Ensign Phillips, and 48 Rangers for Wigwam Martinique. III-148 Returning to Lake Champlain, Rogers ordered Commodore Grant to send the two sloops cruising closer towards Isle aux Noix to detract the enemy, while he landed with the remaining 213 men on the night of June 4, at King's Bay in whaleboats.

Rogers' Journal, Official Report, and Letter-Diary written by an anonymous Ranger officer (probably Lieutenant Simon Stevens) give excellent accounts of what now transpired. II-104 There being a heavy summer rain the next morning, Rogers lay by to conserve his men and provisions. That afternoon the lake became alive with enemy small craft who paddled around Grant's sloops who were cruising off Windmill Point. Fearing that they might be boarded in the night, Rogers rowed out to them after dark, and ordered them back to the Cumberland at Isle La Motte. When Rogers returned to his camp, vigilant eyes perceived him and sent scouts ashore who were able to ascertain his numbers and report to Bourlamaque at Isle aux Noix. However, runners from Rogers reconnoitering parties opposite to the fort returned to Rogers the next morning to excitedly report a force of over 300 were marching on him. Thus forewarned, Rogers, for once was able to deploy his force to advantage and exact, probably, his most successful victory in a pitched battle.

Rogers' detachment consisted of 200 Rangers, including Captains Noah Johnson and Jonathan Brewer, Lieutenant Simon Stevens, Ensign Jacob Farrington, and one of the Sergeants, who was the veteran James Hackett. To add to this poignant force were Ensign Wood, a Sergeant, and 12 Light Infantrymen.

Rogers deployed them expertly. When his scouts relayed the probable point of attack the Rangers and Light Infantry held an ideal battle site on the Pointe au Fer peninsula on the shore of present-day King's Bay. On Rogers' left was the bay with his whaleboats drawn up on the shore. On his right was a bog which Rogers dispatched Ensign Farrington and seventy Rangers through, by the edge of present Griffith Bay, to fall upon their rear. The maneuver had been well timed, for Rogers was informed of the approach of his attackers by his scouts who relayed intelligence right up to the time of the attack. Although the numerical odds were 3 to 2 in favor of the French force, still, Rogers skillfully minimized this factor by the above alertness, and the following elements of surprise. The 300 or more French, Canadians and Indians were well led by the famed Partisans, La Force and Longville. The primeval forests retained their natural hues as Rogers Rangers in their green uniforms blended with Nature's garb. So much so, in fact, that the French were not aware of them until an advance party walked into Rogers' line and were attacked. This happened at 11:30 A.M., and the main body began their attack "with their usual intrepidity and yelling," which was returned with like spirit by Rogers' men.

Rogers had to engage La Force's 300 men with approximately 144 Rangers and Light Infantry, until Farrington, with the other 70, had time to make his way through the swamp and fall upon the French rear. Consequently Rogers had his hands full, and the battle was nip and tuck for several hot moments. A number of Indians took cover behind some of Rogers' whaleboats and he threw a contingent behind the remaining boats. An amusing interlude followed: When the Indians could not reload as fast as the Rangers they started throwing stones, which aroused the competitive spirit of the Rangers, who shouted that they would equalize the weapons and also fight with stones. The Rangers proved to be peers in their speed and accuracy with the stones as well as reloading and firing muskets, for the Indians were so accurately pelted with these primitive missiles that they abandoned the boats with howls. At the same time Farrington fell upon the French rear, on the way they destroyed a number of Indians in the swamp, who were being

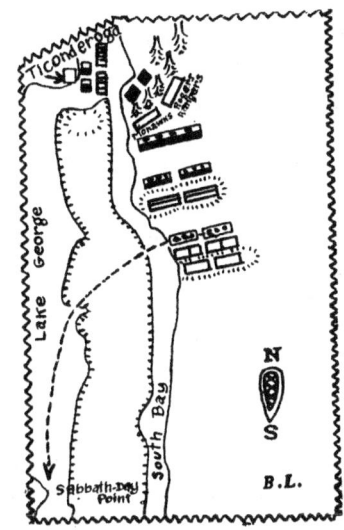

See pages 37-40

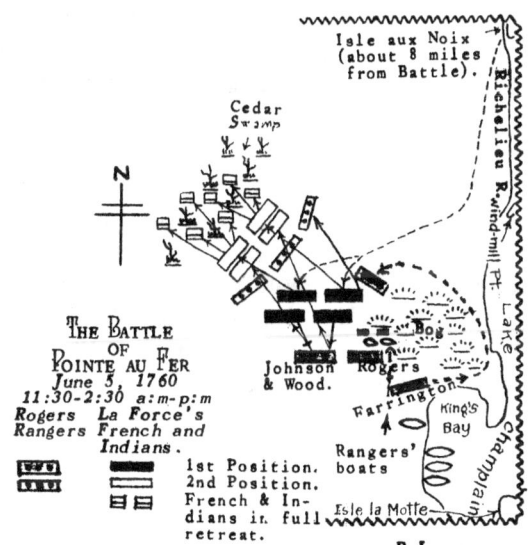

See pages 95-99

exhorted by their medicine-man. As soon as Farrington began his attack, Rogers "pushed them in front, which broke them immediately." The French Grenadiers broke first, then the others followed, retreating in a westerly direction away from Farrington and Rogers. Rogers pursued them with the bulk of his force for about a mile until they entered a thick cedar swamp and split up into small parties and escaped with all of their wounded. It started to rain again very hard, and Rogers immediately gathered his force together at the whaleboats and crossed to Isle La Motte, where he encamped, buried his dead, and sent the wounded back to Crown Point on one of the sloops.

The wounded were attended by the English surgeon, James Jameson. Thanks to the negligence of his superior, Surgeon-General Napier, who dispatched him from Albany without bandages and instruments, many of the wounded died on the voyage to Crown Point, in spite of the heroic efforts of Surgeon Jameson to improvise for them on Isle la Motte before they sailed. Captain Grant and other officers generously offered their linen shirts and Jameson dressed the wounds without applying the non-existent medicines. As a consequence, Captain Johnson, who was badly wounded in three places, died before he reached Crown Point. The Corps lost a valuable officer due to the criminal neglect of Napier in not furnishing Jameson with a medicine chest. The enormity of Napier's folly cannot be overemphasized.

Rogers' losses, besides Captain Noah Johnson, were 16 Rangers killed, and 8 wounded; Ensign John Wood of the 17th Infantry was killed in the first fire and two of his men were wounded. Franch losses were at least 32 killed, among them a noted Mohawk interpreter; and 19 wounded, including both the Commanders. La Force was mortally wounded in the chest, while Longville suffered a slighter wound. Rogers Rangers gathered more than 34 fine firelock muskets, and 3 Indian scalps. They would have gathered more of the latter for the bounty, but the French Indians had beat them to it, and scalped their own brethren before retreating.

This three-hour engagement (from 11:30 to 2:30) was hard fought, and was one of the few pitched battles or bush-fights in which Rogers Rangers were able to completely surprise the enemy. It had been customary for Rogers to be surprised at the outset of his larger forest battles (La Barbue Creek, Rogers' Rock, and Marin's Defeat), and then by skillfully applying his unique methods of defense, retreat, or counter-attack, to extricate his Corps from a ticklish situation, and turn an apparent defeat into brilliant victory, or at least a heroic stand. However, the Battle of Pointe au Fer, the last large scale bush-action of Rogers' during the war, was an exception, and he was able to turn the tables, and completely surprise, defeat, and rout the enemy. Some idea of the intensity of the action can be realized when it was observed that the Rangers had expended most of their sixty rounds of ammunition.

Three days after the Battle of Pointe aux Fer, Lieutenant McCormick joined Rogers with 25 of the belated Stockbridge Company, and a Subaltern, Sergeant, and 30 of the Light Infantry of the 17th Regiment. Captain Solomon had straggled into Crown Point at 10 P.M. on June 3, with only 30 Indians. Since three of them were sick, two more had to remain to care for them, thus reducing the number sent Rogers the next night to Captain Solomon, his Lieutenant and Ensign, and 22 Indian Privates. Even these came close to never reaching Rogers, for a freak storm came up on the sixth (the afternoon of Rogers' battle), and they barely reached the shore in time to escape the pitching lake. Fortunately for the furtherance of Rogers' mission, the Stockbridges escaped another impediment: The day after their departure towards Rogers, Haviland received word from Amherst not to contaminate the Crown Point side with them, rather, to quarter them across the lake at Chimney Point "so they can't get at Rum", and instead of sending them to reenforce Rogers, they were to be employed in scouting toward Number Four.[136]

When Haviland received Rogers' June 8th _Journal_ of the Battle of Pointe au Fer, he believed that the element of surprise was gone, and dispatched orders for Rogers not to proceed on his Richelieu River Valley Raid, instead, to remain with Grant's fleet and "make what show he can to favour Lieutenant Holmes." He wrote Amherst asking if he wanted anything more done by Rogers' de-tachment. Amherst replied on the 10th, apparently confirming Haviland's decision, but the next day wrote that he had just learned of Levi's withdrawal from Quebec, and that Rogers was still to pursue his mission, even if he could not surprise St. John's and Chambly. Rogers was to act "according to his own discretion...and the more he can alarm them the better..." Haviland received the first letter on the 12th and immediately relayed the orders for Rogers to abandon his raid. At the same time assuring Amherst that no time had been lost for he could not send off the sloop sooner than the 10th; as Grant wanted several things from Ticonderoga, particularly biscuits "for the service at the other end of the Lake. As none arrived, I was obliged to bake five days bread here, with that and flour, I desired Captain Grant to make best shift he could and to save what Biscuits he had for Major Rogers' Party. I likewise sent him two Bullocks alive for their refreshment, most of the bread Major Rogers had on shore with him was destroyed by the Rain which was a great loss to them."

A few hours after Amherst's letter of the tenth, Haviland received another dated the eleventh, with news of the relief of Quebec, and orders for Rogers to proceed. The bewildered Haviland immediately dispatched a whaleboat well manned with orders to Major Rogers agreeable to it and am almost certain they will get near as soon as the other Express, as the wind was strong all day and calm when the last set out." Haviland also sent Rogers a reenforcement in the form of 20 Volunteers from a recently arrived Rhode Island Regiment (and 20 more who had sea experience, for Captain Grant). But they arrived too late for Rogers had taken matters into his own hands for he "was determined at all adventures to pursue" his "orders." Rogers landed on the western shore on the night of June 11, and marched to St. John's with 220 officers and men, including Captain Brewer, Lieutenants Simon Stephens, Caesar McCormick, Ensign Jacob Farrington and 159 Rangers; Captain Solomon, Lieutenant Duquipe, Ensign Nunnipad and 22 Stockbridges; and a Subaltern, Sergeant and 30 Light Infantry of the 17th and 27th Regiments. Lieutenant McCormick temporarily commanded the Light Infantry.

Making a forced march, partially through swamps and

streams, they arrived at St. John's on the night of the 15th. While his party rested near the road, Rogers made quick reconnaissance from a distance and found the fort too strong for his force. Nevertheless, he resolved to adopt the plan that he had proposed to Lord Loudoun in 1758 for surprising Crown Point. Lieutenant McCormick, who spoke French fluently, was to march up with the Light Infantry with their coats turned inside out, being lined with white. With this apparent French detachment McCormick was to inform the Gate-guard that he had an express from Montreal for the Commandant. As soon as he had secured the Gate, Rogers would rush in with his Rangers. The plan was ideal, but upon nearing the Fort they observed a large camp on the glasses and a number of vigilant sentries. A consultation of officers resolved to abandon St. John's, instead, to march quickly to Ste. Therese nine miles down the Richelieu at the portage. Ste. Therese was a vital link on the communication with Isle aux Noix, for boats had to dock here to receive supplies and troop transportation for St. John's and Isle aux Noix. Ten A.M. found the Raiders before Ste. Therese. Observing hay wagons about to pass through the Fort's gate, Rogers sent detachments under Captain Brewer and Lieutenant McCormick, who met at the River side and with Rogers rushed in with the hay wagons before they cleared the gate. At the same time without the loss of a man on either side. Fourteen boats and five canoes were found moored under the fort. After firing the village and Fort, Rogers crossed the Richelieu with his 27 French prisoners. The old men, women and children, in all 52, had been set free. Rogers' gleeful humour came to the fore when he gave them a pass to go to Montreal, "Directed to the officers of the different Detachments under my command." Meaning Lieutenant Holmes at Wigwam Martinique and Captain Hazen at Quebec. This bit of galling sarcasm must have infuriated French Commanders who still remembered his hectic "Thank You Note" after his cattle slaughter below the walls of Ticonderoga in 1757.

Safely across the River, the Raiders looked back to see a large body of the enemy upon the Ste. Therese shore. Unknown to Rogers they were English prisoners, under guard, and being sent to Crown Point to be exchanged. The boats which

Rogers' men were now burning were to have conveyed them to Crown Point. A Ranger prisoner, Captain James Tute, was a witness to this vexatious scene, and though he was now forced to walk to other boats at St. John's, still he was admireful of Rogers' handiwork. II-105

Rogers' Raiders followed the eastern shore of the Richelieu until it started to veer west, then they made a southeasterly detour around Isle aux Noix. Near the present settlement of Aird on the Canadian line, Rogers' advance party engaged with a similar party, preceding a pursuit force of 600 men from Isle aux Noix, who were a mile behind. The French advance columns were attacked with such spirit that they were beaten off and Rogers quickened his march to the rendevous at Windmill Point. During the march from Ste. Therese it became apparent that the French Regular prisoners could not keep up with the Rangers' rapid pace, due to the tightness of their breeches. Rogers remedied this by ordering the Rangers to cut off the legs of the French breeches with their knives. Thus unencumbered, the Rangers placed their packs on their captives' shoulders, and the speedy march was continued. On the 20th, the same day of the advance-guard's skirmish, Rogers arrived at Windmill point. A few Rangers had been sent forward to smoke-signal to Grant's ships, and boats were waiting for them at the shore. As they were hastily pulling for the ships, their 600 pursuers burst from the trees to shout frustratedly from the shore. II-106

So ended Rogers' Ste. Therese Raid. This well-planned, well-timed expedition was probably Rogers most successful exploit of the War. Not a man was lost, and still the desired effect was obtained. The French believed that the whole British Army at Crown Point were advancing and the Richelieu River Valley was thrown into a state of nerves and troops were drained from vital St. Lawrence River posts to be rushed to St. Johns.

The day after their safe return to the fleet, Rogers sent his 26 prisoners with 50 men to Crown Point, while he lingered with the balance of his detachment to cover Lieutenant Holmes. Holmes returned that evening on the sloop that was cruising Missisquoi Bay for him. Holmes had failed in his mission. He had followed a River that fell into the Richelieu instead of the

Wigwam Martinique (Yamaska) River. Holmes had found the country alive with roaming bands of Indian hunters, and since he had been privately instructed by Major Rogers not to take any unnecessary risks (Rogers did not want any repetition of the St. Francis retreat of 1759). Holmes rejoined Rogers without effecting anything more than a valuable reconnaissance of the country. [137]

The third arm of Rogers' force, that of Sergeant Beverly's squad, who had volunteered to carry Amherst's message to Quebec, were successful in their 500 mile trek across St. Francis Indian country and safely reached Murray as he was about to advance up the St. Lawrence upon Montreal. Beverly and his squad served temporarily in Hazen's Company of Rogers Rangers and shared in the Company's many skirmishes along the River. [138]

Upon Holmes' safe return, Rogers immediately returned to Crown Point and received orders from Haviland to encamp his Rangers at Chimney Point on the east shore of the Lake opposite to Crown Point. This Point now became known as Rogers' Point, and it was not until some time later, after the War, that the Point regained its original name. [139]

Rogers now found Haviland a Brigadier in command of the reduction of Isle aux Noix. Haviland wasted no time in exploiting his broader authority by endeavoring to have all Regular Majors in his force outrank Rogers. He further planned to form all of his Grenadiers, Light Infantry and Rangers into a provisional battalion under the command of a field officer of the Regulars. By this means Rogers would lose his independent command. Instead, he and his Corps would be subject to a Regular Colonel or Major. Rogers was so indignant at Haviland's proposal that he dispatched a letter to Amherst at Oswego, tendering his commission, thus implying that he would resign if his seniority was not established. Amherst did not wish to lose Rogers' irreplacable services at this late date, and he immediately returned his commission, adding that Haviland had been ordered to put in General Orders that Rogers "was to enjoy" rank of Major from the date of his commission (April 6, 1758). Haviland seems to have given up nettling Rogers when it was driven home that Amherst would back the Ranger in spite of his sly innuendoes and various efforts to reduce Rogers' authority and command to a minimum. It is little short of amazing that Rogers managed to restrain his temper in these various jousts with Haviland during the numerous periods he was under his heckling command.[140]

Amherst's plan for the total reduction of Canada was to advance on Montreal from east, west and south, and crush it as in the jaws of a vice. Murray was to ascend the St. Lawrence from Quebec; Amherst down the St. Lawrence from Oswego and Brigadier Haviland was to force an entrance by way of Lake Champlain. Contingents of Rogers Rangers served in all three expeditions but Major Rogers with six Companys were with Haviland and comprised the bulk of the Corps. These six Companys were captained by James Tute (who led Rogers' Own Company), who had now been exchanged from his second period of captivity; brother James Rogers; the two Brewers, Jonathan and David. Solomon commanded the Stockbridges and Lieutenant Simon Stevens of Quebec-escape fame was promoted to the command of the late Noah Johnson's Company. The choice for this vacancy had been a difficult decision for Rogers to make for there was an expectant candidate in the form of Lieutenant Andrew McMullen. Rogers was forced to disappoint the eager McMullen for the third time, as Stephens was the Senior Lieutenant of the Corps. If Stephens had not escaped from Quebec and re-entered a Company with Rogers at Crown Point, McMullen would have had the Captaincy. In spite of this sad travesty of events, McMullen manfully accepted his loss and remained a Lieutenant for the balance of the War. Amherst writes Rogers that Stephens' appointment was "very just." He remarks that he has not heard from John Stark, but "if he had come he would have course have had this Company."[141]

Rogers recommended other promotions and replacements to Amherst and besides Stephens' commission, the following were signed by the Commander-in-Chief at Oswego on July 11th. The brilliant Ensign, Jacob Farrington of St. Francis Raid and Pointe au Fer fame, was promoted to Lieutenant in Jonathan Brewer's Company when Lieutenant Darcy moved up to fill Stephens' vacancy as First Lieutenant. The Company's Ensign, "Bill Phillips", was the only officer not to profit by Stephens' promotion. Thanks to Abercrombie's contract with Rogers before he would give him his Majority on April 7, 1758, any Ranger Officers reported dead in the Battle of Rogers' Rock who survived to later return, lost their seniority in the Corps. When Rogers signed this stipulation all of the Ranger Officers that did not return with him were reported killed by subsequent French prisoners. This included Phillips, who had surrendered in good faith. He was reported butchered with all of his party by the Indians. Since Phillips was the only captured Ranger Officer to escape, he alone suffered from this curious Abercrombie-Rogers agreement. Amherst approved of Rogers appointment of Caesar McCormick to Lieutenant Joshua Lock's place in David Brewer's Company, since Lock did not rejoin the Corps. One other replacement occurred: Benjamin Hutchings who had served as an Ensign in 1759, and among other achievements had bravely volunteered and carried Amherst's dispatches through Maine to Wolfe at Quebec, had resigned during the Winter upon being promised a Captaincy in the Massachusetts Provincials. He had raised his Company only to find, shortly after his arrival at Crown Point, that a previous Captain had "superseded" him. Endeavoring to get back into Rogers Rangers, he was fortunate enough to be on hand, for he delivered Rogers' recommendations to Amherst, and the General deposited him in Farrington's vacancy. Edmund Munroe, the Sergeant-Major of the Corps, was recommended by Rogers for an Ensigncy, but Hutchings filled the last vacancy, and Amherst informed Rogers that Munroe "must wait another opportunity."

The month of July and the first two weeks of August were a period of bustling activity at Crown Point as Haviland's army prepared to advance. To encourage the temperance of the men Haviland ordered the Sutlers to put all of their barrels of Rum in the Fort's Casemate and they were allowed to withdraw a barrel at a time only with an order from the Colonel of each Corps, in the case of Rogers Rangers, Major Rogers. This excellent practice was observed with "good effects" for over a month until July 3rd. The previous day Haviland had decreed that no Sutler should sell any spirits after the evening gun, but two enterprising Sutlers sold the men Beer and Wine. This was revealed when several of the men became hilariously drunk and started a small riot. Upon which the Sutlers' casks were stove in exciting the following remark from a Provincial witness. "So we have wine and strong beer running down our street..." Unfortunately one of the two Sutlers was one of those attached to Rogers Rangers and he was ordered "To quit Crown Point Emediately" and if he, or the other Sutler miscrepeant, George Morris, were found" in the camp or in any Post between" Crown Point "or Albany they will be shipt and Drum'd out."[142]

Amherst had ordered Haviland on June 1, to send down all of the camp women except two or three for the Surgeon and one to cook for the officers. But as the Sutlers increased in number they managed to slip women in under pretense of being their wives.[143]

On June 17, Captain Brewer "piloted" Captain Jenks of the Provincials with 200 men across the Lake to a Spruce grove that he had previously discovered. Brewer and his detachment of Rangers instructed Jenks' 200 Provincials in the Rangers' method of march, thus making the expedition serve a dual purpose-to protect their march to obtain Spruce for Beer, and to make them more effective fighting force for the campaign. Brewer and Jenks returned laden with Spruce, and without meeting any scalping parties.[III-149] However, an enemy party was reported across the Lake near the mouth of Otter Creek by a vigilant scout of Rangers under Captain James Rogers, and the peril was relayed south as far as Colonel Jacob Kents' New Hampshire Regiment, who were repairing Stark's 1759 road to Number Four.[III-150]

The army was alarmed again the following evening at sunset when a small fire was seen eight miles down the Lake on the west shore. Haviland dispatched Major Skeen, Captains Brewer and James Rogers, and Captain Hutchings (soon Ensign Hutchings of Rogers Rangers) of the Provincials with thirty men in three boats. Before they reached the fire it was out. They remained near the spot until daylight when they fired a shot and were answered from the shore. To their surprise, they discovered two Rangers who had been taken captives the previous Winter, and escaped from Montreal on June 7th. One of them, Christopher Proudfoot was wounded in two places in Rogers' "Three Battles" on March 7, 1759. Given up for dead, he was captured by the French and recovered from his wounds at Ticonderoga and then sent to Montreal. The other Ranger, Ebil Chamberlain, was captured in The Payroll Massacre in February 1760. They had boasted to Captain Tute at Montreal that they would soon be at Crown Point, and he had sent his compliments by them. Tute soon followed these Rangers in for he was exchanged with others shortly after to add to their timely information on Rogers' Battle of Pointe au Fer, and Ste. Therese Riad. [III-151]

In spite of the constant patrols maintained by Rogers Rangers a "flying party" did filter through on July 8, and Rogers' Point was the scene of a bloody half-hour skirmish about six A.M. on July 8, when forty French and Indians fell upon a party of Rangers under Captain Brewer who were making a raft near the Rangers' camp. One Ranger was killed, and Captain Brewer and five Rangers were wounded. "The Rangers returned the fire and beat them off but could not find that they had killed any of them." Rogers sent out a pursuit party who followed them for eight miles before they gave up the chase. Other scouts under Rogers went down the Lake in order to intercept them but to no avail. The six wounded Rangers were taken to the hospital at Crown Point where two of them died two days later. However, Captain Brewer recovered in time to rejoin his Company in the advance on Isle aux Noix. [II-107]

Besides the two Rangers lost in this action, the Corps lost one other courageous Ranger on July 10th. Private Jacob Hallowell died on a sweltering day in the hospital from the wounds he received at the Battle of Pointe au Fer. Another Ranger was lost, but this time to the Regulars. The valuable Lieutenant Abernathan Cargyll of St. Francis Raid fame expressed his desire to purchase an Ensigncy in the 17th Regiment, and Rogers gave him "a very good character..." to Colonel John Darby, who in turn wrote Amherst on July 26, asking him to consider Cargyll. Cargyll entered his Regiment on September 18, 1760.[144]

July 22 and 23, saw Rogers Rangers practicing at shooting at marks.[145] On the 24th Captain Hutchings of the Massachusetts Provincials returned from Oswego with Amherst's promotions in the Rangers (previously mentioned) and rejoined Rogers Rangers as an Ensign.[146] The 25th saw 400

Rangers, Regulars and Provincials boating southward to pick up a load of provisions at the portage at Ticonderoga.[147] The Rangers received their proportion of boats on August 1, and a detail secured them and fitted them out.[148]

On August 4, 284 Provincials from the New Hampshire Regiment were draughted into Rogers Rangers thus swelling the Company to 100 men.[149] The balance of the above recruits were a Company of "Hatchetmen" commanded by Captain Samuel Hodge Jr., and the Corps now had a Company of Pioneers.[150] Major Rogers now had under his immediate command, five companies of white Rangers. Solomon's Company of 70 Stockbridges and Hodges' 100 Hatchetmen. A truly potent and colorful Corps to embark on August 16, to form the advance-guard of Haviland's army.[151]

On the 6th, before embarking, a payroll express arrived from Amherst and the Regulars and Rangers were paid in part. Rogers judiciously endeavored to rectify the shortage of pay by sending a special Ranger Courier the same day to Appy, Amherst's Secretary, the same Courier to return with Amherst's warrants.[152] Amherst had also sent instructions to Haviland to maintain communication with him by sending two or three Rangers via Tute's 1759 route to LaGallete.[153]

On the third day of sailing the army weathered a freak squall of wind and rain, and one of the canoes containing eleven Rangers was split into by the chopping waves. Eight men were drowned before other boats could arrive to rescue the other 3 occupants.[154] The following day Rogers Rangers and the Light Infantry and Grenadiers landed on the east shore unopposed and the army followed. The Rangers established camp on the northern end of Haviland's line, being opposite to the rear of Isle aux Noix. Batteries were erected and fired the next day starting an eight day siege of the Isle. The Rangers figured prominently in the Siege. Their activities were important enough to excite chronicling by Provincial Journalists.[II-111]

On the night of their arrival a whaleboat of Rangers were sent to take soundings of the channel near the French fort. They were observed and a volley of grapeshot greeted them, killing a Ranger and wounding three others, one of whom drowned.[II-110] The Rangers more than made up for this minor loss a week later when they executed a brilliant stroke which brought the siege to an end.

During this week the Rangers had one particular assignment which they had to thank Brigadier Haviland for. Major Rogers was ordered to have piles of wood cut and stacked sixty yards in front of his encampment to be burned every night to draw the enemy fire. The Rangers must have growled at this for such measures invited long-range volleys directly into their camp. The task of cutting the wood was entrusted to Hodge's Hatchetmen and they were ordered to grind their hatchets immediately.[155] The Rangers, however, put their tomahawks to use on the 20th, when 200 Rangers under Captain David Brewer joined a detail of Light Infantry and Grenadiers to cut brush to make fascines.[156] Picket duty for the Rangers consisted of three pickets every night and one during the day to guard the batteaus.[157]

On the 22nd a scout of 9 Rangers brought in four prisoners which they spirited from Isle aux Noix in the early morning. This scout was particularly hazardous, consequently the Rangers were Volunteers and the detail received 37 pounds 16 shillings New York Currency from Haviland the day after they brought in the prisoners.[III-154]

The Rangers' most important achievement occurred about nine A.M. on August 25th. Colonel Darby had proposed capturing the French fleet. As this would destroy Bougainville's lifeline with St. John's, Haviland readily granted him permission to execute the mission. His force consisted of two Companies of Light Infantry, Major Rogers with five Companies of Rangers including the Stockbridges. Dragging three field pieces through the trees, they silently planted them opposite to the unsuspecting vessels in the Richelieu River behind the Island. The French naval force consisted of a rideau, a brig, a sloop and a schooner. A six-pounder opened fire first and by good fortune the first shot cut the cable to the principal ship, the rideau, and a strong west wind drove her ashore into the hands of Darby's Light Infantry. The other vessels hurriedly weighed anchor and made all sail for St. John's but stranded in a bend of the river. Rogers, with his Rangers, hurried along the shore until they came to the stranded vessels. Here, part of the Rangers fired from the shore to cover those who swam out with their tomahawks between their teeth. They boarded and drove the astonished crew down the hatchway or into the water, thus one vessel was captured by this method and the rest were so demoralized that they surrendered to Darby when he sailed up in the British manned rideau.[II-112] This exploit of Darby and Rogers literally brought the siege to an end for the French commander, Bougainville, abandoned the island on the night of August 27, with his garrison, and made his way with extreme difficulty through the dark forest and swamps to join La Pause at St. John's, twelve miles below. Rogers Rangers were sent in hot pursuit of the fleeing Bougainville while Haviland followed with the main army. Arriving at St. John's, Rogers and his Rangers found it in flames.

Leaving 200 Rangers to fortify the log houses that remained standing near the lake side, in order to protect his boats and baggage against a possible return of the enemy. Rogers hurried on with 370 Rangers and Indians and overtook the rear guard of the enemy consisting of 200 men. Rogers' men immediately attacked them and after a hot skirmish, the French and Indians, forming the rear guard, broke and fell back to their main body of 1,500 men. Rogers lost two men killed and two wounded, including Lieutenant Nathan Stone who was wounded through the foot, in this hot engagement.[II-113]

Hoping that Bougainville would make a stand, Rogers pursued them, and hung on their flanks and rear and harassed them constantly until the enemy crossed a river to a fortified camp and drew up the bridge after them, thus putting a stop to Rogers' pursuit. However, Rogers rejoined Haviland with 17 prisoners, among them a French Major and a Captain.

Haviland proceeded as far as Ste. d'Etrese where he encamped his army and erected a strong breastwork. Rogers was sent with his Rangers down the Richelieu to administer the oath of allegiance to his Britannic Majesty among the French-Canadian inhabitants and a Provincial Journalist records that the Rangers "keep bringing in the best of the inhabitants, as they take their choice of them; they also inform us the ladies are very kind in the neighborhood, which seems we shall fare better when we get into the thick settled parts of the country."[158]

After successfully completing this task, Rogers joined Colonel Darby at Chambly, where he was investing the fort with a few light cannon. The fort surrendered on September 1 at two P.M. after receiving one fire.[II-115]

This was the last obstacle, and Haviland's part of the triple attack on Canada was now completed. He opened communications with Murray by a Ranger Officer. At the same time, Murray, who superseded Haviland, sent Ranger Sergeant Luxford Goodwin, with a party of Hazen's Ranger Company, to Haviland. Besides dispatches, they brought Haviland horses for his officers and some French officers.

Murray returned Rogers' officer with orders for Haviland to send him Rogers Rangers and his Grenadiers and Light Infantry to join him at Longueuil and to follow with the balance of his army. However, Haviland had already proceeded to La Prairie under orders from Amherst. He dispatched Lieutenant Benzell of the Regulars and three Rangers to Murray with this intelligence. The three Rangers receiving one pound four shillings each from Haviland for this "Express" service. Rogers and his Rangers were sent to join Murray though, and upon their arrival at Longueuil, Hazen's Company of Rogers Rangers re-joined the Corps after a two-and-one-half year's separation.[159]

Chapter VI
1760

CONQUEST OF CANADA
QUEBEC FRONT

As the fierce weather drove Murray's force from their tented encampment on the plains and into Quebec for the Winter, Hazen's Company of Rogers Rangers were stationed at the extreme advanced post at Lorette, eight miles west of Quebec. Hazen's Company were kept busy in patrolling, woodcutting, [160] and disarming the Canadian inhabitants in the lower St. Lawrence parishes, who after the fall of Quebec, had returned to their homes.

On November 30, Lieutenant John Montressor, an Engineer of distinction, was sent with 12 Rangers to disarm the Canadians on the south side of the lower St. Lawrence and received their oaths of allegiance. They accomplished their work as far as Beaumont where they were forced to turn back because of the severity of the weather. [III-138]

Murray's position was one of dangerous isolation with no prospect of reenforcement until ships could get through in May. Consequently Lieutenant John Butler was sent with four other Rangers across country to New York with dispatches for Amherst. They were obliged to return, after being 10 days in the woods and barely escaping a party of Indians by taking refuge with friendly Canadians. [III-141]

On January 26, however, another attempt was made by a

shorter route, for Murray records: "...it is of the greatest importance to let General Amherst know our situation here, and what preparations would be most necessary to be made for the ensuing campaign..." This time the detachment was trebled to two Sergeants and ten Rangers under Lieutenant Butler, the whole commanded by Engineer Lieutenant, John Montressor, who was also to compute a map of their River Chaudiere route.

This expedition though free of mortal combat was redundant of unparalleled physical hardships which rivalled those of the St. Francis Raiders. They travelled up the Chaudiere to its source at Lake Megantic, then cut directly south, passed between Rangeley and Mooselucmeguntic Lakes and through Maine's Blue Mountains and on until they reached the banks of the Androscoggin which they followed to the Atlantic Ocean. Twelve days before they reached the mouth of the Androscoggin and the first settlement of Topsham their food supply gave out and they were forced to duplicate the extremities of their fellow Rangers in the retreat from the St. Francis Raid, by eating all the spare leather, Indian shoes, and bullet pouches that they had with them. To intensify their sufferings they encountered freezing weather most of the way, and one of the Rangers froze to death. On February 15, Montressor dispatched Lieutenant Butler and one Ranger, "the best traveller, offering a good reward to the latter, "to push on in advance to Topsham for the urgent provisions. Although Montressor later blamed Butler for the necessity of this second attempt to get through to Amherst, he must have been thankful that he and the other Ranger were hardy enough to reach Topsham, Maine five days later and send back two of the inhabitants with provisions. After the Rangers had recovered from their ordeal two of them retraced their steps to Quebec, arriving there on March 13, with the news of the success of the mission. Meanwhile Montressor and Butler rode horseback to Newport where they hired a sloop for New York, arriving there on March 3, delivered Murray's verbal message to Amherst and received his profuse commendation. III-143

On April 19, Butler received orders from Amherst to sail for Boston and pick up the Ranger recruits that Amherst's recruiting parties had gathered for Hazen's Company. Upon

Butler's arrival they embarked in a cattle boat and sailed for Quebec arriving in time to help relieve the besieged city.[161]

From the time when the English took possession of Quebec, reports had come in that Levis had meant to attack it but it was not until April that he arrived from Montreal with his army. In the meantime his advanced parties hovered around the two fortified outposts that Murray had established, one at Ste. Foy and the other farther on, at Old Lorette. Hazen's Company of Rogers Rangers were posted in a house not far from the post at Lorette, and there were several fierce winter actions in which Hazen's Rangers played a prominent part.[162]

The first of these actions occurred in February when a large body of French Grenadiers appeared at Old Lorette and drove off a herd of cattle. Captain Hazen with a detachment of 25 Rangers, a force much inferior in number, charged the cattle rustlers and put the Grenadiers to flight, recovering the cattle.[II-96]

A few weeks later a party of more than 1,000 French, Canadians and Indians, took up a strong position near the church at Point Levi. On February 24, Murray sent over Hazen's C Company of Rangers and a detachment of Light Infantry, all under Major Dalling. They crossed the frozen surface of the St. Lawrence with Hazen's Rangers in the advance. The Rangers secured a footing on the heights and the Light Infantry followed under cover of their protective fire. For the past several weeks Hazen's Rangers had been instructing the Light Infantry in how to use snowshoes, and now they had an opportunity to show the value of their teachings. A sharp fight ensued on the snow. Hazen's Rangers and the Light Infantry routed the enemy and killed and captured a large number on their snowshoes. A third post was established at the church and they returned victoriously to Quebec the same day.[II-97]

In March, Hazen and his Company had a brilliant skirmish. A scouting Ranger came in to the house near Lorette where they were posted, with the information that a large body of the enemy were coming to attack them. Hazen left a Sergeant and 14 men in the house, and set out for Lorette with the rest to ask for a reenforcement. On the way they met the French who tried to surround them, and Hazen told his Rangers to fall back to the house. They remonstrated, saying that they "felt spry," and wanted to show the Regulars that Rangers could fight as well as red coats. Hazen condescended and they charged the enemy, gave them a close volley of buckshot and bullets, and put them to flight. The Rangers had scarcely reloaded, when they were fired upon from behind. Another French detachment had gotten into their rear, in order to cut them off from their house. The Rangers faced about, attacked them, and drove them back as they did at first. The two French parties then joined forces, left Hazen to pursue his march, and attacked the 14 Rangers in the house, who met them with a brisk fire. Hazen and his men hearing the firing, abandoned their march to Lorette, and hastening back, fell upon the rear of the French, while those in the house sallied out and attacked them in front. Again the French were routed and the Rangers chased them two miles, killing six of them and capturing seven. The Rangers received just praise from British Officers for their bravery in this action.[II-98]

Rogers Rangers bolstered British morale in more ways than one. The French at Jacques Cartier had spread false reports among the Canadian populace of Quebec that packets had arrived from France bearing the news of a favorable peace in Europe for France and that heavy reenforcements were on the way. In order to offset this, Murray had a Ranger Sergeant and four Rangers cross the St. Lawrence and come into Quebec as if they were messengers from Amherst bearing dispatches from him and England. This bit of strategy did much to bolster the spirits of the British garrison and quiet the French and Canadian inhabitants of the town.[163]

Soon after this, reports came in of Levis' advance. A deserter from Montreal brought Brigadier Murray a letter from an officer of Rogers Rangers who was a prisoner at that place. He warned that 11,000 men were on the point of marching to attack him. Levis arrived before Lorette late in April and Hazen's Rangers and the British advanced guard fell back to Ste. Foy with Levis' army following. Murray marched out of Quebec on the morning of Sunday the 27th of April with half of his garrison and ten pieces of cannon to withdraw the advanced posts at Ste. Foy, Cap Rouge, Sillery, and Anse du

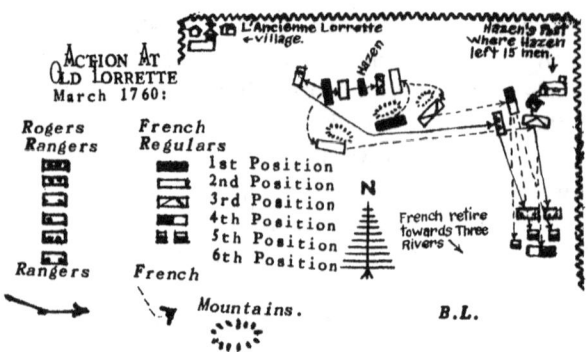

See pages 114-115

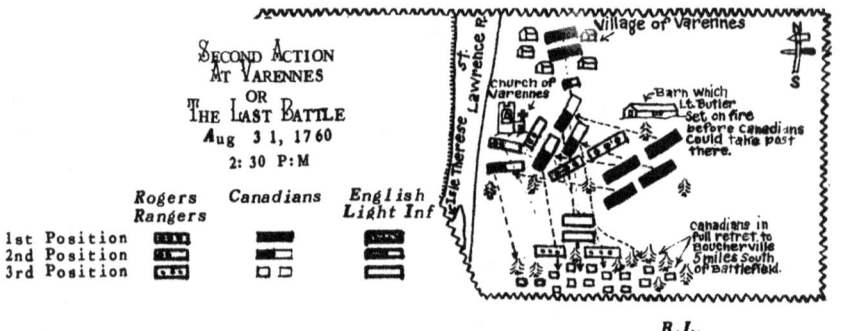

See pages 119-120

Foulon. On reaching Ste. Foy, they opened a brisk fire from the heights upon the woods which now covered the whole army of Levis; the outposts, including Hazen's Company, joined him and they withdrew to Quebec.

Deciding to attack the French army, although his force was much inferior in numbers, Murray marched out the next morning with his whole force of 3,000 men. He met Levis' army advancing to meet him through Sillery Wood, from Ste. Foy. Murray's line consisted of eight battalions, with two battalions in reserve. On the right flank were Dalling's Light Infantry. The left flank was covered by Hazen's Company of Rogers Rangers and a hundred volunteers from the Highlanders under Major MacDonald.

Murray's cannon opened with a telling effect and Levis ordered his left to fall back to the cover of the woods. The British mistaking this movement for a retreat left their favorable position and pushed eagerly forward and engaged with the French in the deep snow where their cannon could not be dragged. As the British cannon ceased to fire, the French charged through the woods onto the British right, overwhelming the Light Infantry who had dashed forward to take a house and windmill occupied by five Companies of French Grenadiers. The French regained the mill and threw the British Light Infantry back in confusion upon their battalions. For an hour more the battle raged for the possession of the windmill.

Meanwhile Hazen's Rangers and MacDonald's Volunteers on the British left received a deadly fire from the Canadians in the woods but they managed to attack and take two adjacent blockhouses but could not hold them. Hazen was wounded, MacDonald was killed and their corps overpowered by sheer numbers. They managed to extricate themselves and fall back on the British battalions. Both of the wings being outflanked and seeing himself surrounded by superior numbers, Murray ordered a retreat while there was still time to reach the gates of Quebec before they were cut off. The French closed in, hoping to cut off the fugitives. Captain Hazen, with his Rangers, was making his way towards the gate, supported by his servant, when he saw at a great distance a French officer leading a file of men across a rising ground. Hazen stopped and told his servant to give him his gun, seated himself on the ground, took a long aim, fired, and brought down his man. A Volunteer who was a witness and who thought at first that Hazen was out of his senses, congratulated him. "A chance shot may kill the devil," replied Hazen; and resigning himself again to the arms of his servant, he reached the town and recovered from his wound. The Rangers' losses, besides Captain Hazen, were two Privates killed and nine Privates wounded. The British lost over a thousand, or more than a third of their number, killed, wounded and missing. The French losses were 833.[II-99]

A rigid siege now ensued until the 17th of May, with the British, officers and men alike, dragging up cannon to their fortifications and working with pick and axe to strengthen the batteries; while Levis and his army entrenched themselves along the stony bank of Buttes-a-Neveu. Every night Hazen's Rangers were advanced between the town and the enemy's works to keep an eye on their movements. They remained on their arms and vigilant until daybreak and then returned to the town. There was hardly a night that went by that the Rangers did not find, or make an opportunity, to carry on the petit-guerre with the enemy's outposts or even on the trenches themselves. On the night of May 4, Hazen's Rangers sallied out and "went up to the enemy's trenches unperceived, poured in a smart volley and returned immediately without having a single shot fired at them."[II-101]

As the siege dragged on, both armies turned anxious eyes down the St. Lawrence, the English for ships from England or Louisbourg, and the French for ships from France.

British eyes were rewarded by the timely arrival of Lord Colville's Squadron in the middle of May.[II-100] It was Lieutenant Patten of Rogers Rangers who discovered the approach of the fleet. On May 15, he was advanced at night close by the river St. Charles with twelve Rangers. Not far from the general hospital they surprised a courier, who swam the river with his horse and was returning with dispatches for Levis "from the lower country, where he was detached for intelligence." By him it was learned that there were some straggling ships in the St. Lawrence and that a British fleet was entering the gulf.[III-146]

Murray, obedient to orders that Ranger Sergeant Beverly brought from Amherst, made preparations for fulfilling his part of the triple attack on Montreal, where Levis had returned with his army. On the 15th of July 2,450 men including Hazen's Company of Rogers Rangers embarked for Montreal. Because of his thigh wound, Captain Hazen was forced to remain behind in the hospital at Quebec. Lieutenants John Patten and Butler led the Company to Montreal with Patten the senior officer. The other Company officer, Ensign Hazen, was still on furlough in New England. Although the Company now boasted 139 officers and men, strangely enough, only 50 men embarked for Montreal.[164]

They advanced slowly, landing from time to time, skirmishing with detachments of the enemy who followed along the shore. On July 18, Hazen's Rangers had a notable skirmish with the enemy: Landing at Point Platon to disarm the inhabitants, the Rangers from the summit of a hill espied a party of 40 Colony troops under Lieutenant Hertel, a noted partisan, who had seen them land and were on the way to attack them. Lieutenant Patten quickly informed the covering party of 200 Regulars that had also landed and an ambush was laid for the unsuspecting Canadians. The Regulars were posted on both sides of the road and the Rangers maintained their position on the hill. When Hertel approached, the Rangers rushed down and drove him back and the two parties of British Regulars closed in. Hemmed in on all sides, the Canadians after a desperate fight were almost all killed, wounded or captured. Lieutenant Hertel was mortally wounded.[II-108] Returning to their ships with their prisoners, they cruised serenely on towards Montreal. Quite often during the journey the Rangers were landed and followed abreast of the fleet, disarming the inhabitants and administering the oaths of neutrality.[165]

On August 27, the British ships were alongside the Isle St. Therese, just below Montreal. The Rangers landed and secured some prisoners for information and learned that there were 200 Canadians with a detachment of French Regulars in the vicinity of the village of Varennes on the eastern shore of the St. Lawrence opposite to the Island. Murray determined to take possession of the village and establish his army on the island until he learned of the whereabouts of Amherst's army. At daybreak on August 31, after sending strong detachments above and below the village, Murray landed with Hazen's Rangers and the Light Infantry. After a spirited engagement they took possession of the Church and drove off the enemy, taking twenty prisoners and inflicting a loss of eight killed and wounded.II-114

Murray reembarked with the two detachments that he had sent ashore above and below the church, leaving the Company of Rangers and two Companies of Light Infantry to fortify the Church and post themselves there until he was ready to advance with the army. About one o'clock in the afternoon the Rangers were disturbed in their work of fortifying the vicinity of the Church when a party of eighty Canadians from Boucherville attacked them. The Rangers left their cover and sallied out. Lieutenant Butler noticed that they were trying to make their way to a barn that stood detached from the chapel. Butler set fire to it, and the enemy, infuriated, endeavored, under cover of the smoke and flames, to cut off the chapel and take post there. They were again foiled, however, when a few Rangers beat them to it and held them off.

By this time a small detachment from the Light Infantry had fallen upon the Canadians' flank and Butler with his Rangers simultaneously pushed them vigorously in front, and they broke and fled. The Rangers with the Light Infantry close behind pursued them for nearly a mile and managed to take seven wounded Canadians prisoners. Besides this loss, the enemy had three men killed and scalped by the Rangers near the chapel. The Rangers' loss in this action was only three wounded. This was the last spirited action that any detachments of Rogers Rangers were to take part in in the French and Indian War. It was the last action of armed resistance by French or English. That a detachment of Rogers Rangers should have brought the last battle of the War to a victorious end, practically by themselves, was not an unusual occurrence for this remarkable Corps. II-116

During the next few days Murray's army was landed on the Island of St. Therese and on September 5, Murray, with Hazen's Rangers, the Grenadiers and Light Infantry marched

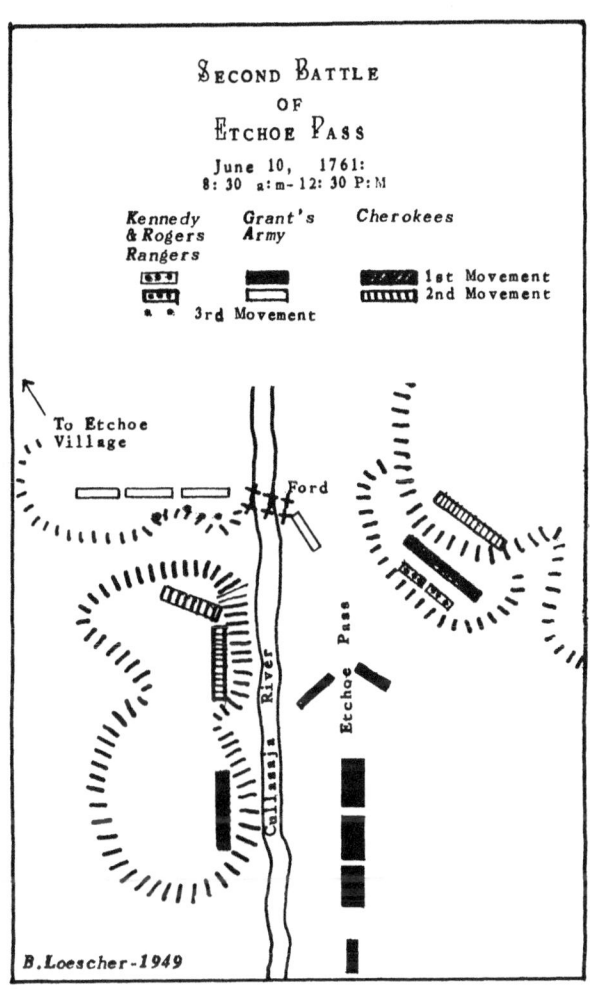

See pages 149-150

to Longueuil directly across from Montreal to reenforce Brigadier Haviland. The next day Major Rogers joined Murray at Longueuil and Hazen's Company joined the main body of Rogers Rangers under their commander, Major Rogers, after an absence of over two years.[166]

Chapter VII
1760

CONQUEST OF CANADA
GREAT LAKES FRONT

Captain Joseph Waite's meager Company of thirty Rogers Rangers stoutly braved the winter at the little post of Fort Brewerton at the west end of Lake Oneida. Their post, though being exposed (being the link of communication between Forts Stanwix and Ontario) was spared from any attacks and the winter and spring were uneventful enough.[167]

Late in February 1760 Waite left the command of his Company to his Ensign, Phineas Atherton, and journeyed to New York where he assured Amherst on February 28 that he could complete his Company by recruiting in his home province of Massachusetts and Connecticut.[168] With his brother, whom he recommended for the Ensigncy of his Company, the two Waites reported to Gage at Albany on April 26 that fifty good recruits were on their way. However, Waite's recruiting Sergeants exceeded his expectations and Waite reported 73 men "Fit for Duty" when Amherst reviewed them at Albany on May 9th. Actually 86 men had been recruited but ten men had changed their minds and deserted. One was left lame on the way to the rendezvous at Albany and two more were sick but present.[169] The same day Amherst ordered Waite to apply to Colonel Bradstreet for batteaus and proceed to Fort Ontario and whip his recruits into shape. On the way he was to pick up his Company nucleus of 30 men at Fort Brewerton.[170]

Waite's Company now numbered 91 officers and men including Captain Waite, Lieutenant Atherton, Ensign Waite and 4 Sergeants.

Captain Amos Ogden, formerly of the New Jersey Provincials and better known as a St. Francis Raider, applied to Amherst to raise a Company of Rangers in New Jersey and he was given 500 dollars advance bounty-money in March. Rogers was informed of this new Company and replied that he was "heartily glad" that Ogden had received a Company of Rangers. Ogden's officers were Lieutenants Richard Van Tyne and Josiah Banck, and Nathaniel Ogden (formerly of Wendell's) received the Ensigncy. Ogden's Company had a slight edge on Waite's in numbers. It totalled 100 officers and men. [171]

Since these two Companies were to serve in Amherst's own advance on Montreal he seems to have taken them under his friendly wing. He tried to round out the knowledge of his future Regular Officers by infusing Ranging methods into them. One, Collingwood, an eager British Volunteer, and two others who had been serving with Eyre, were convinced by Amherst into serving with Ogden as Volunteers. [172]

While Amherst's army of 10,000 Regulars and Provincials gathered at Fort Ontario, daily patrols of Waite's and Ogden's Companies were thrown out from their advanced posts to protect the camp. The Company were mentioned frequently in General Orders and Amherst's correspondence during the campaign. On June 16, two late arrivals for Ogden's Company left Albany for Ontario with the New Jersey Provincials. [173]

On July 15, an officer and 15 Rangers from each of the Ranger Companies were sent in 3 whaleboats to decoy the French brig and schooner to Captain Loring hiding behind an island with his two British snows. The two navies jockeyed about in eastern Lake Ontario for more than a week and when the French ships slipped back into the St. Lawrence on the 23rd the Ranger whaleboats returned to Oswego with Loring arriving on the 27th. [III-152] The same day an officer and eight whaleboat men of Ogden's were dispatched with speed to Captain Wilyamos commanding a detachment of the Royal Americans on an island near the entrance to the St. Lawrence. They had served as a provision base for Loring's fleet and unaware of his return to Oswego they were an easy prey for the French fleet should they venture into the lake again and discover them. III-153

While this exiguous service was being successfully executed Rogers Rangers were again mentioned but not in such a good light. On the 26th Private Benjamin McClean of Ogden's was accused of desertion but was acquitted.[174]

On the same day, in preparation for Amherst's advance, Ogden's Company led the rest of the army in firing two rounds to clean, and most important, to test the accuracy of their firelocks.[175]

On August 7, the bulk of Waite's and Ogden's formed part of Colonel Haldimand's advance force which embarked for the St. Lawrence three days in advance of the army. Hospital and embarkation returns of the 8th and 10th showed five Rangers sick in the hospital and seven officers and 184 effective noncoms and Rangers.[176]

Amherst and the rest of the army embarked on August 10, and officers and Sergeants of the Rangers were employed as whaleboat couriers to Haldimand at Man Island and also to Oswego and back with dispatches.[177]

Upon joining Haldimand, Amherst began the advance down the St. Lawrence to Fort Levis on Isle Royale a little below La Galette.

The 17th saw the French fleet attacked and the following day Fort Levis was invested. On August 23rd the bombardment began from Amherst's three ships, the mainland and the neighboring islands. The Rangers were posted on Isle a La Cuisse opposite to the Fort. The Rangers were entrusted with attacking their 14 whaleboats any enemy craft going or coming from Fort Levis with reenforcements or escaping garrison. On the afternoon of the 25th after a most spirited defense Captain Pouchot, the French Commandant, was forced to surrender. II-109

While Amherst's army were repairing the captured Fort, Captain Jacob Naunauphtaunk, who had been captured with Captain Kennedy before the St. Francis Raid, arrived at night on the 29th with French Indians and a letter from Father Robaud, who was influential among the Indians, offering peace for them. This Jacob had been a prisoner in irons on board a prison ship at Montreal, his release had been secured by the priest and he had been sent back as a measure of good faith by the French Indians who hoped for peace with the British.[178] Amherst now employed Jacob as a peace envoy to the remnants of the St. Francis Indian tribe.[III-155] Jacob delivered the General's speech and a beautiful belt of wampum valued at ten pounds.[179]

On the 31st of August the army left the captured fort which was renamed William Augustus, and proceeded to descend the rapids with the two Companies of Rogers Rangers and Gage's Light Infantry in the advance. The Rangers were disembarked and scoured the woods on both sides of the river so that the army would not be ambushed by any body of the enemy while the rapids were being traversed. This was probably one reason why LaCorne, the usually fearless Canadian partisan, decided not to defend and oppose, with his 200 men, Amherst's advance through the dangerous rapids. A week later the last rapid was behind them and the army was encamped before the walls of Montreal on September 6th. The next day Governor-General Vaudreuil opened negotiations for a capitulation, and on September 8,[II-117] he signed the capitulation by which Canada and all of its dependencies passed to the British.[180]

During the surrender negotiations Waite's and Ogden's Companies were encamped on Isle Perault opposite to Montreal. After the surrender Ogden's Company were relieved by a detachment of Lyman's Provincial Regiment and took post at the Church of the Cedars on September 10th. The day following a Sergeant and twelve men from Waite's were detailed as a "grass-guard;" but the next day Waite's were ordered to rejoin their Corps Commander, Major Rogers, with the following orders: "Waite's and Hazen's Companies of Rangers to march tomorrow under the command of Major Rogers; they are to carry provisions with them to the 20th inclusive and are to receive 18 whaleboats from Mr. Cuyler; they are to be compleated in officers and men from Rogers' Corps."[181]

With these and Amherst's personal orders to Rogers, the difficult task of receiving the capitulations of the farflung western French forts was begun. Difficult, because any body of British troops that were sent on this mission would have to travel through country infested with savages unfriendly to the British arms, and, who for the most part had not yet heard of the treaty, and consequently the changing of masters. This mission of receiving the surrender of Forts Detroit, Miamis, Quatanon, St. Joseph, Michilimackinac, La Baye, and Sault Ste. Marie and administering the oaths of allegiance to the Canadians and Indians was one that called for the utmost discretion and capability of handling. Consequently Rogers and his Rangers were the emissaries chosen for this expedition. Four days after Vaudreuil's surrender Major Rogers received his orders.[II-118]

It would not be amiss to state at this juncture that Rogers anticipated lucrative gains as well as military glory from this commission.

A little-known interlude in Rogers' life was his peculation as a trader, which, contrary to accepted practice, he married with his military career. This dual role had been enacted off and on since the winter of 1757-58, when Rogers had contracted with Albany clothiers for Ranger uniforms. One of Rogers' officers, Lieutenant Andrew McMullen, at one time accused him of being a Sutler to his Corps. It would appear that he was right, for Rogers continued to contract for equipment for his Corps and also special equipment for their various famous raids.[182] Rogers had solidified himself with John Macomb, the Albany supply agent for Greg and Cunningham of New York; and also with Macomb's two young relations, John Askin and James Gordon, who were Sutlers to Rogers Rangers in 1760.[183] But these minor speculations were small fry for one as far-visioned as Rogers.

Consequently, he maintained an alert business eye and when Amherst handed him his orders to relieve the western French forts, he realized that his opportunity had come. The same day he relayed word to Abraham Douw, an Albany merchant and source of ready cash, that "the Tour he had undertaken was exceedingly agreeable to him & he expected to make a Fortune by it" especially since he "has with him the French officer that commanded at Fort DeTroit who has promised him about three hundred thousand wt. of Furs at a very low price—and he desires that if he should have occasion for any Money before he could see you that you would supply him & he will allow as heretofore."[184]

On the 13th of September, Rogers embarked from Montreal at noon in 15 whaleboats with Captains Waite and Jonathan Brewer; 7 Lieutenants, 2 Ensigns, 15 Sergeants and 171 Rangers. In all, 198 officers and men. Also in Rogers' command were Lieutenant Brehme, an Assistant Engineer and Lieutenant Davis of the Royal Train of Artillery. These two specialists were to make a rough draught of distances, terrain and compute the necessary artillery needed at the western forts.

Cruising up the river St. Lawrence, the expedition entered Lake Ontario and, keeping close to the northern shore, they traveled on with the forest primeval for their bed at night. As some of the whaleboats had become leaky and consequently dangerous to travel in, Rogers directed the following order of sailing: "the boats in a line if the wind rose high, the red flag hoisted, and the boats to crowd nearer, that they might be ready to give mutual assistance in case of a leak or other accident." As a result of these precautions, Lieutenant McCormack and his crew were saved when their whaleboat sprung a leak and sank.

Arriving at Fort Niagara the expedtion lingered but one day for the lateness of the season made speed exigent. It was a memorable day for Rogers. While the leaky whaleboats were being repaired, he formed the trading firm of Rogers & Co. His partners were Edward Cole, Nicholas Stevens and Lieutenant Caesar McCormick, the four partners holding equal shares. Purchasing goods to the value of 3423 lbs. 8s. 7d, Rogers stocked the caulked whaleboats with supplies. Rough weather enhanced the firm's business. Captain Brewer lost some of his boats and supplies on the way to Presque Isle and a supply vessel due to arrive at this post was sunk and Rogers sent Captain Waite back to Niagara for more food. After their arrival at Detroit Rogers & Co. found another market for there was a shortage of provisions.[185]

Carrying their re-caulked boats over the Niagara portage, the Rangers launched them once more above the cataract. Rogers and a handful of men hastened southward to Fort Pitt to deliver Amherst's dispatches to General Monckton and receive further orders.

Traveling along the southern shore of Lake Erie, the Rangers arrived at Presque Isle, where Rogers, his errand accomplished, rejoined them. Here the expedition was reenforced by Captain Campbell and a Company of the Royal American Regiment, which had been sent by Monckton. As word was received that a vessel from Niagara bearing supplies for Rogers' expedition had been lost, Captain Brewer was dispatched with a force of Rangers and friendly Indians to drive a drove of forty oxen, presented by Colonel Bouquet, commanding at Fort Presque Isle, along the southern shore to Detroit. Captain Waite was sent back to Niagara for more provisions and ordered to cruise along the north coast of Lake Erie and wait for them about twenty miles to the east of the straights between Lakes Huron and Erie.

On November 7, four days after leaving Presque Isle, the expedition reached the mouth of the Cuyahoga River at the site of the present city of Cleveland, Ohio. The day being dull and rainy, Rogers ordered his party to encamp in the neighboring forest, resolving to rest until the weather should improve.

Soon after the arrival of Rogers' party, a group of Indian Chiefs and warriors entered the camp. They proclaimed themselves an embassy from Pontiac, ruler of all that country and ordered in his name that Rogers should advance no further until they had an interview with the great chief, who was on his way. It is here, for the first time, that this remarkable Indian stands forth distinctly on the page of history. He greeted Rogers haughtily and demanded the nature of his business in his country and rebuked him for entering without his permission. Rogers informed him that the French were defeated, that Canada had surrendered and that he was on his way to take possession of Detroit and restore a general peace to white men and Indians alike. Pontiac listened attentively, but only replied that he should stand in the path of the English until morning. Having inquired if the strangers were in need of anything which his country could afford, he withdrew, with his chiefs, at nightfall, to his own encampment; while Rogers, ill at ease and suspecting treachery, posted a strong guard throughout the night.

In the morning, Pontiac returned with his attendant chiefs and made his reply to Rogers' speech of the previous day. He was willing, he said, to live at peace with the English and suffer them to remain in his country as long as they treated him with due respect and deference. The Indian Chiefs and Rogers and his officers smoked the calumet together and perfect harmony seemed established between them. The crisis was now over, with Pontiac's friendship, Rogers' expedition had nothing to fear from hostile Indians.

Up to this time, Pontiac had been, in word and deed, the fast ally of the French, but he could clearly see that the French power was on the wane and he knew his own interest too well to prop a falling cause. By making friends of the English, he hoped to gain powerful allies, who would aid his ambitious projects and give him an increased influence over the tribes.

A cold storm of rain set in and the Rangers were detained several days in their encampment. During this time, Rogers had several interviews with Pontiac and was constrained to admire the native vigor of his intellect, no less than the singular control which he exercised over those around him. "He puts on," he says, "an air of majesty and princely grandeur, and is greatly honored and revered by his subjects." No doubt, the two great leaders had occasion to talk about the great river "Ouragon" to the westward, which Rogers was soon to long to travel on, as part of the journey to discover the Northwest Passage.

On the 12th of November, Rogers' expedition was again in motion. Within a few days they reached the western end of Lake Erie. Here they learned that the Indians of Detroit were in arms against them and that 400 warriers lay in ambush at the entrance of the river to cut them off. But the powerful influence of Pontiac was exerted in behalf of his new friends. The intended ambuscaders were told to keep hands off and the Rangers continued their progress toward Detroit, now within a short distance.

Approaching the straits of the Detroit River, Rogers received word from friendly Indians that Captain Beletre, the Commandant at Detroit, on hearing of Rogers' approach, had become defiant and to influence the Indians in his behalf he had set up an effigy on a flagstaff of a human head representing Rogers' and a crow surmounting the head, supposed to be Beletre, scratching out Rogers' brains. However, Beletre's gasconade had no effect on the Indians who failed him in his hour of need and allowed Rogers' expedition to approach to the walls of Fort Detroit.

After sending many letters back and forth among them being a copy of Vaudreuil's capitulation and a letter by him directing Detroit to be given up in accordance with the terms agreed upon between him and General Amherst, Rogers finally ordered Captain Beletre to surrender or he would attack the fort, drawing up his detachment in battle formation outside of the fort to emphasize his threat. Beletre acquiesced on November 29, 1760, and the fleur de lis was lowered from the flagstaff and the cross of St. George was raised in its place.

Captain Beletre, his two officers, de Nuit and Vercheres and garrison of 35 French privates were sent to Pittsburg under the care of Lieutenant Holmes and 30 Rangers. From here, Amherst ordered Holmes to bring them to New York via Philadelphia.

The 1,000 or more Canadians at Detroit were allowed to retain their farms and houses on the condition that they swear allegiance to the English Crown. The Canadians readily complied, if for no other reason than that they had 3,000 packs of furs that they were anxious to sell, as they had no opportunity of selling them since Fort Niagara was taken in 1759.

Rogers & Co. might well have been called Rogers Enterprises for his bill presented to the Crown listed a varied collection of debts incurred while carrying out Amherst's orders to relieve the western French forts:

Two Canadian guides, La Fleur and Pannier had been hired as guides from Montreal to Detroit. At Niagara, Presque Isle and Detroit 256 gallons of Rum had been bought from Cole (Rogers & Co.) for "the soldiers on their march." Blanket Coats, to the number of 170 had been purchased from Cole for the detachment, being a gratuity to the soldiers to encourage them to cross the lakes," at 25 pounds apiece, New York Currency. Two Canadians at Detroit, Hertel and Navarre, were of particular service to Rogers. Hertel was "Employed by the Major in taking possession of Detroit and sending away the garrison." Navarre's services were probably greater. Captain Waite had been sent to Niagara for 100 barrels of provisions, but due to a scarcity of boats he could only bring back 36 barrels. Navarre was ordered to send six batteaumen to meet Captain Waite. Navarre supervised a three-week bread-baking for Rogers' force. Flour, firewood and nails being scarce, they were purchased from Navarre. He received an order for hatchets from Rogers and jobbed out the work to Canadian blacksmiths. Seven horses were purchased from the Indians to convey ammunition and provisions for Lieutenant John Butler's detachment sent to relieve Forts Miami and Quantanon. Two more horses were purchased from Cole (Rogers & Co.) "to carry some frozen men to Albany."

Sir William Johnson, the Superintendent of Indian Affairs, had his representative, George Croghan, in the field. Croghan had joined Rogers at Pittsburg. He had sent Indian runners from the Six Nations to the tribes about Detroit in order that their chiefs might be gathered for peace conferences. Rogers ordered Croghan to purchase gifts for the chiefs and since Rogers & Co. were the only firm on the spot they received Croghan's generous order for rum, wampum and vermillion, shirts, coats, double bedgowns, pieces of gimp and stroud blankets as presents for the Indians.

Rogers took an active part in these peace conferences and he cemented the friendship he had started with Pontiac. As a prelude to a meeting, he sent a bottle of brandy by a friendly Indian as a present to Pontiac. The Indians had always been told by the French that the English meant to poison them. Those around the chief tried to persuade him that the brandy was poisoned. In spite of the anxious pleas of his followers Pontiac poured out a cup of the brandy and immediately drank it, saying that the man whose life he had saved had no power to kill him. He referred to his having prevented the Indians from attacking Rogers and his party when on their way to demand the surrender of Detroit.

Captain Waite seems to have been employed promiscuously in these conferences for he ran up a bill of 27 pounds 11 shil-

lings for "disbursements...Whilst on service for Indians."
As the meetings came to an end Captain Waite and Brewer were sent with the bulk of Rogers Rangers to winter at Niagara where provisions were more abundant.

On the tenth of December, Rogers set out to execute the final steps of his mission. While Lieutenant Butler and Ensign Waite were sent to bring off the French garrisons at Forts Miamis and Quatanon; a member of Croghan's party, Alexander McKee, with a French officer, was sent to bring in the detachment of French troops stationed at the lower Shawnee Indian town on the Ohio; the great French-Canadian partisan, Hertel, was sent with another body to bring in the French from the upper Shawnee villages. After seeing these three detachments off, Rogers set out the same night for Michilimackinac, with Lieutenant McCormick and his remaining 37 Rangers. After struggling for six days through Lake St. Clair and the ice-blocked Lake Huron, they could go no farther in their whaleboats and Rogers consulted with a band of Indian hunters at Saginaw Bay on the practicability of reaching Michilimackinac on foot. On being told that it would be impossible without snowshoes, Rogers, to his "great Mortification" was forced to turn back with his Rangers. They arrived at Detroit on December 21st, after a harrowing combat with the rapidly freezing Lake Huron.

During the next year, a detachment of the Royal Americans took possession of Michilimackinac, Ste. Marie, Green Bay and St. Joseph; and nothing now remained within the power of France, except the few posts and settlements on the Mississippi and the Wabash, not included in the capitulation of Montreal in 1760.

Resting for two days, Rogers left all of the ammunition with Captain Campbell and his garrison Company of Royal Americans and set out for Pittsburg with his Michilimackinac party. The march, though occasionally blighted by bad weather, was an idyllic one for Rogers and his Rangers. On the way they met parties of Indians and were happily received and provided with food and new moccasins. They hunted on the way in the magnificent forests, as yet unsullied by man.

On January 23rd, they arrived at Fort Pitt and Lieutenant McCormick was instructed to march the Rangers across the country to Albany where they were disbanded. He suffered a few frozen feet among his wards and had to purchase two horses to convey them to Albany.

Rogers' total loss in his Detroit Expedition was only one Ranger drowned, when he fell overboard and drowned before he could be rescued.

Rogers, after a few days stay at Fort Pitt, set out on horseback with Lieutenant Diederick Brehme, the Engineer, and arrived at New York by way of Philadelphia, on February 14, 1761. Here he received Amherst's congratulations and a Captain's commission in the Regulars as a reward for his extraordinary services during the war.

Chapter VIII
1760-1761

DISBANDMENT AND WINTER SERVICE

Lieutenant John Butler's mission to take possession of Forts Miamis and Quatanon was fraught with as much possible danger as Rogers' intended trek to Michilimackinac; for these little forts were isolated in the wilderness of the Illinois country and were close enough to Vincennes in the Mississippi Valley to receive succour. Consequently, Lieutenant Butler had a right to be apprehensive when he left Detroit on December 10,[186] with his little detachment of Ensign Waite, Sergeants Timothy Farnham, Sanders Bradbury and 18 Rangers, besides a French interpreter employed by George Croghan and seven packhorses.

Although forewarned that the Regular garrisons at the forts were meager, Butler's detachment must have been somewhat surprised that they did not meet any opposition from the Indian hordes, who had sufficient persuasion from the French at Vincennes to destroy them. Fort Miamis was safely reached and English colours raised. The 13 English prisoners found there were released and four of the eight French Regulars were sent to Detroit, guarded by three Rangers, who carried Butler's glad tidings to Commandant Campbell.

Leaving Ensign Waite with a few Rangers to hold Miamis, Lieutenant Butler pushed on to Fort Quatanon and found the fort held by eight French Regulars. From the Canadians, Butler learned that the neighboring Indians had been invited by the French at Vincennes to go there in the spring. After obtaining the oath of allegiance from the Canadians, Butler left the Fort in charge of one of the Canadians and returned to Miamis with the French garrison.III-159

Ensign Waite was now sent to Detroit with three Rangers and the Miamis French officer, who was almost too ill to travel and the remaining part of the garrisons of Miamis and Quatanon. These, and other French prisoners at Detroit, were escorted to Fort Pitt by five Ranger Sergeants. "Because of the unexpected length of their march, they were obliged to trade their personal possessions to the Indians to procure food for themselves and their French prisoners."187

Lieutenant Butler, according to his orders from Rogers, remained at Fort Miamis with two Sergeants and ten Rangers, as it was "a place of great consequence."188 It was originally intended to relieve Butler in the spring with a garrison of Royal Americans, but it was not until October 25, 1761 that the Rangers were able to leave.25

During this eleven months forlornment at Miamis, Butler subsisted his men by purchasing corn and venison from the Indians and Captain Campbell sent him some more ammunition from Detroit. Butler insured an adequate supply of fuel for the winter when he contracted with Lorrain, a Canadian, to cut and cart into the fort 170 cords of wood.189 By May 1st, the Indian corn was exhausted and the Rangers were living solely on wild game which they shot and Butler bought 100 pounds of salt at 6 shillings 11 pence a pound from Lorriane, to salt down the venison. Campbell alleviated their pangs of hunger by sending Butler a canoe with provisions and ammunition. Campbell had expected a reenforcement for Detroit, so that he might relieve Butler, but when this was not forthcoming in the spring and his small garrison was weakened by the necessity of sending men to Niagara for supplies, relieving Butler became out of the question. Butler's forlorn platoon had to remain on. Other difficulties besides hunger beset Butler, for the Indians delivered up some English prisoners and demanded presents for them. The apprehensive Butler had to purchase sundry goods from the Canadian inhabitants at Miamis to satisfy them.

From this same source, provisions for his men had to be purchased out of his own pocket, for the summer droughts made it difficult for Campbell to send canoes with supplies to Miamis.[190]

Finally, on September 10, 1761, Lieutenant Edmund Newland of the 80th and 15 men of the Royal Americans left Detroit to relieve Rogers Rangers at Fort Miamis. Ensign Robert Holmes, of the Royal Americans, formerly a Lieutenant of Rogers Rangers and a member in the Detroit Expedition, was to have command of Miamis but was ill and had to follow later. However, a return of English posts of November 8, 1761, shows Holmes in command at Miamis.[191]

On October 25, 1761, Butler bid adieu to his former officer in arms, Ensign Holmes, and left Fort Miamis with his twelve men.[192]

So ended Rogers Rangers' eleven months cantonment at this farflung British post. Campbell, at Detroit, was generous in his praise of Butler: He writes Amherst on November 8, 1761: "...I recommend Lieutenant Butler of the Rangers to your Excellency's protection for his good behaviour During his Command at Miamis."[193]

Butler's twelve Miamis Rangers preceded him to New York, arriving there on December 4th. The other eight Rangers of his original detachment who, due to illness, had remained at Niagara and Oswego, arrived later in the month. Carrying Campbell's recommendation, Butler soon followed via Sandusky and Fort Pitt, arriving the end of December. On January 2, 1762, he mustered his twenty Rangers and they were paid to January 24th, which gave them a travel allowance to return to their respective homes.

Butler had some difficulty in obtaining the 1,143 pounds 15 shillings that he had laid out "for Sundry goods purchased for presents to the Indians and for the purchase of provisions for the garrison at Miamis and for the support of the French Garrison" he relieved there and to Lorraine for cutting and carting fuel-wood. Amherst questioned Butler's Miamis accounts and inferred to William Johnson that he, or the British Commandants at Detroit, or Fort Pitt, should settle the accounts. Consequently, Butler had to request Major Gladwin, now commanding at Detroit, to hold a Court of Enquiry to delve into his accounts and it was not until January 1763 that he was finally paid.[194]

After the capitulation of Montreal, all of Rogers Rangers who did not accompany Rogers on his Detroit Expedition, returned to Crown Point, where they were employed until October 25th. Their first task upon arrival was to return to St. John's with all of the batteaus and ferry the Regulars to Crown Point. The task was completed by October 2, and two Subalterns and 50 Rangers were ordered the next morning at six o'clock to bail and store them "in a secure place."[III-156]

Rogers Rangers enacted whaleboat postal service when a boatload of Rangers rowed a Regular officer, with dispatches, to Crown Point from Montreal and returned there with a mailbag.[III-157]

Another detachment fetched supplies from Ticonderoga.[III-158]

On September 30, all of the Provincials, who had been drafted into Rogers Rangers rejoined their respective Corps.[195]

Work was continued on Crown Point. On October 15, Ogden's Company and a detachment from James Rogers' Company, under Ensign John Wilson, were assigned to work daily at the Grenadier bastion, from eight in the morning to four in the afternoon.[196]

However, on the 22nd, Ogden's Company were relieved of this unsavory task, when they were ordered to convey Provincial invalids to Chimney Point in batteaus. Four days later, the same Company ferried across fifty discharged Rangers, from six different Companies, who lived in northern New Hampshire and were marching home via Number Four. Since Captain James Rogers was the senior officer during Major Rogers' absence, he handled this finale for the bulk of the Corps, paying the Number Four detachment off on October 25th. The next morning at eight o'clock he reviewed them for the last time at the Grenadier's bastion and one hour later the remainder of the Rangers at Crown Point, with the exception of Ogden's Company, were also paraded and embarked with Captain James Rogers in batteaus for Albany, where they were paid off on November 11th.[197]

Before leaving Crown Point the Rangers had been asked if any of them were willing to enlist into the Regulars and at least one Ranger surprised the Corps by throwing in his lot with Haviland's 27th Regiment stationed for the winter at Crown Point. He was a veteran Ranger named Joseph Fish and evidently regretted his decision, for the following Spring he deserted in a mixed garb of Ranger and British uniform.[198]

The bulk of Ogden's Company were paid off on November 11th. However, a nuclear force signed up again to remain in service, besides the following who were never disbanded.[199] Lieutenant Richard Van Tyne, two Sergeants and twenty-eight Privates remained in service to keep open the communications between Crown Poont and Montreal. This was a unique and extremely hardy duty for Rogers Rangers, for the winter was customarily severe.[III-160]

Lieutenant Van Tyne left Crown Point with ten Rangers on October 18th with dispatches from Amherst to Gage, commanding at Montreal. He had orders to leave his ten Rangers at St. John's, pick them up on his return from Montreal and land at Isle aux Noix to remain there for the winter until relieved. A detachment of Provincials who were still levelling the fortifications upon the island were ordered to leave two or three of the best houses standing and one of them picketted for the security of Van Tyne's provisions and effects against the wild beasts, while he was absent on service or hunting. The Provincials left soon after Van Tyne's arrival and he was alone on this lonely isle with his ten Ranger mailmen. The remainder of Van Tyne's command were a Sergeant and nine Rangers posted at St. John's and a like number at Crown Point. Van Tyne's post at Isle aux Noix, being in the center, was the most forlorn but key station. Besides giving shelter to any winter passengers going through, Van Tyne had the responsibility of forwarding all dispatches, either from Gage at Montreal, or Haviland at Crown Point.[200]

The weather became so belligerent that it became difficult to get the mail through. Amherst realized the hazards of the winter Postal Service. In writing to Haviland on December 7, 1760, he enclosed dispatches to Gage and wrote Haviland "they are not so material as to risk the life of men by sending them down the Lake at an improper time. I should be glad to have them get to Montreal, but not till it can be done with safety.." and in a letter of January 26, Amherst repeated this order.[201]

Lake Champlain froze in January but not thick enough to bear Rangers on skates and the mail had to get through by Rangers on snowshoes, a grueling trek of seven days. Usually two Rangers set out with the mail bag from Crown Point. They delivered the bag at Isle aux Noix and Lieutenant Van Tyne went, or dispatched two Rangers to St. John's and from there it was relayed to Montreal. The same express service being followed in the opposite direction to Crown Point, so that the Rangers had little rest between runs.[202]

When they did find any time on their hands they were reported to have whiled away the time by drinking. This proved disastrous for the Isle aux Noix detachment on February 25, 1761. Van Tyne was "on party" with the mail and the three Rangers remaining took the opportunity of indulging to liberally of liquid spirits and became unconscious. Unfortunately their hut accidently caught fire and they were burned alive. The same accident occurred at Crown Point but did not end so tragically, for the Rangers' hut alone went up in flames.[203]

With the coming of spring the Ranger mail carriers became restless for their homes. On the first of March, the Ranger Sergeant at Crown Point informed Haviland that his detachment had engaged with Captain Ogden to serve not later than this date. Haviland replied that he understood that they were engaged until Amherst saw fit to dismiss them. Five weeks later on April 6, the Sergeant and three of his Rangers packed all their belongings and several days provisions and without leave they went out under the pretense of going hunting and deserted to return home. Three days later, when this conclusion had been reached by Haviland, one of the remaining Rangers brought him the affidavit signed by Captain Ogden on October 18, regarding the March 1st disbandment time agreed to. Haviland enclosed it when writing to Amherst on April 10 when he, true to form, recommended that they all be discharged stating:-"they are scarcely worth the expense particularly in the summer as little more than half of them at any time have been fit for service, as to those at St. John's I know but little of their situation though General Gage informs me once that there were never less than a third of them sick." Amherst replied to the affirmative on the 26th, thriftily noting:- "..I hope we have saved some pay by the Desertion of the Rangers."[204]

Lieutenant Van Tyne came into Crown Point with the mail on May 7, and Haviland ordered him to return to Isle aux Noix and wait for Gage to send down the St. John's detachment and then return with all the mail men and provisions at Isle aux Noix to Crown Point.[205] This mission was eagerly and expediently fulfilled and Van Tyne arrived back at Crown Point on May 18, with all but five of the St. John's detail. They had been confined in the hospital at Montreal with severe frostbite and while there contracted the smallpox. Van Tyne and the other Rangers were discharged by Haviland on May 20, 1761, and paid off at Ticonderoga by Captain Wrightson, paymaster to the 27th regiment, receiving seven days more pay and provisions to see them home.[206]

This interesting interlude of winter Postal Service by Rogers Rangers was a credit to the courageous ability of the Corps. It would have been a more creditable bit of history though, if the fires had not occurred at Isle aux Noix and Crown Point and the Sergeant and three Rangers had not become prematurely homesick.

Lieutenant Van Tyne was very anxious to remain in service. He waited upon Amherst in Albany and fortunately Ogden's Company of Rogers Rangers was being recruited for foreign service and Van Tyne re-joined the Company under Ogden's command.[207]

Chapter Nine
1761-1762

CONQUEST OF THE FRENCH WEST INDIES

After Captains Waite and Brewer returned to Niagra from Detroit in December, 1760, with the 100 or more of Rogers Rangers, they remained in garrison there until the early spring of 1761, then they marched to Albany and New York by way of the Mohawk valley. Here they were mustered out except those that wished to serve in Lord Rollo's expedition against Dominica. Captain Waite, 37 Privates, 4 Sergeants, 1 Ensign and 2 Lieutenants remained in service.[208]

Captain Amos Ogden, whose Company had been partially maintained through the winter, recruited for his Company in New Jersey, during March and April, 1761 and these two Companies, Waite's and Ogden's, though not led by Major Rogers, constituted Rogers Rangers representation in the Conquest of the French West Indies.[209]

Part of Ogden's 4 Sergeants and 62 Privates had been volunteer draughts from Hazen's old Company, who returned with Waite and Brewer from Niagra. Captain Moses Hazen, still recovering from his Ste. Foye wound, was informed by Captain Ogden at Albany on November, 1760, that Ogden had orders to recruit for his Company from Hazen's when they returned from Detroit. Upon this, Hazen quickly put in a futile petition to Amherst, via Secretary Appy on November 19, to allow him to maintain and recruit his Company.[210]

The conquest of Canada now completed, Pitt informed Amherst that some of his unemployed regiments would be needed in the fall of the year for the conquest of Dominica, St. Lucia and Martinique. Amherst was ordered to send 2,000 men to Guadeloupe to cooperate with the Governor for the taking of Dominica and St. Lucia Islands from the French. This force, including Captain Waite's and Ogden's Companies of Rogers Rangers, set sail from New York on May 5, 1761, and by June 1, the first transports began to drop singly into Guadeloupe,[211] the fleet having been separated by a storm. By the third of June, four ships had arrived, together with Lord Rollo, who had been appointed by Amherst to command the expedition. With his four transports and one from Guadeloupe, Rollo sailed for Dominica the 4th of June under the escort of Sir J. Douglass' squadron.[212]

At noon on the 6th of June they arrived before Rosseau, where the French troops were summoned to surrender. The French resisted and manned their batteries and entrenchments. Rogers Rangers landed with Rollo's force, on the beach, and immediately attacked the French in their entrenchments before they had an opportunity to be reinforced in the night. The French were driven out and the commander and his second taken prisoners. No further resistance was made and the next day Dominica swore allegiance to King George.[II-119]

Operations now ceased in the West Indies until the arrival of General Monckton with reinforcements from America to attack Martinique. During this interlude, Barbados was appointed the rendezvous for the expedition and the bulk of Rollo's army went there and rested during the hot season.[213]

However, Waite's and Ogden's Companies were fortunate enough to be sent back to New York during this idle season. Waite's sailed on the Black Prince and Ogden's on the Lyon on July 7th. Lord Rollo states: "...I did not think them necessary here, tho the French both here and at Martinique are terribly alarmed at the thought of Indians." This statement would imply that the French believed Rogers Rangers were all armed Indians.[214]

Captain Ogden carried Rollo's dispatches to Amherst whom he found at Albany, while the Ranger Companies waited at New York on board the ships. Amherst ordered them quartered on Long Island and advanced Ogden and Waite fifty pounds currency "to provide their men with small Necessaries."[215] On August 24, the Companies received four months back pay from May 25th.[216] On November 19, after a three months repose, they sailed with Monckton's army for Barbados.[217]

Arriving at Barbados on Christmas Eve Monckton took command and weighed anchor on January 5, 1762. The transports arrived in St. Anne's Bay, on the southern point of the island of Martinique on the seventh. The troops landed and the army marched over land to Fort Royal, the citadel of the island, three miles away. The road wound through treacherous ravines and deep gullies and the French had erected redoubts at every point of vantage, as well as batteries on a hill beyond, called Morne Tortenson. Monckton was compelled to clear the French out of the ravines and gullies and erect batteries to silence the French guns on Morne Tortenson. For the first task, the two Companies of Rogers Rangers were ideally suited and they adopted their bush-fighting methods and with the Highlanders drove in the enemy's advanced posts and cleared the way for the general advance which took place on the 24th.

Ensign John Carden, a son-in-law of Sir William Johnson's, writes that the Rangers, Light Infantry and Grenadiers led the assault and drove the French back to Fort Royal and Morne Grenier, a higher hill to the north of Morne Tortenson. Waite's and Ogden's Ranger Companies were attached to their old friend, Haviland's brigade. Haviland's and Walsh's brigades had attacked on the north side of the hill. After struggling with great difficulty up the steep mountain the two brigades succeeded in driving the French back to Morne Grenier.

The losses of Rogers Rangers in this battle were:- Lieutenant Richard Van Tyne and one Private Killed; one Sergeant and twelve Privates wounded and two Privates missing.[II-121]

The next day, the British, now being within range, began investing batteries to besiege Fort Royal, but found themselves much annoyed by the French batteries on Morne Grenier on their left. The impetuous French saved the British the trouble of storming the hill when, on January 27, they poured down the mountain on Haviland's Brigade and the Light Infantry and

Highlanders of the army, who were on the left of the British line. In forming for battle the French exposed their flank to Rogers Rangers and the Highlanders and were routed. The two remaining columns gave way and fled up Morne Grenier with the British army in eager pursuit.

The Rangers, Light Infantry and Highlanders were in the van of the pursuit and they plunged down into the intervening ravine at the foot of the mountain after the French and swarmed up Morne Grenier "by every path road and passage where men could run, walk or creep, hunting the fugitives before them." They kept on into the night until they had cleared every French soldier off the hill and gained possession of the batteries at the cost of 100 British killed and wounded. Among these were three Rangers, one killed, one wounded and one missing. II-122

The batteries on Morne Tortenson were now completed, new batteries were constructed within 400 yards of Fort Royal and on February 3, Fort Royal capitulated. In quick succession the rest of the island was conquered and by February 12, the conquest of Martinique was complete. Detachments were now sent to St. Lucia, Grenada, and St. Vincent, which fell without resistance. [218]

Waite's and Ogden's were returned to New York and were disbanded shortly after their arrival on June 16, 1762. They did not serve in Lord Abermarle's Havanna Expedition due to their weakened condition and numbers, besides, Amherst felt that Major Gorham's battalion of Regular Rangers would suffice. [219]

The only ex-members of Rogers Rangers who shared in the reduction of Cuba were Privates George Gardner and Benjamin McLane, who were draughted into the 22nd Regiment at Fort Royal in April and Richard Tervin, taken by the 17th Regiment, all three were of Ogden's. [220]

So ended the foreign service of Rogers Rangers. Their valorous deeds in the sweltering climes of the West Indies were heretofore (before this writing) unrecorded. [221]

Chapter Ten
1761

THE CHEROKEE-ENGLISH WAR

Rogers Rangers reached the height of their fame in the French and Indian War, becoming famous throughout America and even in Europe they were renowned for their exploits. The war in Canada was now over but there were other spheres of operations which had a great need for their talents. The powerful Cherokee Indians, who inhabited a large territory in Georgia, the Carolinas and Tennessee, had aided General Forbes in the expedition against Fort Duquesne in 1758. At the end of the successful campaign they returned to their country by way of West Virginia. Having lost their horses, they considered themselves, due to their past services, free to seize upon any they came across. The owners retaliated by killing several of the marauders. The younger warriors, incited by the French, now began raiding along the borders of the Carolinas and the war was on.

Governor Lyttelton of South Carolina at once prepared to attack them. The Cherokees, who wished to remain on friendly terms, sent 32 chiefs to settle the trouble. Lyttelton made them prisoners and treated them harshly. Among them was Occonostota, or Great Warrior, who was soon released through the intercession of Attakullakulla, or the Little Carpenter, who was the most prominent of the Cherokee Chiefs and who had not been present at the meeting. The captivity of the Chiefs and the activities of Great Warrior upon his release, inflamed the whole Cherokee nation to war. Lyttleton departed to become Governor of Jamaica and was succeeded by Lieutenant-Governor Bull who was more capable of dealing with the Indians.

However, it was now too late to arbitrate and the Cherokee-English War of 1760-61 was long and difficult, owing to the troubles encountered by the British forces in penetrating the country. In 1760, Colonel Montgomery was sent by Amherst, with his regiment of 77th Highlanders or "Royal Scots."

After burning several villages he was ordered to leave four Companies in the inadequately conqured territory and to return to New York before he could complete the conquest.

So matters stood when Lieutenant-Colonel Francis Grant of the 42nd Highlanders was sent by Amherst to bring the war to a speedy and satisfactory close.[222]

Rogers Rangers represented in this conflict were principally Stockbridge Indians, although there were four white Ranger veterans and Lieutenant Jacob Farrington.

When Amherst paid off the bulk of Rogers Rangers at Albany, he prudently kept a few Stockbridges in service. Though Amherst was adverse to employing this type of "gentry", still he thought they might be useful in the Cherokee campaign as scouts.[223] Several Mohawks were on the scene when the Stockbridges were signed up and they also volunteered, numbering, with the Stockbridges, thirty or forty. They were to be under Captain Quinton Kennedy's charge, who was to command a Company of Light Infantry.[224]

As usual, the Stockbridges were detained by liquid spirits in Albany and the sloop sent for them had trouble gathering them. As a result, they arrived late in New York and found Amherst and Captain Kennedy impatiently holding up sail for them (the balance of the transports, with Grant's force, had already left for Charlestown, South Carolina on December 22nd). Finally, they were embarked and arrived in Charlestown on January 7, 1761.[225]

They were followed three months later by another detachment of Rogers Rangers.

Shortly after Rogers arrived in New York from Detroit, Amherst rewarded him for his extraordinary Ranging services with a Captaincy in the Regulars. Amherst, in writing to Grant, states that this was a "Provision which I had so long intended for Major Rogers."[226] Rogers was commissioned Captain from October 25, 1760, to succeed the late Captain Paul Demere of a South Carolina Independent Company.[227]

Lieutenant Jacob Farrington offered to serve in the Company as a Volunteer, until an Ensign's vacancy occurred.[228] Since there were a few Rangers still at Albany who had returned from Detroit with Lieutenants McCormick and Farrington, with Amherst's permission Rogers had Farrington keep in service four white Rangers and ten Stockbridges to serve in his South Carolina Independent Company.[229]

Due to Rogers' lengthy time in gathering together vouchers for the settlement of his Ranger accounts for the concluded war, he could not sail with Farrington and the 14 Ranger recruits.[230]

Farrington and his charges embarked on H.M.S. Greyhound on March 17, and sailed for Charlestown the following day. Farrington's little platoon existed as a detachment of "Rogers Rangers" until Rogers arrived, when they would be absorbed into his independent Company. Since Rogers did not arrive until the campaign was over, the above platoon gathered laurels for "The History of Rogers Rangers."[231]

Much to Amherst's annoyance, the platoon had "...made away with their arms and everything they had" and he "did not think it prudent to trust them with others," as he was "certain they would have gone the same way." Whether their arms had been traded in for rum is not known, but Captain Kennedy outfitted them anew when they joined his command at Grant's Headquarters at Fort Ninety-Six.[232]

Kennedy's provisional "battalion" was a barbaric conglomeration of picked scouting detachments. Besides Farrington's platoon and the other Stockbridge members of Rogers Rangers, who had preceded them, there were details of Mohawks, Chickasaws and Catawbas under King Heigler—ninety in all—besides Lieutenant Wastel, with ten Volunteers from the 17th Regiment and Ensign James Connor with twenty more from Colonel Middleton's South Carolina Regiment.[233]

In spite of their temporary attachment to Kennedy's Corps Farrington's platoon retained their distinction and were designated as "Major Rogers' Rangers."[234]

In May, Grant's expedition set out for the frontiers of South Carolina and the Cherokee country. Arriving at Fort Prince George on the 27th of May, they stopped to gather provisions. This post was the hub of all operations and defense during the war. On June 7 the expedition, 2,600 strong, set out, carrying provisions for thirty days. The main objectives were the "middle settlements" in the heart of the Cherokee country.[235]

Forced marches in order to pass some dangerous defiles brought the army within two days to Etchoe Pass, about six miles from the principal Cherokee village of Etchoe.[236]

An ominous silence greeted them and Grant became wary, for this was the scene of Montgomery's first battle with Great Warrior.

It had been expected that Little Carpenter or Great Warrior would send deputies to sue for peace without evoking bloodshed, when the size of Grant's force became known. Instead, they were greeted the next morning (the 10th) when a party, from a distant hill, fired at their cattle in the rear of Grant's column. This effort of Great Warrior's to detract from his true position—in front of Grant on the hill overlooking the pass —failed, thanks to the sharp eyes of Rogers Rangers and the friendly Indian detachments in Kennedy's Corps, who were thrown out as a buffer in front of the army.

Their sharp eyes detected the main body of Cherokees on the high hill to their right about 8:30 and Rogers Rangers moved forward with Kennedy's command attacking so vigorously that "the Cherokees tho' numerous gave way. But the yelp went from front to rear of the line upon both flanks upon a ridge of Mountains on our right, and on the opposite side of Cowhowee River, which could not be passed on our left," Grant records and adds: "This Indian cry served as a signal for the attack and they began a pretty smart Fire." About one-half mile from the place where the attack began there was a ford and on the opposite side a rising ground. As soon as Kennedy, Farrington and the Light Infantry got over the Cullasaja River, they were posted along the banks to cover the passage of Grant's army, "with orders to cover themselves in the best manner

The best Map depicting the area of Rogers' Rangers platoon in Grant's campaign against the Cherokees in 1761 was J. Lodge's Engraving of: .... A SKETCH OF THE CHEROKEE COUNTRY FOR Thomas Mante's "History of the War in America" as shown below.

Lodge's excellent Engraving was derived from the following: ....

1) In British Museum Additional MS. 57714/16
"SKETCH OF THE CHEROKEE COUNTRY AND MARCH OF THE TROOPS UNDER COMMAND OF Lt. Col. Grant to the middle and back settlements 1761"

2) In British Museum Additional Ms. 140 36e; "A MAP OF THE CHEROKEE COUNTRY" See Also: Alden, John Stuart, pp 113, 365 and Cumming, Southeast, p 231.

3) Also of interest: Louis De Vorsey, De Brahm's Report, Columbia University of S.C., 1971, reproduces seven plans of forts in S.C. & Ga. by De Brahm. See Also: Cummings, Southeast, pp 246-250.
MSS Maps by De Brahm are in the British Museum, Public Record Office London, Harvard University Library and other Libraries.

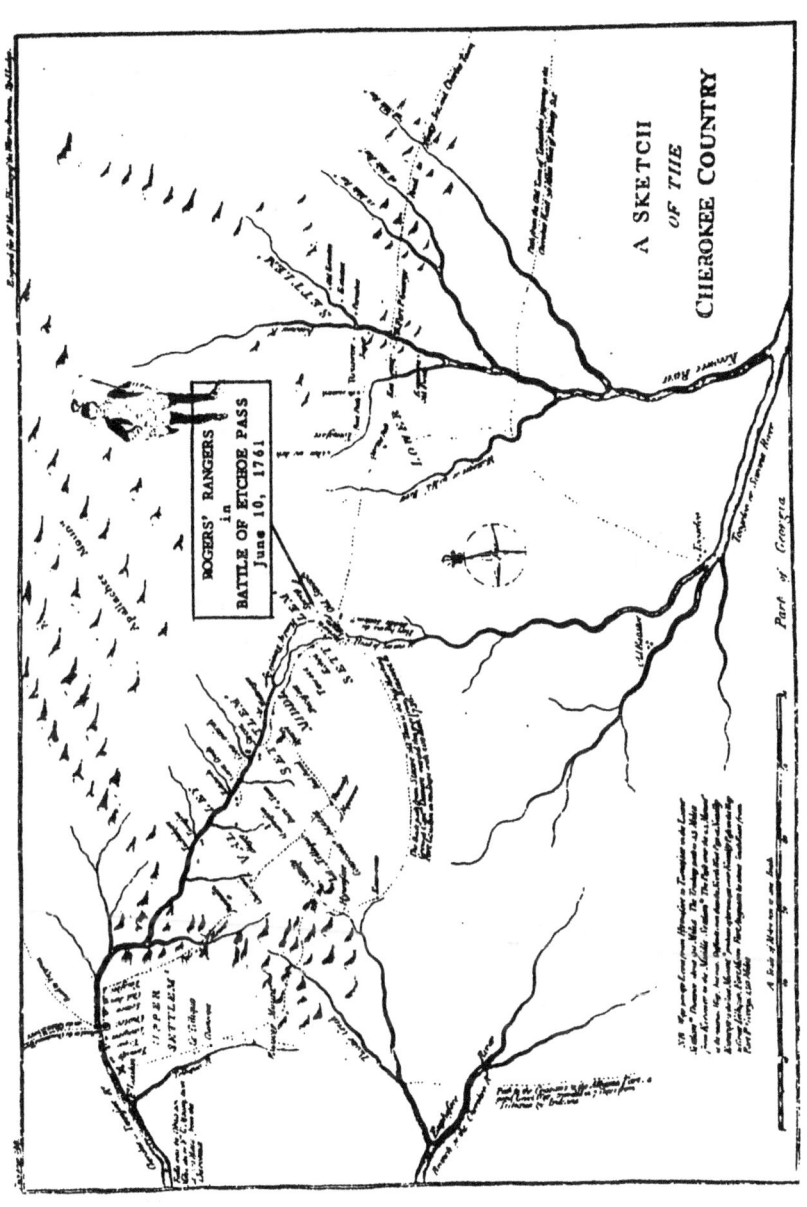

they could and to fire from time to time at the enemy to prevent their drawing nearer and becoming more troublesome."

The firing was hot until noon when most of the Regiments had crossed over and took up positions in columns behind the Light Infantry, allied Indians and Rogers Rangers. The army had thrown in volleys at intervals as they advanced and crossed the ford. The ability of Kennedy and Farrington to employ Indian tactics chagrined Great Warrior. A British officer records that during the heat of the conflict the Cherokees called out in desperation to Captain Kennedy, "to come forward," within reach of their enfilade fire.

The firing slackened after twelve o'clock, for the Cherokees only had a limited quantity of ammunition, but a desultory fire-at-will was maintained until nearly three o'clock, when Great Warrior retired. Kennedy's Corps, due to their skill in bush fighting, suffered only one Indian killed. Their infinite service in covering Grant's crossing was recognized by Grant and his officers. Grant states that they "behaved with great coolness" and another officer notes that "Captain Kennedy and his officers (which included Lieutenant Jacob Farrington) were of infinite service..."[II-120]

The total loss of the invaders in this engagement were 11 killed and 51 wounded.

After burying the dead in the river so that the Cherokees would be less likely to find them, the army proceeded to attack the Cherokee village of Etchoe, which they reached about nine o'clock that night and reduced to ashes.[237]

The next morning Rogers Rangers and Kennedy's Indians "were prevailed upon to go back tho much fatigued," to guard the provisions arriving at the Neweassee Camp, which served as Grant's base camp. This convoy service was safely effected by one P. M.[238]

Fourteen other villages in the middle settlements shared the same fate as Etchoe. Their magazines and 1,500 acres of cornfields were likewise destroyed and 5,000 Cherokees, who had been treacherously goaded into the war by the actions of Governor Lyttelton, were driven to seek shelter and subsistence among the barren mountains. In spite of the hardy spirit that they had shown at Etchoe Pass, the Cherokee warriors did not offer further resistance to Grant's expedition. It could not have been for lack of suitable terrain to waylay the invaders, as the mountain passes that Grant's army had to pass from village to village, offered excellent opportunities; instead, the spirit of Great Warrior and his braves seemed to be broken, either from their lack of sufficient ammunition, or the effect that the size and coordination of Grant's army had on them.

The expedition continued for thirty days in the heart of the Cherokee territories. The towns that Rogers Rangers and Kennedy's Indians figured conspicuously in destroying were Neowee, Canouga, Ayoree and Grant also records on June 17, "...as it was found difficult to pass Cowhitchi River with the troops, the Rangers and Indians were sent to destroy Burning-Town, which was effected that evening. III-161 Some portent of the ruggedness of the terrain and the swollen condition of the streams, which stymied even Rogers Rangers, is expressed by Grant in his Journal for June 18, 19, and 20th: "The Light Infantry with the Rangers and Indians were under orders to destroy Allejoy, the last town upon the Etchoe River, But this could not be effected on account of the River and Creeks which they had to pass, and the roads to Allejoy on the south side of the River were so bad that even our Indians [meaning Kennedy's and Rogers Rangers] could not pass them, though to do them justice they readily attempted it when desired and tried for three days to reach the village."[239]

Only two Cherokee braves were caught up with and they were in the village of Ayoree. One was killed and the other wounded, who escaped. On the 22nd, two more scouts were sent to bring in a prisoner, but to no avail. III-162

Grant notes that near the end of the campaign the men were so fatigued "that they could scarcely crawl—Numbers of them were mounted on the South Carolina Provincial 'Rangers horses—Even our Indians were knocked up."[240] By the time the army returned to Fort Prince George nearly 1,000 men were absolutely without shoes and without the aid of the packhorses, the lame and ailing, who increased daily, could not have been taken care of. There was not much time to lose for Grand had only two days flour left and the Keowee River was not fordable upon their arrival.[241] Upon their return to Fort Prince George the men were so exhausted from their fatiguing march in the rainy season that they were encamped at the fort to recuperate and await the results of the heavy chastisement that they had inflicted on the Cherokees.[242]

They were not long in waiting, for Little Carpenter soon arrived in camp with several chiefs and sued for peace. Grant sent them to Charlestown and Lieutenant-Governor Bull called a council to meet them at Ashley Ferry. A successful treaty followed and the Cherokee-English War came to an end.[243]

Rogers made his tardy arrival at Fort Prince George on August 26, with 18 ex-Rangers for his South Carolina Independent Company. Lieutenant Farrington now joined him with his platoon and Grant sent them all to Charlestown—Rogers being ordered by Grant to take charge of the troops in the town.[244]

When the ten Stockbridges in Farrington's platoon learned that they would have to put on "Red Cloethes," they refused, and since the white members of Rogers' South Carolina Independent Company looked on them with abhorrence, Rogers asked Amherst if he might discharge them, stating that "they are unwilling to put on Red Cloethes..." and "they will not be agreeable to the soldiers of the Company."[245] However, Lieutenant Farrington and his four white Rangers entered the Company, along with the other eighteen, that Rogers brought with him.[246] The ten Stockbridges returned to New York with the other Stockbridges and Mohawks who had served with Kennedy. The fact that the ten Stockbridges were almost incorporated into a British Regular Corps is an interesting counterpart, for it would have been the first and only time in British Military history that North American Indians served as Regular troops.

Thus ended the history of Rogers Rangers in the Cherokee-English War. Though small in numbers, their gallantry at Etchoe Pass had helped to extend the Colonial frontier seventy miles.[247]

THE REVIVALS

1526

Chapter Eleven
1763

PONTIAC'S WAR

Pontiac kept the peace that he had made with Rogers in November, 1760, until the close of 1762. Canada had been won by the English but the treaty to end the Seven Years War was not to be signed until 1763. Being encouraged by the French in the Illinois and Louisiana country that the French would return again to attack the English Pontiac took up the hatchet and so powerful was his influence that he secured alliances with all the former allied tribes of France.

In May, 1763, Pontiac's forces rose and in a lightning campaign of 15 days took 8 English forts, namely Venango, Presque Isle, Le Boeuf, St. Joseph, Miami, Quatanon, Sandusky and Michilimackinac. All of the garrisons were surprised and either massacred or scattered.[248]

Rogers Rangers were non-existent at the beginning of Pontiac's War but were revived by the following circumstances:

Rogers, sweltering in South Carolina and Georgia, had repeatedly petitioned Amherst to allow him to trade Captaincies with a New York Independent Company. His wish was finally complied with and Rogers traded his South Carolina Company for Captain Coventry's New York Company, lately returned from the capture of Havana.[249]

However, Rogers was foiled in his attempt to command a Company of Regulars in the north for the remnants of the New

York Independent Companies were ordered to be disbanded in London on May 18, 1763, almost before Rogers had an opportunity to command his new Company.[250] "This left Rogers a half-pay Captain in the British Army, though he could still act and be paid in addition as an officer of such Rangers as might be raised and used."[251] This soon happened when Amherst decided to send his favorite aide-de-camp, Captain Dalyell, with the remnants of the 55th and 80th Regiments, just arrived from Havana, to the relief of Detroit which was being besieged by Pontiac.

Rogers was greatly chagrined because he was not going to get his New York Independent Company after all and now to lose out in the command of the Detroit relief expedition to a man who had been his junior in several excursions in the French and Indian War, was an added blow. But in spite of this the call of battle was too strong for the restless Ranger and "it was with alacrity that he put himself forward under an inferior officer, nominated to an artificial rank for the occasion, it being matter of indifference to whom the credit of a dangerous enterprise was entrusted, so that he was signalized in a prompt obedience to his country."[252]

Trooping along in Dalyell's expedition, Rogers made up for his lack of a command by reviving his Rangers at Fort Ontario. Here he met his brother James, "whom by a desire of Captain Dalyell," Rogers informs Amherst, "I directly ingaged with some Batteau Men to go forward with us as Rangers. I hope his behaviour will be such that your Excellency will consider both him and the Men that go with him. Everything that I can do to forward the service shall not be wanting."[253]

This little "Platoon," as Gage called it, consisted of Major Rogers, Captain James Rogers and six men: John Steel, Moses Nelson, Hugh Moor, David Beverly, James Falls and James Wonton. This nuclear detachment of revived Rogers Rangers signed up on June 30, 1763, to serve for three months. By July 3, Rogers Rangers were swelled before embarking from Fort Ontario, by a Sergeant and 28 Privates from the New York Provincials stationed at the fort. These Provincials, following the same method practiced in the French and Indian War, were paid by their Provincial Government.[254] Lieutenant Bean, of an Independent Company called "Queen's Rangers"[255] (posted at Niagara and Detroit), joined Rogers Rangers temporarily. In this manner were Rogers Rangers raised anew to serve conspicuously and earn new honours in the bloody Pontiac War.

From Niagara, Rogers Rangers guided the expedition, for some of them had been over the same route with Rogers in 1760. Eventually they reached the charred ruins of the fort at Presque Isle and a few days later Sandusky. Here they landed to wreak vengeance upon a neighboring village of the Wyandottes and after ravaging their cornfields, pushed on again by water for the mouth of the Detroit River. They reached the river's straits in the evening of July 28th. With Rogers and his Rangers to guide them in the dark, the expedition, paddling as rapidly as possible, ascended the river and in the foggy dawn made a final dash for the beleaguered fort. As they reached a spot in the river midway between the village of the Wyandottes and Pottawattamies, the Indian besiegers broke the silence of a fortnight with a hot fusillade and inflicted a loss of fifteen killed and wounded amongst the hindmost boats. The fire was returned with spirit from the boats, the accuracy of the Rangers' fire proving a deciding factor in holding the enemy at bay while the boats gained the shelter of the fort at sunrise.

The defiant, but apprehensive garrison, were greatly cheered by the reenforcement and the fresh supply of provisions and ammunition that Dalyell and Rogers brought, but the fact that this small but capable relief expedition could break through Pontiac's hordes did much more to bolster their spirits. II-123

Major Rogers' old Lieutenant, Caesar McCormick, greeted them at Detroit and he, with other Traders and their servants, "who were obliged to arm at Detroit, had on [Rogers'] arrival, put themselves under his Command for a time."[256] Rogers Rangers now boasted more than forty officers and men."[257]

They were now quartered, with Dalyell's Regulars, upon the inhabitants, but not for long. Dalyell, brave but impetuous and swelled with his success in reaching Detroit, pleaded with Major Gladwyn to allow him to lead a detachment on a sortie upon Pontiac's camp. Gladwyn finally gave his reluctant consent and at two A.M., on July 31, Dalyell and Rogers, with the Rangers and Regulars, numbering in all 250 men, slipped out of the gates and filed two deep along the road, while two large batteaus, each bearing a swivel on the bow, rowed up the river abreast of them. The Indians were well aware of their progress and were lying in wait for them. A mile and a half from Detroit, Parent's Creek—ever since that night called Bloody Run—descended through a wild and rough hollow and entered the Detroit River amid a growth of rank grass. Only a few rods from its mouth, the road crossed it by a narrow wooden bridge. Just beyond the bridge, the land rose in abrupt ridges, parallel to the stream. Along their summits were rude entrenchments made by Pontiac to protect his camp, which had formerly occupied the ground immediately beyond. Here lay a large body of warriors silent as snakes, listening to the approaching column.

The Rangers and Regulars drew near the dangerous pass not totally unaware of danger. The advance guard were half way over the bridge and the main body just entering upon it, when a horrible burst of yells rose in their front and the Indians poured in a deadly fire. Half the advanced party were shot down; the survivors shrank back appalled. The confusion reached even the main body and the whole body wavered. Dalyell and Rogers rallied the men and led them forward to the attack. They received another deadly volley but notwithstanding they charged at a run across the bridge and up the heights beyond. Not an Indian was to be found. The British pushed forward in the darkness but were met with such a harrying fire from the front and flanks from the Indians who had fallen back but were keeping up a guerrilla warfare much to the discomfiture of the Regulars. Rogers Rangers naturally emulated the Indians and took to the cover of trees and bushes. To advance further would be useless and the only alternative was to withdraw and await daylight.

While executing this maneuver they learned from 2 Canadians that the Indians meant to cut them off from the fort and that they had gone in great numbers to occupy the houses which commanded the road below. Dalyell ordered an immediate withdrawal towards the fort. As they passed a large group of barns and outhouses a multitude of Indians delivered a telling volley upon the British rear led by Dalyell himself. Unfortunately Dalyell was among the many who fell. Meanwhile some of the Indians had taken possession of a house from the windows of which they fired down upon the British. Major Rogers with his Rangers burst the door down with an axe, rushed in and drove them out. Hurrying on to another house which commanded the road better, Rogers and his Rangers posted themselves in the windows and covered the British retreat. This house belonged to a Canadian named Campau. It was large and a strong one and the women of the neighborhood had crowded into the cellar for refuge. Many panic-stricken Regulars broke in after the Rangers in their eagerness to gain a temporary shelter. While some of them looked about in fright for a means of concealment, others commandeered a keg of whiskey in one of the rooms and drained it eagerly; while Rogers Rangers, the only level-headed troops present, piled packs of furs, furniture and all else within their reach, against the windows, to serve as a barricade. Thrusting their muskets through the openings they fired upon their lecherous assailants. Old Campau, the master of the house, stood on a trap door to prevent the terrorized Regulars from seeking shelter among the women in the cellar. The cries of the half-smothered women below, the relentless war whoops without, the distracted shouts and oaths of the Regulars, mingled in a scene of distraught confusion, and it was some time before Rogers' authoritative voice could restore order.

In the meantime, Captain Grant (who had succeeded Dalyell) with his advanced party had moved forward about half a mile, where he found some orchards and fences, by means of which he could maintain himself until the center and rear should arrive. From this point he detached all the men he could spare to occupy the houses below; and as soldiers soon began to come in from the rear, being able to do so under cover of Rogers' fire, he was enabled to reenforce these detachments, until a complete line of communication was established with Detroit, and the retreat effectually secured. Within an hour, the whole party had arrived with the exception of Rogers and his men, who were quite unable to come off, being besieged in the house of Campau by full two hundred Indians. The two armed batteaus had gone down to the fort, laden with dead and wounded. Upon word from Rogers, via Lieutenant Bean, that he could not retire without support from the armed batteau, when they returned, Grant ordered them up the river to the relief of Rogers and his Rangers, who had so effectively covered the retreat of the Regulars until they had isolated themselves among a sea of savages. Arriving at a point opposite to Campau's house, the batteaus opened a fire with their swivels, which swept the ground above and below the house and completely scattered the assailants. Major Rogers and his party now dashed out the back door and ran down the road, to unite themselves with Grant. The two batteaus accompanied them closely, and, by constant fire, restrained the Indians from making an attack. Scarcely had Rogers' detachment left Campau's house by the back door with all the Canadian women "showing a clean pair of heels," than Pontiac's warriors entered it by the front, to obtain the scalps from two or three corpses left behind.

Grant and Rogers conducted an admirable retreat to the fort by falling back from house to house. The Indians were unable to make a concentrated attack, so well did Grant choose his positions and so steadily and coolly did he and Rogers conduct the retreat. About eight o'clock in the morning, after six hours of marching and combat, the detachment entered once more within the sheltering palisades of Detroit. II-124

After this defeat, no more sallies of such consequence occurred during the remainder of the siege. However, there were two occurrences that Rogers Rangers figured in which came close to grips with Pontiac:

At three in the morning on August 20, Captains Hopkins and James Rogers led a detachment of Queen's^{258} and Rogers' Rangers and Volunteers to waylay a road between two of the Indian camps much frequented by the Indians. Although four armed batteaus went in an opposite direction to detract from them, they were discovered and had to return to the fort. III-163

Three days later the Indians became overbold and drove in an advanced picket and destroyed their houses, "which the

Commandant thought so insolent that he sent Major Rogers with the picket to take possession again, and upon his appearing the Indians run away and he remain'd there all Night..."III-164

Except for artillery, Pontiac maintained a formal siege of Detroit until November. Two factors determined his withdrawal: A strong British reenforcement was approaching from Niagara, but more crushing was the news on October 21st from the French Fort Chartres, that the Peace of Paris, ending the Seven Years War, had been signed. Consequently, Pontiac could expect no help from the French and he saw himself thrown back upon his own meager resources. His cause was lost and sending overtures to Major Gladwyn at Detroit he withdrew his people and retired with some of his chiefs to the Maumee.[259]

The siege now at an end, Gladwyn shortened his garrison to save provisions. Rogers' detachment of Rangers were part of the 200 men sent to Niagara in November under Rogers' command. Rogers Rangers remained in garrison at Niagara through the winter then were disbanded.[260]

After Pontiac's War, Rogers Rangers ceased to exist. In September, 1765, Major Rogers petitioned the King to allow him the funds to raise and equip 200 Rangers for a three year expedition to discover the Northwest Passage. This proposal was declined due to the stupidity of the home office in failing to realize the value of making further discoveries. Rogers again petitioned the King on February 11, 1772. This time he only asked for the subsistence of 55 men for three years. But once more his proposal was turned down and Great Britain, though not losing the chance to be the discoverer of the fabled Northwest Passage, nevertheless, lost the opportunity of extending her domain in North America, by not sending Rogers and his Rangers to make the discoveries of Lewis and Clark.[261]

For eleven years, "Rogers Rangers" were non-existent, not until the strife of the American Revolution did the Corps awake from its deep sleep to again enter the arena of conflict.

INTERLUDE

MAJOR ROBERT ROGERS, CHARACTER EXTRAORDINARY

While Rogers Rangers slept, their commander had ample time to advance his fortunes, but unfortunately he employed devious means which revealed the shady side of his character. As much as it would like to be chronicled that Rogers' private ventures were as noble as his military achievements, they were not even remotely related. If Major Rogers could have been remembered solely for his splendid accomplishments as a Ranger commander he would have been idolized in history, but the uncovering of his dubious transactions tipped the scales too far in the other direction. It was Rogers Rangers who remained famous in the annals of history, their leader became infamous.

Besides Rogers Trading peculations at Detroit, other ventures, much less honest, became apparent and not even the Crown was free of his attempted extortions. Arriving at New York from Detroit Rogers received his Captaincy in a South Carolina Independent Company, but before sailing south to join his Company Amherst ordered Rogers to produce vouchers to verify his preposterous claim against the Crown for Ranger supplies, pay and debts. Rogers' claims totalled 6,313 pounds, 14 shillings, 2 pence sterling, but much to his dismay he was only allowed one-third of this amount.

The "Articles" that were rejected were:

Alleged claims of Ranger officers and sutlers Rankin and

Morrisson for supplies to Ranger prisoners while in captivity;

Forty-five guns for escaped Rangers who returned to Crown Point;

Cash advanced Lieutenant Kennedy and a Ranger Private who were killed in 1757;

Pay of "Sergeant John" while a prisoner;

Pay of Rogers' 1755-56 winter Company;

Allowance for 459 arms lost during the war by the Rangers in sundry skirmishes (rejected, for men were to supply and stand loss of own arms).

The bulk of Rogers Rangers were reduced on October 24, 1760, but Rogers endeavoured to collect up to November 20, 1760, for five Companies.

Two items that were unjustly rejected were the standby pay of Captains James Rogers and Jonathan Brewer from December 1, 1759 to February 7, 1760; and Ensign Samuel Stark's pay as a Private from March 2, to November 10, 1760, rejected because Stark did not serve as a Private, but as a Volunteer in hopes that a vacancy should offer and he obtain an Ensigncy. This was especially ironic, for Stark had originally been deprived of rejoining his Company in his former Ensign's berth due to a severe fall from a horse while wintering in New Hampshire.

One other article that was almost rejected was Rogers' claim for the Rangers' pay chest that was taken by Langy in the Ranger Recruit Massacre. After much deliberation it was "Allowed because the Enemy...were Considerably superior to the Major's party."[262]

All of the above, with the exception of the last-mentioned and Rogers' claim for his 1755-56 Winter Company, were erroneous claims and must have shocked the honest and thrifty Amherst—putting him on his guard against Rogers.

If this was not sufficient evidence to keep the General wary, similar discrepancies, a la Rogers, occurred while he was recruiting for the Crown in North Carolina in July and August, 1762. Rogers endeavoured to obtain additional bounty that was allowed by Amherst in emergencies, but Amherst's agent, in Charlestown, Lieutenant Ramsay, would not pay it until he heard from Amherst. Upon investigation, Ramsay learned from Rogers' recruiting Sergeant that he never received any second bounty money, only the first, but neglected to give Rogers a receipt for it.[263] Four months later the shocked Amherst was again checking up on Rogers. On December 8, 1762, he queried Smith and Nutt, Merchants in South Carolina: "Mr. Commissary Leake has represented to me that it appears from the provision accounts lately transmitted to him that Captain Rogers of the Independents has drawn 6,672 Rations for some Men during the time they were in Captivity. As this is Entirely unprecedented, I must desire to know whether Captain Rogers drew the said rations in Provisions, or was paid money in Lieu thereof."[264]

All sources of easy revenue were considered and contrived at by the precocious Rogers. He presumed on his popularity and reputation as a renowned Ranger when he convinced the Governor and Council of North Carolina that he was their man for the Superintendent of Southern Indian Affairs and they recommended him to the home office on December 9, 1761.[265] Rogers' ability in handling the Indians is not doubted, but his exactness in balancing the Crown's ledgers for Indian affairs is to be questioned. If allowances could have been made for this extenuating circumstance, Rogers would probably have filled the late William Atkins' boots with success and his ability to cajole the various tribes into a permanent peace might have warranted the Crown's inevitable monetary loss. Six weeks before the North Carolina recommendation, Rogers, in the full flush of his latest brain child, memorialized Amherst on the subject asking him for his "favourable Recommendation and Interest to procure him the office of Superintendant..."[266] Whether Amherst recommended Rogers to London is not known, but it is doubtful, for by this time he had started to receive evidence to doubt Rogers' integrity.

Meanwhile, ever since his arrival, Rogers had been soliciting Amherst to allow him to return to a more moderate climate. At first he merely asked to return home during the 1761-62 winter to recruit for his Company and bring his newly-wed wife back to South Carolina with him.[267] However, his ruse did not work and it was not until the following winter that he returned northward after three insistent petitions on grounds of ill health due to the warm climate. Rogers asked if he might not trade Companies with a New York Independent Captain, but Amherst put him off by stating that these Companies were doing duty in Cuba, a much warmer climate than that of South Carolina.[268] Rogers bemoans his inactivity in another letter, only a month later.[269] Amherst soothingly replies that he shall grant his request "for going on service, whenever I see a proper occasion, as it was always what I intended. I will remove you to the northward but until then you could not be better employed than in raising recruits."[270] Finally, after Rogers' third persistent petition, Amherst reluctantly broke down and wrote on August 23, 1762, "I wish you could remain where you are, but if you think it absolutely necessary for the recovery of your health to come to the Northward, you have my leave to take the first opportunity of proceeding to New York—Providing Governor Boone has no objection to it."[271]

That winter found Rogers in Portsmouth reading a letter from Amherst which stated that he was glad to hear he was enlisting so many men. Rogers was to exchange command of his South Carolina Company with that of Captain Coventry of a New York Independent Company, which was agreeable to Coventry. The General then expressed his candid opinion of Rangers in general, instigated by Rogers' proposal to revive his Corps.[272]

Rogers, however, remained unquenchable and blasted Amherst with yet another proposal. But the General's reply to this last shows how definitely Rogers must have ostracized himself in Amherst's eyes when he asked to be stationed at a distant post with his New York Independent Company to get the command of a Trading Post to alleviate his financial losses. Amherst expressed himself very definitely: "...Although I am really sorry for your circumstances...yet I must Disapprove of the Method you propose, by getting the Command of a trading Post; for I have always thought it unbecoming an officer to be any ways Concerned in Trade, nor could I think of Allowing any such Practices while I have the honour to command."[273]

While Rogers was jockeying about for a lucrative set-up his nefarious transactions were destroying the strength of his famous name. An example of his swindling technique is revealed in barrister John Watts' Letter Book. Rogers was in debt to Smith and Nutt of New York for 23 pounds sterling, but before their Councilor, John Watt, could collect it he skipped off to Boston and Watt had to relay the bill to John Erving, a collector in Boston, adding, "I find there are a preety many other bills on him, and therefore I would get rid of this trifling Business as soon as I can."[274] Irving dispatched an employee named Nevins to collect it. There were hot words in which Nevins gave Rogers some offense, Watt writes Smith and Nutt, "of which I never intended. I meant no more than to get rid of a trifling affair which I was merely acting for another. It's true I had heard there were other Bills on him besides the Inconsiderable one sent to me, but there was no occasion to Tell him so, as it Cou'd be of no Use..."[275]

Rogers paid the bill to Nevins in Boston, not by the customary inter-Province mode of exchange, but in 361 Sterling pieces, 13 of which were defective and lacked 8 shillings sterling. In stating this loss to Smith and Nutt, Watt adds consolingly "...many others have suffered egregiously by that sad Man since..."[276]

All of Rogers' efforts to inveigle financial success were to no avail and each new bubble burst in his face. His trading firm of Rogers & Company was no exception. A rift occurred between two of the partners, Rogers and Edward Cole and no sooner had Rogers returned to New York in 1761 from his Detroit Expedition than he made over his power of attorney to John Askin to collect, or sue for, "...sums due me by Edward Cole."[277] Cole evaded settlement until the spring of 1762 when an employee of Rogers, James Gordon, finally caught up with him at Fort Pitt and settled with Cole after a 2,000 mile chase. In February 1761, John Askin, a former Sutler to Rogers Rangers, was taken into Rogers & Company as a separate partner with Rogers and the firm's name was changed to Askin and Rogers, with Rogers the silent partner. James Gordon, another ex-Sutler to the Rangers, was given a Clerk's berth in the reorganized Company and was given a junior partnership after the successful collection of Cole's debt.[278]

Caesar McCormick and Nicholas Stevens, now minor

partners in the firm, had established trading headquarters at Detroit, receiving the furs from the Traders in exchange for rum and goods for barter with the Indians. The outbreak of Pontiac's War ruined the firm of Askin and Rogers. In August 1763 Askin and Gordon had set out from Albany for Detroit with three boat loads of goods for the Indian trade. Although Johnson (Superintendent of Indian Affairs) had strictly forbidden the trading of rum with the Indians, Askin had cleverly hidden 15 ten-gallon kegs of highly potent rum in the bales of blankets and cloths, the rum to be thinned down at Detroit. However, the War broke out when they reached Niagara and their boats were halted and all traders were restricted to a low point of land between the fort and the lake for the several months duration of the War.

Here, Rogers found them on his way to the relief of Detroit and as he and his partners made their way back to Albany towards the end of the year they found a host of merchants clamoring for their long delinquent accounts for goods they had let out to Askin and Rogers on credit.[279] Thus matters stood for the remaining year and a half that Rogers remained in America.

Rogers seemed to be predestined to failure in civilian matters. Even his honest ventures bore ill fruit. As early as June 1761 Rogers, Captains James Rogers and Hazen of the Rangers formed a Real Estate venture called "Major Rogers & Associates." Obtaining licenses to purchase land on the western shore of the Hudson River above Fort Edward the "Associates" sent a representative to supervise a survey of the land but after waiting on Sir William Johnson he was informed that they could not purchase the land for it was within the boundary of the Mohawk nation.[280] Another land venture by Rogers was equally barren. In 1764 he obtained from Governor Wentworth of New Hampshire a grant of land located on Lake Champlain called Hubbardon and Dunbar but when the boundary line of New York and New Hampshire provinces was settled Rogers' grant fell into New York and the Governor granted the property to others.[281]

It is no wonder that the frustrated Ranger abandoned his native soil to personally solicit the King for civil or military preferment. If Rogers' land ventures had been more success—

ful it is possible that he might have rounded into a solid citizen; as it was, with his Real Estate turning into a will-o'-the-wisp and his house and person perpetually hounded by his creditors for Askin & Rogers accounts, not to mention the incessant nagging of his spouse and in-laws for a more visible means of support, it is no wonder that the harassed Rogers sought refuge in England.[282]

Chapter Twelve

THE AMERICAN REVOLUTION
ROGERS QUEEN'S RANGERS

At the outbreak of the American Revolution there was some doubt as to which side Rogers Rangers would espouse. During Rogers' two periods of residence in London prior to the War he had attempted to promote a Northwest Passage Expedition and to receive the Governorship of military post on the establishment were nil. Emulating his American procedure in monetary pursuits Rogers soon found himself in debt and in the Fleet Prison where he remained until his brother James had paid his debts.[283] Notwithstanding these crushing defeats Rogers' self-confidence and opportunist eye was boundless for, when the American Revolution broke out he was seeking employment against his countrymen. He expressed himself in a petition to George III, making note that he had a more legitimate right to rank than Lieutenant-Colonel Gorham, who was also seeking the command of a Provincial Corps. However, King George was still dubious of the sagacious Robert Rogers, well remembering the incriminating evidence of disloyalty in his Michilimackinac trial.[284] As a result of both Rogers' and Gorham's petitions before him, the King acquiesced in favour of Gorham and Rogers was rejected.[285]

As a consequence of this stinging rebuff Rogers sailed for America but to his amazement he was seized bodily upon landing by the Pennsylvania Committee of Safety and held a prisoner until the following day, September 22, when he was paroled by Congress and allowed to go his way. Rogers' seizure seems to have been prompted by the fact that he was still a British Officer on half-pay. The "Pennsylvania Committee of Safety" were oftentimes more impetuous than diplomatic in their methods.[286]

After his release Rogers' movements were followed closely by agents assigned to the task. Until July 1776, Rogers roamed about the northern colonies and was busily engaged, so he said, in settling debts and visiting relatives.[287] Since his arrival at Philadelphia, Rogers had been suspected of being a spy and a Loyalist.[288] In December 1775, he was visited by John Stark, now a Colonel in the American army. Rogers was at this time trying to obtain an interview with Washington and Stark expressed the belief that if Major Rogers had not been charged with disloyal sentiments before he had expressed them by word or deed, he might have been won to the support of the Continental cause.[289]

It would appear that Stark underestimated the true character of his former Ranger commander, for Rogers, true trader that he was, had played both Howe and Washington for the highest bid. The British Commander-in-Chief had been solicited as early as November 1775. Rogers' letter reached Howe's hands. Howe had superseded Gage as Commander in North America. Rogers offered his services and at the same time implied that the Americans had "...made considerable overtures to him."[290] Howe realized Rogers' invaluability and wrote the Prime Minister from Boston on November 26, 1775, "...I have given encouragement, by desiring him to make his proposals, and by giving an assurance that I am well inclined to do everything in my power to afford him an opportunity of recommending himself to his Majesty's future favour..."[291] To which the Prime Minister replied on January 25th: "...The King approves...your attention to Major Rogers, of whose firmness and fidelity we have received further testimony from Governor Tryon, and there is no doubt you will find the means of making him useful."[292] This restoration of King George's faith in Rogers suggests that he might very well have been employed as a useful agent for the Crown—and the fact that Rogers had offered his services to the King six months before he sought an interview with Washington further implies that his extended tour through New England was of an ulterior nature, detrimental to the American cause.[293]

Rogers' wanderings eventually brought him to Cambridge where he attempted to visit the American camp, but Washington would not allow him to enter the lines. This cold welcome must have stirred Rogers' aplomb for he had written Washington that, "I love America; it is my native country, and that of my family, and I intend to spend the evening of my days in it."[294] Rogers lodged at a Tavern in Medford, where Colonel John Stark, his old Ranger Captain, visited him and supported Rogers in his attempted interview with Washington. But Washington's suspicions remained unshaken. He clearly sets forth his opinion of Rogers in a letter to Congress in January: "I am apt to believe the intelligence given to Doctor Wheelock respecting Major Rogers [having been in Canada] was not true; but being much suspected of unfriendly views to this country, his conduct should be attended to with some degree of vigilance and circumpsection."[295] Accordingly, Washington kept his own agents on Rogers' trail and had Generals Sullivan and Schuyler "strictly examine him." In February Rogers was in New York and made application to Congress for permission to visit the "Duchess of Gordon," the Governor's ship, then in the harbor, in order to transact some private business affairs. Leave was given him. Rogers continued in and about New York during the Spring and early Summer, under suspicious circumstances. Finally Washington ordered his arrest and he was taken at South Amboy. Rogers had his long sought meeting with Washington, although now it was enforced. The General's analytical appraisal of Rogers brought his case to a belated showdown when the ex-Ranger Chieftain was escorted to Congress. The Continental Congress only needed Washington's accompanying letter to bolster their suspicions of Rogers.[296] Consequently Congress resolved on July 6, 1776 "That Major Rogers be sent to New Hampshire to be disposed of as the Government of that State shall judge best."[297]

While confined in Philadelphia Rogers must have realized that he could no longer maintain his role of dual duplicity and he managed to escape to find his way to General Howe who was encamped on Staten Island with his newly arrived army from Halifax.

The new plans of operations were to transfer the seat of war from Boston to New York, capture that city, and seize and hold the line of the Hudson. Rogers was joyously received by Howe and he was empowered to raise a battalion of Rangers and he was given the rank of Lieutenant-Colonel-Commandant. Thus, after eleven years of rest, Rogers Rangers lived again.[298]

In August, recruits were obtained from the remnants of the Queen's Royal Rangers, a Corps from Virginia, which Governor Dunmore, of that Province, followed to New York.[299] From this nuclear force Rogers adopted their name, changing it to "Rogers' Queen's Rangers."[300]

During Howe's preliminary maneuvers to drive Washington out of New York City, Rogers was busily occupied in collecting his men, whom he drew from all the towns in lower Connecticut, Long Island and along the New York shore of the Sound. Besides his magnetic name to draw Loyalists to his standard, Rogers' method of enlistment was that time-honored and serviceable one by which he offered a commission to a chosen few who engaged to bring in a certain quota of Rangers; a method which while it rapidly filled his ranks at the same time gave him a Corps of officers notable chiefly for their inefficiency. Several of Rogers' old Rangers and their sons joined him when they learned that he was re-raising Rogers Rangers, but not as many as were anticipated for the majority of the old Corps were now serving with distinction in the rebel armies.[301]

Those in New England and Westchester County, New York who did hasten to join Rogers had a difficult time in reaching the Corps' headquarters at Huntington, Long Island, as the Americans had heard of the revival of Rogers Rangers and captured scores of would-be recruits and continued to do so as late as January 1777. The Corps lost more men by this means than in all their bloody frays while under Rogers' command.

The first loss occurred on August 29, when Captain Lounsberry, recruiting in Westchester County was killed when he refused to surrender to an American party led by one Flood.

Lounsberry's fourteen Ranger recruits were not as impetuous and surrendered themselves. II-124A

Two months later seven more recruits were taken as they attempted to cross over to Rogers' base camp at Huntington, Long Island. III-165

Heath, one of Washington's Generals, notes that on the night of January 2, 1777 thirty-seven Ranger Recruits all armed with pistols but only two with muskets, were taken in Westchester County. III-167

Heath maintained constant "bloodhound" parties out, especially at night, to intercept the gangs of recruits. As a consequence of Heath's zeal Rogers Rangers lost another Captain on January 3rd. Captain Daniel Strang was captured near Peekskill with Rogers' enlisting warrant sewed in his breeches. Due to this secretiveness Strang was hailed as a spy and judged so by an American Court-Martial. He was hanged with Heath's army drawn up to view the "melancholy" scene. III-168

It would seem that Strang's hanging was a bit of poetic justice, for some time previously a detachment of Rogers Queen's Rangers were instrumental in the similar execution of Nathan Hale of the Americans. III-166 While the Rangers gathered in strength near Huntington, Long Island Rogers established an operative base with a detachment at Flushing, Long Island. With H. M. S. Halifax to convey them Rogers made frequent reconnaissances along the western shore of Long Island throughout September. On such a scout they landed near Flushing Bay on September 21, and came upon Hale about to return to the mainland with maps and notes on Howe's army. Rogers took Hale to the British headquarters at Beekman's Mansion that night and confessing his mission he was hanged without a trial the following morning.

Not long after this unsavory episode Rogers' allotment of 400 Rangers more than made up, he was sent to occupy the extreme right of Howe's front where it was expected his Corps of scouts would be of invaluable service. During the period that Rogers was enlisting his battalion Howe had won the Battle of Long Island and forced Washington successfully from Brooklyn Heights to New York and from thence to White Plains, half way to the Connecticut Line. It was in the attempt to defeat him that Rogers' Queen's Rangers saw their first active fighting in the war.

On the 12th of October, Howe landed a large force of men ten miles up the East River and urged them forward as rapidly as possible past Forts Lee and Washington, while he simultaneously disembarked Rogers Rangers and others on the shore of the Sound, hoping to cut off the communication of the Continental Army with Connecticut. Rogers, while stationed with his battalion during the past fortnight at Huntington, Long Island, had for some time been meditating a descent upon the Colonial stores collected at Greenwich, Stamford and Norwalk, with the inlets and avenues to which his men were perfectly familiar. Washington was aware of this danger and made haste to order Generals Charles Lee, Clinton and Lincoln to form an expedition and descend on Huntington, Long Island and wipe out Rogers Rangers.[302] But the Corps, elusive as old, were away and advancing on the American lines before Washington's orders could be fulfilled.

The first week of Rogers' landing saw detachments of his Rangers doing menial tasks such as sappers entrenching for the Artillery.[303] But not for long. As Howe explored along the front for the possibility of a general advance he shielded his eastern wing with the Queen's Rangers and as Rogers' outpost Corps moved forward towards White Plains, Rogers was finally ordered on the night of October 20, to take a bold station at Mamaroneck only ten miles from the American lines and three miles in advance of the British lines.[304]

Besides establishing post Rogers was ordered to secure the American stores in the town. Accordingly, the following morning at sunrise, he attacked and drove off some militia companies and gained possession of large amounts of Continental Army stores in the houses and mills on the banks of the Mamaroneck; namely rum, molasses, flour and pork.[II-125] Upon his return to the town proper Rogers posted his battalion on the smooth portion of Heathcote's Hill. Commandeering the schoolhouse on the Boston road Rogers magnaminously dismissed the wide-eyed children and established headquarters there. At dusk sentinels were carefully posted in advance along the roads and passes in the direction of White Plains, Harrison and Rye, while the avenues from the British camp were only negligibly guarded; this approach being considered too risky for an enemy advance. Having no tents the Rangers camped around rail fires, made from adjacent fences.[305]

Unbeknownst to Rogers and his Corps natives of the vicinity had gone to the nearest American General, Lord Sterling, with minute information on the exact locations of Rogers' sentries. This enlightenment, with his already abundant knowledge of the neighborhood, determined Sterling to dispatch Colonel Haslet with his crack Delaware Regiment and Major Green with 150 men from the First and Third Virginians to surprise Rogers. Haslet commanded and had 750 veteran men to execute his mission. Sterling received further information on Rogers' situation as late as nine o'clock that night (October 21st) and with his knowledge of the road he was enabled to order the exact approach to be taken by Haslet.

Starting late that night, Haslet's force was led by a force of guides. They marched in silence along the road leading from White Plains to Mamaroneck, until they came to Cornell's Fork; when they took the crossroad leading to New Rochelle and passing by the Quaker Meeting House. They were now within the position taken up by the British right wing the preceding day. Turning to the left, they proceeded along the road from the Quaker Meeting House toward the Sound, until they were within a half mile of the New York-Boston highway. Here they took to the fields, advancing northeasterly on Heathcote's Hill. The guides also served as pioneers removing obstacles that might cause a noise if collided with. About four A. M. they came upon the first Ranger sentry, a young Indian, enlisted by Rogers on Long Island. Major Green of the First Virginia Regiment commanded Haslet's vanguard. After some difficulty in the darkness they discovered the exact location of the Ranger and a party of Virginians pounced upon him. He proved as slippery as an eel and one of the American officers was forced to finish him with a sword thrust. The approach was now open to Rogers' sleeping Corps and the Americans drifted forward in full anticipation of an overwhelming victory. But lady luck, who only smiled on Rogers in danger, stepped forth again to take him by the hand.

Some time after nine that night Rogers had made a meticulous inspection of all his sentry posts. Noting the dearth of sentries on his southwestern side, a sixth sense told him that an attack, though unlikely, might approach by that side if a daring party managed to elude the British camp opposite to him in that direction. Accordingly he ordered Captain Eagles, with about 60 Rangers to take up a position as an advanced guard between Heathcote's Hill and the Indian sentry. After viewing this change with satisfaction Rogers retired to his bed at the schoolhouse.

Eagles' sleeping Company were in the Americans' direct line of approach and they were stumbled upon by Major Greene's advance column. It is to be questioned which side was the most surprised. However, the Americans regained their aplomb sufficiently to demand an instant surrender. Some Rangers complied but a good half resisted, no doubt inspired by the shouts of their Lieutenant Hughson who died fighting to the last. At this juncture Colonel Haslet came up with the balance of his force and Eagles' Company were completely surrounded. The moment was a crucial one for Rogers Rangers, but thanks to the customary resourcefulness of Rogers' officers the Company was saved from annihilation. Greene's Virginians were by this time well mixed with Eagle's Rangers, who like the balance of Rogers Rangers, were un-uniformed. In the darkness American and Ranger appeared the same and Captain Eagles capitalized on this situation and adopted the orders of the Americans to "Surrender you Tory dogs!" Eagles' Rangers quickly picked up his cue and for several moments nothing could be heard but abusive aspersions against Rogers Rangers. The farce was carried further when Ranger grappled with Ranger and friend could not be determined from foe. By these garrulous means Eagles and about one-third of his Company extricated themselves from the melee.

Meanwhile the din of battle had roused the balance of Rogers Rangers from their blankets and they were in battle formation ready to receive Haslet. Although most of the American guides had run off when the action started the determined Haslet quickly gathered his prisoners and their arms and pushed forward in advance of his men up Heathcote's Hill.

Roused from his sleep at the schoolhouse by the firing Rogers burst out the door fusil in hand and running at top speed he joined his Corps at Heathcote's Hill in time to hurl a few encouraging words to his men, as Haslet came up to attack. He bade them hold their fire until the Americans were within range then his gravelly voice could be heard shouting to them to "Fire!" The well directed volley and succeeding continuous fire checked the Americans. This firm resistance in the darkness wilted Haslet's men and they soon envisaged themselves before a well-deployed and numerically stronger force. Haslet wisely resolved to rest on his laurels and immediately withdrew to Sterling's army by the same route he advanced carrying with him 28 Rangers, a pair of the Queen's Rangers colours and 60 stand of arms not to mention a quantity of blankets.

Haslet records his loss as three or four killed and around fifteen wounded. Among the wounded were Major Greene and Captain Pope; Greene was badly wounded in the shoulder, while Pope received a shot in the leg.

Upon counting noses Rogers found that he had lost Lieutenant Hughson and 19 Rangers killed, one subaltern and 8 men wounded and 28 missing (captured). In all, an actual loss of 48, officer and men, besides the 8 wounded. This weakening of the Corps' sinews was offset when 120 Loyalists were spirited out of Connecticut by "one of Rogers' old Captains,"[306] to replenish the Corps.

The participants of the Battle of Heathcote's Hill were buried on the field the next morning by the Rangers. From a dearth of Surgeons, the wounded, both Rangers and Americans remained for some time on the field and contemporaries report that their moans from pain and their cries for water were most distressing. In the afternoon enough ox-carts had been commandeered from the local natives and the wounded were carried to the improvised hospital at the New Rochelle Church.[II-126]

Although Rogers' jealous colleagues in the British army pounced upon this opportunity to besmudge his ability, Howe stood by his friend. Envious officers accused him of disobedience of orders and incapacity; stating that he was ordered to place his Corps only a short distance in advance of the British army, instead of two miles off. They clamored for a court martial, but Howe would not have it, stating that his coolness and courage in the repulse of Haslet, not to mention his vigorous actions and success in capturing the Continental stores were not conducive to a military inquest. Howe reveals his loyalty to Rogers in his account of the action to the Prime Minister when he states that due to "...the carelessness of his sentrys exposed himself to a surprise from a large body of the enemy, by which he lost a few men killed or taken; nevertheless, by a spirited exertion, he obliged them to retreat, leaving behind them some prisoners, and several killed and wounded."306

While General Agnew's sixth brigade moved up to support him, Rogers, with his customary vigor, retaliated in part for his defeat by setting out the very next day to execute one of his traditionally daring coups. He audaciously penetrated to Bedford, Connecticut with a body of Rangers and released and brought off six or eight officers and men of the Royal Navy who were prisoners there. II-127

After this exploit Rogers Rangers formed part of General Knyphausen's command and had a share in the capture of Fort Washington II-130 and the prior battle at White Plains. II-128-129

Three days after their spirited attack on Fort Washington 100 Rangers were detached from the Corps to march with Cornwallis' detachment that was sent in pursuit of Washington. They caught up with Greene and Washington at Hackensac Bridge where the Americans made a brief stand to cover the retreat of the American troops at Hackensac Village, behind the Passaic. II-131 Cornwallis pursued Washington as far as Trenton where he was ordered by Howe to give up the chase and return to the Raritan for winter quarters. The detachment of the Queen's Rangers formed an integral part of Knyphausen's division which guarded New York on the land side. 307

Besides the constant recruiting maintained throughout the winter, Rogers Rangers saw action about ten in the morning on January 18, when General Wooster and 2,500 Americans appeared before Fort Independence and summoned the garrison to surrender. Wooster offered the Hessians good terms but stated that Rogers' Queen's Rangers and Grant's New York Loyalist Companies would not be guaranteed the same treatment. The garrison answered with a brisk cannonade which was returned and maintained for some time until Wooster retired to Courtland's House which the Americans plundered before they established quarters. Two Companies of Rogers Rangers were advanced and posted in a house in front of the fort. On the evening of January 23, five days after Wooster's abortive attack, the Rangers were attacked at their advanced post by a strong party of Americans who thought their numbers were much smaller. The Rangers waited until the attackers approached then turning the tables they sallied out and completely routed the would-be assailants, killing several and taking seven prisoners. II-132

This was the last action that "Rogers' Queen's Rangers" were engaged in for the Corps soon underwent a reorganization. It seems that Rogers was censored for abusing the confidence that had been placed in him by issuing Warrants to very improper persons as inferior officers. The consequence of this was that numberless abuses had taken place, and among others, Negroes, mulattos, Indians, sailors and rebel prisoners were enlisted, "to the disgrace and ruin of the Provincial service."308

"In January, 1777, Colonel Alexander Innes, the newly appointed Inspector-General of the Provincial or Loyalist forces in North America inspected the "Queen's Rangers" and upon noticing these abuses he informed General Howe, who empowered him to discharge all improper persons that had been enlisted. Strict orders were given to prevent any such practices in the future and it was particularly directed that the strictest justice should be done to the non-commissioned officers and privates with regard to their pay and bounty, numberless well-founded complaints having been made by many of them on that subject."309

Although there were undoubtedly <u>undesirables</u> hurriedly enrolled by commission hungry officers, still, the integral composition of Rogers Rangers was no different than it had been in the French and Indian War. Negroes, sailors and Indians had been taken into the Corps then and for the most part had served conspicuously. It seems that the present discrimination had its genesis from a certain clique of British officers who were seeking to oust Rogers from his command and put in their own representative. The command of the Queen's Rangers was a very desirable one. Established as it was as a partisan Corps, it, like no other Corps, was organized for quick daring maneuvers; which, if executed successfully, would bring fame to whoever commanded the Corps. Consequently there were many officers in the British Army who desired the command of the Queen's Rangers. Rogers, finally disgusted with his rank (actually a Captain in the Regular Army) and the intrigue against him, gave up his command and sought advancement under Governor-General Haldimand of Canada.[310]

After his departure the Corps ceased to exist as "Rogers' Queen's Rangers." Though never actually disbanded, the personnel of the Queen's Rangers underwent a complete change and to all intents and purposes a new Corps was formed. The Corps, which, under Rogers' command, had consisted primarily of Loyalists, now took on a British consistency. Most of the original officers of the Battalion were dismissed to make way for several gentlemen from the southern colonies who had joined Lord Dunmore in Virginia and distinguished themselves under his orders. To these were added some volunteers from the British Army, until gradually over two-thirds of the Corps consisted of Irish, English and Scotch.[311]

So ended the brief life of "Rogers' Queen's Rangers," but Rogers Rangers were yet to exist in another form before they stepped from the pages of history.

Chapter Thirteen

THE AMERICAN REVOLUTION
ROGERS' KING'S RANGERS - 1779-84

After relinquishing his command of the Queen's Rangers, Rogers found himself a virtually unwanted orphan. His rough exterior and presuming air were as unwelcome to Haldimand and his staff as it had been to Lord Howe's military family. Rogers' attempts to raise a corps of Rangers in Canada were stymied by Haldimand on the pretext that John Johnson's "Royal Greens" and other Corps had precedence there. Rogers' exact activities in Canada for the summer and fall of 1777 remain a mystery. However, Haldimand readily gave him permission to winter in London. While Rogers' connections might be in the eclipse in both camps in North America, still his political friends in London had not entirely deserted him. Consequently, New York was surprised to see him once again in April 1779, with favorable recommendations to Sir Henry Clinton (Howe's successor) to attempt the recruiting for which Haldimand had withheld permission.

On May 1, Rogers received Clinton's authorization to raise two battalions[312] and six weeks later he was penning a solicitous missive to Lord Amherst in London. The tenure of the letter well expresses how much of a skilled courtesan Rogers had become:

"I had the honour to receive your Lordship's commands that I should write to you on my arrival in America. I have been honoured by the Commander-in-Chief here with a warrant to raise two more Battalions, one of which is called the King's Rangers—so that I shall have the highest happiness, as a Subject, of giving two Battalions to their Majesties. The third will be called Rogers' Rangers...I flatter myself that my good Lord Amherst, will not forget an old soldier, who has had the honour to share in some of his glorious fatigues in America last War—but procure him some little addition to his present rank in the British Army."[313]

Amherst, however, had Rogers well-gauged,[314] for his curt reply in September promised naught.

But Rogers, ever buoyant, had not received Amherst's formal note when he wrote him a vivid portrayal of his expectant campaign. He blandly states that he is: "...Setting out for Annapolis Royal, the rendezvous of my first battalion, which is at present in a most eligible train—from whence I push thro' to Canada, from which place, in a short time, I flatter myself your Lordship will hear of a spirited attack by my Indians and Rangers on the middle frontiers—to the great detriment of the Rebels—and such credit to myself as may entitle me to expect that assistance, Generosity and patronage, I have ever received from your Lordship."[315] This premature credit grabbing was a far cry from the modest Journals of Rogers which he had so accurately recorded during his ascendancy in the French and Indian War.

Unfortunately, Rogers' forecastings fell short of their goal and instead his last historic endeavor degenerated into similar shadows from whence Rogers Rangers had originally sprung in the year 1755. From Rogers' gross overstatements this revival of Rogers' Rangers had the first appearance of all the customary vigor and earmarks of a well-raised Rogers' Corps.[316]

Immediately after his authorization to raise his Rangers Rogers sent out officers to commence enlistments in the northern communities contiguous with the Canadian border. Rogers established his headquarters first at Castine, Maine, then St. John's, New Brunswick and Halifax, Nova Scotia—and even Quebec for a short time. He began to prosecute his enlistments for the King's Rangers along the eastern frontiers of New England and Penobscot. Rogers had secured the services of his brother James to recruit for the Corps.

Upon stating that the minimum number of 600 men were raised, Rogers was given his commission as Lieutenant-Colonel Commandant of both battalions and he appointed brother James Major of the first battalion—designated as the King's Rangers.[317] The bulk of the officers of both battalions had served in the War and were veterans. Nine officers that were gazetted to the Corps were from the six battalions of General Skinner's New Jersey Loyalist Volunteers, a brigade organized in July, 1776. Two more were from Simcoe's Queen's Rangers.[318]

The principal difficulty in raising the Corps was that of rendezvous, for the Rangers were recruited over such a wide area. Ensigns Hill, Andersen and Insley went thru the woods with their recruits to Niagara. Captain Stenson rendezvoused at Penobscot with his forty recruits. Quebec was the principal gathering place and the bulk of the officers (Major James Rogers, Captain John Longstreet, Hatfield, Babington and Walsh; Captain-Lieutenant Breckenridge; Lieutenants Whitworth and Ensigns Robins and Beale) were posted at Old Lorette.[319]

From New York Rogers' recruiting trek took him first to the British post of Castine at the mouth of the Penobscot River in Maine.[320] He was hardly there a week when the invading expedition from Massachusetts appeared. However, in this short time he had raised a few men—enough to inaugurate his new Corps into their first action by assisting in the repulse of the Americans on August 11th.[ll-133] This success so heartened the local Loyalists that Rogers reported "great success in recruiting" and sent the news <u>collect</u> to Haldimand from Fort Howe on the St. John River (New Brunswick), Rogers' next beating ground.[321]

By January Rogers was in Quebec, presumably to gather the officers and recruits for the second battalion to take back to Penobscot. Finding no recruits but a host of destitute Ranger officers, Rogers barraged Haldimand for Batt and Forage money, allowances for contingent men, half-pay and equal rank with British Regulars for King's Ranger officers. All this while he was "so circumstanced as not to admit of [Haldimand] having much conversation with him."322

Rogers delayed his stay in Quebec by informing Haldimand that he was awaiting the arrival of Sergeant Luxford Goodwin and Ranger Private Nulter from Penobscot via the Kennebec and Chaudiere Rivers. The appearance of these two veteran French and Indian War Rangers indicates that Rogers' magnetism still had the power to draw men who had served in his old corps. Rogers proudly notes that he "can depend upon" these two men. Rogers was to meet Goodwin and Nulter (his guides to Penobscot) at the British post on the Chaudiere River, while his detachment of Rangers were ordered to remain on a branch of the Kennebec and await his return by hunting for Moose. III-169

Rogers had informed Haldimand that he had 700 Rangers engaged, 400 at Penobscot (Castine) and the other 300 nearby. Haldimand pressed him to repair there with his officers, for such a large body must need officers and Rogers must be convinced that they were only wasting time in Quebec. Rogers' hesitancy in returning to Penobscot with his officers is understandable for instead of 700 Rangers there and in the vicinity he actually only had forty men raised and he must have realized that there would be a hue and cry sounded as soon as the delinquency was discovered.323

At this juncture Rogers' confidence-man technique gained the ascendancy over his sense of decorum, which in the past had been the thin thread that had left his questionable acts open to conjecture. He lost all sense of propriety when he contracted debts and drew bills from Halifax to as far north as the settlement of Kamouraska on the St. Lawrence. He even managed to fleece Haldimand for 470 pounds when he stated that he needed that amount to defray the expenses of his officers who had resided in Quebec for the winter—and to enable them to proceed to their different rendezvous. Haldimand was only too happy to pay the amount to eject the extravagant Rogers out of Quebec—but the Ranger Chieftain was still lingering ten days later and applying for carriages for part of his journey. Naturally Haldimand refused Rogers' request and expressed his surprise that he was still in town.[324] Realizing that he could procrastinate no longer Rogers set out with two of the Captains of his second battalion up the Chaudiere River with Sergeant Goodwin to guide them.

What were the thoughts of the tortured mind of this strange contradiction of a man as he traveled southward on his last scout? Was he thinking of how his repeated indiscretions had left him without friends and fortune—but most important, without a wife or son?[325] His nefarious peculations began with his advent as a Ranger in 1755. For six fame-growing years his violent physical exertions as an unparalleled Ranger commander had kept his nefarious deeds to a respectable minimum. If Rogers could have been continually employed as an explorer in search of the fabled Northwest Passage or more tangible discoveries he would not have had time for his indiscreet leanings to gain the ascendancy. The close of the French and Indian War saw the beginnings of the steady decline of "Major Rogers." His vacillations snowballed in proportion until his friends and family—at first shocked and then angry, deserted his standard leaving his life an empty vacuum.

Rogers' trek to Penobscot and his subsequent actions were probably the most critical of his violent career. He was literally <u>on the fence</u> and the direction of his falling was a fulfillment of his "extraordinary conduct." Realizing that he must reach Penobscot in advance of his officers before they discovered the negligible number of Rangers there, Rogers made himself obnoxious to the two Captains (Hatfield and Walsh) in his party—so much so that they feigned illness two leagues from the "Grand Portage" (Portage Lake) and "alledg'd they were incapable of marching," and returned to Quebec.[326] Rogers breathed more easily and pushed on with the faithful Sergeant Goodwin, met the detail of Rangers Moose hunting on the Kennebec and pushed on for Penobscot. Upon arriving there he immediately took boat for Halifax.

Rogers had penned his last letter to Haldimand from the "Lake over ye Grand Portage" on March 20, stating that if he has offended him in any way he hopes that it will be overlooked as he only had the good of the service at heart.[327] This phrasing was particularly galling to Haldimand for by the time Rogers reached Halifax shock had set in from the flood of his creditors who were petitioning Haldimand for his delinquent accounts. If Haldimand was shocked at Rogers' financial intemperance he was aghast at the response to his suspicious queries to Brigadier Maclean, commanding at Penobscot, respecting the true numbers of Rogers Rangers there. Upon receiving word that there were only forty men raised, instead of 700, his anger surged.[328]

Rogers must have been psychic, for he never made the error of again encountering Haldimand. He remained in Halifax, safely out of Haldimand's province, executing nothing spectacular, instead, stretching his credit taut to the end of the war when his gravy train came to an end and he crossed the Atlantic for the last time to die a few years later in hospitable London—a dreary victim of tavern-room loquacity on his past exploits.[329] As so frequently happened Rogers' debauchery affected brother James who had to face his creditors. Although Robert had penned him a hasty letter on April 26, stating that he was sending orders by Mercure, a Canadian courier, for the settlement of all debts—still his outstanding debts remained unsettled and honest James impoverished himself to meet Robert's bills.[330]

As if this was not enough of a burden to shoulder, James had to face the sly aspersions and innuendoes cast against Robert. Although Haldimand assured him that his brother's "extraordinary conduct" would not prejudice him, still the situation became unbearable and on May 10, 1780, James wrote Haldimand that he was determined to resign his pretensions to the King's Rangers and to put himself under the King's protection. He asked that he might be appointed to some other Corps. Haldimand eased the situation by recommending patience and assuring him of every protection that could reasonably be expected.[331]

Meanwhile the Corps had slowly started to take form. After Rogers left for Penobscot in March, Major James Rogers left for St. Johns on the Richelieu River to establish quarters to recruit for his battalion. Although the authorized strength of his battalion had been originally set at ten Companies of sixty men each, still he was never able to muster more than four Companies with a total of 183 men by the end of the war.[332]

Despite the fact that Major Rogers' battalion was ordered to serve under Haldimand's command, still they were actually a part of the army of General Clinton at New York and this unique status caused no end of misery to the officers and men. The supernumeracy of officers for the meager quantity of Privates engaged were continually embarrassed for want of subsistence funds. When the officers arrived in Quebec in July and August 1779, they sent Haldimand a deluge—and finally, in September, he "advanced the officers a certain amount to prevent them from suffering distress."[333] When Lieutenant Colonel Rogers was about to set out for Penobscot, Haldimand instructed him to furnish Major Rogers with credit on the Paymaster-General at Halifax. However, Major James Rogers' Battalion was out of the Paymaster's province and besides he was already burdened with settling the extravagant accounts of Lieutenant-Colonel Robert Rogers, made more difficult by his ingenious method of scattering his credit.[334]

Consequently, Major Rogers' King's Rangers were dumped into Haldimand's lap and became his indefinite charges. He still hoped for word from Clinton as to paying them—until then, and upon his own authority, Haldimand placed the battalion upon his own establishment. A scale of half-pay was arranged in April, 1780.[335] Haldimand and the battalion officers waited impatiently for three years before positive word was received from Clinton stating that the King's Ranger battalion was to be part of Haldimand's command.[336]

At first the Corps was quite "naked" from want of even sufficient clothing much less uniforms. Gradually a semblance of a uniform took shape when the men all wore blanket coats through the rigors of winter. Finally by February, 1782, Major Rogers' battalion were all clothed in green cloth coats and breeches (woolen for winter and linen for summer) with red facings; linen shirts; stockings; moccasins (two pair); black tri-cornered cocked hats; and the Sergeants wore the British regulation cut suit with right-shoulder strap designation of rank.[337]

From this time forward, Major James Rogers' battalion garrisoned the post of St. John's on the Richelieu River, sharing the barracks there at first with the 34th and subsequently with the 29th Regiments.[338] In spite of Lieutenant-Colonel Robert Rogers' debauchery, he still retained his command, for his commission had been given him by Clinton and it was not in Haldimand's power to revoke it. Major Rogers in spite of disagreeable quarrels with officers enlisting for rival branches, especially Johnson's "Royal Greens" and Jessup's "Loyal American Rangers," devoted himself manfully to completing his Battalion and in spite of manifold jealousies and difficulties, before the war was over had rostered and equipped four Companies of Rangers. His Battalion never numbered over 200 men, however.[339]

The King's Rangers under Major James Rogers were principally a garrison Battalion, though frequently they were active in outstanding raids and Secret Service scouts. James Rogers' long apprenticeship in Ranging warfare and his intimate knowledge of the country in which his Battalion was stationed stood him in good stead at this frontier post of St. John's in Quebec, which fort had ironically often been his object of reconnaissance and destruction when a Captain of Rogers Rangers in the French and Indian War. Various schemes of reconnaissance and attack were from time to time submitted by him for Haldimand's consideration and approval. His advice was often asked and taken, on more than one occasion he was employed, where a field officer's services were demanded, upon missions of delicacy and importance.[340]

After their defeat at Saratoga, the British had evacuated Ticonderoga and fallen back to St. John's, Quebec, and greatly improved the works there. This post now remained the frontier line of defense for the British in Canada.

The Corps had just graduated from its nuclear state when it was called upon to take part in its first and only expedition of consequence which called for more than a mere scouting detail. Haldimand, ever fearful of an American invasion by way of Lake Champlain, had decided to send out an expedition to destroy the American forts which had been established in Rogers Rangers old home ground at the head of Lake George and on the route from the Hudson to Lake Champlain, which was beginning to take a threatening position. Major Christopher Carleton was given the command of the expedition which consisted of a Company of the King's Rangers, a Company of Jessup's Loyal Rangers; fifty of the 34th and fifty of the 53rd Regiments, besides a party of Indians, in all over 200 men. On October 8th at the ruins of Ticonderoga, Carleton dispatched fifty men of the 53rd up Lake George against Fort George at the head of the lake. At the same time Carleton, with the King's Rangers and the rest of his force, traversed South Bay at night. With the veteran members of Rogers Rangers to guide them through the swampy bay. Their objective was rebuilt Fort Anne on Wood Creek. Advancing boldly, the Fort was surrounded on the tenth of October and the garrison of 75 officers and men surrendered and the fort burned. II-135

Carleton, not deeming Fort Edward sufficiently important to delay his attack on Fort George, at nine in the morning started his march to the lake. At five that evening his force had arrived within nine miles of Fort George, where they halted for the night. An officer and twelve Rangers were detached down the Hudson to burn the mills and to forage as far as Fort Miller; to act similarly on the western side of the stream; to remain in concealment, and then to make a push and if possible burn the mills and barracks at Saratoga. This small detachment of Rogers Rangers was sent as they were less likely to be seen than a larger force. They fulfilled Carleton's orders almost to the letter and near Saratoga had a brush with a superiod body of American militia. Carleton likewise sent a party of Jessup's Rangers directly across the river to burn some mills in operation there. II-136

Rogers' King's Rangers rejoined Carleton from their Saratoga Raid about seven o'clock and proceeded with him in his advance against Fort George. They had arrived within a mile and a half of the fort when their presence was discovered by two men passing along the road, who had stumbled on the Indians in the advance; they managed to escape and carry the information to the garrison. Ranger scouts sent out by Carleton reported that fifty of the garrison were coming along the road. They had been sent out to attack the Indians who had been seen on the supposition that they were the only enemy present. Carleton moved forward with fifty of the 34th and 25 Rogers' King's Rangers. The Indians had placed themselves between the detachment and the fort and had begun an unequal fight. The arrival of Roger's King's Rangers and the Regulars soon decided the contest. In half an hour all was over. Twenty-three men were killed and scalped by the Indians and seven prisoners were taken. Carleton's loss was a private of the King's Rangers and a Regular killed; a Sergeant and a private of the 34th wounded and one Ranger of Jessup's Corps; besides two killed and one wounded of the Indians. II-137

Carleton summoned the fort. The surviving garrison of 46 officers and men surrendered as prisoners of war. The fort was destroyed and the expedition returned to St. John's.

In the spring of 1781, a detachment of the King's Rangers served in St. Leger's (Commandant of St. John's) well equipped expedition that advanced up Lake Champlain to the Hudson to divert the attention of the continental troops from the more important expedition of Major Ross from Oswego. In order to oppose St. Leger, a large force of Americans was collected at Albany and Saratoga to operate against him and it was thus kept inactive during the expedition undertaken by Major Ross. II-138

However, Captain John Myers was detached with a party of King's Rangers to Ballstown in the Mohawk valley where he took a number of prisoners. He rejoined St. Leger with them at St. John's on July 8th. A Ranger recruit arriving behind Myers reported that Myers had been pursued by 200 Rebels, who followed him as far as the Socondoga River. II-139

These were the only campaigns of consequence that were launched from St. John's during the King's Rangers cantonment there; but the battalion, besides their garrison duty at St. John's, were constantly engaged in Secret Service scouts, which were probably redudnat of more mortal danger, for, being in disguise, they were subject to treatment as spies and the few that were caught were hanged as such. Aware that Vermont was partially disaffected from the American cause due to the refusal of New York and Congress to allow her statehood, Haldimand set up an "underground" to penetrate into her northern townships. Captain Justus Sherwood and Doctor George

Smyth, proven experts in this type of duty and both Loyalist refugees from Vermont, were given the command of these espionage scouts.

While Doctor Smyth operated from St. John's, Sherwood first set up headquarters at Isle aux Noix and by July 1781 was boldly established at "The Loyal Blockhouse," a well situated post which he had built on Lake Champlain at Dutchman's Point.[341] Sherwood, at one time, had as many as 47 scouts penetrating into Vermont.[342]

Although officers and men from Jessup's and McAlpin's Corps engaged in these scouts, at least eight officers and noncoms of the King's Rangers served conspicuously in this duty. Of these, Captain Azariah Pritchard was the most noted and was one of Sherwood's principal agents.[343]

Pritchard was engaged in intelligence work as early as June 1779, before he secured a Captaincy in Roger's King's Rangers. On June 8, a Major Pritchard at Poughkeepsie offered him employment as a spy, to remain in Canada and forward information. He accepted and the same month was located at St. John's, Quebec. For the next four months he was furnishing information as to rebel sympathizers in Canada and proposing plans for obtaining intelligence. On September 16, at Chambly, he was petitioning Major Carleton to intercede for him in securing "a situation in the Rangers." When he was assured of a Captain's berth in Major Roger's battalion if he raised his quota of men, Pritchard, not one to be lacking in enterprise, seduced men from McAlpin's recruits by getting them drunk at St. Ours, Quebec and promising them commissions and higher pay. Since it was illegal for King's Ranger officers to enlist men in the province of Quebec, not to mention by such piratical methods, Pritchard was stopped, but managed to raise his quota in the summer and winter of 1780 from the Loyalists in Vermont and received his commission.[344]

Pritchard was employed constantly as a spy and even had Loyalist agents working for him. As early as October 1780 he was asking for funds to carry on his work which had been conducted entirely at his own expense; adding that this activity engrossed so much of his time that he was unable to fill up his Company, "although many would join him" if he could devote a little time to recruiting. When this belated time was granted him, Pritchard, with a Captain from another Corps, enlisted 53 men. One of Pritchard's agents of unusual daring and ability was Abner Barlow whom he rewarded with a Corporal's berth in his Company.[345]

By February 1781, Pritchard was reporting on Ira Allen's demands on the Continental Congress for statehood for Vermont. In March he penetrated to the eastern part of Vermont and brought back a prisoner named Thomas Johnson, who offered to attempt to bring all of Eastern Vermont to neutrality.[III-174]

Pritchard's record was punctuated with vigorous activity. In August 1781, he captured a rebel scout near Corinch consisting of a Corporal and two Privates.[II-141] In October a daring rebel scout was reported and Pritchard was sent to intercept them. On October 17th he met the rebel scout of a Sergeant and four men in the woods. After a short brush, two of the Americans ran off. One, the guide, was mortally wounded and the Sergeant and a Private were taken prisoners.[II-143] From the guide Pritchard learned of the movements of the Lovel family, who were noted rebel spies. Pritchard was granted permission to intercept them, which he successfully effected the first week of November, bringing in two of the Lovels.[III-176B] Immediately upon his return he was assigned to lay plans to bring in General Bailey, the prize catch of Loyalist baiters in Vermont. Pritchard's groundwork to set his trap was conducted with such diligence that on one preliminary scout he was closely pursued. Spy-Chief Sherwood reported that he was "indefatigable" in his assignment and recommended him to Haldimand. Finally, on June 4, 1782, he received his belated orders to set out for Newberry, Vermont to capture General Bailey. With only nine King's Rangers he operpowered a Sergeant and twelve men comprising Bailey's night guard at his home. But all their efforts were to no avail and Pritchard returned empty-handed for the wily General did not sleep in his own house.[II-145]

In August and September of the same year Pritchard made a daring scout to General Carleton at New York to arrange a better method of exchanging dispatches with Haldimand at Quebec. While there he pinned Clinton to an answer on the status of Major James Rogers' King's Rangers. After a day's deliberation the General informed him that "Major James Rogers in Canada, did not belong to this army, but to General Haldimand's, and that he would write to General Haldimand to take Major Rogers under his patronage to form and commission as he thought proper."III-183

Pritchard's invaluable services were minimized when it was implied in June 1783 that he had been engaged in exporting black market beef and counterfeiting money to distribute in Canada. Pritchard denied the charges in July but by December Sherwood had received money and a pamphlet proving him the instigator of trade from Vermont and Loyalist leaders in Vermont requested that Pritchard not be allowed to come in again as he had impaired the projected beef-trade with them. Pritchard's character was further impugned when Sherwood learned that he had enlisted a deserter from the King's Rangers into his own Company under a false name. In February it was learned that Pritchard had been selling British tea up the lake at one dollar a pound and had employed one Baldwin to retail it for him.[346]

Notwithstanding these shortcomings, Pritchard seems to have escaped scot free from these charges, no doubt due to his extraordinarily good services as a spy.

Other King's Rangers who risked their lives as spies were Captain John Myers; Captain-Lieutenant James Breckinridge; Lieutenants Israel Ferguson, Soloman Johns and William Tyler; Ensigns Roger Stephens and Caleb Green, Sergeant Peter Taylor; Corporals Abner Barlow, Moses Williams and P. McCoy—and Private J. Miller.[347]

Captain John Myers had asked for permission to return to New York which was granted him and he arrived there in April 1780; from then until December 1780 he served in Colonel Ludlow's Provincial Regiment. In December he surprised everyone by appearing in St. John's with five recruits "for Major Rogers." Believing that he would be of more service at St. John's than in New York, he had resigned from Ludlow's to rejoin Rogers Rangers. He stated that he had engaged almost a full company among Loyalists in the colonies and hoped to bring them in the next spring. Captain Myers had originally been chosen by Lieutenant-Colonel Robert Rogers for his battalion, consequently his Company maintained a detached status from Major Rogers' battalion until September 1782, when it was put under Haldimand's command and he included it in Major Rogers' Battalion.[348]

In July, 1781, Myers' petition to bring off certain ringleaders of the rebels who had been persecuting the loyalists was granted and he penetrated to the neighborhood of Albany, New York, arriving on the 29th. He remained a week until a hue and cry for a King's Ranger scout under Beatie had died down.[II-140A] On the night of August 7, he attempted to capture his "object," name Blake. Covering both doors to his house he moved in with his detachment of King's Rangers. Myers states that after entering the house he "met with an opposition of Iron men in which a skirmish issued which lasted near a quarter of an hour, in which I and my party killed one and wounded two and took two prisoners, and the other two made their escape..." Their object, Blake, also managed to escape through a window during the fight and alarmed the town, but Myers managed to make the long trek back to St. John's unmolested. Haldimand was satisfied that Myers had done his best to capture Blake and he reassured the crestfallen Captain.[II-142]

The energetic Myers had hardly recuperated from this lengthy scout when he returned—this time to Saratoga to make an attack on General Schuyler's house, from which his Rangers removed some valuable silver plate.[II-142A]

Captain-Lieutenant James Breckenridge was another officer appointed by Robert Rogers. He and his brother Ensign David Breckenridge had been left in Quebec by the Colonel to act as the liaison to forward recruits to Halifax for his battalion. Since they never had the opportunity to indulge in this duty, recruits not forthcoming, they were sent to join Major James Rogers at St. John's in September 1780, for he was in sore need of them to recruit for his battalion. James Breckenridge became the Captain Lieutenant of Major Rogers' own Company, while David Breckenridge received the Ensigncy of Henry Ruiter's Company.[349]

James Breckenridge's fiery temper is revealed when he used some very abusive language to the Commandant of St.

John's when he returned his commission a year later than it actually was. His fiery nature would suggest that he even quarrelled with Major Rogers on occasion, for on June 11, 1782, James Rogers was writing Haldimand to grant Breckenridge leave to go to Halifax, "where he would be more useful than here." However, Haldimand replied that he was to remain where he was.[350]

Before being assigned to Major Rogers' battalion, Captain-Lieutenant Breckenridge had been employed as a spy. With a Sergeant and Private of the 31st Regiment, all in the guise of deserters, he was sent to discover the inhabitants of the province of Quebec who received and protected deserters, rebel emissaries, spies and disaffected subjects. His mission was very successful. Breckenridge continued in the secret service after his assignment to Major Rogers' Company at St. John's and operated under Doctor Smyth.[351]

In July, 1781, he was penetrating into Vermont and reporting on the scarcity of powder and lead there. In the same month of 1782 he was in Bennington, Vermont collecting news of Washington. Upon his return he sought an interview with General Haldimand and delivered to him the secret terms of propositions from Vermont for reunion with the Crown. In September and October he was again in Vermont following up this proposed break. His brother Ensign David Breckenridge entered the plot and was stationed for a time at Crown Point to relay messages from General Allen in Vermont. On May 23, 1783, David arrived at the Loyal Blockhouse with a verbal message from Allen who still hoped to return Vermont back to the King in spite of the rumours of peace.[III-175]

Captain Breckenridge's espionage work seems to have ended at this point for he became involved in a serious quarrel with Doctor Smyth's son which developed into blows being exchanged. In the Court of Inquiry held at St. John's through the latter part of August Smyth senior asked for an investigation of the Captain's conduct to him personally, for Breckenridge had made aspersions against his ability. Breckenridge retaliated by making charges against Doctor Smyth and he collected a host of witnesses to substantiate his charges. As a result of the growing aspects of the Inquiry, it was thought best, for the good of the service, that all three of the principals should be cleared of all charges.[352]

Ensign Roger Stephens was a constant secret agent. On November 2, 1781, he returned to Sherwood with letters and papers from Doctor Olden, a Loyalist confederate in Vermont.[III-177] Again, on December 10, 1781, he left St. John's for Vermont on a hardy winter scout. On the way he captured along with one Sutherland, who had joined him, seven rebels digging iron at Crown Point. He waylaid another rebel at Chimney Point and chased him across the lake to Crown Point, recovered his pack of ample provisions, which Stephens' party needed badly, and continued to Vermont. He effected his business and upon his return trailed a rebel scout to Canada. On the second day he came up to their previous night's camp and plundered it of all their provisions which they had left to carry them back to Vermont. After this series of odysseys Stephens arrived back at St. John's on the 31st, in time to see the New Year in.[III-179]

Stephens' energy was boundless for he was scouting again in a few days to return on January 30, with reports of the movements of Washington and offered a plan for obtaining intelligence. On February 28, 1782, he was reporting on the conduct of the Vermonters and recommending the services of his uncle as an agent. Stephens was untiring for two weeks later he was again penning vital information on rebel gold shipments and preparations for a Canadian invasion.[III-180]

During March and April he was operating in the region of Onion River Falls looking for rebels to capture. He managed to surround a scouting party of four at Monckton while they slept. One escaped, the others were captured, but managed to escape one night on the return march, due to the laxness of one of Jessup's men who was guarding them.[II-144]

By May 15, Stephens with a catch of furs, under the guise of a trapper, penetrated as far as Massachusetts where he spied for Haldimand.[III-182]

On Augst 3, he arrived at St. John's from another informative scout towards Saratoga, New York.

Stephens returned from a particularly daring scout in October and hoped to be sent personally to Haldimand with his report and thus gain some small reward. But the envious spy-chief, Doctor Smyth, sent his report by someone else, although Stephens had risked his life to get the information and had specifically asked to be sent to Quebec with them. Stephens, however, sent Haldimand duplicates of his report, deploring Smyth's conduct and adding that although he was worn out with so much scouting he was willing to go on an expedition to carry off the men who were so troublesome to him in his scouts and to the Loyalists of Vermont. III-184

Stephens' differences with Doctor Smyth continued. The chief bone of contention seems to have been the reluctance of the Spy Chief to pay him for his numerous scouts. Smyth seems to have been particularly vindictive of Stephens for he made false aspersions to Haldimand when he wrote of "the uselessness and avarice of Stevens." Stephens' account was still unpaid as late as June, 1783. 353

Other King's Rangers, who were equally daring, but less sustaining in the frequency of their secret scouts were Lieutenant Israel Ferguson, who made an expedition in July, 1780, to New York state and arranged with a confederate to receive news weekly from Albany. III-171 In August, 1781, he almost managed to seize a Loyalist agitator named Mitchel of Ballstown, but was discovered and pursued by such a strong party that he had to adopt an old Ranger technique of separating his Rangers to elude capture. III-176A Another infrequent secret agent was Lieutenant William Tyler. He made a scout for a similar objective at the same time as Ferguson. Although he failed to seize his object (Squire Palmer), he managed to overpower a small American scout, who had discovered them—taking all prisoners. II-140

Ensign Caleb Green was reported as having "behaved well" on a January, 1783 assignment into Vermont to Poughkeepsie, II-146 bringing back a number of prisoners to the Loyal blockhouse. Private Jonathan Miller was an active agent in Ballstown in July 1781. III-176 Major James Rogers, on April 28, 1782, was ordered on a mission of utmost secrecy in which he was to contact a Loyalist Judge "but the business of Rogers proved abortive by want of secrecy."III-181

Probably the most unique espionage service that Roger's

King's Rangers were engaged in was that of two Privates, John Lindsey and William Amesberry, when they volunteered in November, 1781, to burn a 74 gun ship building at Portsmouth, New Hampshire for Captain John Paul Jones. Captain Pritchard had also asked to be sent on this mission but it was felt that Lindsey and Amesberry were more acquainted with the task to be done, both having worked as ship carpenters. "After considerable fattegue & risque" the two Rangers arrived in Portsmouth, where, finding the 74 gun ship on the stock on a small island in the bay and not likely to be finished until the fall, they hired themselves out as ships carpenters for four shillings per day. The ship was being built at the expense of France and when finished would join the French line, to be commanded by John Paul Jones. As the greatest damage would be done if the ship was set afire upon near completion, the two arsonists worked diligently on her hulk for six months when they were scheduled to return to St. John's. Telling Captain Jones that they had to go to Boston to obtain some back wages and promising to return in August or September bringing with them some ships carpenters, they made their way to St. John's. Upon their arrival Lindsey made out a report in which he asked permission to return with Amesberry to complete their task when the ship was completed. Lindsey stated that "...if we do not succeed we will not expect any pay, but we dare almost engage at the forfeiture of our own lives, that we shall succeed." Regardless of their zeal, Haldimand felt that the risk was now too great, especially now with the probable prospects of peace in the offing. III-178

The only reported loss to the King's Rangers in their various secret service scouts was that of Ensign Beatie who was captured with two others in Vermont. The latter two turned state's evidence, but Beatie stood steadfast and was hanged as a spy, becoming a martyr to the Loyalist cause, rather than reveal the names of Vermont Loyalists. II-140A

Besides their daring secret service scouts Major Rogers' battalion at St. John's maintained their routine of garrison duty in spite of the jealous manifestations of Jessup and McAlpin, commanding similar Loyalist Corps.[354]

Jessup and McAlpin even recommended, in January 1783

to merge the Loyal and King's Rangers, Major James Rogers shrewdly went along with them when he wrote Haldimand that he had no objection to this as it would facilitate the King's service. If agreed to, he believed that he could complete a battalion in a reasonable time. Haldimand replied that, although it had been contemplated for some time to join his detachment to the Loyal Rangers, but that at the present can not be arranged. Major Rogers, however, must have felt that it would be advantageous to be annexed with another Corps for on May 7, he and other officers of the King's Rangers were applying to Sir John Johnson, for their Corps to be admitted to his second battalion which was not yet completed. This proposal proved equally void due to the prospects of peace.[355]

The second battalion of the Corps, termed Rogers Rangers, was scattered during their service throughout the maritime provinces. With headquarters at Halifax, where he was contiguous to the Paymaster, Rogers swelled his nucleus of forty men to four Companies which were stationed at Halifax, Penobscot, Prince Edward Island and George's Island to the northeast of Cape Canso, Nova Scotia, to guard the British shipyards there.[356]

After their repulse of the Massachusetts expedition at Penobscot in 1779, Rogers Rangers were in no more battles of consequence for campaigning practically ceased even in this debatable terrain. However, one Company of Rogers Rangers was stationed at Castine on the Penobscot River and saw more action than all the other Companies of the battalion. The Ranger Captain of the Penobscot Company was a dashing character and his exploits soon established him as the most famous officer in the battalion if not the whole Corps: John Jones by name, he hailed from Concord, Massachusetts. Settling in Pownalboro, Maine he became a noted surveyor. In 1763, he surveyed Mount Desert Island for Governor Bernard of Maine in preparation for a settlement to be made there at Southwest Harbor. In September, 1774, his Loyalist tendencies caused him to be visited by rebels who insisted on his joining the cause by signing the covenant. Stripping open his shirt he told them they might stab him to the heart before he would join the rebels. His callers then seized him and after binding him threw him into the Kennebec River and then dragged him about by a rope until they almost tore him to pieces. He was then thrown into Casco gaol for six months and escaped a probable conviction of a proposed trial by the absence of the Judge who had fallen on the ice while traveling to the trial. Upon his release Jones moved to Vassalboro, Maine but on October 7, 1777, he was haled before the magistrates and banished as a Tory to Concord, Massachusetts. Here he met Colonel Campbell, a prisoner of the Americans, who gave him a letter of recommendation to General Piggot at Newport. At this time, 1778, Jones turned smuggler and fitted out a vessel sending her to Newport loaded with stores for the British. On his second trip he was discovered by an American ship and after a losing race he was obliged to destroy his ship. Undaunted, Jones fitted out another ship and slipped through to Rhode Island. He received instructions from Admiral Gambier and General Prescott to return to Boston and bring in two similar vessels loaded with provisions. But upon landing in Boston Jones, who was by this time suspected by the American council, was seized and thrown into Boston gaol. After five weeks of confinement he escaped and made his way to Quebec via Lake Champlain.[357]

After petitioning Haldimand on August 29, 1779, for some "...Employ where I might be of service to Government, and get Retalliation for the repeated abuses I received from the Rebells," Jones met Colonel Rogers in Quebec and received a Captain's commission in his battalion. Haldimand sent him to Penobscot after writing to Brigadier Maclean, the British commander, that he "...should be watched." Jones soon dispelled any doubts by completing his Company and thus insuring his Captaincy.[358]

Jones' swarthy complexion gained for him the names of "Black Jones" and "Mahogany Jones." He was small of stature, compactly built and possessed of a resolute determination to avenge his persecutors. His uncanny knowledge of terrain due to his experience as a Surveyor made him a valuable courier across Maine to Quebec.[III-172] But "Black Jones" gained his real fame from his several forays to the Kennebec. From his headquarters at Bagaduce (on the Penobscot River) called Fort George, Jones lost no time in exacting retribution. In

1780, his first year in Rogers Rangers, he made two raids to Kennebec, "one by land, the other in a whaleboat." In his inimical style Jones describes his two raids: "... First by land, I went up and down till I found where to strike. Thought best to bring Brigadier Charles Cushing off. The way I proceeded was as follows: I surrounded his house in the morning very early; sent two men to rap at the door; on his crying out 'who is there?' I answered 'a friendl' 'A friend to whom?' I answered 'to Congress, and we are from George's River with an express, for the enemy has landed fifteen hundred troops from three ships.' He jumped up and came down with his breeches on, lit a candle and opened the door. We immediately seized him. On his making some noise his wife came running down stairs, but soon returned and put her head out of the chamber window and hallooed 'murder!' I told her if she did not hold her tongue my Indians would scalp her. Away we hauled her into a boat we had prepared, and up the river about a mile above Gardinerstown landed him and gave him a pair of shoes and stockings, and marched him to Fort George through the woods in four days. The whole country was alarmed, and was about six hours after us. In two or three days Roland Cushing came in with a flag. In two or three days after three men came in and informed us how matters were. Joseph North has gone to Boston. Bowman keeps guard every night, and all the people are much frightened. Roland keeps guard and Major Goodwin sleeps every night at the house [all of the above had been Jones' principal persecutors]. Many of our friends have been threatened, but no one is touched or hurt, for great is their fear. Many of the inhabitants don't cut their meadow [for fear of being captured]... When by water we went and cut out a vessel and brought her safe. I have had several scoutings since I have been here. Have always got the better of the rebels."III-173; II-134

Jones had at least one close call. Returning privately to Hallowell, he was secreted by Amos Pollard in his Tavern. The Americans in the neighborhood learning of this assembled, under the lead of Captain Nathaniel Hearsy, and filled the Tavern with "infuriated men," but so effectual was the concealment that he was not discovered. After this Jones openly returned under the protection of the treaty of peace and lived with his wife in a house when he built near the lower factory boarding-house, where he died August 16, 1823, eighty years old.[359]

The other Companies of the Rogers Ranger battalion were principally garrison Companies but occasionally certain officers were engaged in assignments redundant of danger:

Captain John Stinson was captured while on a secret assignment in 1782.[III-185] Lieutenant John Dean Whitworth "was ordered in 1780 on the recruiting service between Quebec and Halifax and made a journey of sixty days on foot in snowshoes through the snow suffering great hardships and losing the sight of an eye.[III-170] His afflictions obliged him in 1783 to obtain leave to sail for England." The talents of Benjamin Bradford of "Black Jones" Company were utilized when he became employed as a pilot in the Royal Navy and served on many occasions in privateers and armed ships.[360]

Finally, in November 1783, Clinton and consequently Haldimand received the King's order for the disbandment of the Loyalist troops and Rogers' two battalions were mustered out by December 24th. However, due to the lateness of the season the Loyalists were provided for until the following spring when they could go to their land grants. The officers were put on half-pay and each field officer was to receive 5,000 acres of land; each Captain 3,000 acres; each subaltern 2,000; and each non-com and private 200 acres. The Rogers Ranger battalion was mustered out on the St. John's River, now in the Province of New Brunswick in October 1783. The majority of this battalion settled in this region, while part of them went to Prince Edward Island and induced others to do likewise.[361] But James Rogers' King's Rangers battalion, though disbanded on December 24, 1783, remained on at St. John's, Quebec throughout the winter and made preparations for the move westward in the following year. By spring all members of the battalion who had families in the colonies were granted leave to bring them out.[362]

Returning with his wife and children to St. John's, Rogers granted leave to a number of unincorporated Loyalists and an officer of the King's Rangers, with a detachment of ten or twelve men to go to Cataraqui to reconnoitre.[III-186] The strain that the more ignorant members of the Corps were under, is revealed by Major James Rogers when he notifies Haldiman of a report which he had discovered among his own Corps, that he, Rogers, was going to have them taken to Cataraqui and there made slaves. In spite of this incredible suggestion confidence was restored and most of Roger's King's Rangers migrated with him into the wilderness.

Over 200 of the battalion accompanied their Major in that heroic advance into the wilderness in search of a new home. Several of the officers remained at St. John's buying the ground on which their late barracks stood. The bulk of the battalion that accompanied Rogers into the wilds of Canada settled on the third township of the Frontenac district upon the shores of the Bay of Quinte, James Rogers and his Rangers occupying what is known as the township of Fredericksburg, as well as a part of an adjoining township.[363]

So ends the saga of "Rogers Rangers," a Corps whose name, in spite of its Acadian exiled-like ending, still today implies the essence of fearless, daring men, whose achievements did much to win America's Independence and also to expand the frontiers of Canada.

The epitaph of the Corps might well read:

> *They won Canada from France so that the American Colonies might be free to win their Independence from England; and then strove to defend Canada from American occupation so that two great countries might be born. The United States and Canada can both proudly claim Rogers Rangers.*

APPENDIX I
BATTLE HONORS OF ROGERS RANGERS

ISLE OF MUTTON, *September 29, 1755*
LA BARBUE CREEK, *January 21, 1757*
FIRST DEFENSE OF FT. WILLIAM HENRY,
  March 19-23, 1757
FRESHWATER COVE, *June 8, 1758*
SECOND SIEGE OF LOUISBOURG,
  June 9-July 26, 1758
TICONDEROGA FALLS, *July 6, 1758*
MARIN'S DEFEAT, *August 8, 1758*
FORT FRONTENAC, *August 27, 1758*
THE THREE BATTLES, *March 7, 1759*
LOUISBOURG WOODS, *June 1, 1759*
BEAUMONT, *June 30, 1759*
ST. JOSEPH, *June 30, 1759*
POINT LEVIS WOODS, *July 1, 1759*
L'ANGE GARDIEN, *July 8, 1759*
LANGLADE'S AMBUSCADE, *July 8, 1759*
ROGERS-CAMPBELL MANOUVER, *July 12, 1759*
HAZEN'S POST, *July 15, 1759*
TICONDEROGA BRIDGE, *July 22, 1759*
SIEGE OF TICONDEROGA, *July 23-26, 1759*
MONTMORENCI FORD, *July 25, 1759*
ST. FRANCIS RAID, *September 13-November 1, 1759*
POINT LEVI, *February 24, 1760*
OLD LORETTE, *March, 1760*
SECOND SIEGE OF QUEBEC, *April 28-May 17, 1760*
POINTE AU FER, *June 6, 1760*
FORT STE. THERESE, *June 11-20, 1760*
POINT PLATON, *July 18, 1760*
SIEGE OF FORT LEVIS, *August 18-25, 1760*
SIEGE OF ISLE AUX NOIX, *August 19-27, 1760*
VARENNES, *September 1, 1760*
DETROIT, *September 13-November 29, 1760*
ETCHOE PASS, *June 10, 1761*
CAPTURE OF DOMINICA, *June 6, 1761*
MORNE TORTENSON, *January 24, 1762*
MORNE GRENIER, *January 27, 1762*
DEFENSE OF DETROIT, *July 29-November, 1763*
WHITEPLAINS, *October 28, 1776*
FORT WASHINGTON, *November 16, 1776*
DEFENSE OF FORT INDEPENDENCE, *January 18-23, 1777*
DEFENSE OF CASTINE, *August 11, 1779*
SIEGE OF FORT ANNE, *October 10-11, 1780*
FORT GEORGE, *October 11, 1780*
BALLSTOWN, *June 13, 1781*

APPENDIX II
SOURCES AND SELECTIVE DOCUMENTS ON THE ACTIONS,
AMBUSCADES AND MAJOR EXPEDITIONS OF ROGERS RANG-
ERS - MAY 1758 to JANUARY 1783

23. (p. 2) JACOB'S WOODCUTTER AMBUSCADE, May 4, 1758: Most complete source: Malartic, May 15, 27, 1758. Also Rogers, p. 108; News-Letter, May 25, 1758.
Bougainville, pp. 204, 208, substantiates Rogers' account and establishes the date of the ambuscade.

24. (p. 3) ETOWAUKAM'S DEFEAT, May 27, 1758: This action took place six miles south of Ticonderoga on the west shore of the "Drowned Lands" (Lake Champlain) Malartic, June 2, 1758. It is the only Ranger fight which actually occurred in the "Drowned Lands."
Other accounts in News-Letter, June 15, 1758; March 15, 1759 copy describes the odysseys of two of the Indian-Rangers who were captured: "A few days ago a Vessel arrived at New London from Monte Christo, in which came two Passengers, Indians, one of the Stockbridge, the other of the Mohegan Tribe; They give the following account: 'viz.: That they were under the command of Captain Jacob, and taken by a Party of Canada Indians, last Spring, near South Bay; and by them sold on board a French Man-of-War of 24 Guns, at Quebeck, and from thence sent to Cape-Francois [France] in August or September, where they were again sold, and kept to extreme hard labour, upon slender Diet, with the Negroes; but happening to discourse with an honest Spanieard who spoke English, they communicated their story to him; whereupon the Spanieard in a friendly manner, advised them to make their Escape to Monte-Christo where he did not doubt they might get a passage home in some English Vessel, which advice they put in Execution, after stealing a Gun Ammunition and 2 large Knives and made off to the Woods, and after 13 days travelling they arrived at Monte Christo..."
FRENCH ACCOUNT: Bougainville (Jrn., 205, 209, 210) reveals new data on leadership, size and the best French account: Chief Kisensik (shared command with the Canadian Outetat) left Montreal for Ticonderoga on May 16, with 25 Nipissings intent on making red "with English blood the ashes of his father, dead last fall." Determined to earn the gorget personally presented to his father by Louis XIV. Augmenting his force to 40 Nipissings Kisensik and Outetat met Etowaukam near the falls of the Chicot River, on the right bank. Of Etowaukam's party of 18 Ranger Indians and 5 white Rangers Kisensik took four scalps (two English and two Indians), and nine prisoners (two white Rangers, two Delawares, four Mohawks and a Mahican). The two [white Rangers] stories under interrogation were so conflicting that the French could make nothing out of them. Kisensik returned to Montreal arriving June 4, with nine prisoners that the Indians wanted to kill. The Abinakis objected and the lively squabble was quieted.

25. (p. 31) LANDING AT FRESHWATER COVE, June 8, 1758: Principal sources: McLennan; Knap, June 11, 1758; Knox, III, p. 5; Wood; Pichon, p. 284; Macdonald; Robertson, June 8; Thomas Geofery's Map of the Landing, published in London Oct. 9, 1758; Budd, June 8; Downey, 154-158 and Hamilton (1), pp. 232-233 give lively accounts. Hibbert, 24; Long; News-Letter, July 6, prints Brigadier Lawrence's commendation of Rogers Rangers and adds the following official army press release, which surprisingly gives the Rangers their due credit, whereas private British Journals credit the Light Infantry and Major Scott: "Published by order—Part of a Journal of the Fleet and Army... but on a Body of Rangers and Highlanders getting on their flanks, which they forgot to cover, they immediately gave ground, which gave our Soldiers an opportunity of getting into the Cove and taking Possession of their works,...we found the Body's of 100 odd French Regulars and two Indians which our Rangers Scalped. We took their magazines of Powder and their Sutlers grand Tent for supplying their army entrenched from Louisbourg...the soldiers got 2,000 Loaves, and 7 bags of Bread, 100 Kegs of Wine...100 of Brandy, also $700 and other things..."

Montressor, June 8, states that the War Chief killed by the Rangers "was a stout fellow with large limbs and features." One of the most important accounts is related by a Rogers Ranger participant, Sergeant Benjamin Wait (brother of Captain Joseph Wait). Sergeant Wait commanded one of Wolfe's landing boats and when his Rangers instinctively crouched down in the boat to screen themselves from the heavy French fire, Wait told them "to stand up to their work or take to the water!"-- Jones, M.B., pp. 5-6.

26. (p. 31) LOUISBOURG PATROL FIGHT, June 10, 1758: Montressor, June 10; News-Letter, July 6, 1758.

27. (p. 32) GALLOWS HILL, June 13, 1758: Best account— Montressor, June 13, he states that "We killed and wounded 40, one of which we brought in..." Robertson writes, "...our Picket...attack'd by a party from the woods, which was repulsed with the loss of 7 men killed and one taken prisoner. On our side we had 2 men killed and one officer wounded." W. Amherst notes, "A little skirmishing upon the hills opposite to the center of the Camp, between a picket and some Irregulars of ours and 5 pickets of the enemy. They were drove back into the town."

A picket consisted of a hundred men. News-Letter, July 6, gives the best account relative to the Rangers, "...About 500 French and Indians advancing from the City some small distance, to draw our troops within Cannon fire, they were attacked and fired upon by some of our Rangers, who killed 7, and wounded several others, upon which they retreated precipately to the City. Four of the Rangers were wounded in the Action..."

28. (p. 5) BATTLE OF TICONDEROGA RIVER, June 15, 1758: Rogers, pp. 109-110; News-Letter, July 6, 1758; Cleaveland, June 20, 21; Abercrombie to Pitt, June 29, 1758; Hervey, p. 49; Macomb, June 20, to Wilder, gives an example of the exaggerated accounts; "Yesterday we had an acct of Major Rogers' party to the number of 50 being all cut off save 5, and himself wounded in 2 places." The same story was repeated to General Forbes in Philadelphia on June 27, with the addition that Rogers was "mortally wounded." He writes Abercrombie the same date: "...I have just now heard some confused tale of Rogers having been worsted and mortally wounded. I shall be very sorry if it proves true, as I take him to be too good a man in his way, to be easily spared at present."
FRENCH ACCOUNTS: Malartic, June 19; He also pens Wolfe's flag visit to Abercrombie's camp. He erroneously states that Wolfe only had 30 men and that he killed one-half of Rogers' force besides taking some prisoners. Vaudreuil to Bourlamaque, Montreal, June 23, 1758, expresses his pleasure at Wolfe's success against the enemy, but adds that none would have escaped had the Indians been sober. He will do his best to rescue Ensign Downing from the Indians. Fate of the 2 Rangers taken is unknown. Bougainville states: Wolfe's force numbered 37 (30 French and 6 Indians). Wolfe was a half-pay officer of the Bentheim Regiment.--Bougainville, 213-214; 97.

29. (p. 8) CAPTURE OF STEVENS AND STONE, June 25, 1758: Stevens gives the best account in his Journal: Lieutenant Simon Stevens was ordered by Rogers on June 24 to scout down Lake George in two whaleboats to Northwest Bay. His force consisted of Lieutenant Nathan Stone (commanding one whaleboat), 2 Sergeants and 18 Privates. They embarked at 1 AM and shortly after Stevens landed a Sergeant and 3 Rangers to go to Ticonderoga to attempt to take a prisoner. Rowing along the east shore Stevens landed the balance of his party on a small island at the First Narrows about daylight. He immediately prepared a Sergeant and three Rangers to go to the mainland in a whaleboat, to cross the mountains and scout to South Bay. But before they embarked the island was surrounded by 4 canoes with 20 French and Indians in each. Stevens weighed the possibility of running his two whaleboats to the mainland only 60 yards away; but being outnumbered more than 5 to 1, he wisely surrendered his party of 18 men to Langy on a promise of good quarters. They were bound and taken to Ticonderoga the same day. Stevens and Stone were threatened with being turned over to the Indians if they did not reveal the strength and situation of Abercrombie's army. The two Ranger officers replied that they were officers of King George the II...and Commandant Bourlamacque might act his pleasure but he would receive no account from them. Stone was given to the Indians but Stevens was taken to Montreal and later Quebec.
Only four of the eighteen who surrendered were recorded to have returned to the British:
   Lieutenant Stevens escaped from Quebec May 1, 1759
   Lieutenant Stone was sold to the French by the Indians and

exchanged on November 15, 1759.
Private Isaac Rice - exchanged Nov. 15, 1759.
Private Littlefield Nash - exchanged Nov. 15, 1759.
Rogers, 110-111, states 300 captured Steven's men.
FRENCH ACCOUNTS: A newly discovered Manuscript Journal in W.O. 34 reveals that Langy was dispatched by Bourlamacque from Ticonderoga on June 23, with 60 Indians to reconnoiter towards the end of Lake George and attempt to take some prisoners.
Evidently all of Steven's party of eighteen were still alive on July 24, 1758, for Montcalm wrote Abercrombie on that date about the capture.

30. (p.33) THE BLOCKHOUSE SORTIE, June 26, 1758: Amherst, June 26, 1758. Amherst to Pitt, June 26, '58.

31. (p.32) CROFTON'S AMBUSCADE, June 29, 1758: Montressor, June 29, 1758, states only 3 Indians were attacked by Crofton. On March 29, 1759 he states "a body of Indians.." News-Letter, July 20, 1758 quotes 3 Indians. Amherst to Pitt, July 6, 1758; Budd, June 29, 1758. Scene of Crofton's exploit was one of Wolfe's blockhouses eight miles from Louisbourg.

32. (p.33) BARACHOIS RIDGE SORTIE, July 1, 1758: Amherst, June 30, July 1, 1758; Knox, July 1st.

33. (p.9) MONTCALM'S LANDING, July 6, 1758: Rogers, p. 112; Goodenough, p. 886; Cobb says 7 French, 2 Rangers K.O

34. (p.9) PAIGE-MAXWELL ADVENTURE, July 6, 1758: Maxwell, gives the principal account; Rogers, p. 113. Ranger Morris O'Brian.

35. (p.11) BATTLE OF TICONDEROGA FALLS, July 6, 1758: Bougainville, 226, 228-229: gives the exact details of Langy's force but gives the incredible excuse for his defeat by stating that he became "lost." Sieur de Langy has been detached with 130 volunteers to take post between Mount Pelee and the lake... Trapezac, captain in the Bearn Regt. supports him with three light companies... However the 350 man detachment which Sieur Langy led, abandoned by the few Indians who served it as guides, went astray in the mountains and after 12 hours marching came into contact with an English column which was proceeding toward the Bernetz River. About four o'clock in the evening we heard a great musketry fire and we perceived an hour later the remains of this unfortunate detachment pursued by the English. A few companies of grenadiers at once crossed the rapids at the Falls to lessen the [pressure of] the enemy's pursuit and several of our people favored by their fire got across by swimming. We lost out of this detachment Sieur de Trepezac, dead the next day from his wounds... Enemy suffered considerable loss in death of Brigadier General Lord Howe... He was march-

ing toward us when Sieur de Trepezac's detachment ran blindly into his column. At the first shots he ran up and was killed. His death stopped the advance [of Abercrombie]. The disheartened English gave us 24 hours delay and this precious time was the saving of us and of the colony."
Rogers, pp. 113-14; O'Conor, pp. 103-107; Lyon, July 7; Goodenough, p. 886, was a Ranger participant and adds a few new factors. He states that prior to the action: "Rogers men ...had a most desperate fight with some French who were minded to stop us but we shortly killed and captured most of them." Langy's Defeat he notes: "We again fell in with them that afternoon and were challenged 'Qui vive' but answered that we were French, but they were not deceived and fired upon us, after which a hot skirmish insued..." British losses were 25 killed. News-Letter, July 13th. Provincial participant Benjamin Jewett gives Rogers exemplary credit. Jewett, 62-65. The present landmark of the portion of the battlefield where Howe was killed is the high land one-quarter mile S. of the Catholic Cemetery in the village of Ticonderoga. Ticonderoga M. Bul. II, n.8, p. 53.
RETURN OF FRENCH PRISONERS TAKEN: Captain Bonneau, Guienne Regiment, Lieutenants Jaubert, Bearn Regiment; Le Rochelle, Guienne Regiment; Le Chevalier de Resie, Marine; Le Chevalier de Barnard, La Reine.
Three Cadets and 143 Privates. --AB 424.

36. (p. 13) BATTLE OF TICONDEROGA, July 8, 1758: Rogers, pp. 114-16; O'Conor, pp. 92-115; News-Letter, July 13; W.O.1: Vol. I, f 339, gives Ranger losses. Mante, map depicts Rogers Rangers as being on the extreme left of British line and in front of the French Regiments of Bearn and La Reine. Ranger Goodenough, p. 886 writes: "I was once carried right up to the breastwork, but we were stopped by the bristling mass of sharpened branches...I have...been in many battles and skirmishes, but I never have witnessed such slaughter and such wild fighting..." The folly of not first commanding Mt. Defiance with artillery and Burgoyne's success by doing so in 1777 are adequately described by Moore, pp. 92-93. Remington did an excellent drawing depicting Rogers Rangers in the attack. -- Remington, 885. Embleton did a fine color plate of the Black Watch attacking for the cover of Tradition, no. 19, 1967.
It was an odd coincidence but Captain Abercrombie was killed at the Battle of Bunker Hill while charging Stark's position on the hill.

37. (p. 33) CAP NOIR SORTIE, July 9, 1758: Montressor, July 15; McLennan; Amherst, July 9th.

38. (p. 33) REPULSE OF BOISHEBERT, July 15, 1758: Amherst, July 15; McLennan; Long; Boishebert; Webster gives best account of Boishebert's impotent attempt to relieve Louisbourg, mostly thru no fault of his: Charles Deschamps De Boishebert left his base at St. John's Fort at the mouth of the same River on the Bay of Fundy on June 17, 1758 for Shediac where

he had arranged to receive boats and supplies from Villejouin, Commandant on the Island of St. John. On the 26th the force arrived at the Gut of Canso. They eluded two British frigates at the south end and reached Port Toulouse (St. Peters) on the 28th undiscovered. After baking bread there they set out for Mire arriving on July 1st. There they were joined by Villejouin and 200 badly equipped men, 100 of them without shoes. His attempts to harass the enemy resulted in a series of small inconsequential raids from his force of not more than 600 men (see p.   ) There is some doubt whether Boishebert led the attack on Northeast Harbour on July 15, for Amherst notes that after the French were driven off a deserter came in and gave a "very intelligent" report stating that the attackers consisted of 100 from Boishebert, who was still at Mire with 203 men which was the balance of his force. Amherst adds: "Major Scott pursued, the Deserter shewing him the road but he could not get up with them. They went off in a great hurry. If he could have overtaken them after their Ammunition was fired and in their retreat and a river to pass to joyn Mosr. Bolisbere, he might have had great advantages by this Deserter.." However, Boishebert and Vaudreuil to the Minister (Arch. Rept., 1905, Vol. II, p. 365): give Boishebert credit for leading the attack. Vaudreuil was very belittling when he wrote that Boishebert had only burned a house serving as a British guard house, killed a sentinel, took a prisoner near the head of the British camp and took some tents -- losing himself two men and several wounded.

Boishebert's force had dwindled in half by desertion by the time of this attack and continued rapidly after July 15th. His men had lost heart. They were fatigued and a number fell ill. His Indians abandoned him and the Port Toulouse Acadians left in a body. He soon had only 140 effectives left when Louisbourg fell on July 26th. Boishebert departed on the 29th, the Bras d' Or Lakes being crossed in boats and canoes. Port Toulouse was reached the next day. On August 1, he reembarked in boats which had brought them from Miramichi to St. John's Fort. Boishebert states that while at Shediac he went to the Peticodiac River and had a fight with a large British force, losing 15 men and the enemy more, then left for Miramichi arriving on August 8th.

<u>39</u>. (p. 34) FIFTY GUINEAS SCOUT, July 15, 1758: Evidently Boishebert claimed to have led this detachment for Vaudreuil to Massiac, Montreal, Sept. 28, says that: "Sieur de Boishebert was not at the head of the 50 Acadians, who after being in the neighborhood of Louisbourg, were pursued by a detachment of 200 English. These Acadians had themselves elected their chief and equipped themselves at their own expense, as I have the honor to report to M. Moras."
Knap, July 16: "Our Rangers Brought 1 Indian prisoner that they took last night." Amherst, July 15.

<u>40</u>. (p. 40) LA CORNE'S AMBUSCADE, July 28, 1758: Rogers, p. 117; Abercrombie to Captain Wrightson, July 24, 1758

--AB 941; Same to Colonel Montressor from Camp at Lake George, July 29; AB 484; Same to Colonel Massey, July 30-- AB 490; Captain John Wrightson to Abercrombie, Halfway-Brook, July 30, --AB 489; Captains Burbank and Rutherford were sent with 150 Rangers and Regulars on July 30, to bury the cattle, etc., and Burbank was instructed to follow La Corne's back trail for a distance to pick up anything they may have dropped. Cleaveland, July 31st; Kingsley, IV, p. 178; Rea, July 31st records that 150,000 pounds sterling (apparently a payroll) was taken by La Corne in the affair. But Rea is the only one to state this. Colonel Hart was courtmartialed and Lieutenant Andrew McMullen and Ensign Archibald Campbell, Jr. were the principal witnesses against him. Their Depositions are in W.O. 34, Vol. 75, ff 173-176, 181. All of the Ranger officers and Sergeants who served in Burbank's skirmish were sent up to Lake George to testify. They were Lieutenants McMullen, Morris, Ensigns Campbell, Stone, Sergeants Bolton and Wellesley.--AB 539. Of the 13 Rangers ambuscaded by La Corne at least 2 survived. Private John Terry was captured and exchanged on November 15, 1759. The Historian, Francis Parkman, received a relayed first-hand account by Hoyt of Private Catlin's escape; Catlin was in the lead and immediately before La Corne's attack he spotted a crow pecking dung in the road, which ran thru a low swampy place. Thinking he would shoot the crow he took to the bushes until he approached opposite to the bird for a shot. The crow enticed him further away by flying further down the road until it came to rising ground and when Catlin reached him he flew away. At that moment he heard La Corne's attack below him and thanks to his interest in the crow Catlin escaped to the post at Halfway-Brook.--Wade, 191.

41. (p.16) HACKETT'S MESS-TIME FIGHT, July 31, 1758: Wrightson to Abercrombie, Half-Way-Brook, July 31, 4 PM. --AB 491. The above was dispatched immediately upon Hackett's return. Farmer-Moore, relates Ranger William Moore's account of his captivity: "William Moore, of Stratham, N.H., was one of Rogers Rangers. He, with ten others, was sent out on a scouting party; and while partaking of soldier's fare, at a table spread in the wilderness, they were surrounded by a party of savages. A desperate fight ensued; 17 of the Indians were killed and 8 of the Rangers. [Sergeant Hackett, the only survivor to escape from the massacre, made his way to Halfway-Brook.] Moore was taken, but not till he had wrenched the tomahawk from the Indian who first seized him and buried it in his brains. The other survivor was murdered in cold blood on the battlefield; his heart was taken from his body and forced warm into the mouth of the prisoner, who had been his companion and friend. The Indians were of a tribe residing far to the west; and returning to their homes, they carried Moore with them for torture. At Montreal, the French understanding for what fate he was reserved, endeavored to redeem him, but in vain. His captors resolved to exercise on him their cruelty and revenge the death of the warrior whom he slew. On their

arrival at their own country great preparations were made for his lingering execution. When all was ready, Moore was made fast to a tree. He was deliberately cut and stabbed all over his body and limbs in more than 200 places and splinters of pitch and wood were put into every wound. To these his tormentors were about to apply the fire when the Mother of the Indian he had killed, declared she would take him as her son, instead of the one she had lost. Upon this, he was immediately unloosed; the splinters were extracted, and some medicinal herbs applied, as soon as they could be gathered, to his wounds. Such was the efficacy of their applications, that in 3 or 4 days he was free from pain, and able to travel as usual, though he retained the scars to his death. He was not adopted into the family of the squaw, whom he was to call his mother, and by whom he was treated as a son. He lived with her about 6 years and went out with the tribe in their hunting, fishing and fighting expeditions. He was too remote from the civilized settlements to venture an escape; but was too earnest to return to his freinds, not to make some attempt to visit them... He hoped by alarming their fears to obtain permission to leave them. His mother, alarmed, said, "You Spit blood—You die!" Moore said, yes, he must die, unless he could see an English doctor who could easily cure him. The Indians tried all their remedies in vain, for the stick would still produce blood and he was obliged to apply it so often that he became pale and debilitated. Despairing of his recovery without the aid of a white physician, his mother and two Indians set out with him on a visit to the whites—Moore assuring them that when the English Doctor had cured him and he returned to the tribe again; he should make a better hunter and braver warrior than ever. They first went to a French physician, to whom Moore made known his object and the French directed him to an English Doctor, who, he said would better understand the disease. The Englishman was attached to the army and on Moore's arrival, secured him and sent the Indians away. The old squaw appeared to mourn as sincerely and lamented as loudly, as if the child of her adoption had been the child of her blood..."Vol III, p.87-8.

42. (p.20) MARIN'S DEFEAT, August 8, 1758: Rogers, pp. 117-120; Thomas Barnsley to Bouquet, Albany, Sept. 7, 1758, Bouquet Coll., A, 13, Vol. I, p. 262—describes the giant Indian. Colonel Montressor at Fort Edward was the first to receive word of the battle. At 2:30 p.m. two Rangers arrived from Rogers. Montressor sent Rogers 40 of Brewer's Mohegan Rangers, 26 Highlanders, 76 Royal Americans, and 260 Provincials. Montressor to Abercrombie, Aug. 8, AB 514. Champion, July 29-Aug. 8; Spaulding, Aug. 29; Price, Aug. 20; Abercrombie to Delancey, Camp at Lake George, Aug. 14— W.O. 34, Vol. 30, f 27; DeLancey to Abercrombie, N.Y., Aug 7-W.O.34, Vol. 29; Abercrombie to Brigadier Prevost, Aug 10-AB 521; Rogers and Dalyell returned to Abercrombie's camp escorting a supply train. Abercrombie to DeLancey, Aug. 10-AB 522: blames the Connecticuts"... Putnam's Men

were his own choice from among the Connecticut Troops who scatter'd so much that they cou'd not be collected in due Time so as to pursue the Enemy..." Abercrombie to Stanwix, Aug. 12—AB 531; DeLancey to Abercrombie, N.Y., Aug. 20—AB 550; Also condemns the Connecticuts. Commends the others and states Marin's Defeat should let the enemy know they can be handled in the woods. News-Letter, first notice by Colonel Goffe in Aug. 24th copy; second notice Aug. 31, states "The Regular officers gave Rogers a very good character and say he behaved extremely well..." Third notice Sept. 7: "...Two Deserters came in the night before last [Aug. 25th], who informs, that the Indians immediately after Rogers' late Battle went all home, except 30 which got so drunk that they could not travel." Fourth notice Sept. 7, gives a harrowing account of Lieutenant Worster of the Connecticuts: "...He being in the front with Major Putnam...the enemy fired upon him and 8 bullets lodged in him, 3 of which are taken out; he had also 3 wounds by a Tomahawk, 2 of which were on his head and the other in his Elbow. His head was flayed almost, the hair part off. He was sensible all the while the Enemy were scalping him and finding himself wounded in so many places that he could not run and the Enemy close upon him, he fell on his face and feign'd himself Dead...however, they gave him 2 blows on his head but not so hard as to deprive him of his senses and then Scalp'd him, during all which time he made not the least resistance...He is yet alive and likely to recover..." Abercrombie to Pitt, Official Report, Aug. 19, 1758, in Corr. of Pitt, I, pp. 318-322. W. Parkman, states battle lasted 2 hours and 10 minutes. Maxwell, a Ranger present gives his version. Boston Weekly-Advertiser, Letter from Lake George, signed by Captains Maynard and Giddings—participants in the battle. Livingston, pp. 86-92. Cleaveland, Aug. 9-16; Rea, July 30-Aug. 12.

SITE OF MARIN'S DEFEAT: On Clear River, the west branch of Wood Creek, about a mile northwest from the ruins of Fort Anne. —Lyon, p. 28, n.

NUMBERS OF CORPS IN ROGERS' FORCE:

ROGERS RANGERS—80 (including Rogers, Lt. Tute, etc.)

DALYELL'S DETACHMENTS FROM THE 80th & 44TH— 60 (including Capt. Dalyell, Lt. Eyers—4th, Ensign William Irwin, 80th, Volunteer Lieutenant Thomas Barnsley.)

PUTNAM'S CONNECTICUT PROVINCIALS—300 (Major Putnam, Lieutenants Durkee, Tracy, Worster—also called Peter Wooster, etc.)

PARTRIDGE'S ROYAL HUNTERS—40

MASSACHUSETTS PROVINCIALS—50 (Captains Giddings and Maynard.)

Partial list of Connecticut losses: Privates Lemanuel Dean, Caleb Atwater and Joseph Bewel, Jr., wounded. Rufus Chapman captured—later exchanged. War, Vol. 8, pp. 171,178,181, 234; Vol. 9, p. 143. There are no lists of Rogers Rangers losses.

FRENCH ACCOUNTS: Bougainville's (Journal, 258, 260, 261-262): account is enlightening but as usual, excuses a French defeat: Marin left Ticonderoga on August 4, for the South Bay-Wood Creek area with 219 Indians and 225 Canadians. They were issued food and equipment but several Indians sold theirs and returned asking for more, as there was no record of the stores issued. Because of the ebbing and flowing of his Indians, Marin's exact strength at the moment of the battle is not exactly known. A few of his Indians returned to Ticonderoga, "saying they were indisposed." However, a detachment of Sault St. Louis Indians also joined Marin, so his force probably numbered around 500 men. Bougainville writes: "the game was not even..." After the battle Marin withdrew in good order leaving 13 dead, 5 of them Indians and carried off their 10 wounded. They took Major Putnam and 4 prisoners. Marin claimed that the bulk of his Canadians were "of the bad sort..." He claimed the militia commander gave him these because of professional jealousy. Marin arrived back at Ticonderoga on August 10th. Pouchot, I, 123, erroneously states Rogers' losses at 100 men, "while the French had 4 Indians killed, 4 wounded; 6 Canadians killed and 6 wounded, among whom was an officer and a cadet." Montcalm, p. 432; Doreil to Marshall de Bellex Isle, In Docs. X, p. 818, 851; Malartic, Aug; Levis p. 145; Malartic states that Marin heard 3 shots which led his scouts to Rogers' force. Doreil, pens"... Marin... perceiving that... the Indians, who feared that they would not be able to carry off some wounded, demanding to retire, he was obliged to think of retreating, which he did in good order and without being pursued, after having, for an hour, longer kept up a fire with such picked men as he had, who performed prodigies of valor. The Indians, in general, have also behaved well; but of 100 Canadians, more than 60 deserted Marin, no one knows wherefore at the very moment when the English were wavering. This somewhat astonished the Indians and prevented that brave officer deriving all the advantage he could from the circumstance..."

Marin's force consisted of 50 Troops de la Marine, 100 Canadian Militia and 300 to 350 Coureurs des Bois and Indians.

<u>43</u>. (p. 34) SPANISH BAY EXPEDITION, Aug. 7-20, 1758: Amherst, Aug. 6, 7, 20; Montressor, Aug. 7th. Spanish Bay, now called Sydney Harbour. Principal purpose of expedition, besides receiving capitulation, was to bring prefabricated frames there for the barracks at Louisbourg. Dalling returned with 450 pieces of squre timber, 1600 plank, 120,000 shingles. He had to leave behind 800 pieces of square timber, 1500 piquets & 1200 loads of wood.

<u>44</u>. (p. 34) ISLE ST. JEAN EXPEDITION, Aug. 8, 1758: Amherst, Aug. 7-8. Now called Prince Edward Island.

<u>45</u>. (p. 22) THE COLLISION FIGHT, Aug. 21, 1758: Rangers' Letters, Rogers' Island, Fort Edward, Aug. 23, 1758.

45-a. (p. 26) FORT FRONTENAC, Aug. 27, 1758: Stanwix to Abercrombie, Aug. 15, 1758. "Return of Troops detached from the Oneida Station [for Bradstreet's Expedition]. AB 541. List of French Prisoners taken. —AB 565. Terms of Surrender— AB 566. Johnson Papers, II 889-90. Williams, Bull, Bass, Door, Aug. 14-30; Hamilton (1), Phineas Atherton from E. A. Jones, Loyalists of Mass., 10-11. AB923—1 & 2.

46. (p. 34) FORT ST. JOHN EXPEDITION, Aug. 30-Nov. 11, 1758: A return of McCurdy's, Stark's and Brewer's at Ft. St. John on Sept. 24, totals 314 officers and men. 250 were sick but present, 7 were sick in Hospital and 2 had died, apparently of smallpox. —AB 949; W.O. 34, Vol. 43. Monckton; Scott; Monckton to Abercrombie, Oct. 15—AB 764; Amherst, Aug. 24-26, 30; Northcliff 13.

47. (p. 23) HOLMES' CANOE AMBUSCADE, Sept. 5, 1758: Rangers' Letters, Sept. 11: says "a beautiful gun & sundries" was taken from the canoe. A French version is revealed in Bougainville's Journal Sept. 5:..."A few Indians who were hunting along the sides of the Pendu River [ed. note: probably East Creek across the lake in Vt.] have been attacked by an enemy party; one Indian was slightly wounded, the others ran away to Carrillon. M. de St. Luc followed the enemy's tracks with almost all the Indians in camp and returned two hours later to tell us that they [the tracks] seemed to be those of some 30 men [actually Holmes had only seven Rangers] several of them in French shoes [this must have confounded the French!] the rest Indians. Thirty of our men will leave tomorrow morning to run after this party which they expect to meet the day after, and not on their guard, provided that they then do not expect to be pursued." Bougainville, 273.

48. (p. 22) ROGERS' PATROL TRAP SCOUT, Sept. 9, 1758: Rea, Sept. 9, 11, 14, 18.

49. (p. 23) FORT EDWARD ROAD AMBUSCADE, Sept. 9, 1758: Rea, Sept. 9; Rangers' Letters, Sept. 11: says Sept. 6. Champion, Sept. 9th. Bougainville's account RE: pursuit of Holmes after his 'Canoe Ambuscade' (see above) may will be the French force that engaged in this ambuscade. —Bougainville, 273.

50. (p. 24) MORRIS' CROWN POINT AMBUSCADE, Sept. 25, 1758: Rangers' Letters, from Albany, Nov. 12th.

51. (p. 24) TUTE'S HUNTING EXPLOIT, Nov.   , 1758: Rangers' Letters, Nov. 12th.

52. (p. 34) CAPTURE OF MCCORMICK, Nov. 15, 1758: Monckton, Nov. 16; Monckton to Governor Pownall, Nov. 20, 1758— Northcliffe, Vol. 13; Knox, Jan. 20, 1759: McCormick was removed from Miramichi to Restigouche. Pierre Du Calvet,

the keeper of the stores seems to have treated him kindly although the several letters he wrote were apparently done under pressure, or at least without his knowledge of how the French capitalized on them.

53. (p.37) FEBRUARY FIRST AMBUSCADE, Feb. 1, 1759: News-Letter, Feb. 15, states fight occurred near the Royal Blockhouse at Fort Edward. Amherst to Pitt, Feb. 28, Corr. of Pitt, II, 43-4; Gage to Amherst, Albany, Feb. 5—W.O. 34, Vol. 46A, f 7, gives Haldimand's report. The Indians were in two parties of about 30 each. The second party waylaid some Regulars in search of wood, killing one and capturing a Corporal. "That having but 16 Rangers, the rest being employed in escorting sleys, Haldimand sent them to watch the enemy till 190 Regulars were sent in pursuit." which they did so closely that the Indians dropped their blankets and other objects the better to escape.

54. (p.71) HAZEN'S ST. ANNE'S RAID, Feb. 18-March 5, 1759: Amherst to Gage, Apr. 2, 1759—W.O. 34, Vol. 46A, f 154; Lt. John Butler to Capt. Danks, Ft. Frederic, Mar. 6, in Knox, I, Apr. 5, 1759; Amherst to Pitt, Apr. 16—Pitt Corr.

55. (p.37) THE THREE BATTLES, March 7, 1759: Rogers, pp. 127-134: After crossing the drowned lands Rogers discovered Indian tracks totalling 50 headed for South Bay. Tute informed Haldimand and signal guns were fired which supposedly were heard by the Indians near Ft. Miller, 8 miles below Ft. Edward and scared them off. Haldimand wrote Rogers when sending him the relief sleds: "I congratulate you heartily on your good success..."
Amherst to Gage, N.Y., Mar. 12, 1759—W.O. 34, Vol. 46A, f 145; Same to Same, Mar. 19,—W.O. 34, 46A f 149; Same to Same, Mar. 26—Ibid, 46A, f 150; Same to Same, Apr. 2—Ibid, 46A f 154; Gage to Amherst, Albany, Feb. 25, 1759—W.O. 34, Vol. 46, f 13; Same to Same, Mar. 5—Ibid, 46A, f 15: relates dispute between Rogers and Williams. Alst states that the Mohawks were greatly diminished in numbers from the time they left Johnson to their departure from Fort Edward with Rogers. Same to Same, Mar. 13—Ibid, 46A, f 19; Same to Same, Mar. 17—Ibid, 46A, f 20; Same to Same, Mar. 19—Ibid, 46A, f 21: Encloses Rogers' official Journal, examination of the prisoners and Lieutenant Brehm's "Draught and Paper Reference." Gage to Haldimand, Feb. 23, 1759, f 19, approval; and Mar. 12, f 23, congratulations.
Rogers' original Journal of the expedition is in the Gage Papers, Clement's Library—in his own handwriting. He gives a breakdown of the officers and Corps in his force:
ROGERS RANGERS—Major Rogers; Lieutenants Tute, Robert Holmes, Archibald Stark, David Brewer; 7 Sergeants and 79 Privates.
1ST REGT. "Royals"—Lieutenants West and Cootz; 4 Sergeants, 1 Corporal and 40 Privates.

60TH "Royal Americans"—Capt. Williams; Lieutenant McKay; Ensigns Brown and Monins; 4 Sergeants; 4 Corporals; 110 Volunteer privates. Lieutenant Turnbull; 3 Sergeants; 2 Corporals; 41 Privates and Lt. Brehm, Engineer of Colonel Prevost's Battalion.

MOHAWKS—Captain John Lottridge and 50 warriors.

Rogers' losses were 2 Rangers killed, 1 Mohawk and the only Regular in the battles, badly wounded. The sleds and reenforcements were under Captain McBean. Rogers records: "Both officers and men behaved with great bravery in particular Captain Lottridge and Lieutenant Holmes... who excelled in their courage..."

Provincial Newspaper accounts: Boston Gazette and Country Journal, Mon., Mar. 26, no. 208; News-Letter, Mar. 29: says Rogers took 5 prisoners and 6 scalps. Amherst to Pitt, Mar. 29, Pitt Corr., II, 79: writes that Rogers took 7 prisoners and 4 scalps in the first battle, but was obliged to kill 2 of the prisoners who could not keep up with his Rangers. Lt. Thomas Barnsley to Bouquet, Mar. 12,—Bouquet Coll., 14. FRENCH ACCOUNTS: Hebecourt to Bourlamacque, from Carillon, Mar. 10,—Lettres Variarum, IV, 309-12, Vaudreuil to Berryer, Montreal, Mar. 28—Docs., X, 946. Although Rogers states he killed 30 of the enemy, the French admit no losses in the second and third battles. They claim that only 4 Marine privates and 2 of de Berry, and Cadets Charpentier and Louvisons were captured in the first battle. Three Privates of Berry and one Abenaqui Indians killed. Two Abenaqui wounded and a Canadian Interpreter, a Private of Berry and two Abenaqui scalped. Although the Berry Private was scalped, received two tomahawk blows in the skull and had his thigh broken and part of his arm chopped off, he recovered without any fever. One Ranger, Cris Proudfoot, of the two left for dead by Rogers, was captured, recovered and later escaped. The French never admitted more than 7 killed, 3 wounded and 8 taken prisoners. In all, 18.

<u>56</u>. (p.72) LAKE LABRADOR RAID, March 13, 1759: News-Letter, Apr. 19, 1759.

<u>57</u>. (p.42) HURLBURT'S HUDSON RIVER FIGHT, May 1, 1759: Deposition of Daniel Hurlburt and Robert Hewitt, May 2, 1759 —Northcliffe, XXVII, Que, 10, p. 206; Knox, May 3, 1759.

<u>58</u>. (p.43) THE PIGEON-HUNT AMBUSCADE, May 7, 1759: This is the first recorded mention of an action of Wendell's Company—Amherst, May 9: "...I had an account from Fort Stanwix of a scouting party of Lt. Stevens and 16 Rangers who were discovered by the enemy's Indians as they had been shooting Pidgeons & were surprised; Tiebout, a Volunteer and 4 men killed, 1 man taken prisoner & Sergt. Kenedy wounded..." Tiebout, or Tribout, was not killed for he was promoted to a Lieutenant in Wendell's and passing thru Albany with recruits by May 22, 1759—Amherst to Eyre, Albany, May 22, 1759—W.O. 34, Vol. 54, f 129.

59. (p.43) BURBANK'S DEFEAT, May 11, 1759: Rogers, 137: writes "I returned to Ft. Edward the 15th of May, where I received the melancholy news that Capt. Burbank with a party of 30 men, had in my absence been out on a scout and were all cut off. This gave me great uneasiness, as Mr. Burbank was a gentleman I very highly esteemed, and one of the best officers among the Rangers, and more especially as I judged the scout he was sent out upon by the commanding officer at the fort was needless and unadvisedly undertaken." News-Letter, May 24, 31st. Capt. James Abercrombie to Loudoun, Ft. Edward, June 20, 1759—LO 6115: condones Burbank. Amherst to Governor DeLancey, Camp of Lake George, June 23, 1759—W.O. 34, 30 f 52; Amherst to Pitt, May 19—in Knox; Amherst to Eyre. Albany, May 19—W.O. 34, 54, f 127: reveals that Rogers offered a plan for retaliation by waylaying convoys above Ticonderoga: "Major Rogers' proposal of laying in Ambuscade for the Enemy is exactly what might have been executed with great success, when Captain Williams was with him I approved of it entirely and that he should have the command of the party. If Langy and his people is gone to Montreal it will facilitate this scheme of Rogers, which should not be put in execution if there is appearance that the garrisson has been reenforced, which I imagine is not yet done and the former garrisson will not at this time venture out many people..."
Eyre to Amherst, Ft. Edward, May 17—W.O. 34; Amherst to Eyre, May 24—W.O. 34, 54, f 130; Eyre wrote Amherst another letter on May 20, with a return of the buried members of Burbank's party, but it cannot be found in the Amherst Papers, W.O. 34. Amherst to Eyre, May 22—W.O. 34, 54, f129; DeLancey to Amherst, N.Y., May 28—W.O. 34, 39, f 73: offers his partially accurate opinion"...The party of Rangers missing have most probably been taken as you observe; for I have remarked from several of their own accounts that they never were properly upon their guard until they approached near Ticonderoga—and this ill-imagined security will always expose them to a surprise..." N.Y. Mercury, June 11; Reverend William Patrick's Historical Sermon, Oct. 27, 1833, in History of Canterbury, N.H., I, p. 41, describes the harrowing melee of the Shepherd brothers in the ambuscade. Provincials on their march to Lake George received disconcerting accounts of Burbank-Henshaw, May 21, 1759. A droll incident occurred when one of the captives, Christian Shamburn, was employed by the Indians as a means of barter when they realized that French power was waning in 1760. A Conondago Indian in an effort to restore friendly relations with the English brought in Ranger Shamburn and set him free, taking care, though, to hide him in the bottom of his canoe when they passed other French Indians. --Haldimand to Johnson, May 19, 1760. --Johnson Manuscripts, III, p. 241. Anonymous (Ranger officer diary) comments, May 13, 1759 entry.
Burbank's widow finally despaired of his return and printed the following notice in the N.H. Gazette, on Jan. 11, 1760: "All Persons that have any just Demands on the Estate of Captain

Jonathan Burbank, late of New Hopkinton (so called) In N.H., deceased, are desired to bring in their accounts to Ruth Burbank of New Hopkinton aforesaid Administratrix of said Estate: And all who are indebted to said Estate are desired to make speedy Payment, or to renew their Bonds, to prevent further trouble--New Hopkinton, December 27, 1759."
Farmer-Moore, I, 286: describes Burbank's death.

LIST OF RANGERS CAPTURED: (exchanged Nov. 15, 1759)*

-William Farris	-Joseph David
-Oliver Gauph	-Samuel Robertson
-William Walker	-Samuel Shepherd
-Isaac Butterfield	-Samuel Hall
-Timothy Bowing	-John Adams
-Abner Chase	-Joseph Brady
-John Farrington	-Jonathan Clay
-John Gray	-Isaac Walker
-Nicholas Brown	-George Shepherd
-John Butler	-John Dewey
-Ebenezer Tincomb	-Jacob Hooper
-Isaac McKay	-Christian Shamburn, given up by Indian May 19, 1760
-Isaac Burton	
-Samuel Moore	*W.O.34, Vol. 8, ff18-19

60. (p.77) STEPHENS-STOBO ESCAPE & STEPHENS' PORT DANIEL NAVAL COUP, May 22, 1759: Prisoner Witherspoon on May 2, 1759: notes that there was "mist" which must have aided their escape from Quebec. He adds that the French "... sent a command of men after them with speed both by sea and land, but hitherto to no purpose for they could not be found which keeps a stir in this place.--p. 41. For the Port Daniel Coup see: Stephens, May 22; Stobo, p. 37-8; News-Letter June 29. Besides Stephens, see also Alberts for escape, etc.

61. (p.74) LOUISBOURG WOODS, June 1, 1759: Knox, I p. 354. Rogers Rangers alone served in this action, for Goreham's Company were on board one of Admiral Durell's Ships gone to the mouth of St. Lawrence and Dank's Company had not arrived yet.

62. (p.78) BEAUMONT, June 30, 1759: Three days after the landing on Isle Orleans Brigadier Monckton was sent with his Brigade and a detachment of Rogers Rangers and Goreham's to establish a fortified camp on the heights of Point Levi, opposite Quebec. The Rangers and Light Infantry crossed over on the night of June 29, and took possession of the Church of Beaumont, the tide was out by this time and Monckton's Regulars lay on their arms on the Isle of Orleans. In the early morning the Rangers were attacked at Beaumont by a force of Colony troops and after a contested action were driven off. The Ranger and Light Infantry loss was 2 wounded, while the enemy lost 7 killed, who were scalped by the Rangers and 5 were taken prisoners.--Knox, I, p. 396.

63. (p.78) ST. JOSEPH, June 30, 1759: Action occurred when Monckton moved up from Beaumont to Point Levis and he strove to take possession of the fortified church of St. Joseph south of the point. The church exchanged hands several times until Monckton settled the issue by attacking simultaneously with Rangers, Highlanders and Grenadiers on three sides. After a stout resistance, the French were almost surrounded when they gave way and retreated. The British and Rangers lost 30 killed and wounded. Enemy loss unknown.--Knox, I, pp. 380-81.

64. (p.78) POINT LEVIS WOODS, July 1, 1759: A Company of Rogers Rangers and Goreham's Rangers were the ambuscaders.--Knox, I, p. 381.

65. (p.45) JACOB'S DEFEAT, July 5, 1759: Amherst, July 4, 8, 9, 11, 12th; W. Amherst, July 8, 9, 17-18: On the 18th, by a flag of truce it was learned that Jacob and some of his party were taken to Montreal. News-Letter, Aug. 2: adds that Jacobs, at his request had been sent out to avenge the massacre of the N.J. troops on July 2nd. True, July 12th. Lemuel Wood, July 9, 11: States a Volunteer Provincial Joseph Fisk (of Boxford) was killed or taken in the action. Also, the reluctance of Stockbridge survivors to return to camp: "July 11, this Day another man of Capt. Jacob's Company came in almost starved ..." Anonymous (Ranger officer Diary) comments.

66. (p.79) L'ANGE GARDIEN, July 8, 1759: Knox, I, 195.

67. (p.79) LANGLADE'S AMBUSCADE, July 8, 1759: Knox, I, pp. 196-7; Wolfe, July 9th.

68. (p.46) ROGERS-CAMPBELL MANEUVER, July 12, 1759: Webster, July 12; Hardy, July 12; Amherst, July 12; Wood, July 12th states Rogers returned shortly after sunset and that he lost a Sergeant and a Regular killed and a Stockbridge wounded. Hardy, writes that Rogers burnt the small wooden breastwork that the French had so impudently erected on the island. French losses are unknown but one of their batteaus was shot in two by Rogers' musketry. Anonymous (Ranger officer Diary) July 12, 1759, entry.

69. (p.79) HAZEN'S POST, July 15, 1759: Lane, July 15, a Ranger participant, gives the best account. Wolfe, July 14th.

70. (p.47) TICONDEROGA BRIDGE, July 22, 1759: Rogers, p. 139; Webster, July 22; Amherst, July 22; Hawks, July 22, states the 2 prisoners were from the Berry Regiment—the four killed were scalped by the Rangers. Rogers' continuous fire-power seems to have disconcerted the French for they deserted Bournie after the first volley. Amherst "expressed great satisfaction..." at Rogers' possession of such a strong position. Amherst, states the Rangers lost 1 killed and 1 wounded. W. Amherst, July 22, writes: an officer of the Mi-

litia and 2 privates were taken by Rogers. J. Robertson to Loudoun. Carillon—LO 6126.

71. (p. 80) AMBUSCADE OF BUTLER, July 22, 1759: Ranger Lane, July 22, was a participant.

72. (p. 47) BREWER'S NORTH ENTRENCHMENT CAPTURE, July 23, 1759: Rogers, p. 140.

73. (p. 80) HAZEN'S JULY 24TH BLOODHOUND SCOUT, July 24, 1759: Lane, July 24: 50 Rangers in Hazen's scout.

74. (p. 47) BREWER'S INDIAN SALLY FIGHT, July 24, 1759: W. Amherst, July 24th.

75. (p. 80) MONTMORENCI FORD, July 25, 1759: Wolfe, July 25.

76. (p. 80) PATTEN'S CAPTURE, July 25, 1759: Lane, July 25.

77. (p. 48) ROGERS' BOOM-CUTTING FROLIC, July 26, 1759: Rogers, pp. 141-42; News-Letter, Aug. 16; Amherst, July 26; Merriman, July 26; Hawks, Amherst's General Orders to Rogers to cut the boom, "as well as to amuse them on that side." See name index volume III for an exploit by Morrisson on the same night.

78. (p. 80) HAZEN'S JULY 26TH BLOODHOUND SCOUT, July 26, 1759: Lane, July 26th.

79. (p. 48) FLETCHER'S POSSESSION OF CROWN POINT, Aug. 1, 1759: Amherst, Aug. 1; News-Letter, Aug. 16; Merriman Aug. 2nd.

80. (p. 80) HAZEN'S 'BOON-QUARTER' SCOUT, Aug. 2-4, 1759: Two of Rogers Rangers give the best accounts: Lane, Aug. 2-4: "Capt. Hazzen imbark'd on board 2 flat bottomed boats with about 90 men in order to go about 15 miles down the River..."—4th—We landed on the N. side of the River. We took 1 prisoner, the Enemy presently attack'd us, Killed 1 Lieut, 1 Private & Wounded another. We soon drove them and returned to camp the same day." Ranger Perry, elaborates giving more interesting details: "... We landed in the morning and secreted ourselves in small parties in the woods beside the road. I was with the Lieutenant's party. We had a man by the name of Frazier in our party, who enlisted under Captain Peck, in Boston and he was a pretty unruly fellow. There came along three armed Frenchmen near where we lay concealed and Frazier saw them and hallooed to them 'boon quarter' whereupon one of them levelled his piece and shot him thru the head and killed him instantly. The Captain hearing the report, came and inquired how it happened. We told him we could not keep

Frazier still; 'well,' said he, 'his blood be upon his own head.'
We now expected to have some fighting. We left our blankets
upon the dead man and took the road the Frenchmen came in
and after marching about half a mile we came into an open field
with a large number of cattle in it; and on the opposite side of
the field, just in the edge of the woods, were great many little
huts, full of women and little children, with their hasty-pudding
for breakfast of whom I partook with them; but their little children scampered into the brush and could not be got sight of
again, any more than so many young partridge. We did not,
however, wish to hurt them. There were 3 barns in the lot
filled with household goods; we took as many as we could of
these and drove the cattle back the way we came to where the
dead man and blankets were left, which we took up and were
proceeding with our booty to the river when the enemy fired
on us and killed Lt. Meech of Danks' company and wounded one
other. In the meantime, the cattle we had taken all ran back;
but we drove off the enemy and got our goods, etc., aboard the
boats and returned to camp."

81. (p. 81) POINTE-AUX-TREMBLES, Aug. 8, 1759: Knox,
V, 45; Wolfe to Monckton, Aug. 4—Northcliffe Coll., p. 149.

82. (p. 51) KENNEDY-JACOB ST. FRANCIS MISSION, Aug. 8,
1759: Rogers, 144; Amherst, Aug. 8, 11, 19, Sept. 10-12;
Stockbridge Rangers captured were: Captain Jacob Naunauphataunk—released in 1760; Privates John Jacobs, and Abraham, also released. Others unknown.

83. (p.81) DALLING'S SCOUT, Aug. 9, 1759: Journal of the
particular transactions, Aug. 13th.

84. (p.81) GOREHAM'S ST. PAUL RAID, Aug. 10-18, 1759:
Goreham's official report to Wolfe, Camp at Pt. Levis, Aug.
18—Northcliffe Coll. pp. 140-141; Out of Goreham's force of
281 men, 1 was killed and 8 wounded. St. Anne's on the south
shore was fired on the 15th and a large store of grain was destroyed. Gorcham returned with his boats loaded with cattle.

85. (p. 81) MONTGOMERY'S MASSACRE, Aug. 23, 1759:
Lane, Aug. 22-24; Ranger Perry describes Hazen's ruse:
Montgomery's force landed at St. Joachim, "As soon as it was
light Capt. Hazen told his men to stroll back a few at a time,
undiscovered into the woods. As soon as we had done this the
regulars marched by fife and drum in a body round a point of
the woods, in order to draw the enemy there and we kept still
until they got between us and the regulars, when we rose and
fired on them and put them to flight immediately. Our orders
from Captain Montgomery were to 'kill all and give no quarter'
..." Fraser, Aug. 23: gives detailed account of massacre
and condemns Montgomery. Knox, Vol. II, p. 32; Parkman,
II, 261-2.

86. (p. 52) TUTE'S OTTER RIVER AMBUSCADE, Aug. 23, 1759: Mercury, Sept. 3, 1759, No. 368, gives best account. Amherst, Aug. 23, entry is critical.

87. (p. 53) FLETCHER'S FIGHT & CAPTURE, Aug. 27, 1759: Fletcher's official report to Amherst, Montreal, Sept. 4, 1759 —W.O.34, Vol. 78, f 10; Gazette-Journal, Sept. 17, No. 233; James Grant to Amherst, Montreal, Oct. 28, 1759—W.O.34, Vol. 78, f 105. Of the 5 Rangers taken and redeemed by the French from the Indians, only Lieutenant John Fletcher and Sergeant James Hackett were exchanged on November 15, 1759. The other 3 escaped prior to that time.—W.O.34, Vol. 8, ff 18-19; Tute to Amherst, Montreal, An Account of Money Disbursed to the Rangers then Prisoners at Montreal—W.O.34, Vol. 51, f 85. Amherst, records an interesting account of the affair on various dates as he received bits of information from other Ranger scouts and Fletcher's survivors who escaped; Aug. 31—"...Four Rangers who had been with Sergt. Hopkins came back with an account that the Lt. was going to be attacked & must have lost several men."
Sept. 4—"...A man of Ruggle's came in who was left with Lt. Fletcher's whale boat. He says some Indians came on him and another man who was left with the boat; took the other and he made his escape. At night an Indian came in from Lt. Fletcher's Party, said the Lieut was attacked by a great number and that he escaped; thinks the Lt and others taken. The French Prisoners declare one man was taken at the boat & brought on the Island; the other who was left with the boat is come here last night and two men from the Lieut when he was surrounded, so that he can have but five men left with him."
Sept. 10—"...By the Flag of Truce I had a Letter from Lt. Fletcher...I believe they behaved well."
News-Letter, Sept. 20, gives account and on Oct. 26: states that Lieutenant Lee of Whiting's Provincial Regiment was killed with 2 Rangers in the fight.

88. (p. 56) TUTE'S LA GALLETE MISSION, Aug. 26-Sept. 22, 1759: Moreau St. Thery Coll., Vol 13, f 308—Translation of orders and instructions of Amherst to Captain Tute; Bourlamaque Coll., Vol 5, ff 85-8—Copy of Tute's report to Gage relating his difficulties. Amherst's orders to Tute, Crown Pt, Aug. 26—W.O.34, Vol 80, f 151, states: "...as you have two men with you who have resided there for some time you may by their help reconnoitre it thoroughly without risk...Inform no one of these instructions." Amherst's orders to the Serjt and 5 Rangers who were to meet Tute with provisions, Crown Pt, Sept. 22—W.O.34, Vol 81, f 34. Gage to Amherst, Oswego, Oct. 2—W.O.34 Vol 46A, f 51; James Grant to Amherst, Montreal, Oct. 28 W.O.34, Vol 78, f 105; Amherst, Aug. 26, states that a "Mr. Swetenham", evidently a guide, went with Tute; Sept. 18, he received letter of distress from Tute, who also mentions that the weather had been extremely bad. Only 2 Rangers captured with Tute were exchanged with him on Nov.

15, 1759. They were: Sergeant McKane and Private Timothy Hopkinson. The fate of the other three is unknown—W.O. 34, Vol 8, f 6-7. During his seven weeks captivity at Montreal Tute maintained an active loan business with fellow Rangers. He loaned 15 Rangers a total of 1,060 pounds to assist them in buying necessities—W.O. 34, Vol 51, f 85.

<u>89</u>. (p. 56) THE ST. FRANCIS RAID, Sept. 13-Oct. 4—Nov. 1759: While the account in this work is comprehensive we must recommend our exhaustive account in the separate limited edition volume entitled: "ABENAKI APHRODITE—Rogers' St. Francis Raid—Fact, Legend and Lost Treasure."

RANGER ACCOUNTS: Rogers, 144-160, gives his official account to Amherst relating from his arrival at St. Francis. However, he fills in the gaps in the text of his <u>Journals</u>. Rogers' original document dated Nov. 1, is not among the Amherst Papers. The sufferings of the Rangers in their retreat is related by Lieutenant George Campbell to Captain Thomas Mante who recorded it in his <u>History</u>; Also, Sergeant Evans who gave two different versions to the historians, C. Stark and Potter, pp 161-62 and p 335 respectively. The owl eating episode is related by an anonymous Ranger to Hoyt, p 306, ftn. A Ranger of Sergeant Phillips' party tells of their hunger to Hoyt p 335. Stark, p 449, writes: "One Ranger, instead of more important plunder, placed in his knapsack a large lump of tallow which supported him on his way home, while many, who had secured more valuable plunder, perished with hunger."
Loescher's "Abenaki Aphrodite," reveals an Anonymous Rogers Ranger Diary with much new and valuable data on the Raid, the 'Aphrodite,' the routes of Rogers' divided parties, and the fate of Marie-Jeanne. Verbatim documentary accounts. Complete calendar of newly discovered English and French accounts. The lost and buried treasure of Saint Francois. Several St. Francis Abenaki accounts, and considerable more. The most complete and definitive study of the Raid.
LEGEND OF THE SILVER MADONNA: "L'histoire a verite; la legende a la sienne" from Drake, Chapter VI, pp 263-66. Probably one of the Indians escaped from the mission before it burned to the ground and was able to give an account of the poignant drama that was enacted in the chapel. After a curse was laid upon them from a voice from the dead, the Legend relates that a singular phenomenon occurred—as Bradley's party were leaving the chapel they had fired they heard the bell tolling ominously from the belfry, although there was no living person in the chapel. Although the firing of the Mission was wanton destruction and inexcusable, still it probably would have caught fire from the burning town and been consumed anyway. All the precious objects except the Silver Madonna were destroyed or taken. In 1700 the St. Francis Indians (Abenakis) sent the Dean of the Chapter of Chartres a collar of beads and porcupine quills and he responded by sending them the image

of the Blessed Mother in silver, exactly like the one the Dean had in his subterranean church. In 1749 he also sent a silver chemise which was destroyed. From C. Stark's (pp 160-61) and Bouton, (p 194) it appears that Sergeant Bradley (aged 21) died on the site of the present town of Jefferson, N.H. Before he expired he probably gave his 3 Rangers—Hoit, Pomeroy and Jacob, the negro—directions how to reach Concord, N.H. His one grave error was in mistaking the Upper Cohase for the lower Cohase. Apparently Bradley's directions to his Rangers were accurate enough, even though his calculation of the distance was far off, for they got as far as Lake Winnipesaukee, which was in the general direction of Concord and would no doubt have reached their destination if two had not succumbed to starvation. Sources: Bishop de Pontbriand to a Bishop of France Montreal, Nov. 5, 1759—in D.R.C.H.N.Y., X, 1058; Stone, II, p 108; Roberts, II, p 45.

PARTICIPANTS IN THE ST. FRANCIS EXPEDITION: ROGERS RANGERS—Major Robert Rogers, Captain Joseph Wait, Lieutenants Jacob Farrington, Abernathan Cargyll, George Campbell, George Turner, Andrew McMullen,** "Bill" Phillips, Sergeants Benjamin Bradley,* Evans and Wait, Privates Robert Pomeroy,* Stephen Hoit,* Andrew Wansant; Sergeant Phillip.

PROVINCIALS—Captain Amos Ogden commanded the Provincials, besides 9 of his Company of the N.J. Regiment, there were Captain Butterfield,** Lieutenant Noah Grant (of Connecticut), Jenkins,* Ensign Elias Avery of Fitch's Connecticut Regiment; Sergeant Moses Jones of Preston, Conn., in Capt. Crary's Connecticut Company—held prisoner for two months; Corporal Frederick Curtiss of Canterbury, Conn., in Fitch's Regiment—captured with Jones about Sept. 30th and held prisoner until middle of June, 1760. Privates Hewet, Lee and Ballard also captured with them but made their escape, except for Ballard who was killed. Private Samuel Fugard lost. Private Ebenezer Wheeler killed or died. Fifteen unidentified Provincials returned sick to Crown Point with Captain Butterfield.

REGULARS—Captain Williams of the Royals,** Lieutenant William Dunbar of Gage's 80th,* Volunteer Hugh Wallace of 27th. A Sergt of the 80th. 10 Privates of 80th,* Private Andrew McNeal of 27th. 2 Privates of the Royals,** 2 of the 80th,** 1 42nd Highlander,** 1 Montgomery Highlander,** all returned with Williams.

* denotes participants who were killed.

** denotes participants who were sent back and did not take part in the raid.

Unfortunately all the names of the raiders cannot be ascertained. The above incomplete list is gleaned from Rogers, Amherst, Stephen's Courtmartial Proceedings, Provincial War Records, Wheeler, Dibble.

BRITISH ACCOUNTS: Amherst, Sept. 10-14, 18, 19; Oct. 3-4, 9, 18, 25, 30; Nov. 2, 3, 7-8, 21. Amherst's Journal-Letters to Pitt in Corr of Pitt, II, pp 187, 195-6, 219-20, 224 amplify his original Journal.

Considerable correspondence on the raid was discovered in the Amherst Papers, W.O. 34: England.

A complete calendar of the English documents relative to the Raid are in the Appendix of Loescher: 'Abenaki Aphrodite—Rogers St. Francis Raid.' See also Notes 81-84 of this book ('Genesis') for partial listing.

PROVINCIAL ACCOUNTS: are many and redundant of praise— N.H. Gazette, No 175, Feb. 8, 1760, writes: "What do we owe to such a beneficial Man; and a man of such an enterprising genius." The N.Y. Mercury, No 380, Nov. 26, prints Rogers' official report to Amherst with the interesting addition that Rogers arrived at Number Four with "Capt. Gordon and 1 man more." The paper signs "R. Rogers" with a half inch spread and adds, "The indefatigable and brave Major Rogers." The same paper, No 371, Sept. 24, reports Rogers either killed or wounded—So conflicting were the first accounts that preceded Rogers' official report. No. 372, Oct. 1, states that "Captain Williams... and a few more were wounded in stepping over some logs by their Pieces going off, but slightly. They were sent back." News-Letter, Sept. 28, states that Captain Ogden commanded the Provincials under Rogers. On Oct 4, the paper guessed that Rogers' goal was the destruction of a small settlement at St. Peters. By Nov. 8, the paper was receiving accounts from Rutland, etc. of the raid and Rogers' arrival at Number Four. The Feb. 7, 1760 copy states that the Indian boy captured by Rogers was left in N.Y. in a School. The two young girls also captured died of smallpox in Albany. Moore, I, 234, writes that the boy was Sabatis, a brother to the famous Mrs. Johnson, who was captured five years before and held captive at St. Francis until 1757. A Ranger recovered a bundle of her husband's papers and returned them to her at Number Four where she was living in 1759. Wells, pp 13-14: offers conflicting accounts derived from participating Rangers on the exact spot of Lieutenant Stevens' hurried departure. However, Stevens' Courtmartial reveals that he was ordered by Amherst to await Rogers at Well's River. Stevens and his party offered the lame excuse that the Connecticut was too rapid above Cohase to hazard provision-laden canoes (actually there are no rapids). Consequently, from his base at Cohase, Stevens, or three hired men, went daily to Wells' River, which was three miles by land, and fired signal guns.

FRENCH ACCOUNTS: Governor Vaudreuil at Montreal wrote Bourlamaque, Commandant at Isle aux Noix, 8 anxious letters respecting Rogers' Raiders: 2 letters on Oct. 3, 1759; one on Oct. 5, 6, 7, 8, 15, Nov. 10th. Bourlamaque, II (Lettres Vaudreuil), pp 393-400, 401-404, 405-408, 413-416, 409-12, 417-20, 421, 424, 491-94. Other Documentary Sources: Pontleroy to Bourlamaque, Three Rivers, Oct. 6—Bourlamaque, III pp 159-60; Rigaud to Bourlamaque, Montreal, Aug. 23, Bourlamaque, IV, 105-08; Ibid, Sept. 20, pp 145-8. Anonymous French Diary in D.R.C.H.N.Y., X, 1042. Evenements de la Guerre en Canada, 1759, p 72. Levis, V, pp 47, 49, 55. Vaudreuil to Minister, Oct. 26th. Pouchot, I, 222-23. A complete calendar in Loescher, Abenaki Aphrodite-Rogers' St. Francis Raid.

NORTHWEST PASSAGE, Special Limited Edition, Volume II, comprises the Appendix to this unequaled Novel. Besides other pertinent material on Rogers it contains the 'Pennoyer Narrative,' an interesting account by a surviving St. Francis Indian chief, who for some unexplainable reason states that Rogers ambushed his pursuers inflicting a crushing defeat on them. Documentary comments on this may be found in Loescher, 'Abenaki Aphrodite-Rogers St. Francis Raid...'

90. (p. 66) BURBANK's SHIPWRECKERS FIGHT, Oct. 9-23, 1759: Amherst, Oct. 9, 23rd.

91. (p. 66) DALYELL-BREWER FEINT ON ISLE AUX NOIX, Oct. 20, 1759: Amherst, Oct. 18: "...One of the Enemy's Sloops was so far repaired of all the damage done to her that ...I sent Capt Dalyel with 100 of Gage's & as many Rangers to Capt Loring to assist in looking into any of the bays for him that the Schooner may not escape..." Oct. 23: "...Capt Dalyel came in...He had been with the Brig at the Isle La Motte & had reconnoitred to the Isle au Noix where the Schooner was got in by going round the Grand Isle. They fired one shot at them from the Island...They will concluded Dalyel was with the advanced Guard & have expected the Army..."

92. (p. 61) ENSIGN AVERY'S FIGHT, Oct. 16, 1759: Rogers, 149.

93. (p. 61) TURNER-DUNBAR MASSACRE, Oct. , 1759: Rogers, 157, Amherst to Pitt, Nov. 21, 1759. Text Correction: Dunbar was the only officer killed.

94. (p. 67) NOVEMBER FOURTH ISLE AUX NOIX SCOUT,1759: War Office 34, Vol 8, ff 18-19.

95. (p.84) RANGER PAYROLL MASSACRE, Feb. 12, 1760: Rogers, pp 160-61; Gage to Amherst, Albany, Feb. 19, 1760 —W.O.34, Vol 46A, f 87; Same to Same, Feb. 27, Vol 46A, f 90; Amherst to Gage, N.Y., Feb. 22—Vol 46A, f 211; Haviland to Amherst, Crown Point, Mary 24—Vol 51, f 13; states that Rogers found Langy's "Combustibles" (to burn the British shipping) when he returned to the scene of the holdup the next day. Robert Rogers to Amherst, Albany, May 23—Vol 82, f 219. One of the Four Rangers taken alive to Montreal was Sergeant Thomas Beverly.
Haviland to Amherst, Crown Point, May 8—Vol 51, f 19; James Tute to Amherst, Vol 51, f 85.
The N.H. Gazette, No 178, Feb. 29, 1760, deviates from Rogers Journal by stating that he owed his escape to being in the first sleigh which Langy let pass in order to surprise the rest. News-Letter, Feb. 28, Mar. 13; Pitt, II, 263-64. Capt Tute's Account of goods for Major Rogers' Co. taken...Feb. 12... certified by Rogers—Vol 199, f 91

96. (p.114) HAZEN'S COWBOY EXPLOIT, Feb. 9, 1760: Knox, II, Feb. 10: "...A detatchment of French Grenadiers under M. Dumas are skulking in the neighborhood of our post at Lorette; Captain Hazen with 25 Rangers only, surprised a large party of them, two nights ago, who were driving off some cattle, when they found they were discovered, they took to their heels in the most precipitate manner, without firing a shot, the Rangers pursued them above a mile, calling after them to stand and fight him (For says he my fellows feel bold at the repeated success of the regulars and wish for an opportunity to distinguish themselves in like manner); but the Captain perceiving they retired towards a strong defile and apprehending a snare might there have been laid for him, thought proper to discontinue the pursuit and contented himself with recovering the cattle, which were returned to their respective owners..."

97. (p.114) Point Levi, Feb. 24, 1760: Knox, II, eb. 24.

98. (p. 115) OLD LORETTE, Mar. ___, 1760: Ibid, March. Rangers suffered 3 men wounded. Hazen burned their house and retired to Lorette where they were less isolated.

99. (p.118) BATTLE OF STE FOY, Apr. 28, 1760: Knox, II, Apr. 28; Revue Candienne, IV, 865, for Hazen's marksmanship. Fraser, Apr. 28; Johnson, Ibid. News-Letter Aug. 28, 1760: "...Captain Hazen...who behaved in a most gallant manner and was wounded in his thigh is since recover'd..."

100. (p.118) SECOND SIEGE OF QUEBEC, Apr. 28-May 17, 1760: Knox, Apr.-May.

101. (p.118) MAY FOURTH SALLY, 1760: Knox, May 5th.

102. (p.90) THE MAIL-PATROL HOLDUP, May 9, 1760: John Campbell to Amherst, Ticonderoga, May 9—War Office 34, Vol 50, f 13. Amherst, May 12-13th.

103. (p.91) DECOY AMBUSCADE AT POINTE AU FER, May 10, 1760: Lieutenant Alexander Grant to Haviland, eight miles opposite Ile aux Noix on H.M. Brig The Duke of Cumberland, May 15, W.O.34, Vol 51, ff 24-5; Haviland to Amherst, Crown Point, May 18—Vol 51, f 22.

104. (p.95) BATTLE OF POINTE AU FER, June 6, 1760: Rogers, 179-181. Anonymous Ranger Account in News-Letter, Sept. 4, 1760. Amherst's orders to Rogers, May 25, 1760, Albany—W.O.34, Vol 84, f 204; Amherst to Haviland, June 10, 11-Vol 52, ff 46-7. Haviland to Amherst, Crown Point, June 8-Vol 51, ff 45-7 (two letters). Surgeon James Jameson to Amherst, on board the brig Cumberland, June 18—Vol 82, ff 246-7. Amherst to Monckton, Albany, June 11—Northcliffe Coll, Vol XVI. Amherst, May 26, 27; June 4, 10-11. Vaudreuil to Dumas, Montreal, June 11, writes a skillfully worded account in which he neither claims a victory or defeat. Can.

Arch. Rep. 1905, I, 45. Ranger Goodenough, a participant gives a good account.

<u>105</u>. (p. 102) THE STE. THERESE RAID, June 11-20, 1760: Rogers, pp 181-188. Haviland to Amherst-W.O. 34, Vol 51, f 47; Same to Same, June 13, 29, 24—Vol 51, ff 48, 52, 63. Robert Rogers to Amherst, on Board the Duke of Cumberland, June 21, 1760 (official report of Raid)—Vol 51, f 55. Capt. Alexander Grant to Haviland, Island Mote, June 21—Vol 51, ff 59-60.
Ste d Etrese dated from 1664. In that year Captain de Salieres of the Carignan Regiment was ordered with two other Captains to build forts on the Richelieu River to block the Iroquois avenue of marauding. M. de Salieres built his fort nine miles above Chambly which he named St. d Etrese, because it was finished on St. Theresa's feast day. St. d Etrese was the rendezvous for many French and Indian raids to the Mohawk settlements. Relations de ce qui s'est passes en la Nouv France en Annes 1665-6. As a consequence of Rogers' Raid not only Isle aux Noix was reinforced but the regiments of La Reine and Royal Rousillon were sent to Saint John's and strengthened by a detachment of militia from Montreal. Kingsford, IV, 398. Subsequent French prisoners revealed that the French Indians suffered heavily at Pointe au Fer and that they all returned to their villages to bury their dead. News-Letter, July 10.

<u>106</u>. (p. 102) MISSIQUOI BAY (ADVANCE GUARD ACTION), June 20, 1760; Rogers, 185.

<u>107</u>. (p. 107) POINT ROGERS, July 8, 1760: Haviland to Amherst, Crown Point, July 21—W.O. 34, Vol 51, f 67. Frost, July 8, 11. Holden, July 8, 9. Jenks, July 8, 9, 10. N.H. Gazette, No 199, July 25.

<u>108</u>. (p. 119) POINT PLATON, July 18, 1760: Knox, II, Ibid.

<u>109</u>. (p. 125) SIEGE OF FORT LEVIS, Aug. 18-25, 1760: Amherst, Aug. 18-25. Amherst's Orders, Aug. 20-V.85, f 50.

<u>110</u>. (p. 109) SOUNDING PATROL MISSION, Aug. 18, 1760: Heath, Aug. 10. Holden, Aug. 18. Heath, Aug. 19.

<u>111</u>. (p. 108) SIEGE OF ISLE AUX NOIX, Aug. 19-27, 1760: Rogers, 188-192, Holden, Aug. 18-28. Hodge, Ibid. Heath Ibid. Colonel Haviland's Journal from Crown Point to opposite Montreal, Aug. 11-Sept. 3, 1760—W.O. 34, Vol 77, ff 130-31. Jenks, Aug. 28, states: that Haviland would allow no Ranger, Provincial or Indian on the captured Isle aux Noix. This was considered "a very high-handed affair." There is a rare map in the Clements Library MSS: "Montressor Maps, Map No. 15 —Fort Isle aux Noix, 1760."

<u>112</u>. (p. 110) CAPTURE OF FRENCH FLEET, Aug. 25, 1760: Rogers, 190-191. Jenks, Aug. 25: "... We have not lost a man

in this affair, altho the action was very sharp. We have killed a field officer of theirs who was on board and have taken their commodore and about 20 men prisoners." Haviland, Heath, MacClintock, Aug. 25.

__113__. (p. 110) PURSUIT OF BOUGAINVILLE, Aug. 30, 1760: Rogers, 192-3. Holden, Aug. 30. Jenks, Ibid.

__114__. (p.120) FIRST ACTION AT VARENNES, Aug. 31, 1760: Knox, II, Aug. 31.

__115__. (p.111) FORT CHAMBLY, Sept. 1, 1760: Rogers, 194.

__116__. (p.120) THE LAST BATTLE (SECOND ACTION AT VARENNES), Sept. 1, 1760: Knox, Sept. 1.

__117__. (p.126) MONTREAL, Sept. 8, 1760: Rogers, 195-6. Amherst, Sept. 7-9.

__118__. (p. 127) EXPEDITION TO RECEIVE SURRENDER OF WESTERN FRENCH FORTS, Sept. 13-Nov. 29, 1760: Amherst's order to Robert Rogers, Montreal, Sept. 12—W.O.34, Vol 85, f 34. Amherst to Major Walters, commanding at Niagara. Sept. 12—Vol 23, ff 41-2. Brehm, Sept. 13-Feb. 23, 1760-61. Account of Pay for the Detachment of Rangers that went under... Major Rogers to Detroit, Oct. 25, 1760-Mar. 24, 1761 (151 days), Vol 199, f 95. Amherst, Sept. 12, 1760; Jan. 18, Feb. 4, 14, 1761.
There are three existing copies of Rogers Journal of his Expedition, all have variations. His printed account in his Journals is on pp 197-236. Major Robert Rogers Detroit Journal to General Robert Monckton, N.Y., Feb. 27, 1761, edited by Victor Hugo Paltsits,1933. The official account to Amherst is in W. O.34, Vol 7.
On March 3, 1761, Major Rogers at New York presented his bill for the expenses he incurred on his expedition. He titled the 882/8/8 statement: "The Government to Major Rogers—W. O.34, Vol 199, ff 173. In the "Abstract of Major Rogers' Claim against the Crown while in command of H.M. Independent Companies of Rangers," May 18, 1761-Vol 199, ff 213-14—Rogers asks for 16/12/10 for Lieutenant Holmes' expenses in bringing away part of the garrison of Detroit—and 11/1/1 for his five Ranger Sergeants "who marched with the French Prisoners from Detroit, because of the unexpected length of their march, they were obliged to trade their personal possessions to the Indians to procure food for themselves and their French prisoners."
News-Letter, Jan. 22, Feb. 12, 1761. Bouquet Coll.: Robert Rogers to Bouquet, Dec. 1, 1760—A. 14 B.M. 21, 645, Vol III; Bouquet to Lt. Holmes (to proceed to Philadelphia with French prisoners), Ft. Pitt, Dec. 27, 1760. Johnson Papers:

Amherst to Johnson, N.Y., Feb. 1, 1760, III, 316; George Croghan to Johnson, Presque Isle, Nov. 1, 1760-III, 276; Ibid, Ft. Pitt, Jan. 13, 1761—III, 301-3. Croghan's Journal was published in the Pa. Mag. of History, Oct. 1947.

Eighty-two Ranger officers and men remained at Niagara until Christmas 1760. They marched to Albany in January 1761 and were mustered out. The two Captains, Jonathan Brewer and Joseph Waite, journeyed to New York where they waited on Amherst. Amherst's Warrants, Feb. 2, 1761, to pay Wait to Dec. 24, 1760, for himself, Lt. Atherton, 2 Sergeants and 20 Privates—W.O. 34, Vol 199, f 41; Warrant of Feb. 4, to pay Brewer, 4 Sergeants and 53 Privates to Dec. 24—Vol 199, f 43.

CHEROKEE-ENGLISH WAR

<u>120</u>. (p.150) SECOND BATTLE OF ETCHOE PASS, June 10, 1761: Grant, June 10. N.Y. Mercury, Aug. 3, 1761, No 470: Extract of a letter from an officer in Col. Middleton's Regiment. Extract from a letter of a Regular officer—Losses of Rogers Rangers, if any, are unknown. Philopatrios, March 26, 1762. Corkran, pp 236-254, French, June entries.

CONQUEST OF THE FRENCH WEST INDIES

<u>119</u>. (p.143) CAPTURE OF DOMINICA, June 6, 1761:

<u>121</u>. (p.144) BATTLE OF MORNE TORTENSON, Jan. 24, 1762: W.O. 34, Vol 55, f 58. Return of Joseph Waite's Company, Ft. Royal, Apr. 17, 1762-Vol 200, f 254.

<u>122</u>. (p.145) BATTLE OF MORNE GRENIER, Jan. 27, 1762: Ibid, Vol 55, f 60.

PONTIAC'S WAR

<u>123</u>. (p.155) RELIEF OF DETROIT, July 29, 1763: Rogers, July 29; McDonald, Ibid.

<u>124</u>. (p.158) BATTLE OF BLOODY BRIDGE, July 31, 1763: McDonald, July 31. T. De Couagne to Wm. Johnson, Niagara, Aug. 24, 1763—Hough, Siege of Detroit, 60-61; 56.

AMERICAN REVOLUTIONARY WAR

<u>124A</u>. (p.170) CAPTURE OF LOUNSBERRY, Aug. 29, 1776: Heath. Cuneo (4), pp 67-68: Lounsberry between 50-60 years old made a heroic stand in a cave and held off his attackers with a club until he was dispatched by seven bayonets.

<u>125</u>. (p.172) ROGERS' MAMARONECK RAID, Oct. 21, 1776: Hadaway, pp 20-1.

<u>126</u>.(p.175) BATTLE OF HEATHCOTE'S HILL, Oct. 22, 1776: Hadaway, pp 20-26: gives most detailed account. Hough, F.

O.: Chapter VIII, Heathcote's Hill, pp 165-184, portrays a dramatic but accurate account. Ranger Devoe, p 118. Jones J.E., Manuscript. Cuneo (4), pp 70-71.

RANGERS CAPTURED: Joseph Dean, Stephen Law, Elijah Carle, John Angevine, Joseph Carle, Walter Brown, Gillbert Myers, Frederick Devoie, David Lawrence, James Angevine John Charlick, Moses Travis, Elnathan Appleby, Jacob Cadwell Burr, Reuben Stives, David Travis, Josiah Worden, Elijah Bartoe, Jonathan Asten, Francis Besly, James Tharpe, Solomon Parent, Jonathan Ecly, Stephen Travis, James Kennedy, Abraham Brown, Jedediah Davis, Wm. Washburn. They were marched to New Hampshire and confined in gaol. American Arch. III, p 470.

AMERICAN ACCOUNTS: Colonel Haslett to General Rodney, Oct. 28, 1776—Sparks, IV, 526. Washington to the Continental Congress, White Plains, Oct. 25—Sparks IV, 524. Tench Tilghman to Wm. Duer, Oct. 22, 1776—Amer. Arch., III, 576. Ward, pp 78-82, 559. Cuneo's: Early Days of the Queen's Rangers.

<u>127</u>. (p.176) ROGERS' BEDFORD RAID, Oct. 23, 1776: Mackenzie, Oct. 26, 1776.

<u>128</u>. (p.176) BATTLE OF WHITE PLAINS, Oct. 28, 1776: Almon, IV, 205. The Corps apparently suffered no losses—Howe's official list in Amer. Archives, II, 1056.

<u>129</u>. (p.176) ENGAGEMENT ON NORTH ST., Oct. 31, 1776: Hadaway, 62: "... Captain Van Wyck, who commanded a company of American Rangers attached to General George Clinton's brigade, was unfortunately killed. He went out in the morning with about thirty men, to patrol upon the enemy's right. At a house in North Street, he fell in with a detachment of Rogers Rangers and instantly attacked them, although superior to him in numbers. Having discharged his musket, he was in the act of reloading. While so engaged one of Rogers Rangers shot him through the brain... In a moment after, his death was avenged by his lieutenant, who killed the hostile ranger and brought off the Captain's body..."

<u>130</u>. (p.176) BATTLE OF FORT WASHINGTON, Nov. 16, 1776: Hannay, p 125.

<u>131</u>. (p.176) HACKENSAC BRIDGE, Nov. 21, 1776: Kemble, I, p 411, Greene, F.V., pp 59-60.

<u>132</u>. (p.177) DEFENSE OF FORT INDEPENDENCE, Jan. 18-23, 1777: Kemble, I, 108.

<u>133</u>. (p.181) DEFENSE OF CASTINE, Aug. 11, 1779: Robert Rogers to Haldimand, Ft. Howe, River St. Johns, September 26, 1779—Haldimand, B. 160, p 17.

134. (p.199) BLACK JONES SECOND KENNEBEC RAID, June ___, 1780: John Jones to Reverend Bailey, Sept. 4, 1780—North, J.W., p. 158.

135. (p.187) CAPTURE OF FORT ANNE, Oct. 10-11, 1780: Kingsford, VII, 40-43. Tic. Mus. Bul., July 1946, p 3-12. Mathews to Major James Rogers, Que., Sept. 4, 1780—Haldimand, B160, p 64; Major James Rogers to Mathews, Chambly, Sept. 8—Ibid, pp 65-8.

136. (p.187) SARATOGA RAID, Oct. 10, 1780: Kingsford, VII, 40-3. Tic. Mus. Bul., July 1946.

137. (p.188) BATTLE OF FORT GEORGE, Oct. 11, 1780: Ibid.

138. (p.188) ST. LEGER'S EXPEDITION, May 1781: Ibid.

139. (p.188) MYERS' BALLSTOWN RAID, June 13, 1781: Ibid. Names of the people taken prisoners by Myers on June 13th—Haldimand, B161, 275. John Myers to Mathews, St. John's, July 8—Ibid, 283.

140. (p.195) TYLER'S SQUIRE PALMER MISSION, July 1780: Lt. Tyler's official report—Haldimand, B.182, p 421.

140-A (p.192) CAPTURE OF BEATIE; July, 1781: B.177-2, p 399. B.177-1, p 171.

141. (p.190) PRITCHARD'S CAPTURE AT CORINTH, Aug. 1781: Sherwood & Smyth to Mathews, Loyal Blockhouse, Aug. 11—Haldimand, B.176, p 209.

142. (p.192) MYERS' ENGAGEMENT AT BLAKE'S HOUSE, Aug. 1781: John W. Myers to Mathews, St. John's, Aug. 18—Haldimand, B.161, pp 316-7; Ibid, 319. Mathews to Myers, Que., Aug. 23-Ibid, B.163, p 111.

142-A. (p.192) MYERS' RAID ON SCHUYLER'S HOUSE, Sept. 1781; B.182, p 431.

143. (p.190) PRITCHARD'S SPY CAPTURE, Oct. 17, 1781: Pritchard to Mathews, St. John's, Oct. 21—Haldimand, B.161. pp 338-9.

144. (p.194) STEPHEN'S CAPTURE AT MONCKTON, April 1782: Roger Stephens to Matthews, Loyal Blockhouse, April 5—Haldimand, B.177-1, pp 178-80.

145. (p.190) PRITCHARD'S FIGHT AT BAILEY'S HOUSE, June 1782; Smyth to Mathews, St. John's, June 1—Ibid, B.177-1, p 330. Ibid, B.177-2, p 364. Pritchard to Mathews, St. John's, June 21—Ibid, pp 367-70. Joseph White to Mathews, St. John's,

July 7—Ibid, 378. Smyth to Mathews, St. John's, July 17—Ibid, 388.

The American accounts clarify the failure of Pritchard's daring odyssey: "The Bayley family, in this region (Newbury, Orange County, Vt.), a role similar to that performed by the Allens on the other side of the Green Mountains. The rear wooden section of the Ox-Bow Antique Shop, at the south end of Newbury Village, was Jacob Bailey's residence. Bayley was plowing on the day that... Lieutenant Pritchard, and his Tory followers came to capture him. Thomas Johnson, on parole from the British, was aware of the plot but unable to warn his friend personally, because the Tory ambuscade overlooked the Bayley meadow. Johnson contrived the warning by sending another man to the field, not to speak to Bailey, but to drop a slip of paper bearing the following message: 'The Philistines be upon thee, Samson.' Bayley escaped across the river to Haverhill, but that evening Pritchard took four prisoners from the Bayley home, including one of Jacob's sons. But for the courage of a defiant housemaid who barred their entrance, [Pritchard] would have seized more captives."—Bearse, R., p 296.

146. (p.195) GREEN'S POUGHKINSIE SCOUT, Jan. 1783: Sherwood to Mathews, Loyal Blockhouse, Jan. 31—B.178, 46.

NOTE: Actions 1-22 are in THE HISTORY OF ROGERS RANGERS, The Beginnings, 1755-Apr. 6, 1758, by Loescher.
From 23-146: Ninety were victories, thirty-eight were defeats (numbers 24, 28, 29, 34, 36, 37, 40, 41, 45, 48, 49, 52-3, 57-9, 65, 71, 81-3, 87-8, 90, 92-5, 99, 102, 107, 110, 124-124a, 126, 131, 138, 140a).

APPENDIX III
SOURCES AND NOTES FOR EVERY RECORDED SCOUT,
EXPEDITION AND INDIVIDUAL FIGHT, APRIL 1758-1783
*Designates successful Scouts and Expeditions

48.* (p 28) HALIFAX WOODS PATROLS, Apr. 12-May, 1758: Cutter, Ibid.

49.* (p 20) SHEPHERD'S SOUTH BAY SCOUT, May 1758: Rogers, p 105.

50.* (p 20) BURBANK'S SCOUT, May 1758: Ibid.

51.* (p 20) ROGERS' MAY FIFTH CROWN POINT AMBUSCADE; Rogers, pp 106-7. Pitt Corr, I, p 255.

52.* (p 26) STARK'S MAY FIFTH TICONDEROGA EXPLOIT: Rogers, pp 105, 108.

53.* (p 29) RANGERS' JUNE FIFTH LANDING FEINT: Amherst, June 5, 1758.

54.* (p 31) JUNE 11TH BLOODHOUND SCOUT: Montressor, J., June 10-11.

55.* (pp 32-8) CONSTRUCTION OF THE LIGHTHOUSE BATTERY, June 12-19, 1758: Brigadier Wolfe's Intentions at the Lighthouse Point. Wolfe to Amherst, June 19--

56. (p 7) HARTWELL'S ACCIDENTAL SCOUT, June 20, 1758: News-Letter, July 6.

57. (p 7) KERR'S ACCIDENTAL SCOUT, June 24, 1758: Ibid, July 13.

58.* (p 8) JUNE 23RD PRE-INVASION SCOUTS: Rogers, 110-11. Lyon, June 23.

59.* (p 8) HOLMES' RECONNAISSANCE, July 5-6, 1758: Rogers, 111-12.

60.* (p 12) JULY SEVENTH COURIER CAPTURE: News-Letter, July 13.

61.* (p 14) ROGERS' SOUTH BAY SCOUT, July 15, 1758: Rogers, pp 116-17.

62.* (p 14) JACOB'S MONTCALM LANDING SCOUT, Ibid.

63.* (p 21) BREWER'S SIXTY GUINEAS SCOUT, July 15, 1758: Amherst, July 15. Knap, July 16. Bougainville, 273.

64. (p 15) ROGERS' PURSUIT OF LA CORNE, July 29, 1758: Rogers, 117. Cleaveland, Rea, July 31. Hart was acquitted as well as Davis-Rea, Sept. 4.

65. (p 20) ROGERS' FORT MILLER SCOUT, Aug 11, 1758: Rogers, 119.

66.* (p 18) THE POST MORTEM SCOUT, Aug 15, 1758: Rogers, 119. Rea, Aug. 16.

67.* (p 21) FORT EDWARD ALARM, Aug. 16, 1758: Rea, Lyon, Aug. 16: Rangers report French at S. Bay.

68. (p 20) THE BARKING DOGS SCOUT, Aug. 21-30, 1758: Rea, Aug. 21, 30.

69.* (p 22) SHEPHERD'S TICONDEROGA RECONNAISSANCE, Aug. 31-Sept. 2, 1758: Rea, Ibid.

70. (p 22) DALYELL'S WOOD CREEK SCOUT, Sept. 2-7, 1758: Lyon, Rea, Sept. 4, 7, 9.

71.* (p 22) ROGERS' SUBSTANTIATION SCOUT, Sept. 3-7, 1758: Lyon, Rea, Sept. 3, 7.

72.* (p 23) SEPTEMBER 9-26TH CROWN POINT SCOUT, 1758: Rea, Ibid.

73.* (p 23) FORT ANNE SCOUT, Sept. 11, 1758: Lyon, Ibid, Josh Barrit and a Ranger made the uneventful scout.

74.* (p 23) WOOD-CREEK SCOUT, Sept. 26-8, 1758: Lyon, Sept. 26-8.

75. (p 34) GOREHAM'S CAPE SABLE RAID, Sept. 1758: Two Lieutenants, 1 Ensign, 2 Sergeants of McCurdeys and W. Stark's and 56 Privates of Stark's were in the expedition. Monckton's Sept. 24th Return—AB 949.

76. (p 23) ROGERS' LAST 1758 SCOUT, Sept. 24-9: Rea, Sept. 24-30: 200 Rangers in whaleboats.

77.* (p23) NUMBER FOUR, N.H.SCOUT, Oct. 4, 1758: Lyon, Oct. 4.

78. (p 24) SCALP LIFTING AMBUSCADE, Oct. 30, 1758: News-Letter, Nov. 2.

79. (p 24) CAPTURE OF BLAKE, Nov. 1, 1758: W.O. 34, Vol 8, ff 18-19.

80.* (p 34) MCCURDY'S JEMSEG RAID, Nov. 6, 1758: Monckton, Nov. 6.

81.* (p 34) BREWER-DANKS' GRIMROSSE RAID, Nov. 6, 1758: Monckton, Nov. 6.

82.* (p 34) SCOTT'S PETICODIAC RAID, Nov. 11-18, 1758: Knox, Nov. 17. Monckton, Nov. 15.

83. (p 35) CROFTON'S ATTEMPTED RESCUE SCOUT, Nov. 16-17, 1758: Monckton, Nov. 16-17.

84. (p 24) CAPTURE OF FLAGG, Dec. 22, 1758: W.O. 34, Vol 8, ff 18-19.

85.* (p 37) JOHNSON'S CROWN POINT SCOUT, Feb. 16-Mar. 10, 1759: Captain Noah Johnson's official report, in Haldimand to Gage, March 16, 1759—Gage Mss. Gage suggested sending Johnson, he being a "good woodsman," Rogers being so often on scout that he should be spared. He ordered Haldimand to recall Johnson (on Feb. 18) to avoid his party's colliding with Lottridge's Mohawks en route to Ft. Edward. —Haldimand Coll., folio 7, 15.—Canadian Archives.

86. (p 74) MONTRESSOR'S LAKE LABRADOR SCOUT, Mar. 27-Apr. 3, 1759: Montressor, J.

87.* (p 42) HERWOOD-RANGER TICONDEROGA SCOUT, May 13, 1759: Herwood, a Volunteer from the Royal Regiment, accompanied the Rangers but "...his make was by much too Corpulent for a Speedy March..." and he died from fatigue.—W.O. 34, Vol 45, f 45—Amherst to Gov. DeLancey, Albany, May 24, 1759.

88.* (p 43) CROWN POINT INTELLIGENCE SCOUT, May 13, 1759: Amherst to Pitt, May 14. DeLancey to Amherst, N.Y., May 28—W.O. 34, Vol 29, f 73. Anonymous (Ranger officer Diary)—Commands Scout—May 14, 16, 20, 22 entries.

89. (p 44) ROGERS' ATTEMPTED REVENGE-AMBUSCADE, May 25-27, 1759: See p 350, line 19. Rogers' party to attempt to waylay French convoys above Ticonderoga comprised 300 men (Rangers, Indians and Light Infantry of the 55th). They left Ft. Edward on May 25, with 10 days provisions but were discovered the next day.—Amherst to Eyre, Albany, May 27—W.O. 34, Vol 54, ff 131-2; Same to Same, May 29—Ibid, f 133.

90.* (p 44) FOUR MILE POST PATROLS, May-June, 1759: Robert Rogers to Amherst, no date—W.O. 34, Vol 77, ff 76-7. Rogers' opinion of sending daily scouts from the Four Mile Post was adopted. His plan consisted of one daily scout East "as far as Ft. Anne Road, then bear from it Northwardly to Scoon Creek and from there to reconnoitre up the south side as far as the ponds from which place they will steer southeasterly to the post they set out from. A second scout to go Northwest from the encampment to Scoon Creek near the Ponds, from there to reconnoitre down the north side of the Creek while near Ft. Anne and from thence bear their courses to the Blockhouse on the hill near Ft. Edward. A third party to be sent from the Four Mile Post to where Scoon Creek and Wood Creek meet, where they will cross to the north side and march to the falls, then cross the Mountains that overlooks South Bay as far west as Diskeau's River and return back on the west side of it. Besides constant parties to reconnoitre for 3 or 4 miles Round the Fort. A fourth party from Half Way Brook to go north about 18 miles which will bring them opposite to South Bay and about 4 miles west of it, then to go east as far as Wood Creek and return by the Four Mile Post. A party daily to reconnoitre from the Half-Way Brook to Scoon Pond and from that four miles east and return across the woods. Besides constant parties to reconnoitre daily for 3 or 4 miles round the Post, a party likewise to go across to Hudson River near the mouth of Sacondago. The officers of the Rangers at those posts will be able to judge the proper quantities of provisions for those Scouts."

91.* (p 44) SACONDAGO RIVER SCOUT, June 6-13, 1759: Amherst, June 6, 13: Discovered fresh Indian trail.

92.* (p 44) OSWEGATCHIE RIVER SCOUT, June 7, 1759: Amherst, June 7: "...A German of the Marine brought Prisoner by a Scout from..." Oswegatchie on the River St. Lawrence.

93.* (p 44) MARTIN'S TICONDEROGA SCOUT, June 11, 1759: Amherst, June 11. Henshaw, June 24.

94.* (p 44) CROWN POINT PRE-EMBARKATION SCOUTS, June 12, 1759: Amherst, June 12, July 8: One of the two scouts sent, under Lieutenant Holmes, returned without any prisoners on July 8. On his return he was a witness to Jacob's Defeat on the Lake.

95.* (p 44) LAKE GEORGE SCOUTS, June 22-26, 1759: Amherst, June 22: "Sent out scouts to both sides the lake." Wood, June 24, 26. Anonymous (Ranger officer Diary) account, June 22, 1759, entry.

96.* (p 44) CONVOY DUTY, June 23-July 6, 1759: Wooster, June 23-July 6, from Ft. Edward to the Lake.

97.* (p 44) STARK'S RESCUE OF VOLUNTEER TRUMBULL, June 23-4, 1759: Amherst, June 23-4: "Mr. Trumbal of R. Highlanders and Paterson of Gages in a batteau a fishing had got too far out and were pursued by 3 boats, one of the three very wisely trying to get between them and the camp, and got ashore as soon as they did. So soon as they got ashore they run for it and Paterson came in about four in the afternoon and imagined the others would get in. I sent Capt. Stark out with a party to secure their retreat and try to catch the enemy." June 24: "The party came in in the morning. Mr. Trumbal had joined them as he was coming to camp, for on finding himself cut off he thought 'twas best towards Ticonderoga and he had with him got into a little Island where they intended to defend themselves..."

98.* (p 44) ROGERS-SHEPHERD SCOUT, June 24, 1759: Henshaw, June 24.

99. (p 45) STARK'S FISHING DECOYS, June 25, 27, 29, 1759: Amherst, June 25, 27, 29.

100.* (p 78) HAZEN'S ISLE ORLEANS BLOODHOUND SCOUT, July 2, 1759: Knox, July 2.

101. (p 44) PURSUIT OF N.J. MASSACRERS, July 2, 1759: Amherst, July 2: "About ten o'clock I heard several dropping shots; found immediately twas a party of Indians. I sent instantly to a Company of Light Infantry and Rangers and they were out as soon as possible. I saw the shots on the right of the rear of the camp and the officer commanding the Post on the right fired ten or a dozen shots before the Light Infantry or Rangers could get down. I added two more Companies of Light Infantry and three of Grenadiers to sustain, but before the first could get to the place where the firing was the Indians had made off. They creeped on a Sergt., Corporal and sixteen men of the Jersey Troops who were cutting brush. The Sergeant and five privates escaped and got into camp; six privates were killed and one Corporal and five privates missing. The Rangers pursued but could not overtake. Saw enemy off in 11 canoes. Anonymous (Ranger officer Diary) account, July 2, 1759 entry.

102. (p 44) CAMP PROTECTION SCOUTS, July 4, 1759: Amherst, July 4: "Sent a Light Infantry Company to the right and one to the left of the Lake with a party of Rangers to each Company to scour the woods and remain out all day to try to cut off any scalping party..."

103. (p 78) SCOTT'S RIVER CHAUDIERE SCOUT, July 6, 1759: Wolfe, July 7: pithily records "Major Scott returned without seeing the Etchemins River and la Chaudiere, some scattering shott from the woods and the sight of a few Indians determined him to retire." Bell, July 7, is also critical.

104. (p 44) CAPTURE OF RANGER TRIO, July 8, 1759: W. O.34, Vol 8, ff 18-19: Privates Juda Bills, Joseph Fisk and John Boyd were captured on Lake George. They were exchanged on November 15, 1759.

105.* (p 79) HAZEN'S NAVAL INTELLIGENCE SCOUT, July 9, 1759: Wolfe to Monckton, July 8—Northcliffe Coll, Vol XXII, p 146.

105A. (p 79) MCCORMICK'S BLOODY SCOUT, July 9, 1759: Knox—Ibid.

106.* (p 44) ROUTINE SCOUTS, July 16, 1759: Amherst, July 16.

107. (p 44) DECOY SCOUTS, July 11, 1759: Amherst, July 11.

108. (p 44) JULY 15TH-16TH MANEUVER, 1759: Amherst, July 15-16.

109.* (p 47) EMBARKATION SCOUT, July 19-20, 1759: Amherst to Governor DeLancey, July 20—W.O.34, Vol 30, f 61. Lieutenant Holmes led the reconnaissance.

110.* (p 47) SERGT WELLS' BREAD CONVOY, July 23, 1759: James Montressor to Amherst, Camp at Lake George, July 23 —W.O.34, Vol 77, f 105: "...If the Post doesn't come in before this Party is ready I shall send this to your Excellency by Wells' of Major Rogers' Company, who I send with 16 more Rangers in a Batteau with Bread that had been forgot. The rest of them here with two officers are all sick or pretend to be so. The same as many more men here who are a dead burden to the Community. All the sick certified by the Doctor were sent in empty Sutlers' wagons back to Fort Edward."

111.* (p 47) RANGERS SHARPSHOOTING DISTRACTION, July 25, 1759: Wooster, July 25.

112.* (p 80) CHAUDIERE RIVER EXPLORATION, July 26-28, 1759: Knox, July 26-8.

113. (p 48) SCALPING OF ENSIGN JONAS, July 28, 1759: News-Letter, Aug. 16.

114.* (p 49) ROGERS-ABERCROMBIE SECRET ROAD SURVEY, Aug. 1, 1759: Amherst, Aug. 1. A map was discovered in the British Crown Collection, untitled but with the endorsement: '1757. Mr. Abercrombie. A sketch of Ticonderoga.' There is mention of his working on this map in 1757—LO 5159. The map has a dotted line from Lake George to Wood Creek with a note stating "here Captt Rogers carried his boats across to Wood Creek." Abercrombie may have become first aware of Rogers' Water Passage in November 1757 from John Stark when they scouted together.—LO 4915, LO 5132; Loescher (1) p 355. Now he had a firsthand account surveyed tour by Rogers himself of his famous secret route. The route probably started near present day Huletts Landing and continued through the valley between Hogback and Spruce Mountains to the brook flowing into Wood Creek, passing north of Dresden Center to the inlet north of Chubbs Dock. For Rogers Rangerists seeking to follow the 'secret route' be sure to refer to a geodetic map showing the contours and elevations namely, the New York -Vermont, Whitehall Quadrangle, Geological Survey U.S. Department of the Interior, July 1902 map, reprinted in 1942.

Bougainville, after much surmising in five different theories finally, after reports by ascertaining expeditions, stated: "It is very likely that the armed barges came from the Chicot (Wood Creek) River, passing under the forts of Carillon and St. Frederic (Crown Point) by night. This idea is made more likely because several of the oars were bound with cloth."—pp 46-48, 51. Of course the French never did discover that Rogers' secret passage started in Lake George. See map on end pages of Loescher, The History of Rogers Rangers, The Beginnings, p 411; and text pp 76-79 and footnote 54.

115.* (p 48) CROWN POINT BLOODHOUND FEAT, Aug. 2, 1759: Webster, Aug. 3. Amherst, Aug. 3.

116.* (p 48) BREWER'S MARCH INTO CROWN POINT, Aug. 4, 1759: Rogers, p 143.

117.* (p 49) CONSTRUCTION OF TICONDEROGA-CROWN POINT ROAD, Aug. 5-8, 1759: Amherst, Aug. 5-8.

118.* (p 49) ROGERS WOOD-SURVEY HUNTING SCOUT, Aug. 5, 1759: Amherst, Aug. 5. Anonymous Orderly-Book of the British Regiments at Ticonderoga and Crown Point, Aug. 1-10, 1759.

119.* (49) ROGERS' GRAND HUNT, Aug. 8, 1759: Ibid.

119A.* (p 50) HUTCHING'S QUEBEC MISSION Aug. 7-Oct. 9, 1759: Amherst, Aug. 7-Oct. 9. Boston-News-Letter, Oct. 11; Sept. 13. Pargellis-Mil. Affairs—N. Amer.

120.* (p 51) WILSON'S ISLE AUX NOIX SCOUT, Aug. 8-19, 1759: Amherst, Aug. 8-19.

121.* (p 51) BUILDING OF STARK'S ROAD, Aug. 9-Sept. 9, 1759: Amherst, Aug. 8, Sept. 9: "Capt. Stark returned with his Party from No. 4; 14 of his men deserted, six left sick behind. He said he had made the Road & that there were no mountains or swamps to pass & as he came back it measured 77 miles. It may be much shortened..." This was the beginning of the famous 'Crown Point No. 4 (Charlestown) N.H. Military Road,' which was much shortened and improved in later years.

122.* (p 51) JOHNSON'S OTTER RIVER EXPLORATION, Aug. 13-24, 1759: Amherst, Aug. 13: "...Ordered Capt. Johnson with ten Rangers to march to the Otter River to the Place Captain Hawks crosses it in his Road to No. 4 and then to proceed down the Otter River to explore the whole and return here by the Lake..." Aug. 24: "Capt. Johnson returned with his Party from exploring the Otter River. He found eight falls instead of three and mostly very bad ones; the sides of the River for the most part very swampy, and he says the most impracticable impassible River that he ever saw. This is the River that many People have run away with the notion that it would have been the Route for the war to have been carried on and talk of it as if they knew it, when they are totally ignorant of every part of it."

123. (p 51) INDIAN ALARM, Aug 20-21, 1759: Amherst, still undoctrined to the exigencies of Rogers Rangers, recorded his usual cryptic report: Aug. 20: "...In the evening some Rangers reported they had seen seven Enemy Indians; it may be, but unlikely. I ordered a Party after them. Aug. 21: "...Part came back and reported they had tracked them, & left the rest pursuing; their reports very likely to be false. At night the remainder came back, could not overtake..." Anonymous (Ranger officer Diary), August 21, 1759 entry.

124.* (p 51) ABERCROMBIE-HOLMES HUDSON RIVER EXPLORATION, Aug. 20-24, 1759: Amherst, Aug. 20: "...This morning Capt. Abercromby, with Lt. Davis of the Artillery and Lt. Trumbul & 24 men of the Light Infantry and Lt. Holmes and six Rangers, went to the West to explore the upper part of the Hudson River & the country about there. Aug. 24: "...Capt Abercromby returned in the Afternoon with his Party..."

125. (p 51) INDIAN PURSUIT, Aug. 22, 1759: Amherst, Aug. 21: "...At night two men of late Prideaux's missing who had contrary to orders been on the other side of the Lake." Aug. 22: "...A Scout I sent on the East side of the Lake brought back a French gun case of an officer, who I suppose comes from their shipping to try to see what we are about and popped upon the two fools of Prideaux's Regt who were out of all bounds and without Arms..."

126.* (p 53) HOPKINS' FISH-STORY EXPLOIT, Aug. 22-Sept. 1, 1759: Amherst, Aug. 22, 31; Sept. 1st. News-Letter, Oct. 26; Sept. 20. Boston Gazette & Country Journal, Sept. 17, No. 233.

127. (p 54) MCKENZIE'S SCOUT, Aug. ___-Sept. 1, 1759: Amherst, Sept. 1. Anonymous (Ranger officer Diary), Sept. 1, 1759.

128.* (p 81) SCOTT'S LOWER ST. LAWRENCE RAID, Sept. 1 19, 1759: Scott's Official Report, dated Sept. 19, is in the Northcliffe Coll, Vol XXI, Que V, p 144. Landing at Kamouraska they marched back 52 miles destroying 998 buildings, 2 sloops, 2 schooners, 10 Shallops and several small craft. Killed 5. Had 1 Regular and 2 Rangers killed. 3 Rangers wd.

129. (p 55) HOPKINS' SLOOP BURNING ASSIGNMENT, Sept. 4-14, 1759: Amherst, Sept. 4, 14. Amherst's orders to Sergt. Hopkins, Crown Point, Sept. 4—W.O. 34, Vol 81, f 2. Amherst to DeLancey, Sept. 18—Vol 30/80 News-Letter, Oct. 26, No 2043. Meloizes, 9/12/1759 entry—best French account.

130.* (p 55) FLEET PROTECTION SCOUTS, Sept. 6-7, 1759: Amherst, Sept. 6-7.

131.* (p 65) WILSON'S LA BARBUE CREEK EXPLORATION, Sept. ___-15, 1759: Amherst, Sept. 15.

132.* (p 65) DARCY'S WOOD CREEK-SOUTH BAY SURVEY, Sept. ___-Oct. 2, 1759: Amherst, Oct. 2, Roberts, Vol II.

133.* (p 65) JOHNSON'S AMBULANCE SERVICE, Oct. 7, 1759: Amherst to Noah Johnson, Crown Pt., Oct. 6—W.O. 34, Vol 81, f 58.

134.* (p 65) ROSIER'S POINT AU FER SCOUT, Oct. 9-23, 1759: Amherst, Oct. 9, 23.

135. (p 66) AMHERST'S ADVANCE ON ISLE AUX NOIX, Oct. 11-18, 1759: Amherst, Oct. 11-18.

136.* (p 63) BREWER'S CHARRED-HULL DISCOVERY SCOUT, Oct. 25, 1759: Amherst, Oct. 25. Rogers' landing place is known thanks to a survey made of Lake Champlain in 1762 which revealed the charred whaleboats. —Brazier.

137.* (p 67) BLOODHOUND SCOUT FOR BOSTONERS, Nov. 3, 1759: Amherst, Nov. 2-3. Dibble, Nov. 3.

138.* (p 112) THE DISARMING SCOUT, Nov. 30, 1759: J. Montressor, Nov. 30.

139. (p 70) ABDUCTION AT RIVER-HEAD BLOCKHOUSE, Dec. 1759: Rogers, 171. Haviland to Amherst, Dec. 24—W.O. 34, Vol 51, f 3.

140.* (p 70) THE 100 TOES EXPEDITION, Dec. 25, 1759: Same to Same, Jan. 5—Vol 51, f 4. 38 Rangers frostbitten.

141. (p 112) BUTLER'S ATTEMPTED N.Y. SCOUT, Dec. 26-Jan. 6, 1759-60: Knox, Murray, Dec. 26-Jan. 6.

142.* (p 88) STONE'S PROVISION MISSION, Jan. 1760: Haviland to Amherst, Crown Pt., Jan. 24—W.O. 34—V 51—f 5.

142.* (p 113) MONTRESSOR-BUTLER MESSAGE TO AMHERST EXPEDITION, Jan. 26-Feb. 20, 1760: Lt. John Montressor's Journal of an Expedition in 1760 Across Maine from Quebec for the Fixing The Plan for The Junction of the Army at Montreal.

144.* (p 88) COWBOY SCOUTS, March-May, 1760: Haviland to Amherst, Crown Point, May—W.O. 34, Vol 51—f 28. Same to Same, Jan. 24-Vol 51, f 5.

145. (p 85) TUTE'S SECOND CAPTURE, March 31, 1760: Hav-

iland to Amherst, Apr. 4—W.O.34, Vol 51, f 15, describes capture and chagrin at consenting to allowing them to fish, Same to Same, Apr. 12—Vol 51, f 16, again expresses mortification. Same to Same, Apr. 17—Vol. 51, f 17, learns from 4 French deserters that all the prisoners are safe. Amherst to Haviland, Apr. 20—Vol 52, f 24, consoles Haviland.

146.* (p 118) PATTEN'S FLEET RELIEF DISCOVERY, May 15, 1760: Knox, May 16.

147.* (p 95, 103) BEVERLY's MESSAGE TO MURRAY MISSION, June 3 ___-___, 1760: Amherst, May 27: "... I wrote a letter to Governor Murray upon a very small piece of paper which Rogers is to send by 2 or 3 men across the Country from Mississquoi Bay to Quebec." Amherst to Haviland, Albany, May 26—W.O.34, Vol 52, f 36. Amherst to DeLancey, June 1 —Ibid, Vol 30, f 105. Contingencies, N.Y., March 1, 1762— Ibid, Vol 200, ff 47-8: "11: To Luxford Goodwin a Ranger who went thro' the woods with Letters to Governor Murray from General Amherst, a gratification by his order—5 pounds sterling." Luxford Goodwin to Haviland, Crown Pt., Aug. 30, 1761—Ibid, Vol. 51, f 198.

Stark's Reminiscenses, pp 154-8 records Ranger John Shute's own account: "From the dangerous nature of the undertaking, a reward of fifty pounds was offered to any four who would volunteer for the service. Sergeant Thomas Beverly, although he had just escaped from Montreal, volunteered and led the detachment of veterans, namely, Luxford Goodwin, Joseph Eastman and John Shute. Eastman and Shute both came from Concord, N.H. They were companions and messmates. These four, with Beverly in command, took charge of the despatch together with a large number of other letters from officers at Crown Point to their friends in the army at Quebec and on June 3, they were landed at Missisqui Bay. From there they were ordered to proceed to the river St. Francis, by the same route the Rangers pursued when they destroyed St. Francis the year before. Rogers ordered them to keep in the woods, avoiding all settlements and upon no occasion to cross the St. Francis River in the day time, for fear of discovery by the Indians. With these instructions they left Rogers at Missisqui Bay and journeyed many days thru wet marshy grounds where they could scarcely find a dry spot to encamp at night. They reached the St. Francis one Sunday morning, striking the river just above a rapid. In crossing the river their raft became unmanageable in the swift current and they lost all the letters and the dispatch when Beverly and Goodwin were carried over the rapids. They traveled on with scarcely any provisions, until several days later when they came in sight of a small village. All the inhabitants were in the village church, so they entered a house, helped themselves to provisions and clothing and returned to the woods.

From here they followed a foot path which soon brought them to a log house, against the gable end of which a ladder rested leading to a door fastened with a padlock, which breaking open with their hatchets, they discovered a large chest, filled with woman's clothing of the richest quality. Shute made himself a rifle frock of one of the gowns, helping themselves to a share of the plunder, they pursued their march in the woods, avoiding all roads, until nearly night when they ventured again to approach the settlements on the Chaudiere River. After the village had settled down for the night, the four travelers entered a barn in quest of a hog for food. As they opened the door they were almost knocked over by a calf which galloped thru them. They eventually caught and killed it, dividing it into four parts. Then climbing into the garden of a gentleman's house, they rifled it of what vegetables they could use. Retiring with their booty about four miles into the woods, they kindled a fire, refreshed themselves with part of their loot and dried the remainder in the smoke and made moccasins of the skin. Continuing their journey they reached the top of a high hill on the third day and from the height they saw for the first time the St. Lawrence River, with a large encampment of Regular troops upon the bank. This was about 20 miles above Quebec and they were in doubt as to whether the army was French or English. Sergeant Beverly decided to descend the hill and find out and make signal if they were the enemy. The three Rangers watched his progress, saw him stopped by the sentry and after a moment's pause, enter the camp, where several officers shook hands with him. Upon this they hurried down the hill and were received with open arms by the English. After stating their business to the commander, he put them on board a boat to proceed to headquarters at Quebec where they arrived at midnight and were conducted to General Murray's kitchen. There they slept upon the floor until morning, when they were conducted into a large hall in which were about 100 officers. There, says Shute, 'each man received a glass of liquor, such as I have never tasted before nor since, nor have I ever drank any thing so good in my life.' After this they were ordered to tell their several stories, which as they had previously agreed upon a statement of facts, coincided very well although they were examined separately. The four Rangers joined Murray's army in its advance on Montreal receiving four guineas each, extra pay." Rogers, 176-8 prints his instructions to Sergeant Beverly stating that General Murray, upon application, would pay the fifty pounds reward. Murray did not pay it and it took Amherst to settle the account in 1762.

148. (p 95-102) HOLMES' WIGWAM MARTINIQUE MISSION, June 3-21, 1760: Rogers, 175-6, 188. Amherst to Haviland, Camp at Oswego, July 11—W.O. 34, Vol 52—f 69.

149.* (p 106) BREWER-JENKS SPRUCE BEER SCOUT, June 17, 1760: Jenks, June 17.

150.* (p 106) OTTER CREEK MOUTH PATROL, June 17, 1760: Kent, June 17.

151.* (p 107) CAPTIVE RESCUE SCOUT, June 19, 1760: Holden, June 18-19. Intelligence of Rangers Proudfoot and Chamberlain, Crown Pt., June—W.O. 34, Vol 51, f 47. Haviland to Amherst, June 19—Ibid, Vol 51—f 51.

152. (p 124) THE DECOY CRUISE, July 15-23, 1760: Amherst, July 15, 24.

153.* (p 125) RELIEF OF WILLYAMOS MISSION, July 27, 1760: Hervey, Amherst, July 27.

154.* (p 109) ISLE AUX NOIX KIDNAPPING SCOUT, Aug. 22, 1760: Jenks, Aug. 22. Haviland's Disbursements in 1760 Campaign—W.O. 34, Vol 198, f 249.

155.* (p 126) JACOB'S ST. FRANCIS PEACE MISSION, Aug. 30, 1760: Amherst, Aug. 29. Jacob Naunauphtank's Claim for back pay and St. Francois Wampum belt—W.O. 34, Vol 198, f 309. Although the above Jacob delivered the belt and Amherst's speech he found that the principal members of the tribe had dispersed throughout the woods for the winter. The Johnson Papers (Vol III, pp 281, 353, 402-3, 623, 660) and Doc. Hist. N.Y. (Vol IV, pp 303, 196) reveal the difficulty of establishing a Stockbridge-St. Francis peace: When Jacob was captured by the St. Francis Indians in 1759 prior to Rogers' St. Francis Raid one of his Indian Rangers was tortured and killed. The executioners felt justified in this act for the Indian had been a married member of the St. Francis tribe but finding an opportunity to desert his tribe he joined the Stockbridges. When captured he had refused to rejoin the St. Francis Indians and was consequently killed. The elder Jacob refused to see the justice of his death. The St. Francis Indians anxious to "drop the affair into oblivion" purchased an 18-year old Pawnee Indian to present to Jacob in lieu of the Indian killed. Jacob stubbornly refused to accept him and it took nearly a year and a half of negotiating, assurances by the tribe that the executioners had moved to the Oswegatchie tribe shortly after (hence the St. Francis inhabitants of the year 1762 were not liable for their actions), and finally, pressure by Johnson, the Indian Superintendent, before the matter was settled. —Johnson to the Stockbridge Indians, Johnson Hall, March 29, 1762— "Children of Stockbridge. When I saw you last at Albany, I told you I would give you notice when the Canada Indians were coming. They arrived here at my House in the Woods two days ago, without my having any previous notice thereof. Yesterday they finished what they came about, and delivered over the Prisoner to me, in Room of the Man of Yours which was killed in Canada; also performed the Ceremony usual on such Occasions and behaved extremely well thru the whole Ceremony. Your Uncles the Mohawks were present at ye Meeting and others of the Six Nations. I would have two or three of your Soberest Men come immediately and fetch your Prisoner from here. He is a Young Man about 25 years of age, and seems very well contented at the change..."

156.* (p 138) FERRY DUTY, Sept. 22-Oct. 2, 1760: Holden, Sept. 20, 22, Hobart, Oct. 2.

157.* (p 138) WHALEBOAT POSTAL SERVICE, Sept. 14, 1760: Amherst to Haviland (at Longueuil), Montreal, Sept. 14—W.O. 34, Vol 52, f 83.

158.* (p 138) SUPPLY FERRY DUTY, Sept. 28, 1760: Holden, Sept. 28.

159.* (p 136) BUTLER'S EXPEDITION TO RECEIVE CAPITULATION OF FORTS MIAMIS & QUATANON, Dec. 10-___, 1760: W.O.34, Vol 199, ff 73-4. Captain Campbell to Amherst, Detroit, Jan. 23, 1761—W.O. 34, Vol 49, f 17. Same to Same, Feb. 14—Vol 49, ff 19-20. Rogers Rangers in Butler's Expedition were: *Lieutenant John Butler, Ensign Waite, Sergeants *Timothy Farnham and *Sanders Bradbury; Privates *Samuel Jewell, *James Dickey, *Derry Jellison, *Daniel Webster, *Ashel Andrews, *William Latterly, *William Thompson, *Elijah Wood, *Frank Beard, *Adonijah Edwards, Paul Higgins, Samuel Rose, James Campbell, William Hogg, Patrick Coborn, John Spear, John Craig, William Anson.—W.O. 34, Vol 200, f 1; Account of Pay due to the Detachment of Rangers under command of Lieutenant John Butler... N.Y., Jan. 4, 1762. *Names asterisked garissoned Miamis with Butler, others left at various times to escort prisoners to Niagara and Oswego and remained sick at these posts.

160.* (p 139) WINTER POSTAL SCOUTS: See ftns 200-202.

161.* (p 151) RAIDS ON NEOWEE, CANOUGA, AYOREE & BURNING TOWN, June 1761: Grant, June.

162. (p 152) BLOODHOUND SCOUTS FOR CHEROKEES, June 22, 1761: Grant, June 22.

163. (p 158) HOPKINS-J. ROGERS SALLY, Aug. 20, 1763: Ibid, p 63.

164.* (p 159) MAJOR ROGERS' PICKET SALLY, Aug. 23, 1763: Hough, Detroit, Jrn., p 64.

165. (p 171) OCTOBER 28TH RECRUIT CAPTURE, 1776: Heath, p 77.

166.* (p 171-6) ROGERS' CAPTURE OF NATHAN HALE, Sept. 21, 1776: Bamford, Sept. 22. Halifax Log, Sept. 16-21; 30. Seymour, Documentary Life of N. Hale.

167. (p 171) JANUARY 2ND RECRUIT CAPTURE, 1777: Heath, Jan. 3, 1777.

168. (p 171) CAPTURE OF STRANG, Jan. 3, 1777: Hough, Rogers' Jrn., 277-8. Heath Papers, Heath to Washington, Peekskill, Jan. 4, 1777.

169.* (182) GOODWIN'S PILOT SCOUT, March 1780: Robert Rogers to Haldimand, March 20—Haldimand Collection, B.160, p 34.

170. (p 200) WHITWORTH'S RECRUITING SCOUT, March 1780: Jones, 280.

171.* (p 195) FERGUSON'S N.Y. STATE SCOUT, July 1780: Ferguson to Mathews, St. John's, Aug. 3—Haldimand Coll, B.161, p 104.

172.* (p 198) JONES' PENOBSCOT-QUEBEC COURIER DUTY, 1780-1781: Haldimand to Gov. Hughes, Que., Nov. 16—Haldimand Coll., B.150, pp 95-6. Mathews to Major J. Rogers, Que., Jan. 1, 1781-Ibid, B.160, p 85.

173.* (p 199) JONES' CAPTURE OF BRIGADIER CUSHING, Aug. 1780: North, J., p 158.

174.* (p 190) CAPTURE OF THOMAS JOHNSON, March 8-13, 1781: Johnson, T., March 8-20. Sherwood to Mathews, Isle aux Noix, Mar. 11—Haldimand Coll., B.176. Same to Same, Mar. 23-4—Ibid, B.176, pp 55, 58-61.

175.* (p 193) BRECKENRIDGE'S DIPLOMATIC SCOUTS, July 1781: Smyth to Mathews, St. John's, July 21—Ibid, B.176, p 169. Sherwood to Mathews, Dutchman's Pt., July 21 (Return of Breckenridge), Ibid, p 171.

176. * (p 195) MILLER'S BALLSTOWN MISSION, July 1781: J. Miller's Report, July 11—Ibid, p 150.

176A. (p 195) FERGUSON'S BALLSTOWN SCOUT, Aug. 1781: B.182, p 417.

176B.* (p 190) PRITCHARD'S CAPTURE OF THE LOVELS, Nov. 1781: B.163, p 118.

177.* (p 194) STEPHEN'S DOC OLDEN SCOUT, Nov. 2, 1781: Sherwood to Mathews, Tic., Nov. 2—Ibid, 1 326.

178. (p 196) ATTEMPT TO BURN MAN O' WAR, Nov. 1781— Aug 17, 1782: Smyth to Mathews, Nov. 10—Ibid, p 333. Smyth to Haldimand, Nov. 21—Ibid, p 359. Smyth to Mathews, Dec. 12—Ibid, p 365. John Lindsay's Report, Aug. 17, 1782—Ibid, B.177-2, pp 442-5. Mathews to Sherwood, Nov. 15, 1781—

Ibid, B.179, p 155.

179.* (p 194) STEPHEN'S CHIMNEY PT.-VERMONT SCOUT, Dec. 10-31, 1781: Roger Stephens to Mathews, St. John's, Feb. 6, 1782—Ibid, B.161, p 391.

180.* (p 194) STEPHEN'S WINTER ESPIONAGE SCOUTS, Jan.-Feb. 1782: Sherwood to Mathews, Loyal Blockhouse Feb. 24—Ibid, B.177-1, p 74. Roger Stephen's Report, Feb. 28—Ibid, p 85. Sherwood to Mathews, Jan. 30, River La Colle—Ibid, p 21.

181. (p 195) MAJOR JAMES ROGERS' MISSION, Apr. 28-May 1782: J. Rogers to J. Mountain, St. John's, Feb. 16—Ibid, p 55. Sherwood to Mathews, Loyal Blockhouse, May 18—Ibid, p 295. Haldimand to Major Rogers Apr. 28—Ibid, B.160, p 107-8 (2 letters). Major Rogers to Mathews, Loyal Blockhouse, May 2—Ibid, p 109.

182.* (p 194) STEPHEN'S MASSACHUSETTS SCOUT, May 1782: Sherwood to Mathews, Loyal Blockhouse, May 15—Ibid, B.177-1, p 289.

183.* (p 191) PRITCHARD'S N.Y. CITY SCOUT, Aug.-Sept., 1782: Pritchard's Report, St. John's, Sept. 17—Ibid, B.177-2.

184.* (p 195) STEPHEN'S HAZARDOUS SCOUT, Oct. 1782: Stephens to Mathews, St. John's, Oct. 15—Ibid, B.161 1 456.

185. (p 200) CAPTURE OF STINSON, 1782: Parole of Captain John Stinson, Aug. 10—Ibid, B.160, p 115. J. Rogers to Mathews (giving account of Stinson's capture) Aug. 21—Ibid, p 116. Mathews to J. Rogers, Aug. 26—Ibid, p 117.

186.* (p 200) THE LAST SCOUT, Apr. 1784: J. Rogers to Mathews, St. John's, March 28, 1784—Ibid, p 161: Since numbers of the King's Rangers have asked leave to set out to reconnoitre the lands about Cataraqui as soon as possible, there being various accounts of the country. Asks that Lt. Ferguson and 10 or 11 of the most confidential men should obtain leave so as to find at least a good landing place for the boats where huts could be built.

NOTE: See Loescher (1) for Scouts 1-47 (Appendix III).

APPENDICE IV

UNIFORMS OF ROGERS RANGERS 1758-1783

This study will continue the definitive descriptions detailed in our HISTORY OF ROGERS RANGERS-The Beginnings[1] to cover the newly discovered evidence thus enabling the author to draw the most comphrehensive plate.

ROGERS RANGERS-Ranger-1758-1761: Depicted in full marching uniform and gear. Short-tailed jacket and vest of an inexpensive green frieze (a rough heavy woolen fabric with a shaggy nap.) The jacket not quite as short as those of the light infantry as Rogers Rangers had to wear them the year round, except for very hot summer when they went out in their vests or Indian hunting shirts. The latter sometimes worn over the vests and on occassion over their jackets to preserve their uniform as well as protection in the brush. The jackets were lined with green serge. The short green collar and cuffs of serge contrasted enough from the nappy frieze jacket to give a distinct facing. A double row of white metal buttons on the front of the jacket and four on each sleeve. The insignia or badge of Rogers Rangers as inspired by Lord Howe was inscribed on the buttons of Rogers' own company and probably the other companies before the war was over. An 'ANONYMOUS DIARY OF A ROGERS RANGER OFFICER' in possession of the author best describes the 'Insignia Button':

'Ye Majors Co. still have ye white buttons with ye Rogers Rangers marked so on ye face Ye Major says Lord Howe sug(g)ested it before his untimely death. The R's standing back to back - ye top of R's form ye Kings Crown signif(y)ing his Majestys Independant Co's of Rangers. Some have contrived this design as a Badge wearing it on ye bullit pouch or ye waist Belt buc(k)el.'[2]

The Scotch Balmoral bonnet was much favored and worn by the privates and non-coms. The same Diarist records the 'ornamentation' upon them:

'Rogers Rangers favo(u)r ye Squir(r)el or Bucks tale (tail) on ye green Balmoral Bonnet rathir than ye evirgreen sprigs much used by ye Light Inf. I must concur with my men that ye sprigs dry out to(o) fast and ye sap sticks to ye Bonnet when fres(h) cut. By setting ye length of ye tales (tails) Major Rogers has kept a uniform look. To shorten ye cut is don(e) at ye root end. Ye Major (Roger)s Co. all have ye squir(r)el tale (tail).'[3]

He comments further on the length of the jackets:

'Our coats are not quit(e) as short as some of ye other Regts (Regiments,)as ye Rangers must wear them ye year round. I fear ye men wou(l)d not be akin to a stoppage for 2 uniforms....'[4]

The Rangers wore buckskin breeches ending just below the knee (shaped much like our modern 'knickers'). Over these they wore green Indian leggings usually of rattan material. The leggings were fastened to the breeches belt at the top and strapped under the instep at the bottom with garters just below the knees to further avoid 'slippage'. The Ranger officer Diarist relates a most humorous facet regarding the Leggins:

'Most of our (Rogers) Rangers favo(u)r ye true Indion (Indian) Leggins which come quit(e) high on ye legs & tye (tie) to ye breeches belt & with strap under ye feet so ye Leggins will not slip up ye legs. With Garters directly below ye knee ye Leggins are quit(e) snug.

'Our Rangers are not quit(e) as barbaric as Gorhams (Rangers,)who are reported wearing no breeches under their Leggins - Only a kilt (a)round ye outside.[5] Certain of our Rangers would have worn only ye Breechcloth fore and aft in ye Summer instead of breeches under ye Indion Leggin(g)s stating they wou(l)d have more freedom for action. Ye Major (Rogers) put it down & told ye men at General Muster that there wo(u)ld be no op(p)ortunity for wenching in ye brush & ye on]y -Freedom for Action- wo(u)ld

Sergeant Goodwin. Illustration by Gary Zaboly.

Ranger Officer. Illustration by Gary Zaboly.

Duke Jacobs. Illustration by Gary Zaboly.

Old French print of Robert Rogers

be needed further down in ye Feet! I daresay this provoked unduly loud lafter (laughter) amongst ye Rangers which shoc(k)ed certain Regular officers present. I fear ye English Officers will nevir (never) understand ye Majors (Rogers) way of Level(l)ing ye men. He deals with a new breed of men. They are more free than evin (even) ye Scots Clans.'[6]

Moccasins on the feet with an extra pair in the pack or blanket roll completed the uniform. The shirt under the jacket was the pull-over type usually white although checked shirts could have been worn as there is no definite evidence of uniformity in the shirts. A stock of leather or dyed cloth or linen was worn around the shirt collar, especially in inclement weather. This protective 'scarf' enhanced the military effect.

WEAPONS: Consisted of the shorter 42 inch barrel Brown Bess; The short knife bayonet; The round or oval eyed Tomahawk; A long Scalping-Knife (the Deer antler handles were favored - as shown in the plate).

ROGERS QUEENS RANGERS-Ranger-1776-1777: Recruited in part by and of former Rogers Ranger officers and men the advent of this revival as a Loyalist corps saw the uniform greately influenced by the dress and gear of the French and Indian War. These old veterans or their sons brought whatever items of uniform or gear that survived when they made their secret if not hurried exodus from the New England coast across the sound to Rogers' recruiting headquarters on Long Island at Huntington.

Rogers ordered the same colors for his uniforms except the coat facing and cuffs were blue.[7] The green coat with white metal buttons was cut the same as the British army Light Infantry, short tailed and double-breasted lapelled front, green waistcoat. The white bindings were maintained on the eventual black tri-corne hats.[8] It is not definitly known whether this uniform reached Rogers from England during the life of the corps while it existed as Rogers Queens Rangers during the winter of 1776-77.

Until they arrived, the corps wore the uniform as depicted in the plate. Their raids on the American storehouses contributed clothing items and gear to allay the shortage until the ships arrived from England. It is no wonder that their active Fall campaign of 1776 in Westchester County evoked exclamations of alarm from the patriots for by all appearances 'Rogers Rangers' lived again.[9]

ROGERS KINGS RANGERS-Ranger-1779-1783: The last half of this last revival of Rogers Rangers saw them finally uniformed as shown in the plate. Green cloth British Light Infantry cut coats and vests with the short regulation 'knickers' underneath the Indian Leggings-green and moccasins on the feet. The green beret (Scotch Balmoral bonnet) for privates and cocked tri-corne black hats for non-coms and officers. The coats and breeches were woolen for winter and linen for summer. Linen shirts, stockings and two pair of mocassins were issued. Sergeants wore the regulation right shoulder strap designation of rank. The Ranger is depicted called on alert hastily slipping into his green blanket coat, which normally would be underneath the waistbelt and cartridge box but is shown half open so the 1782-83 uniform can be seen underneath. The first years, 1779-1781 saw the corps wearing the green hunting shirts instead of the British cut coats and vests. They resembled the Queens Ranger figure except for the green beret. The blanket coat was one of the first items issued and presented a uniformity of dress during the winter.[10]

NOTES: [1]*Loescher (1)*, pp 271-286 Appendice B, ROGERS RANGERS UNIFORMS & EQUIPMENT, 1755-1783. This study contains excerpts from all the contemporary documents. The color plates depict the 1755 to 1758 uniform.

[2]*Anonymous, Rogers Ranger Diary* (in possesion of the author) 10 June, 1759 entry. Symbols: () used for editing by author in lieu of [ ]

[3]*Ibid*, 13 June 1759. Evidence of the 'Bonnet' being worn as early as September, 1756, is revealed by *Bougainville, 9/11/1756 Journal* entry:-

Little parties of **Rogers** Rangers (mistaken for 42nd Highlanders) in Balmoral bonnets with Stockbridge Rangers were observed continually peering into Ticonderoga from the surrounding heights.-E.Hamilton, trans & edit.
⁴Op. Cit., 14 June 1759.
⁵Ibid, 15 June 1759. Evidently this report was a disparaging rumour started in humour against a rival corps for Gorham's Rangers did wear clothing under their kilts. A contemporary description scotches the rumour: 1759-Gorham's Rangers wore '..linen, or canvas drawers..'-Loescher (5), p 11, also see plate by the author, frontispiece of same source. The leather breeches (under Leggings) sustained a party of Hazen's company when starving 'on Party' in February 1760.-Montressor, Feb 15, 1760.
⁶Op. Cit.; Boston News-Letter 10/4/59: notes a drowned Ranger deserter was found wearing only 'Indian' Leggings and 'Moggasens'.

ROGERS QUEENS RANGERS (NOTES)

⁷Blue, chosen for the Queen's Royal blue. The plate depicts a veteran Rogers Ranger wearing his outgrown hunting shirt. The two-short sleeves reveal the blue-cuffed British cut coat beneath which might very well been worn underneath. The hunting shirt providing warmth for the Rangers vigorous fall and winter campaign of 1776.
⁸The Ranger wears the Light Infantry hat issued to the Light Company of the Queen's Rangers. The Ranger retains his squirrel tail insignia from the French and Indian War, which he wore on his Balmoral bonnet in that war. Other evidence of his veteran service record are revealed in the 1758 'R.R.' belt buckle insignia and the deer antler handled scalping knife. The wooden canteen retained the vintage of two decades prior.
⁹Their somewhat barbaric appearance while alarming to the American patriots, was abhorred by the British army. When Rogers could not cloth his Rangers in the uniform he ordered due to the non-arrival of the ship bearing them from England, the British officers aspiring to command this active partisan corps, which would advance them, seized upon this opportunity to discredit Rogers.

There is pictorial evidence of the uniform Rogers ordered and which was adopted and modified by Rogers successors early in 1777 when the regiment ceased to exist as 'Rogers Queens Rangers'. See Charles M. Lefferts, Uniforms of the American, British, French, and German Armies in the War of the American Revolution 1775-1783, pp 222, 230. Also Cecil C P. Lawson's Uniforms of the British Army, See chapter on Loyalist corps

ROGERS KINGS RANGERS (NOTES)

¹⁰See Index this book, 'Uniforms, Kings Rangers'. Also footnote 337. Alley, II, page 5.

COMMENT ON THE PLATE

The theme depicts the life of Rogers Rangers in the unique mannerisms of their uniform. The 'Genesis' is portrayed in the items of dress which bound the revivals (Queens Rangers and Kings Rangers,) to their more famous ancestry in the French and Indian War. The Balmoral bonnets,the: 'R.R.' insignia, the Indian Leggings, the moccasins, the squirrel-tails on the headgear and last but not least the horn-handled scalping knifes
The Queens and Kings Rangers hurry to follow in the footsteps of Rogers Rangers before the close of the American Revolution ends the life of Rogers Rangers.

HISTORICAL NOTES

To avoid repeating the full title of a source citation most citations have been made by the use of key words, usually the names of the writers or editors of the works cited, such as 'Loescher (1)' for History of Rogers Rangers—The Beginnings, 1755-Apr. 6, 1758. All key words appear in the bibliography of Principal Sources following these notes.

CHAPTER I
1758—ABERCROMBIE'S EYES
Pages 1 - 26

p-ix [1] For 'The Beginnings' of Rogers Rangers see Loescher (1).

p-1 [1a] See Loescher, Vol I, pp 261-2.

p-2 [2] News-Letter, May 25, 1758.

p-3 [3] Rogers, p 108.

p-3 [4] Rogers, p 110. Brigadier Lord Viscount George Howe, able second in command to Abercrombie.

p-5 [5] Ibid.

p-5 [6] Engagement of the Stockbridge Indians, Feb. 1758—LO 5799. Burbank's Company to June 24, 1758—AB 922-1. Provision Warrant for Moses Brewer's Company, July 3, 1758—AB 929-1. Pay Warrant for Same to June 24, 1758—AB 929-2.

p-7 [7] Ibid. Brigadier Lawrence to Abercrombie, Apr. 12, Boston—AB 147. Abercrombie to Lawrence, N.Y., Apr. 30—AB 216. Wentworth to Abercrombie, Portsmouth, N.H., May 19—AB 270. Numbers of Rangers and Provincial Recruits for each Company are listed in: AB 590—(Burbank's, Shepherd's, M. Brewer's, J. Stark's, R. Rogers'). Numbers of J. Stark's, Shepherd's and James Neale's are in—AB 930, 931, 932, 911, 934, 590. Besides Rogers' seven Companies at Lake George there were six others in his Corps: James Neale's Company at Fort Miller, Henry Wendell's Company at Fort Stanwix in the Mohawk Valley and John McCurdy's, Jonathan Brewer's, James Rogers' and William Stark's Companies on the Louisbourg front.

p-7 [8] Anonymous British Journal, in W.O. 34.

p-8 [9] Ibid, June 25.

p-8 [10] Namely Langy's Defeat at The Battle of Ticonderoga Falls. See text, pp 32-34.

p-8 [11]Anonymous French Diary in W.O. 34.

p-8 [12]Rogers, pp 111-12.

p-8 [13]Ibid, p 112.

p-9 [14]Ibid, pp 112-13.

p-11 [15]O'Connor. Rogers, p 114.

p-12 [16]See Loescher, Vol I, 193-7.

p-12 [17]Rogers, 114-15.

p-20 [18]Rea, Aug. 13, 1758.

p-20 [19]Cleaveland, Aug. 11, 1758.

p-20 [20]Ibid, Aug. 16.

p-20 [21]Rea, Aug. 1. The Rogers' Rock survivor was Private David Vander Heyden, Jr., of Bulkeley's. The Stockbridge was Private Aaron Ninhem. Both had been prisoners at Conosedago, the Indian Castle 25 miles above Montreal and had escaped the middle of July.—Declaration of Heyden and Ninhem, Camp at Lake George, Aug. 2, 1758—W.O. 34, Vol 75, ff 179-80.

p-21 [22]Abercrombie to Sir Wm. Johnson, Camp at Lake George, Sept. 26—AB 699: The Mohawks indulged so heavily in liquor that their scouts never reached Ticonderoga, for they became sick and returned to Camp. One even deserted from a scout led by Rogers.

p-21 [23]Champion, Sept. 7, 30, 1758.

p-21 [24]Rea, Sept. 1, Aug. 17, 1758.

p-21 [25]Munroe, Sept. 4, 1758.

p-22 [26]Ibid, Aug. 28.

p-22 [27]Rea, Sept. 3, 1758.

p-24 [28]Abercrombie to Paymaster Mortier, Camp at Lake George, Sept. 11—AB 641: Although discharged the Stockbridges had to wait till sterling arrived.

p-24 [29]Amherst, Champion, Oct. 6, 1758.

p-24 [30]Pay Warrants, June 25-Aug. 24—AB 590.

p-25 [33]Rogers, 126-7. W.O.34, Vol 197, f 318.

p-25 [34]Returns of Ranger Companies, Nov. 4, 1758 to June 28, 1759: W.O.34, Vol 197, ff 306; 305; 304; 303; 302; 301; 300; 299; 298; 297; 296; 295; 294; 291; 289; 290; 288; 264; 236; 199; 382; 376; 370; 366; 325; 324; 323; 322; 326; 320; 319; 318; 317; 309.

p-25 [35]Champion, Oct. 20. Abercrombie to Pitt, N.Y., Nov. 25, 1758—AB 828. Loescher (3): Chapter VII, Ranger Goodwin's Easter Rum.

CHAPTER II
1758—LOUISBOURG FRONT
Pages 27 - 35

p-27 [36]There were also 100 American Carpenters under Colonel Meserve. Rogers Rangers were the only fighting Americans in the expedition—Cutter, Apr. 3.

p-28 [37]Major Robert Rogers' account against the four Ranging Companies gone to Cape Britton enclosed to Lt-Gov. Monckton, June 30, 1758—AB 16. Abercrombie to Gov. Pownall, N.Y., March 20—AB 56. Same to Same, March 30—AB 91.

p-28 [38]Charles Lawrence to Abercrombie, Boston, Apr. 2, 1758—AB 99. Loring to Abercrombie, Apr. 3, Boston AB 108. Lawrence to Abercrombie, Boston, Apr. 5—AB118. Hopson to Abercrombie, Apr. 7, Halifax—AB 126.

p-28 [39]Hopson to Abercrombie, Halifax, Apr. 12—AB 148. Scott was brevetted Major for this command.

p-31 [40]See Loescher, Vol I, pp 90-91. Browne, pp 13, 14: states that "Sergeant Beau de Bien, Captain Wm. Stark's Wolf dog, accounted for his French name from the fact that Stark, while on a northern hunting trip, found a French officer beating the dog. Stark, who loved dogs, intervened and a fierce duel ensued between Stark and the Frenchman, in which Stark was the victor. The dog gladly attached himself to his new-found defender. Stark named him Sergeant Beau de Bien but it was soon shortened by the Rangers to Beaubien, while he was most generally known as "The Sergeant." He lived to a ripe old age and though he never boasted of his deeds he was considered a hero."

p-32 [41]Amherst, June 19, 1758.

p-32 [42]News-Letter, July 20, 1758.

p-33 [43]Amherst, June 21, 1758.

p-34 [44]Munroe, Aug. 28. Stark, C., Reminiscences,p 160: states that Sergeant Philip, a Pequawket Indian of Rogers Rangers, was the first man to enter the Fortress of Louisbourg after its capture. However, this has not been substantiated by any other contemporary account.

p-34 [45]James Rogers' Company continued the Corps custom of shooting at marks while stationed at Louisbourg, which had fatal results on Oct. 8: "There was a Lt. of ye Rangers was a fireing at a mark and shot a young man that belonged to Lunenburg that he Dyed directly." Knap, Oct. 8, 1758.

p-35 [46]Amherst's List of Winter Quarters, Dec. 18, 1758—C. O., 5/54, f 23. Monckton's Report of the St. John Expedition, Nov. 20—Northcliffe Coll.

CHAPTER III
1759—AMHERST'S ADVANCE GUARD FOR CONQUEST
Pages 36 - 71

p-36 [47]Rogers, 121-2.

p-36 [48]Gage to Amherst, Albany, Jan. 28, 1759—W.O. 34 Vol 46A, f 4.

p-36 [49]Same to Same, Jan. 29—Ibid, Vol 46A, f 6.

p-40 [50]Rogers, 124-127. Gage to Amherst, Albany, Feb. 18, 1759—W.O.34, Vol 46A, f 11: Received 4 letters from Rogers relative to raising Stockbridges but will not do anything without Amherst's approval—Casts Disparaging remarks on Stockbridge Rangers and Rogers' leadership of them: "...These Indians were last Campaign so great a nuisance to the Army and did no Manner of service. Some people say they were not properly managed. I own myself ignorant of the management that is proper for those gentry; can only say that neither orders or Entreatys could prevail on them to do service, always lying drunk in their Hutts, or firing round the Camp..."
Same to Same, Albany, March 19—Ibid, f 21: "...Capt Jacobs arrived here since my last, but would proceed no farther, insisting that Rogers should meet him here; no arguments could prevail on him to stir further. As Rogers from being frost-bit in his last scout, was of no service at Fort Edward, I desired Col. Haldimand to order him down here if able to ride and he arrived accordingly last night and this day the two Chiefs hold their Conference and I suppose matters will be settled upon much the same terms as last year. But Mr. Jacob has given me some hints that money must be advanced him to raise his People which I am by no means inclined to grant him. I rather choose to see his people first."
Same to Same, Albany, March 25—Ibid, f 23: "...Rogers is here and has fixed matters with Jacobs, who is set forward to raise his Company. The other Jacobs is also wrote to, as well

as King Uncas of the Mohegons to raise two other Companies.." Amherst to Gage, N.Y., March 26—Ibid, f 150: "Capt Jacobs has behaved just like himself and all the Drunken good for nothing Tribe. I hate them all but as things are, they may do some good by doing Mischief, of which we have a great deal to do, to be at par with the French." Jacobs' insistence on advance pay from Amherst spread thru the army and became a standing joke.—R. Putnam, July 26, 1759: "But I was not so prudent as the Indian, Captain Jacobs, in another case, to request the General to put his promise on paper."

p-40 [51]Gage to Amherst, Albany, March 19—Ibid, f 21 pithly adds: "...They are a mixture of good and bad men, though the latter not in very great numbers..."

p-41 [52]Gage to Haldimand, Albany, March 27—Haldimand Papers, B.2-1, p 28: "...Major Rogers should be sent back to you immediately, but he has got a Disorder, that many of the profession are subject to. I am informed however that he may set out in five or six days..." Gage to Haldimand, Apr. 4—Ibid, p 33—His decree respecting the Rangers. Ibid, p 17, Gage to Haldimand, 2/20/1959: If forced to decide rank disputes it must be against the Ranger Officers. Ibid, p 27: Evidently Rogers Rangers' winter quarters in Ft. Edward were very limited which did not ease the tension. Gage stated that the Regulars must make room for the new Ranger recruits.

p-41 [53]Gage to Amherst, Albany, Apr. 9—W.O.34, Vol 46A, f 27. Rogers left for Fort Edward with orders to put his Companies in order. "...but as I know him to be a true Ranger and not much addicted to Regularity I had before sent directions on this head to Colonel Haldimand and Colonel Eyre [who has left to relieve Fort Edward]." Rogers' proposal to taking Mohawks into his Corps promising but impractical "was it practicable they would certainly be preferrable to all the Rangers on the Continent. Rogers is a good man in his way, but his schemes are very wild and he has a new one every Day...I enclose you a scheme for putting the Rangers in some better order."

p-41 [54]The Rangers' first crisis was their Whipping Post Mutiny. See Loescher, I, pp 201-210, 304-11.
Amherst's first impression of Rogers Rangers' carefree attitude is revealed in Amherst to Gov. DeLancey, Camp at Lake George, June 23—W.O.34, Vol 30, f 52: "...I am sorry to say I do not give the least credit to any Ranger Reports; from all I have seen of them they are the most careless, negligent, ignorant Corps I ever saw, and if they are not beat on all occasions I really cannot find out the reason they are not—M. Rogers a good man, but I must Rub his Corps up, or they are worse than nothing. I don't mean that you should think I want Rangers, I think I have full enough of them..."

p-41 [55]Gage to Amherst, Apr. 2, 1759—Ibid, Vol 46A, f 25: makes indirect aspersions against Rogers' leadership: "... There is such Confusion in the Ranging Companies that it is difficult to ascertain their numbers. They have no person among them enough acquainted with Regular Service to put them in a proper order. Gen. Abercromby gave them an Adjutant, who is an idle Drunken fellow [William Steward], who instead of introducing some regularity among them, makes more confusion..." News-Letter, Apr. 26, 1759, records a mail-courier ambuscade on Apr. 3. The courier threw his pack in the bushes, escaped, and recovered his pack the next day. This incident delayed mail delivery to Fort Edward.

p-43 [56]Rogers, 138. Loescher, I, 261-2, 437. Gage to Amherst, Albany, March 5, 1759—W.O.34, Vol 46A, f 15: "... The Rangers have never taken any Rank till last Campaign. They then assumed the same rank as Provincials and as it was judged necessary that they should have rank equal with the Provincials with whom they are generally on Duty, it was winked at; and from that time they insist on their Rank or refuse to serve. Their commissions signed by the Commander-in-Chief without being confirmed by his Majesty or sent home for that purpose entitles him to no Half-Pay or Rank. According to the general opinion the matter is loose and wants to be fixed. I must say they much better deserve Rank than the Provincials.."

p-43 [57]Amherst to Rogers, N.Y., Apr. 1—W.O. 34, Vol 54, f 122.

p-43 [58]Amherst to Gage, Apr. 2—Ibid, f 154.

p-43 [59]Ibid, Apr. 6—Vol 46A, f 156. Same to Same, Jan. 14, 1760—Ibid, f 198: Waite owed Rogers 111 pounds "by a promissory note of hand for necessarys furnished that Company." Gage to Amherst, Albany, Feb. 12, 1759—Ibid, f 9: "... Capt. Wendell was ordered to his post [at Ft. Stanwix]." Same to Same, Apr. 2, Ibid, f 25: Wendell's Company men time up, men anxious to be discharged so can recruit in Provincial Regiments for high bounty, only one-half will reenlist with Wendell. Just heard from Wendell, none of his Company will reenlist. Wendell and two of his officers wish to retire. Same to Same, Apr. 9—Ibid, f 27: Sooner Wendell can be replaced the better, recommends Captain Ogden of N.Y. Provincial Ranger Company, who has petitioned for a Company of his Majesty's Rangers; Ogden's brother was a Lieutenant in Wendell's, two officers and 27 recruits passed thru to Ft. Stanwix for Wendell's; one officer still recruiting. Early in 1760 Wendell penned Amherst a Memorial (W.O.34, Vol 82, f 43) stating that he left the Command of his Company of Rangers upon Amherst's leave because he had such bad men who deserted daily. When the Company was mustered by Colonel Massey at Ft. Stanwix and asked why they deserted and if Wendell treated them well, they said that he treated them well. When he resigned and gave up his command to Captain Waite he gave him a list of the deserters, but Waite did not bother with them. One of them, George Wendecker, accosted Wendell and demanded payment for the time he had deserted (18 months). Wendell threw him out of doors and told him to join Waite's Company and serve his time out. Wendecker immediately got a lawful writ of 500 pounds against Wendell and recommended to all the other deserters to do the same. Wendell had paid all Rangers who served without deserting. Recommends Amherst to look into this matter. Also he seeks to serve next campaign (1760) as he is a half-pay officer. Amherst replied that he was amazed at Wendecker's audacity and recommends Wendell to seek legal procedure.—Ibid, Vol , f . Amherst to Wendell, Albany, May 16, 1759—Ibid, Vol 79, f 114: Directing him (since his resignation) to acquaint Waite, upon his arrival, with the Company's Numbers, pay, etc.

p-43 [60]Amherst to Rogers, N.Y., Apr. 1, 1759—Ibid, Vol 54, f 122. Upon being exchanged McCormick served in one of Rogers' Companies with Wolfe at Quebec and did not enter Rogers' own Company until 1760.

p-44 [61]Alex Schomberg of the 'Diana' to Amherst, N.Y., May 11, 1759—Ibid, Vol 42, f 226. Enclosed (f 227) Major Rogers' Report to Schomberg, May 11th.

p-44 [62]Major Rogers' Own Company, J. Stark's, Burbank's, Johnson's, Shepherd's (now Tute's), M. Brewer's, Lieutenant David Brewer's, Jacob Cheeksaunkun's, Jacob Naunauphtaunk's and Waite's at Fort Stanwix.

p-44 [63]Account of Pay for Rogers' Companies, Aug. 31, 1759 —W.O. 34, Vol 197, f 404; Lt. Brewer's Company had only 17 Privates on May 1, and 3 Sergeants and 55 men by Aug. 24th. Amherst to Joshua Lock, Albany, May 11, 1759—Ibid, Vol 79, f 112.

p-44 [64]Captain Jacob Naunauphtaunk was scheduled to march from Albany on May 6, however Amherst notes that "... Capt. Jacob's drunken crew did not quit this place so soon as I ordered, but they are at present all out of town and I hope will arrive Sober to you. The Captain promises great things..." Amherst to Eyre, Albany, May 9—Ibid, Vol 54, f 125. Same to Same May 5—Ibid, f 123: gives a return of the Company—1 Captain, 1 Lieutenant, 1 Ensign, 2 Sergeants, 1 Clerk, 45 Indian men, 5 Indian Boys, 4 White Men. Amherst notes that one of the above Indians was discharged this morning (May 5th). The Company shrunk from 59 to 44 by June 24, and to 27 by Oct. 27, 1759 when the Company was discharged.—Amherst's Notes on Losses in Stockbridge Companies, Oct.—Ibid, Vol 81, f 199. Amherst to Lt. Solomon Uhhaunwaunwaumot of Captain Naunauphtaunk's Company, Crown Point, Oct. 27—Ibid, f 92.

p-44 [65]Amherst, May 27. Amherst to Eyre, Albany, May 27 —Ibid, Vol 54, f 131-2. Same to Same, May 29, Ibid, f 133. On May 27, 1759, Jacob Cheeksaukun's Company had a paper strength of 52 officers and men. Actually there was 1 Captain, 1 Lieutenant, 1 Ensign, 2 Sergeants and 26 Privates (4 of these were boys). The absentees, who never joined the Company, were 1 Clerk and 7 Privates said to be at Ft. Edward. Ten Privates with Sir Wm. Johnson. Three Privates not joyned from Stockbridge. By Oct. 27, 1759, the Company only numbered 15, all told.

p-45 [66]Appy, June 28, 1759. John Appy, besides being Amherst's Secretary, was Judge Advocate of the army.

p-46 [67]Willard, July 17. Wooster, July 17.

p-46 [68]Wooster's Orderly Book gives an excellent picture of the activities of Rogers Rangers to July 21, when the army embarked for Ticonderoga:
-June 22, Camp at Lake George: "After Orders—Major Rogers is on all Detachments to take rank as Major according to the date of his commission as such next after the Majors who have the King's commissions or one from His Majesty's Commander-in-Chief."
-June 23, "All extraordinarys in...the Rangers to be reported to the Colonel of the day..."
-"...2 officers and 40 Rangers to march under the command of the Captain of Gage's which he will dispose of as he thinks proper, the whole to take two days provisions with them and march at 5 in the morning and remain till the evening. One subaltern and 30 of Gage's and 2 officers of the Rangers are to join their detachment...the whole to go in their waistcoats and take 1 days provision with them (to escort Cannon Cartridge wagons)..."
-June 24, "...Gage's and the Rangers to furnish the same escort on the Posts on the road to Ft. Edward for the wagons as ordered yesterday and to be posted in the same manner..."
Same order—June 25-29 and July 4-6 (viz., 1 officer and 40 Rangers).
-June 27, after orders give complete details on formation of covering parties to Stark's Fishing Decoy, "Major Rogers to furnish as many Rangers and Indians [as he can]..."
-June 28, "...When the Rangers and Indians draw provisions each Company must make a return of their effective present, signed by the Commanding Officer of the Company and Major Rogers will sign for the whole. They are always to receive provisions two days before it is due, that there may be a sufficiency in their camp to supply scouting parties..."
-June 29, "...The Companies of Indians and Rangers in Camp are to be under arms tomorrow morning at 5 o'clock to be inspected by Brigadier Gage. The officers commanding each Company will have returns ready agreeable to the form that will be sent them by the Major Brigade..."

-July 2, The Rangers received their provisions first at 5 A. M. July 5, Regulars and Rangers received 8 days provisions and "if the weather should be warm the men must dress all their provisions that it may not be spoiled." July 8, "..It is repeated that the Rangers always receive provisions 2 days beforehand and for 4 days and 3 days alternately..."

-July 9, "...tomorrow morning if a fine day, the men to be in their waistcoats with their arms and ammunition...and no man to straggle towards Fort Edward. The Rangers and Indians must be observant to this order, if they are straggling in the woods they will be shot..."

-July 10, "...Tomorrow the Indians to receive 2 days provisions at 6 o'clock for their effective numbers, hereafter to receive every 2 days for 2 days..."

-July 13, "...Regulars and Rangers to receive flour for 5 days which they are to get baked tomorrow and kept..."

-July 14, "...The Rangers and Indians to fire off their pieces tomorrow morning at 5 o'clock in the front of their Camp at Marks, they will afterwards put their arms in the best order they can. It is repeated the men are on no account to touch the 5 days bread they were ordered to keep..."

-July 15, "...The Bread must now be eaten that it may not be spoiled and they will continue baking the flour they receive so that they will always have 5 days Bread ready when the army embarks. The Rangers that fired this day are to complete their ammunition by applying to Major Ord, commanding officer of the Artillery..." "...As shots and shells fired or left by the enemy may be of use in sending back to them again—To those who pick them up and deliver to Commissary of Artillery Stores will receive for: a 13 inch shell-$1.00; 10-inch shell-a half-Dollar; 8-inch shell-quarter of a Dollar; large Shot-2 pence; smaller Shot-1 Penny; 5 Shillings for every good or repairable firelock brought into Headquarters."

"After orders:...an officer and 150 Rangers to conduct Provincial troops to a post on the West side of the Lake. The men to take one days provision, marching in their Waistcoats and Blankets..."

-July 16, "...8 of the Provincial Battalions are to give 13 men each and 2 of the Provincial Battalions 14 men each for the Ranging service. The men to be told they will receive the difference betwixt the pay. Commanding officers of those Battallions to turn out all Volunteers willing to serve in the Rangers tomorrow at 1 o'clock. Major Rogers will attend and choose the numbers each Regiment to furnish out of such Volunteers ..."

-July 18, "...Every man to have a good flint in his firelock and a spare flint in his pocket. Major Ord will furnish them... Volunteers from Provincials to join Rogers at 5 PM, must take no tents but live in huts in the same manner as the Rangers do. To take their provisions they have for tomorrow inclusive and they will afterwards draw with the Rangers and not be included in the provision return of their respective Regiments."

-July 19, "...Received flour again and ordered to bake it..."

-July 20, Embarkation orders: "...Col. Haviland to command Rangers, Light Infantry and Grenadiers in the attack...The men to land in their waistcoats, as light as possible, carrying only their blankets and provisions; no hurrying,no Huzzaying, upon any account whatsoever and no man to fire without orders from his officer...The men must row in turn and when not rowing to sleep..."

p-46 [69]Amherst to Captain John Shepherd, Lake George July 12, 1759—W.O.34, Vol 80, f 76: Shepheard also recommended Tute, who was his First Lieutenant.
Shepherd's Company was stationed at Half-Way-Brook during June "for scouting."—Ibid, Vol 23, f 24. Amherst to Eyre, June 20. Shepherd made at least one scout while here, for the British Commandant, Payson, sent him with 60 Rangers in pursuit of a lurking enemy party. The prowlers eluded Shepherd. —Ibid, Vol 77, f 87, H. Payson to Amherst, Halfway Brook, June 22.

p-46 [70]Lieutenant Andrew McMullen to Amherst, Ft. Royal, July 16—Ibid, Vol 77, f 97.

p-47 [71]Rogers, 139-40.

p-48 [72]See Loescher, I, p 405, ftn 13.

p-48 [73]Wooster, July 26: "...Enemy Indians firing in the rear..." July 27: "Rangers, Light Infantry, Grenadiers, Lyman's and Wooster's to entirely destroy the Road they have in their front by laying logs across and cutting some trees if necessary so as to make it impossible from Lake Champlain to the road leading to the saw-mill..."

p-48 [74]Rogers, p 140.

p-49 [75]Rogers, 143.

p-49 [76]Bouton, pp 195-6: "Tradition by J. Eastman."

p-50 [77]See p 351, Note 60, of this Volume.

p-54 [78]Webster, Sept. 15, 1759.

p-64 [79]Dibble, Nov. 19, 1759: Records that 20 Rangers died of starvation and 20 were killed.

p-64 [80]Pouchot, I, 222-23. See page 361-Appendix.

p-64 [81]Haviland to Amherst, Crown Point, Dec. 14, 1759—W.O.34, 51, f 2. Wallace was commissioned Lieutenant in Robert Rogers' New York Independent Company on June 25, 1763.

p-64 [82]N.Y. Mercury, No 380, Nov. 26, 1759.

p-64 [83]Rogers to Amherst, Dec. 12, 1759—W.O. 34, 78, f 182. "The misfortunes attending my Retreat from Saint Francois causes me great uneasiness, the Brave men lost I most heartily lament, and fear your Excellency's censure as the going against that place was my own proposal, and that I shall be disappointed of that Footing in the Army which I have long endeavored to merit..."

p-65 [84]Same to Same: "Lieutenant Stephen's Misconduct in coming off with the Provisions hurt me greatly and was the cause of so many perishing in the woods. I put him under an Arrest and also a Sergeant of Genl. Gage's Regiment for aspersing my Character by spreading a False Report that I took away from Dunbar's party Provisions and gave it away to others who had loaded themselves with Plunder after the place was destroyed. I hope Your Excellency will be pleased to order a Court Martial that I might have justice done me as I have nothing to depend on but my character."

Gage to Amherst, Albany, Dec. 17, 1759—Vol 46A, f 64: "Major Rogers is here demanding Court-Martial on Lieutenant Stephens of the Rangers for non-obedience of orders and Sergeant Lewis of my Regiment for false assertions. I have offered to comply with his requests, but his Evidences are so scattered thru all parts of the Country that it seems no easy matter to collect them. He tells me he has wrote you explaining everything..."

Same to Same, Vol 46A, f 69: Delivers Amherst's letter to Rogers "who has been here some Days. In Respect of the Court Martial I don't find they are more likely to be concluded than when I last wrote you, on which account I have given Lt. Stephens the liberty of the town 'till I hear that the Witnesses are collected..."

Amherst to Rogers (2 letters), Dec. 24, 1759—Vol 81, ff 200, 201: "I am Sorry to see you have so many Men Missing; this will, I hope, be a Lesson to all other Partys to Secure Provisions and themselves instead of Loading themselves with Plunder, by which they must be Lost, if an Enemy pursues... I Disapprove entirely of Lieut. Stephen's Conduct, and I have Wrote to Brigr. Genl Gage, that if the Evidences can be Collected without prejudicing the Service, it would be but right that a Court Martial should Sit for his Trial. I have no Objection neither to One on Mr. Gage's Serjeant, if You absolutely Chuse it, but the Evidences are so dispersed, that before they can be Assembled, a great deal of time must Elapse... but to tell you the truth, I do not think there is any Occasion for One, as, from anything I have heard of the Affair, it is not in the power of that Serjeant to hurt Your Character."

As a result of this letter Rogers waived his suit against Sergeant Lewis of Gage's.

Gage to Amherst, Albany, Jan. 20, 1760-46A, f 74: "When Major Rogers arrives here [in a day or two] he must decide whether Lieutenant Stephens can be tryed at present or not. He must know by this time if the necessary Evidence can be procured..."

However, it was not until three months later, on April 23, 1760, that Stephens was Courtmartialed at Crown Point and found guilty "...of Neglect of Duty, in not taking his Canoes up to Well's River according to his Orders from General Amherst & that therefore he be suspended during the General's pleasure." Lieutenant Samuel Stephens fades out of the Corps' history with an undated Memorial to Amherst stating that he has not received his pay from Nov. 25, 1759 to May 24, 1760, when he was dismissed from the service at Crown Point. —Vol 100, f 18.

p-65 [85]Wilson; Oct., 1759.

p-66 [86]Amherst to Lt. Solomon Unhaunwaumot, Crown Point, Oct. 27, 1759—W.O. 34, Vol 81, f 92. In Amherst's private notes on the losses in the Stockbridges—Vol 81, f 199: he notes that 12 went home on October 19, the day he abandoned his march on Isle aux Noix. In his Journal, Oct. 28, he comments on the remaining: "...as idle good for nothing a crew as ever was..." Amherst's instructions to Captain Sterling, Crown Point, Oct. 28—Vol 54, f 151, reveals his anxiety for his batteaus: "As some of the Indians that are going home are, I am told, Sick, You will furnish them with one Batteau and no more to carry them down to Albany, for which purpose you will give them a pass, setting forth, that upon their arrival there they must apply to Lieutenant Coventry and deliver the Batteau to him." Amherst to Colonel Willard at Ticonderoga, Oct. 27— Vol 81, f 95; Amherst to Colonel Miller at Ft. George, Oct. 27, Vol 81, f 94.

p-66 [87]Amherst to Lieutenant D'Arcy, Crown Point, Oct. 27 —Vol 81, f 93.

p-67 [88]Forsey, the Corps' principal uniform maker, was no longer in business—N.Y. Gazette.

p-67 [89]W.O. 34, Vol 81, f 199: "A Sergt & 8 Private Indians who were in Rogers' St. Francis Expedition returned home on Nov. 25th from Crown Point.

p-68 [90]Vol 8, f 6, 17-19. Amherst, Nov. 15th.

p-68 [91]Evenements de la Guerre en Canada 1759—p 79.

p-68 [92]Amherst to the officer commanding the Party of Rangers at Stillwater, Crown Pt., Nov. 2-81, f 113.

p-68 [93]Amherst's Journal to Pitt; Amherst, Nov. 22.

p-68 [94]Amherst to Robert Rogers at No. 4, N.H., Nov. 24— Vol 81, f 185.

p-68 [95]Amherst to Colonial Office, Dec. 15—C.O. 5/54 Amherst to Major Bellows at No 4, Crown Point, Nov. 10—Vol 81, f 149.

p-69 [96]John Stark to Amherst, Dec. 7, 1759: "The Ranging Officers with their places of abode in New England"—Vol 84, f 47. Amherst to Rogers, Nov. 24—Vol 81, f 185, expresses his candid opinion of certain Rangers: Hopes the officers "will be able to Raise better men than those who now demand their Discharges, of which the greater part is the worse trash that I believe was ever Collected in any Corps..."

p-69 [97]Amherst to Lieutenant Small at No. 4, Nov. 24, 1759—Vol 81, f 186.

p-69 [98]Amherst, Dec. 3, 1759.

p-69 [99]John Stark to Amherst, Albany, Dec. 7—W.O.34, Vol 78, ff 170-72. N.H. Gazette, No 176-Feb 15, 1760.

p-69 [100]Robert Rogers to Amherst, Albany, Dec. 17, 1759—W.O.34, Vol 78, f 188.

p-70 [101]See 'Interlude', pp 269-78 of this volume, Chapter IV—1759: Wolfe's Scouting Arm—pages 72-82.

p-72 [102]Amherst to Gage, Apr. 2—Vol 46A, f 154.

p-72 [103]Abercrombie's Ranger Commissions, N.Y., April 7, 1758—AM 124. Amherst to Gage, Apr. 2-46A/154.

p-73 [104]Ibid.

p-74 [105]James Rogers enlisted several Rangers in Boston and adjacent towns but at least 17 deserted. Captain Rogers offered a ten Dollar reward to "Whoever will apprehend any of the above Deserters and commit them to any of His Majesty's Gaols so as that they may be delivered to any officer of the Rangers shall have TEN DOLLARS Reward for each man."—News-Letter, Apr. 6, 12, 1759.

p-74 [106]Embarkation Return, June 5, 1759:
Goreham's--7 officers, 88 NCO's and Rangers.
W. Stark's--3 officers, 92 NCO's and Rangers.
J. Brewer's--3 officers, 82 NCO's and Rangers.
M. Hazen's--3 officers, 86 NCO's and Rangers.
J. Rogers'—4 officers, 108 NCO's and Rangers.
Dank's Company not arrived at date of return--3 officers and 90 men.--Mahon, p 95.

p-78 [107]George Scott to Amherst, Bost—Nov. 11-78/144.

p-78 [108]Perry.

p-78 [109]Knox, I, June 28-29th.

p-79 [110]Ibid, July 5th.

p-82 [111]George Scott to Amherst, Boston, Jan. 14, 1760—W. O. 34, Vol 82, f 15. Same to Same, Nov. 24, 1760—Vol 83, f 222-3. Monckton to Amherst, Sept. 25, 1759—Vol 43, f 34. Same to Same, Vol 43, f 38.

p-82 [112]George Scott to Amherst, Boston, Nov. 11, 1759—Vol 78, f 144-5. Same to Same, Jan. 1, 1760—Vol 82, f 1. Same to Same, Vol 82, ff 16-17. Ibid, Feb. 11, 1760—Vol 82, f 37. Amherst to Scott, Nov. 19, 1759—Vol 78, ff 174-5.

CHAPTER V
1760—CONQUEST OF CANADA—LAKE CHAMPLAIN FRONT
Pages 83-111

p-85 [113]Rogers, pp 161-166.

p-86 [114]Amherst to John Stark, March 1, 1760—W.O.34, Vol 84, f 52. Same to Same, March 19, 1760—Vol 84, f 61. Amherst to James Rogers, N.Y., March 19—Vol 84, f 65. Amherst to Jonathan Brewer, Same date f 66. John Stark to Amherst, Derryfield, N.H., Apr. 12, 1760—Vol 82, f 120. William Stark to Amherst, Derryfield, Apr. 12—Vol 82, f 119.

p-87 [115]Amherst to John Stark, N.Y., Apr. 24, 1760—Vol 84, f 109. James Rogers to Amherst, Boston, Mar. 31, 1760—Vol 82, f 100. David Brewer to Amherst, Boston, Apr. 18, 1760—Vol 82, f 130. Jonathan Brewer to Amherst, Boston, April 18, 1760—Vol 82, f 131.

p-87 [116]Amherst to William Stark, N.Y., Apr. 24—Vol 84, f 110. William Stark to Amherst, May 31, Londonderry, N.H. —Vol 82, f 222.

p-87 [117]Amherst to John Stark, March 1, 1760—Vol 84, f 52. Amherst to Robert Rogers, March 9, 1760—Vol 84, f 54.

p-87 [118]Robert Rogers to Amherst, Crown Point, April 24, 1760—Vol 39, f 126: offered a proposal to fill up the Corps' ranks with draughts from the Provincials which was adopted by Amherst.

p-87 [119]See footnotes 122 and 129.

p-88 [120]Haviland to Amherst, Crown Point, April 26, 1760— W.O.34, Vol 51, f 18.

p-88 [121]Same to Same, April 17, May 10—Vol 51/17, 20.

p-88 [122]Same to Same, Jan. 24th—Vol 51, f 5. Amherst to Haviland, March 9—Vol 52, f 18. Haviland to Amherst, Feb. 24—Vol 51, f 8.

p-88 [123]Amherst to Rogers, N.Y., March 9, 1760—Vol 84, f 54. Rogers to Amherst, Crown Point, Mar. 20, Vol 51, f 12. Rogers, p 167. Rogers to Amherst, April 24—Vol 39, f 126.

p-89 [124]Amherst to Rogers, Albany, May 30—Vol 84, f 237. Amherst to Captain Solomon, May 30—Ibid, 239.

p-89 [125]Haviland to Amherst, Crown Point, May 8, 1760—W.O.34, Vol 51, f 19.

p-90 [126]Amherst to DeLancey, Albany, May 15—Ibid, Vol 30, f 102. Same to Lt. Grant, April 13—Vol 84—f 99.

p-91 [127]Haviland to Amherst, Crown Point, May 18—Ibid, Vol 51, f 22. Same to Same, June 13—f 48.

p-91 [128]Amherst to Robert Rogers, May 14—Vol 52/27.

p-92 [129]Robert Rogers' Memorial to Amherst, Albany, May 23, 1760—Ibid, Vol 82, f 219.

p-92 [130]Amherst, May 26-27, 1760.

p-93 [131]Haviland to Amherst, May 30—Vol 51, f 33.

p-93 [132]Haviland to Amherst, May 28—Ibid, ff 30-1.

p-93 [133]Haviland to Amherst, May 30—Ibid, ff 33-4. Amherst to Haviland, June 3rd—Vol 52, f 41.

p-93 [134]Haviland to Amherst, May 30—Ibid, f 35-6.

p-94 [135]Samuel Stark to Amherst, Derryfield, April 12—Vol 82, f 118. Amherst's List of Ranging Officers May 24, 1760—Vol 84, f 192. Robert Rogers to Abercrombie, N.Y., Apr. 7, 1758—AB 124.

p-99 [136]Haviland to Amherst, June 6—Vol 51, f 39. Same to Same, June 7—Ibid, f 42. Amherst to Haviland, June 3—Vol 52, f 40.

p-103 [137]Even Haviland believed that Holmes effected all that was possible: "...I am sorry that Lieutenant Holmes could not find the place he was ordered to, I have so good an opinion of him that I am sure he did all that was in his power..." Haviland to Amherst, Crown Point, June 24—W.O.34, Vol 51, f 63.

p-103 [138]One of the Courier Squad, Luxford Goodwin, received a Sergeantcy in Rogers Rangers as a result of his services—W.O.34, Vol 51, f 198—Goodwin to Haviland, Crown Point, Aug. 30, 1761.

p-103 [139]The anonymous Ranger Journalist writing for the Boston-News-Letter in 1760 dates his articles from 'Point Rogers.' Haviland to Amherst, June 24, 1760—W.O.34, Vol 51, f 63.

p-104 [140]Amherst to Major Rogers, Camp at Oswego, July 11, 1760—Vol 52, f 72. Amherst to Haviland, Ibid, f 69. Haviland to Amherst, Crown Point, June 24—Vol 51, f 63. Same to Same, July 26, f 76.

p-104 [141]Amherst to Major Rogers, July 11—Vol 52, f 72. Amherst's Succession of Rangers in late Johnson's Company, Three Rivers, July 9—Vol 85, f 2. On May 25, 1760, Lieutenant Simon Stevens was ordered by Amherst to join Rogers at Crown Point with his recruiting Sergeant and the nineteen men they had recruited in New England.—Amherst to Rogers, Albany, May 25, 1760—W.O.34, Vol 84, f 205.

p-106 [142]Amherst to Rogers, July 11—Vol 52, f 72. Jenks, July 3, 1760. Holden, July 2-3rd.

p-106 [143]Haviland to Amherst, June 7, 1760—Vol 51, f 42. Same to Same, June 13—Ibid, f 48: "...Our Ladys set out this morning for Albany..." The Provincial, Captain Jenks, notes in his journal on July 24, the smuggling in of one of the supposed 'wives' by an unidentified Sutler: "There is one of my men that was stationed at Ticonderoga that come up with a Sutler who has brought up a very fine mistress with him. On their passage they fell into disputes. At length he struck her, which inraged hir so that after several fits and efforts jumpt over board. This cooled her courage, for her sweetheart held her under water until she was almost expiring. They then took her in, stript off her cloaths and drest anew, and so the fray ended. I wish it were the fate of all these sort of ladys that follow the army. She apeard prety likely and was very well drest..."

p-107 [144]Colonel John Darby to Amherst, Crown Point, July 20—Vol 51, f 75. Ford.

p-107 [145]Jenks, July 22-23, 1760.

p-107 [146]Holden, July 24, 1760. Robert Rogers to Amherst, May 4—Vol 82, f 172. Amherst to Robert Rogers, July 11, 1760—Vol 52, f 72.

p-108 [147]Holden, July 25, 1760.

p-108 [148]Ibid, Aug. 1, 1760.

p-108 [149]MacClintock, Aug. 4, 1760—Goffe's N.H. Regt. However, on Aug. 26, 41 Provincials were drafted out of the Massachusetts Regiments to join Major Rogers "...in Lieu of that number of the New Hampshires that was not fit for Rangers..." Holden, Aug. 26th.

p-108 [150]Hodge, Orderly Book, 1760.

p-108 [151]Rogers, Haviland, Aug. 16, 1760.

p-108 [152]Holden, Aug. 6, 1760. Robert Rogers to Appy Camp at Crown Point, Aug. 6—Vol 51, f 83.

p-108 [153]Amherst to Haviland, July 29—Vol 52, f 74.

p-108 [154]Rogers, p 189. MacClintock, Aug. 14: states that 3 of the Rangers drowned were draftees from Goffe's N. H. Regiment.

p-109 [155]MacClintock, Aug. 26th. Hodge, Aug. 18th.

p-109 [156]Hodge, Aug. 20th.

p-109 [157]Ibid, Aug. 20th.

p-111 [158]Rogers, p 194. Jenks, Sept. 3, 1760.

p-111 [159]Goodwin to Haviland, Aug. 30, 1761—Vol 51, f 198. Holden, Sept. 5. Haviland's Disbursements in 1760 Campaign —Sept. 14, entry.—Vol 198, f 249.

CHAPTER VI
1760—CONQUEST OF CANADA—QUEBEC FRONT
Pages 112-122

p-112 [160]Knox, Vol II—Nov-Dec. 1759.

p-114 [161]Amherst to Lieutenant John Butler, N.Y., Apr. 19, 1760—W.O.34, Vol 84, f 103.

p-114 [162]In spite of the determination of these partisan bands there were 14 French deserters who acquiesced and General Murray ordered them into Hazen's Company on a probationary Ranger status. They served in the Company for 54 days.— Hazen to Amherst, Nov. 17, 1760, W.O.34, Vol 3, ff 55-56.

p-115 [163]Murray, April 2-4, 1760.

p-119 [164]Knox, II, p 459, 463. Hazen to Amherst, Albany, Nov. 18, 1760, Vol 3, f 40-51: The strength of Hazen's Company for 1759-60:
-Apr. 25-June 24, 1759—99 Officers*and men.
-June 25-Aug. 24, 1759—98 Officers and men.
-Aug. 25-Oct. 24, 1759—141 Officers and men.
-Oct. 25-Dec. 24, 1759—141 Officers and men.
-Dec. 25—Feb. 24, 1760—138 Officers and men.
-Feb. 25-Apr. 24, 1760—138 Officers and men.
-Apr. 25-June 24, 1760—145 Officers and men.

-June 25-Aug. 24, 1760—139 Officers and men.
-Aug 25-Oct. 24, 1760—123 Officers* and men.
*The number of Officers and Sergeants during this period (1759-60) were: 1 Captain, 2 Lieutenants, 1 Ensign and 4 Sergeants. Sick lists for April and June 1760 report:
-14 Rangers sick in the garrison on April 24.
-1 Captain and 16 men sick & wounded on June 15th.

p-119 [165]Knox, Murray, July-Aug-Sept. 1760.

p-122 [166]Murray, Sept. 6, Rogers, Sept. 6th. Ensign Hazen of Rogers Rangers carried the dispatches from Murray to the Lake Champlain front arriving there on Sept. 5.

CHAPTER VII
1760—CONQUEST OF CANADA—GREAT LAKES FRONT
Pages 123-134

p-123 [167]Amherst's List of Winter Quarters 1759-60, Wood, L., C.O., Vol 5, f 54.

p-123 [168]Amherst to Rogers, March 1, 1760—in Rogers p 161.

p-123 [169]Rogers to Amherst, Apr. 24th-Vol 39, f 126. Gage to Amherst, Albany, Apr. 27th—Vol 46A, f 118. An Effective Roll of Captain Waite's Recruits at Albany, May 9, 1760—Vol 82, f 181. Allowance for Recruiting Provisions—Vol 198, f 215.

p-123 [170]Amherst to Joseph Waite, Albany, May 9th—Vol 84, f 128.

p-124 [171]Rogers, pp 164-66. Rogers to Amherst, Mar. 20—Vol 51, f 12. Allowance for Recruiting Provisions Vol 198, ff 125-27, 301. Ogden's Company arrived at Albany on May 26th. —Amherst, May 26, 1760.

p-124 [172]Amherst to Eyre, Albany, June 5—Vol 23/27.

p-124 [173]Amherst, May 29th. Hervey, June 16, Aug. 5.

p-125 [174]Hervey, July 26th, Ft. Ontario.

p-125 [175]Hervey, Aug. 5, Ft. Ontario.

p-125 [176]Ibid, Aug. 7-8, Ft. Ontario.

p-125 [177]Amherst to the Serjt. of Ogden's, Aug. 15,—Vol 85, f 44. Lt. Charles Robertson to Amherst, Aug. 16—Vol 42, f 262. Amherst, Aug. 14th.

p-126 [178]Amherst, Aug. 29, See Appendix, p 383.

p-126 [179]Jacob Cheeksaunkun to Amherst, Albany, Nov. 16, 1760—Vol 198, f 309.

p-126 [180]Amherst, Woodhull, Plant, Vail, Hervey, Aug. 31—Sept. 8.

p-126 [181]Hervey, Sept. 10-12th.

p-127 [182]See ftn 70; Macomb, Letter-Book.

p-127 [183]Mayer, p 392. Macomb.

p-128 [184]Mayer, p 389.

p-128 [185]Rogers Papers; Edgar Papers.

CHAPTER VIII
1760—DISBANDMENT AND WINTER SERVICE
Pages 135-141

p-135 [186]Rogers, p 229.

p-136 [187]The Government to Major Rogers—W.O. 34, Vol 199, ff 173-4. Ensign Benjamin Wait relates the abject coldness and suffering of his three Rangers escorting the French officer from Miamis to Detroit: "...the men, becoming disheartened and benumbed with cold, would beg him [wait] to shoot them, instead of which he switched their legs with sticks until aroused by anger they resumed their march..." Jones, M., 10

p-136 [188]Capt Donald Campbell to Amherst, Detroit, Jan. 23, 1761.—Vol 49, f 17.

p-136 [189]Same to Same, Feb. 14—Vol 49, ff 19-20. Lt. John Butler to the Crown, N.Y., 1762—Vol 201, f 45—Butler had paid Lorrain 149 pounds on Sept. 23, 1761 for his wood and salt.

p-137 [190]Lt. John Butler to the Crown, N.Y., Dec. 31, 1761—Vol 200, f 7. Capt Campbell to Amherst, Detroit, May 10, 1761—Vol 49, f 31. Same to Same, April 18—Vol 49, f 35. Ibid, May 22—Vol 49, f 36. Ibid, Aug. 9—Vol 49, f 46. Return of Provisions at Detroit, Sept. 16, 1761.—Vol 49, f 57: "Forwarded to Miamis at Sundry times - 17 Barrels of Flour; 10 Barrels of Pork; 21 Bushels Indian Corn.

p-137 [191]Campbell to Amherst, Detroit—Vol 200, f 39. Same to Same, Sept. 10, 1761—Vol 49, f 51. Capt Henry Balfour to Amherst, Detroit, Sept. 9, 1761—Vol 49, f 49. A Return of the Detroit Posts, Nov. 8, 1761—49 f 65.

p-137 [192]Campbell to Bouquet, Detroit, Oct. 12, 1761. Bouquet Coll—A. 17, p 240. Butler to Amherst—49/166.

p-137 [193]Campbell to Amherst, Nov. 8—Vol 49, f 63.

p-138 [194]Amherst to Johnson, N.Y., Dec. 30, 1761; Johnson Papers, III, p 597. Johnson to Amherst, Ft. Johnson, Jan. 7, 1762—Ibid, p 600: backs Butler's claim. Campbell to Amherst, Jan. 10, 1762—Vol 49, f 68. Butler to Amherst, N.Y., Jan. 1, 1762, "Sundries supplied the Miamis garrison Dec. 6, 1760 to Oct. 25, 1761."—Vol 49, f 166. Same to Same—Vol 49, f 170.

p-138 [195]Holden, Sept. 30th.

p-138 [196]Hobart, Oct. 15th.

p-139 [197]Ibid, Oct. 25th. Amherst, Nov. 11th. Amherst to Capt James Rogers, Crown Point, Oct. 25—Vol 52/92.

p-139 [198]Ibid, Oct. 25th. N.Y. Mercury, June 8, 1761.

p-139 [199]Ibid, Amherst to Major Skene, Albany, Nov. 20, 1760.—Vol 52, f 99. Amherst to Haviland, Montreal, Sept. 21, 1760—Vol 52, f 87. Same to Same, Oct. 24.—Vol 52, f 90.

p-139 [200]Amherst to Lt. Van Tyne, Crown Point, Oct. 18, 1760—Vol 85, f 149. Amherst to the Sergt of Ogden's Rangers that is to command during the Winter at St. John's with 9 Rangers, Crown Point, Oct. 19.—Vol 85, f 167.

p-140 [201]Amherst to Haviland, Dec. 7, 1760, N.Y.—Vol 52, f 103. Ibid, Jan. 26, 1761—Vol 52, f 107.

p-140 [202]Same to Same, Feb. 1, 1761—Vol 52, f 108. Haviland to Amherst, Crown Point, Jan. 9, 1761—Vol 51, f 104. Same to Same, Jan. 19—Vol 51, f 105.

p-140 [203]Amherst to Haviland, N.Y., March 15, 1761—Vol 52, f 160. Loescher (3): Chapter V, Ranger Goodwin's cure.

p-141 [204]Haviland to Amherst, Apr. 10, 1761—Vol 51, f 115. Winter Rangers' Contract with Capt. Ogden, Oct. 18, 1760—Vol 51, f 117. Amherst to Haviland, N.Y., Apr. 26, 1761—Vol 52, f 115.

p-141 [205]Haviland to Amherst, May 7, 1761—Vol 51/122.

p-141 [206]Same to Same, May 19—Vol 51, f 127. Capt. Wrightson's Account of Winter Rangers' Pay, Ticonderoga, March 1761—Vol 199, f 128. Account of the Pay of Van Tyne's Detachment for 1760-61, Tic., May 22, 1761—Vol 199, f 234. Amherst to Haviland, Albany, May 27, 1761—Vol 52, f 123:

writes: "Lt Van Tyne is arrived here; his men would at first Enlist, but were afterwards off; they are always tired of the place they are in. I was in hopes of getting the best of them into Regular Corps..."

p-141 [207]Amherst's Warrant to Ogden, Mar. 16, 1761, N.Y., —Vol 199, f 105.

CHAPTER IX
1761-1762—CONQUEST OF THE FRENCH WEST INDIES
Pages 142-145

p-142 [208]Boston News-Letter, Feb. 12, 1761. Account of Pay for Waite's Company, Mar. 25-May 24, 1761—Vol 199, f 187.

p-142 [209]Amherst's Warrant to Ogden, N.Y., Apr 28, 1761— Vol 199, f 185. Amherst, May 3rd.

p-142 [210]Moses Hazen to Amherst, Nov. 19, 1760, Albany— Vol 83, f 203-4.

p-143 [211]Amherst, May 3rd. Fortescue.

p-143 [212]Fortescue.

p-143 [213]Ibid.

p-143 [214]Lord Rollo to Amherst, Dominique, July 7, 1761— Vol 55, f 12.

p-144 [215]Amherst to Monckton, Albany, Aug. 6, 1761—Vol 43, f 183. Amherst to Mortier, Aug. 6, 1761—Vol 199, f 277. Anonymous 74th Private Diary, Oman, editor.

p-144 [216]Returns of Ogden's and Waite's showed 1 Captain, 1 Lieut, 1 Ensign, 4 Sergts and 62 Privates in Ogden's. 1 Capt, 1 Lieut, 4 Sergts and 35 Privates—Vol 199, ff 286, 310, 352.

p-144 [217]Amherst, Nov. 15, 19, 1761.

p-145 [218]Fortescue. Lord Rollo's Correspondence to Amherst —in W.O. 34, Vol 55. Gordon, Journal no. 2.

p-145 [219]Amherst, June 16-17, 1762. A Muster of Ogden's Company on board the Backell Transport, June 16, 1762, N.Y. —Vol 200, ff 244-46. Ibid, Waite's - on board the Rachel.— Vol 200, f 256.

p-145 [220]Musters of Waite's and Ogden's at Ft. Royal Apr. 17, 1762—Vol 200, ff 254, 250.

p-145 [221]So ended Waite's Company of Rogers Rangers which had existed since the spring of 1758.

CHAPTER X
1761—THE CHEROKEE ENGLISH WAR
Pages 146-152

p-147 [222]McCrady, pp 325-30. Amherst, Feb. 12, 1761. Corkran, D.H.: The Cherokee Frontier—1962, U. Okla. Press for his definitive Chapter 17, pp 236-54 on Grant's expedition.

p-147 [223]Amherst's Instructions to Grant (relative to Stockbridge and Mohawk Rangers), N.Y., Dec. 15, 1760.—W.O.34, Vol 48, f 39.

p-147 [224]Grant's Queries to Amherst and Answers (relative to employing the Indian Rangers), Dec. 21, 1760.—Vol 48, ff 50-51.

p-147 [225]Amherst to Grant, N.Y., Dec. 22, 1760.—Vol 48, f 55. Amherst, Feb. 12, 1761. S.C. Gazette, Jan.

p-148 [226]Amherst to Grant, N.Y., Feb. 27, 1761.—Vol 48, f 64.

p-148 [227]Ford; Foote (1)

p-148 [228]Amherst to Grant, Feb. 27, 1761.—Vol 48, f 64.

p-148 [229]Amherst to Grant, 'List of Recruits belonging to Captain Robert Rogers Independent Company,' N.Y., March 17, 1761.—Vol 48, f 71: Lt. Jacob Farrington, Privates William Miller, Lowris Vesteroot, Daniel Nepash, Daniel Whiteham, Billy Cooper, Frederic Cahon, Wonk Napkin, Samuel O'Brien, Samuel Mamenash, David Way (all Stockbridge Privates). Richard Aspinwell, Joseph Chandler, Abraham Fowler, Thomas Clish (four veteran white Rangers).

p-148 [230]Ibid, f 70.

p-148 [231]Amherst to Jacob Farrington, N.Y., March 17, 1761. Vol 48, f 69.

p-148 [232]Amherst to Grant, Mar. 17—Vol 48, f 70. Loescher (3): Chapter III, Ranger Goodwin's Cherokee Rum.

p-148 [233]N.Y. Mercury, June 29, 1761, and July 6th. Corkran, p 244.

p-149 [234]Ibid, June 29, 1761.

p-149 [235]Philopatrios: Middleton to Grant, July 10, July 19, 1761. Grant to Middleton, July 10. Gov. Bull to Grant, Apr. 10, 1761. McCrady, pp 229-30.

p-149 [236]Grant's Journal of the March of Operations of the Troops from Fort Prince George against the Cherokees, June 7-July 9, 1761.—Vol 40, ff 95-98.

p-150 [237]Ibid, June 10, 1761.

p-150 [238]Ibid, June 11, 1761.

p-151 [239]Ibid, June 18-20, 1761. Corkran, 251: Kennedy & Farrington were sent with 500 men to dispose of a reported gathering of warriors at Joree. But after a steep back route climb they found Joree empty.

p-151 [240]Ibid, June 28, 1761.

p-152 [241]Ibid, July 9, 1761.

p-152 [242]Grant to Amherst, July 1761—Vol 47, f 96.

p-152 [243]Amherst to Grant, Aug. 26, 1761—Vol 47, f 100. McCrady, pp 233-4. Amherst, July 31st.

p-152 [244]Amherst to Grant, July 13, 1761.—Vol 48, f 81. Rogers to Wife, Betsy, Charlestown, Nov. 9, 1761.

p-152 [245]Rogers to Amherst, Charlestown, Oct. 17, 1761.—Vol 47, f 110.

p-152 [246]Ibid. It is unknown in what capacity Jacob Farrington served in Rogers' Company. Lieutenant Nathan Stone petitioning Amherst received an Ensigncy in another S. C. Company.—Amherst to Grant, Aug. 1, 1761—Vol 48, f 84. Ibid, Feb. 4, 1762.—Vol 48, f 95. Ibid Apr. 30, 1762.—Vol 92, f 106. Nathan Stone to Amherst, Albany, July 1, 1761.—Vol 87, f 1.

p-152 [247]McCrady, pp 335-40.

CHAPTER XI
1763—PONTIAC'S WAR
Pages 153-159

p-153 [248]Amherst, May 28; June 16, 21, 29; July 12, 23, 26; Sept. 27, 30; Oct. 4; Nov. 1, 7th.

p-153 [249]Amherst to Rogers, Dec. 26, 1762.—Vol 93/272.

p-154 [250]Pargellis, The Four Independent Companies of New York.

p-154 [251]Supposition of S. M. Pargellis.

p-154 [252]C.O.5, Vol 154, no 18.

p-154 [253]Rogers to Amherst, Ft. Ontario, June 20, 1763.—Vol 19, f 230.

p-154 [254]Rogers to Wife, Betsy, Ft. Ontario, June 21, 1763. —Robert Rogers-Elizabeth Rogers Corr. Return of Rogers' Men, Ft. Ontario, June 20, 1763.—Vol 39, f 357. Dalyell's Embarkation Returns, Ft. Ontario, July 3, 1763.—Vol 39, f 358.

p-155 [255]"His Majesty's Independent Company of Foot or The Queen's Royal American Rangers" were raised in Pennsylvania in May, 1762 and served conspicuously at Niagara (the bulk under Lt. Abraham Cuyler) and Detroit (Capt. Joseph Hopkins, Ensign Perry and 24 rank and file).—Hopkins to Amherst, June 24, 1762, Vol 200, f 190. Ibid, Nov. 23, 1762—Vol 49, f 131-33.

p-155 [256]Carter, II, p 376.

p-155 [257]Carter,—Gage to Barrington, Jan. 15, 1766—Corr of Gage, II, 331-2. Among the traders and merchants who joined Rogers' command at Detroit were Rangers Caesar McCormick, James Sterling, Samson Fleming (who was Deputy-Commissary of Detroit).—Declaration made to Caesar McCormick, June 11, 1763.—W.O.34, Vol 39, f 364.

p-158 [258]Hough, Siege of Detroit, p 56.

p-159 [259]Parkman, Conspiracy of Pontiac, Vol I, 317-329; Vol II, 115-118.

p-159 [260]As late as 1766, Rogers in N.Y., was petitioning the home office for the pay and subsistence of his Pontiac War Rangers. Gage, Commander-in-Chief in North America, wrote Sec'y of State Barrington two letters respecting Rogers' claim stating that he could find no evidence that Rogers' Company of Rangers existed. It appears that Gage was deliberately attempting to cut Rogers out of his just claim for he admitted disbanding "the Platoons and Rangers" in January, 1764. Rogers' Muster roll and Correspondence to Amherst from Ft. Ontario in 1763 clearly defines the Company. Rogers claimed that he drew 320 pounds 7 shillings from Joseph Knox, a Merchant at Niagara to pay for 1 Sergt, at 4 shillings per day and 13 Privates at 3 shillings per day from Dec. 3, 1762 to May 1, 1764. —Carter, Corr of Gage, II, pp 218, 331-2, 376. Gage Papers, Vol 8G9, f 66. See ftn 254-255 of this Volume.

p-159 [261]Elliot.

CHAPTER XII
INTERLUDE
Pages 160-166

p-161 [262]Abstract of Major Rogers' Claims against the Crown while in command of H. M. Independent Companies of Rangers, May 18, 1761. —Vol 199, ff 213-14.

p-162 [263]Lt. W. Ramsay to Amherst, Charles Town, June 28, 1762. —Vol 47, f 123. Ibid, Aug. 10th—f 129.

p-162 [264]W.O.34, Vol 93, f 252.

p-162 [265]Chatham Papers, Vol 96, from the Governor and Council of N. Carolina, Wilmington, Dec. 9, 1761.

p-162 [266]Capt. Robert Rogers to Amherst, Charles Town Oct. 24, 1761 (answered Nov. 21st)—W.O.34, Vol 47.

p-162 [267]Rogers to Amherst, Charles Town, Oct. 17, 1761. —Vol 47, f 110. Rogers to Wife, Betsy, Nov. 9, 1761. —Rogers-Elizabeth Rogers Corr.

p-163 [268]Amherst to Rogers, N.Y., June 28, 1762. —Vol 92, f 241. (Receives Rogers' letter of March 20th).

p-163 [269]Same to Same, July 5, 1762—Vol 93, f 16. (Receives Rogers' letter of April 29th).

p-163 [270]Ibid.

p-163 [271]Same to Same, Aug. 23, 1762. —Vol 93, f 89.

p-163 [272]Same to Same, Dec. 26, 1762. —Vol 93, f 272.

p-163 [273]Ibid, May 3, 1763. —Vol 96, f 125.

p-164 [274]Watts to Smith and Nutt, N.Y., Nov. 3, 1762. Watts, p 93. Watts to Maj. Robt. Rogers, N.Y., Nov. 15, 1762. — Watts, p 95. Watts to John Erving, N.Y., Nov. 29, 1762. — Watts, p 99.

p-164 [275]Watts to Smith and Nutt, N.Y., Dec. 2, 1762. Watts, p 103. Watts to John Erving, N.Y., Dec. 22, 1762. —Watts, p 111.

p-164 [276]Watts to Erving, Jan. 11, 1763—Watts, p 114. Watts to Smith & Nutt, Feb. 12, 1763—p 125. Ibid, Aug. 31, 1763. — p 180.

p-164 [277]Rogers Papers.

p-164 [278]Ibid. Askin Papers. Gordon MSS.

p-165 [279]Rogers Papers. Their outstanding creditors were Cornelius Glen, Shipboy and Henry, John DePeyster, and John A. Lansing of Albany and Henry Agnew, Alexander Stewart and Greg & Cunningham of New York. These creditors, particularly Greg & Cunningham, were responsible for Robert Rogers' term in Fleet Prison.

p-165 [280]Johnson Papers—Johnson to Cadwallader Colden, Ft. Johnson, June 18, 1761.—Vol 3, p 409.

p-165 [281]Robert Rogers to the King, London, Dec. 21, 1769. —C.O. 5:1074, ff 385-387.

p-166 [282]Rogers left for England in March 1765.

CHAPTER XIII
AMERICAN REVOLUTION—ROGERS' QUEENS RANGERS
Pages 167-178

p-167 [283]Rogers was confined in the Fleet Prison from June 1770 to June 1773.

p-167 [284]Major Robert Rogers to the King.—George III, Corr, Vol II, Letter No. 814. Rogers to Dartmouth, Mar. 13, 1775— Hist MSS Commission.

p-167 [285]Jones, J.E., part two.

p-168 [286]Amer. Arch., 4th Series, Vol III.

p-168 [287]Nevins, pp 160-165; Potter, pp 489-493.

p-168 [288]Ibid.

p-168 [289]Moore, H.P., pp 214-15.

p-168 [290]Howe to Dartmouth, Boston, Nov. 26, 1775. Amer. Arch., 4th Series, III, p 1674.

p-168 [291]Ibid.

p-168 [292]Germain to Howe, London, Jan. 5, 1776.—Amer. Arch., 4th Series, IV, p 575.

p-169 [293]Rogers to wife, Betsy, Medford, Dec. 17, 1775.— Rogers-Elizabeth Corr.

p-169 [294]Potter, p 490.

p-169 [295]Moore, H.P.; Potter, pp 490-93.

p-169 [296]Washington-Congress, June 27, 1776.—Writings of Washington, V, p 185. Potter, pp 491-3.

p-169 [297]Congress to Washington, July 6, 1776.—Ibid V, p 184.

p-170 [298]Sparks, IV, p 520.

p-170 [299]Jones, E., ed; A Letter Regarding the Queen's Rangers.—Va Mag of Hist, Oct. 1922, 368-376.

p-170 [300]Jones, J. E.

p-170 [301]See Sketches, Vol III, check name index.

p-172 [302]Washington to Gov. Trumbull, Sept. 30, 1776; Trumbull to Washington, Oct. 13, 1776—Writings of Washington, IV, pp 128-9. General Lee to Washington Camp at Phillipsburg, Nov. 12, 1776—Amer. Arch., III, p 653. Lee to Col. Reed, Camp, Nov. 24, 1776—Ibid, pp 833-4. Lee to Washington, Peekskill, Nov. 30, 1776—Ibid, p 932.

p-172 [303]Kemble, Oct. 17, 20, 1776.

p-172 [304]Hadaway, p 20. Nevins, pp 165-66.

p-173 [305]Ibid. Devoe, p 118.

pp-175, 176 [306]Captain John Shepherd. Howe to Germain, N.Y., Nov. 30, 1776.—Amer. Arch., Vol III, p 922.

p-176 [307]Hough, pp 277-8.

p-177 [308]Jones, E., ed: Letter Regarding the Queens Rangers.

p-177 [309]Ibid. Jarvis, Jan.-Mar., 1777.

p-178 [310]Rogers to Haldimand, Sept. 26, 1779—Haldimand Coll., B.160, p 17. Clinton to Haldimand (no date) referring Rogers and his officers and men to him.—Haldimand Papers.

p-178 [311]Hannay, pp 125-30. Clinton Papers, f.15.

CHAPTER XIV
AMERICAN REVOLUTION—ROGERS' KINGS RANGERS
Pages 179-201

p-179 [312]Rogers to Haldimand, Sept. 26, 1779—"...I can but return you most respectfull thanks for the favour you did me the Last winter in Granting me leave to go to England, by which means I got provided for."—Haldimand Coll, B.160, p 17. Clinton's Commission to Lt.-Col. Robert Rogers, N.Y., May 1, 1779—Haldimand Coll., B.160, p 1.

p-180 [313]Rogers to Amherst, N.Y., June 16, 1779—W.O.34, Vol 115, f 71.

p-180 [314]Amherst to Rogers, Whitehall, Sept. 10, 1779.— Ibid, Vol 231, f 273.

p-180 [315]Rogers to Amherst, Halifax, Sept. 11, 1779—Ibid, Vol 155, f 181.

p-180 [316]Rogers to Haldimand, N.Y., July 17, 1779.—Haldimand Coll, B.160, pp 8-9. Haldimand to Rogers, Que., Sept. 18, 1779.—Ibid, p 12.

p-181 [317]James Rogers to Haldimand, Que., Oct. 20, 1779.— Ibid, p 20. Rogers, W., pp 49-50.

p-181 [318]Stryker, pp 50, 60, 62, 65. Jones, E.A.

p-181 [319]J. Rogers to Haldimand, 'List of Officers,' Sept. 14, 1779.—Haldimand Coll, B.160, p 11. Cornet Daniel Bissonet to Haldimand, Sept. 24, 1779.—Ibid, p 14. John Longstreet to Haldimand, Lorette, Nov. 23, 1779.—Ibid, p 21.

p-181 [320]Rogers to Haldimand, Ft. Howe, Sept. 26, 1779.— Ibid, p 17.

p-181 [321]Same to Same, Ft. Howe, Sept. 29—Ibid, p 18.

p-182 [322]Haldimand to Rogers, Que, Feb. 10, 1780.—Ibid, pp 27-8. Rogers to Haldimand, Que, Feb. 22.—Ibid, pp 29-30. Same to Same, Que, Feb. 25.—Ibid, p 31. Haldimand to Clinton, Que, Jan. 31, 1780.—Haldimand Papers (Mich), Vol 19, p 496.

p-182 [323]Haldimand to R. Rogers, Que, Feb. 10, 1780—Haldimand Coll, B.160, pp 27-8.

p-183 [324]R. Rogers to Haldimand, Que, Feb. 25, 1780.—Ibid, p 31. Haldimand to Rogers, Mar. 7.—Ibid, p 32. Ranger Captain Longstreet to Haldimand, Que, Mar. 10, 1780:—Complains that Col. Rogers has not paid him the money drawn on his account.—Ibid, p 33.

p-183 [325]Elizabeth Rogers to The Council House of Representatives of N.H., Feb. 11, 1778.—Rogers-Elizabeth Rogers Corr; Sabine, II, pp 234-36. As a result of Elizabeth's above petition she obtained a divorce from Robert and the custody of their son.

p-183 [326]Rogers to Haldimand, Lake on the Grand Portage, Mar. 20, 1780.—Haldimand Coll, B.160, p 34.

p-184 [327]Ibid.

p-184 [328]Haldimand to Brigadier Maclean, Que, Jan. 30, 1780. —Ibid, B.150, p 52. Same to Same, Jan. 30:—Rogers says he has 700 men enlisted, 400 being at Penobscot; has different accounts from others; desires to know the real state of affairs. p 56. Haldimand to Lt.-Gov. Hughes, Feb. 28, 1780.—Ibid, p 59. Haldimand to Brigadier Maclean, May 28, 1780.—Ibid, p 61. Haldimand to Major J. Rogers, Apr. 24—Ibid, 44. Maclean to Haldimand, Que, Mar. 7, 1780.—B.149, p 570.

p-184 [329]Robert Rogers' elusive trail would have commanded the best tracking efforts of a modern James Bond. Rogers' 'dossier', although scanty, is enough to piece together an incredible story: Apparently word had preceded him for his reception in Halifax left much to be desired. Undaunted, Rogers cast a speculative eye towards Newfoundland, the last probable source of credit. Robert Rogers to Amherst, Halifax, May 8, 1780: "As I shall have a number of Recruits to bring from Newfoundland the approaching Autumn, therefore desire your Lordship will give orders to the Military officer commanding in that place to give me or my officers all the assistance he can, which will much promote his Majesty's service."—W.O. 34, Vol 163/129. The slowness of communication to and from England precluded the swift assistance needed from his old commander and Rogers was gaoled in Halifax for debt by June of 1780. Managing to eventually obtain his release he turned up on the Penobscot Bay front about the time that his Ranger Captain, Black Jones, was emulating Rogers' own daring forays of the French and Indian War (see text pp 329-332). It is possible that Rogers had a hand in his Ranger battalions happenings on the maritime provinces front for the balance of 1780 at least as there is evidence that he was on the front. On September 14, 1780 (no location), Rogers wrote on a two of diamonds playing card a pass for one 'Reegawiskom' to pass to the front of the lines. —HM 13473. The Penobscot region was the only front of consequence at this time, where Rogers would be employed. The beginning of 1781 started a new, if not ironic chapter in his falling star. Boarding a schooner bound for New York harbour the ship was captured by the brigantine Patty under Captain Read on January 10, 1781. Since she was a Pennsylvania Privateer Rogers ended up in the new gaol in Philadelphia.—Pennsylvania Gazette, 10 January, 1781. Rogers' repeated efforts to arrange an exchange were to no avail until the spring of 1782.

Reported with the British on May 10, 1782. January, 1783. — Major James Rogers to Haldimand, St. John's, Que. —Haldimand Coll, B.160 pp 125-6: Robert Rogers apparently still held the reins of his King's Rangers for brother James was receiving word that Colonel Rogers had no objection to Major James Rogers' battalion at St. John's, Quebec being under Haldimand's command. Colonel Rogers probably was instrumental in the final mustering out of his battalion on the St. John's River in present New Brunswick province, before he made his last crossing to England. The final twelve years of his life were tragic to say the least. In and out of debtors' prison, at least four years of his remaining life he was in debt for his half pay was assigned to creditors for the years 1784, 1788, 1793, and 1794. Southwark resounded to his drinking bouts during his last days. He was completely in hock to his landlord, John Walker. Apparently he developed tuberculosis of the lungs and a severe fall damaged his mind, hastening his last scout which came on May 18, 1795. Two days later he was buried in the southern part of London. The old inn, Elephant and Castle, still stands by the churchyard. —The Morning Press Administrative Act Book 1796. He left no will. His Estate of 100 pounds was assigned to his landlord, John Walker.

p-184 [330]Haldimand to Major J. Rogers, July 31, 1780. Haldimand Coll, B.160, p 59. Major J. Rogers to Haldimand, St. John's, Aug. 4, 1780. —Ibid, pp 60-61.

p-184 [331]Major J. Rogers to Haldimand, St. John's, Apr. 29, 1780: "...The conduct of my brother of late had almost unmanned me. When I was last in Quebec often wrote to and told him my mind in regard to it and as often he promised to reform. I am sorry his good talents should so unguarded fall a prey to intemperance..." Same to Same, St. John's, May 10, 1780. —Ibid, pp 49-50. Haldimand to J. Rogers, May 18, 1780—Ibid, pp 51-53.

p-185 [332]Major J. Rogers to Haldimand, St. John's, Mar. 27, 1780. —Ibid, pp 35-6. Same to Same, St. John's, Dec. 13, 1783. —Ibid, pp 142-3.

p-185 [333]J. W. Myers to Haldimand, Montreal, July 1, 1779. —Ibid, B.161, p 21. On Aug. 17, he was repeating his request for money for his subsistence. —p 30. Lt. Michael Smith to Haldimand, St. John's, Mar. 29, 1780. —Ibid, B.160, p 37. Haldimand to J. Rogers, Apr. 6, 1780. —Ibid, p 38. J. Rogers to Haldimand, St. John's, Apr. 9, 1780. —Ibid, p 39. Same to Same, Aug. 11, 1781. —Ibid, pp 93-4. Also pp 95, 96, 98, 99, 100, 101, 103, 111 (widows of deceased officers received 20 pounds a year), 129, 130, 134, 132. B.161 pp 239, 286, 337, 340. B.162: p 57. B.163: pp 7, 52, 105, 128, 137.

p-185 [334]Haldimand to R. Rogers, Feb. 10, 1780. —B.160, pp 27-8.

p-185 [335]Haldimand to J. Rogers, Apr. 6.—Ibid, p 38.

p-185 [336]Capt. A. Pritchard to Haldimand, St. John's, Sept. 17, 1782.—Ibid, B.177-2, pp 492-3.

p-185 [337]J. Rogers to Haldimand, St. John's, Sept. 18, 1780. —Ibid, B.160, pp 70-71. Haldimand to J. Rogers, Sept. 21, 1780.—Ibid, p 73. Also pp 93, 95. Haldimand to Duport, A.Q.M.G., June 28, 1781: Ordering him to send the enclosed list of clothing for the use of scouts.—Ibid, B.188, p 116. Haldimand to Carleton, June 28, 1781: He is to issue clothing to a party of Ranger recruits brought in by Capt. John Myers at St. John's. The men to serve under him.—Ibid, B.188, p 114. Lt. I. Ferguson to Haldimand, St. John's, Nov. 9, 1780.— B.161, p 181. Return of Clothing issued out of the Quartermaster General's store to (Rogers' King's Rangers and others), Sorel, Feb. 21, 1782.—Ibid, BM 21,849, p 141.

p-186 [338]Rogers, W., pp 5-10.

p-186 [339]Nairne to Haldimand, Vercheres, Dec. 26, 1780: He reviewed Rogers' King's Rangers and carefully examined all the prisoners who had been recruited; all passed but three. He remarks on different recruits, the good opinion he has formed of Major James Rogers and of his method of dealing with his men, but he has little assistance from his officers, so that he should have the help of a quartermaster and adjutant. Sends pay lists with above remarks.—Haldimand Coll, B.161, pp 213-17.
Correspondence of Major James Rogers and other King's Rangers officers relative to their many recruiting scouts (written to Haldimand and vice versa) is in the Haldimand Coll:—B.160, pp 35, 39, 40, 41, 42, 44, 47, 54, 55, 57, 58, 60, 62, 105, 107, 109, 112-13, B.183; p 99, 105; B.161, pp 218, 243, 320, 323, 325, 326, 333, 340, 389, 397, 429; B.162, pp 12, 25, B.163, p 152. B.167, p 337. B.178, pp 15, 46, 112, 91, 360.

p-186 [340]Haldimand to J. Rogers, Montreal, Apr. 28, 1782 (2 letters)—Ibid, B.160, 107-8, 166. Also: B.177-1, p 252.

p-189 [341]J. Sherwood to Haldimand, Loyal Blockhouse, July 29, 1781: Has built a good blockhouse; it is the best place on the frontier for secret scouts, and easily defended.—Ibid, B. 176, pp 183-185. Preceding this letter he wrote Haldimand on July 1, from 'Dutchman's Farm,' describing his arrival, building of an oven, the hutting of his men and preparations for building the blockhouse; states the situation and description of Dutchman's Point; its natural suitability for a post.—Ibid, pp 142-4.

p-189 [342]Same to Same, Loyal Blockhouse, May 2, 1782.—Ibid, B.177-1, pp 254-7.

p-189 ³⁴³See p 318. Sherwood and Smyth had their principal agents established in Vermont use the following code names: 'Plain Truth,' 'Corn Cob,' 'Whapping Boards,' 'Intelligencer,' 'Z L,' 'G (with crosses),' and Smith labelled himself 'Hudibras,' while Sherwood used the above mentioned 'Plain Truth.'—Plain Truth to Haldimand, (no date), Ibid, B.177-1, p 301. (Gives explanation of names).

p-189 ³⁴⁴Brigadier Powell to Haldimand, St. John's, June 12, 1779.—Ibid, B.181, p 181. Also: B.205, pp 58, 66, 79, B. 185-2, pp 336, 338, 350, 352; B.161, p 148.

p-190 ³⁴⁵Pritchard's 'Intelligence' duty: B.182, p 308; B.176, pp 30, 45, 137, 228, 222, 231, 238, 239, 277; B.179, pp 89, 157, 165; B.180, pp 117, 120; B.183, p 204; B.177-1, pp 100, 101, 106, 114; B.177-2 pp 492, 494, 499, 500, 510, 516, 527, 588.

p-191 ³⁴⁶Pritchard's 'Black-Marketing' and 'Counterfeiting are in: B.162, pp 58, 68-70, 599, 611, 614, 618, 620, 623, 632, 690, 692, 695; B.178, pp 15, 44, 46, 67, 76, 153, 253; B.183, pp 275-9.

p-191 ³⁴⁷See pp 318-325 of this Volume.

p-192 ³⁴⁸Capt. Myers to Haldimand, St. John's, Dec. 1780. —Haldimand Coll, B.161, p 218. Also B.160—p 168.

p-192 ³⁴⁹Haldimand to J. Rogers, Sept. 4, 1780.—Ibid, B. 160, pp 64-5. Ibid, Sept. 13.—p 69. Lists of J. Rogers' and H. Ruiter's Companies, St. John's, Jan. 27, 1784.—B.160, pp 153, 155. Ibid, p 103.

p-193 ³⁵⁰J. Rogers to Haldimand, St. John's, June 11, 1782. —Ibid, p 110. Haldimand to J. Rogers, June 17, 1782.—Ibid, p 111.

p-193 ³⁵¹J. Breckenridge's Secret Service duty is recorded in the following documents: Breckenridge, J., Journal—B.184 -2, pp 528-34. Also pp 520, 545. B.182 p 481. B.176, pp 169, 171. B.177-2, pp 399, 415, 532. B.178, pp 203, 205.

p-194 ³⁵²Ibid, B.178, pp 237, 240, 249, 251.

p-195 ³⁵³Ibid, p 217. B.177-2, pp 625, 632.

p-196 ³⁵⁴WOOD CUTTING DUTY: On Dec. 11, 1782, Major Campbell ordered 20 of the 29th Regt and 38 King's Rangers to cut wood for the garrison of St. John's, the men to be paid the same as agreed on in Greave's contract. They have their arms, etc., and are to lodge in the woods.—B.190, p 62.
KING'S RANGERS-JESSUP'S CORPS QUARREL OVER SHIRKING OF GARRISON DUTY: B.161, p 228.

p-197 [355]B.160, pp 125, 127, 136. As early as Sept. 18, 1781, a board of officers recommended that Rogers King's Rangers should be kept distinct from the others, having been raised by order of Sir Henry Clinton and that the other different corps of Loyalists should be joined into one consisting of 8 Companies of 50 men each. —B.167, p 328. See p 394.

p-197 [356]Sabine, Capt. Edward Mainwaring, Lt. John Throckmorton, Ensigns Peter Anderson and John Robbins were stationed at Prince Edward Island (Isle St. John). Also Ensign Joseph Beers. Capt. John Jones served at George's Island.

p-198 [357]John Jones Memorial to Haldimand, Que, Aug. 29, 1779. —Pub. Arch. of Can., B. Series, Vol 214, p 130.

p-198 [358]Ibid, Also: B.181, pp 231-4. B.150, pp 59, 95, 96, 202. B.160, pp 32, 85.

p-200 [359]Siebert, p 15. Acadiensis, July 1907, p 276. North, J.W., pp 110-112.

p-200 [360]Jones, p 50.

p-200 [361]Haldimand Coll, B.162, pp 295, 372, 392. B.160, pp 140-168. Bryce, pp 9, 12-13. B.162, pp 148 (Myers and Pritchard petitioned for a land grant on the east side of Missisquoi Bay), 179 (Myers petitions for a township with others on Cape Breton) 206, 208, 214, 249, 254, 270, 272.

p-200 [362]Ibid.

p-201 [363]Ibid. Rogers, W.

BIBLIOGRAPHY OF PRINCIPAL SOURCES
(With Key Word by which cited
in Appendix & Notes)

PRINCIPAL MANUSCRIPTS

Key
W.O.34 WAR OFFICE CLASS 34: *AMHERST PAPERS*,
Public Record Office, London, England.
All Volumes covering Amherst's service
in North America (1758-1764) have been
consulted and Volumes 115, 155, 163 and
231 (Rogers-Amherst Correspondence in
the American Revolution).
This vast Collection was the principal
source for this Volume.
AB   *Abercrombie Papers*, Huntington Library
Haldimand Coll *HALDIMAND COLLECTION*, Public
Archives of Canada, Ottawa, Ontario:
Vols:
B.160-Correspondence with Lt.Col Rogers, Major J. Rogers & King's Ranger Officers.
B.149-Letters from Governors of Nova Scotia & commanders at Halifax, 1777-1784.
B.150-Letters to above.
B.161-Letters from Loyalist Officers 1776--1782.
B.162 Ibid; 1777-1785 Vol II.
B. 163-Letters to above.
B. 167-Loyalist Corps Musters 1778-85.
B.176-Letters from Capt. Sherwood & Dr. Smyth
B.177-1-Ibid. 1777-84.
B.177-Ibid.
B.178-Ibid.
B.179-Letters to above - 1780-83.
B.180-Capt. Sherwood on Secret Service 1780.
B.181-Secret intelligence from various parts.
B.182-Ibid; 1775-82. Vol. II.
B.183-Corr relating to Rebel prisoners 1778-83.
B.184-2-Papers relating to State prisoners & suspects in Canada 1775-84.
B.185-2-Ibid. 1777-84.
B.190-Barrackmaster General Dept.papers
B.205-Papers relating to Calvet & Pillon.
B.3 B.M., 21,663-Vol 2nd-Corr with Gage 1758-1777 (relating to Rogers 1768) p.104
B.2-1.B.M.,21,662-Ranger officers'1759 rebellion, pp 28, 33.

Haldimand Papers	British Museum, Additional MSS 21,800, 21,810, and 21,820.
Brazier, William	Draughtsman: *A Survey of Lake Champlain,* 1762, Clements Library, Ann Arbor, Michigan.
Clintor Papers	Clements Library. *Sir Henry Clinton Hdqrt Papers,* (letters from James Rogers).
Ibid	Ibid. a separate notebook: *Journal of an Expedition to the S. Colonies* ..., in particular an entry re: the Queen's Rangers.
Gage Papers	Clements Library. Frequent mention of Robert Rogers in 1759, 1763,1766, 1767, 1768 and 1774.
Ibid	*Letters Winter Quarters 1759* Letter Copy Book MSS.
Rogers, Robert	*Papers, 1759-1832:* 52 items in Clements Library from Rogers to his wife Elizabeth Browne from America and London, etc. Described in Guide to the MSS collection in Clements Library, compiled by H.H. Peckham (1942). Also in the catalog of Charles F. Heartman, no. 237, June 11, 1932 and in the Month at Godspeed's VII, no.9, 1940.
Ibid	*Papers, 1766-1769, Frontiersman and Soldier.* Copies of a journal of council proceedings with the Indians at Michilimackinac, together with the proceedings of a general court-martial held at Montreal in October 1768 for Rogers' trial on charges of treason. 198 pp. in State Historical Society of Wisconsin Collections.
Ibid	*Rogers' Papers.* MSS relating to Robert Rogers in the N.Y. Public Library. Namely: British Officers Account Book 1759-60. John Askin's Travel Accounts, Detroit to Albany, 1762. Edward Cole's Detroit Expedition (1760) Account of merchandise shipped from Niagara to Detroit. Amherst's permit to Askin & Gordon, May 27, 1760 to act as Sutler to Rogers' Corps of Rangers. Paul Burbeen to Abraham Douw on financial success of Rogers' Detroit Expedition. Rogers' Power of Attorney to Askin to collect money due him from Edward Cole. A photostat copy of the recollections of James Gordon referring to trade with Rogers at Montreal.Rogers' Detroit Journal (copy sent to Monckton).
Anonymous	*Rogers Ranger Diary.* See Loescher, *Abenaki Aphrodite-Rogers St. Francis Raid...*

MANUSCRIPT AND PRINTED DIARIES,
  JOURNALS, NARRATIVES, LETTER-BOOKS,
  ORDERLY BOOKS, ACCOUNT BOOKS
    LETTERS AND SECONDARY SOURCES:
Key:
Acadiensis *A Lake Champlain Gunboat of 1760*
            (with contemporary illustration)
            Mag. American History,Vol 8, p.498.
            July, 1907, p. 276.
Alberts,   *The Most Extraordinary Adventures*
R.C.   *of Major Robert Stobo*, 423 pp.1965,
            Houghton Mifflin, Boston, Mass.
Alexander,Ensign Thomas of Northfield, Mass.
            Military Journal May-Oct, 1758, Ti-
            conderoga, in A History of North-
            field by Temple & G. Sheldon, Al-
            bany, 1875, pp 303-305.
Alley,   *Loyal Provincial Regiments* (Uni-
H.R.   forms) Loyalist Gazette,II, p 5.
Almon's   *Remembrancer*, Volume IV.
Altieri,   Lt. James J.: *Darby's Rangers*,151
            pp., ill. Ranger organization Fund,
            1922 Medary Ave., Phila., Pa.
American Archives 4th Ser., III & IV; 5th
            Series, III.
Amherst,   *Journals* ed, J. Webster, Chicago,
Jefferey   1931.
Amherst,   *Journal 1758-60*. J.C. Webster, ed.
William
Anonymous   *British Journal, L.George & Ticon-*
(1)   *deroga, 1758*.MSS in W.W.34. Public
            Record Office, London.
Anonymous   French *Journal-Ticonderoga, 1758.*
(2)   Ibid source.
Anonymous   *Letter-Diary of a Ranger Officer* at
(3)   Ticonderoga, Crown Point, & Point
            Rogers, 1759-60. Boston News Letter.
Anonymous   Oman, Sir Charles: *On the Diary of*
(4)   *a Private of 74th Foot-West Indies*
            1760-64, London Times, 7/25/36, pp
            15-16.
Anonymous   *Journal of an Indian Trader - 1761-3*
(5)   J.W. Jordan, ed. in Pa. Mag. Hist.
            37:1-47, Jan. 1913.
Anonymous   *Orderly-Book of the British Regi-*
(6)   *ments at Ticonderoga & Crown Point,*
            Aug 1-10, 1759, MS in Library Con-
            gress.
Anonymous   *Provincial Officer's Diary, May 3-*
(7)   *Nov 14,1758*. Nova Scotia Historical
            Collections, Vol. 13.
Anonymous   *Genuine Letters from a Volunteer in*
(8)   *British Service at Quebec*. London,
            1759.
Anonymous   *Journal of the Siege of Quebec*.Lon-
(9)   don, 1759.

Anonymous (10) *Journal of an Expedition up the St. Lawrence R.* Boston 1759.
Anonymous (11) *Provincial Orderly Book, L. George, 1759.* Copy in Lib. Cong.
Anonymous (12) *Ibid, Schenectady-Ft. Edward.* MS in Library Congress.
Anonymous (13) *General Orders, June 12-20, 1758, Albany-Ft. Edward.* In Connecticut Historical Society.
Anonymous (14) *Provincial Diary, L. George 1758.* Antiquarian Society.
Anonymous (15) *Mass. Provincial Journal, Nov. 1758, from Brimfield to Boston to Casco.* Connecticut Historical Society.
Anonymous (16) *Provincial Diary, Crown Point, 1759.* Amer. Antiq. Soc.
Anonymous (17) *Provincial Orderly-Book, Ticonderoga 1759.* Conn. Hist. Soc.
Anonymous (18) *General Orders-Aug. 20-22, 1760.* Conn. Hist. Society.
Anonymous (19) *Account of a Journey from Crown Point to Quebec.* MS Tic.
Anonymous (20) *Journal of an Officer during the Siege of Ft. Detroit.* London, 1858, Sabin.
Anonymous (21) *Military Journal (Provincial officer) May-Nov. 1758* in N.N.Y. in History Mag. ns.X-1871, pp 113-122.
Anonymous (22) *Journal, Que. June-Aug., 1759.*(Fraser's Regt.?) Ibid IV.
Ashton, J. *The Fleet* (Prison).
Askin Papers M.M. Quaiff, editor
Atkins, C.T. *British Forces in N. America, 1714-1781, their distribution and strength.* Journal Soc. Army Historical Res, XVI.
Bagley, Col. Jonathan *Orderly Book, L. George 1758.* Amer. Antiquarian Society, April, 1881.
Bangs, Sergeant Nathaniel *Orderly Book, Castle William-Ft. Edward 1759-60.* Mass. Historical Society.
Barrows, Abner *Diary, 1756-58, L. George.* Soc. Mayflower Descendants.
Bartlett, William S. *The Frontier Missionary.*
Bascom, R. *The Fort Edward Book.* N.Y., 1903.
Bass, Lt. Benjamin *Diary, Ft. Frontenac Expedition 1758.* N.Y. Hist. XVI, Oct. 1935, pp449-452
Bayley, Captain Jacob *Diary-Ticonderoga 1759,* in History of Newbury, by F. P. Wells.
Beatson, Col.R.S. *Notes on the Plains of Abraham,* Gibraltor, 1858.
Beckles Wilson *Life & Letters of James Wolfe;* London, 1909.
Beverly, Sgt.Thomas *Recollections;* in C. Stark (1), pp 154-8.
Bird, Harrison K. *Navies in the Mountains--The Battles on the Waters of Lakes Champlain & George, 1609-1814,* Oxf. Univ. Press.

Ibid, (3) *Battle for a Continent*, Oxford University Press.
Bird, Harrison K. (1) & Frederick T. Chapman: "Rogers Rangers," 1756-1760, being Plate No. 97 in Military Collectors & Historian Journal, VII, No. 1, Spring 1955 pp. 18-20.
Bougainville, Louis Antoine de: *Journals in America, 1756-1760* ("Adventure in the Wilderness") excellently edited and translated by Edward P. Hamilton, Univ. Oklahoma Press, 1964.
Boishebert, Charles des Champs: J.C. Webster, editor.
Bond, William: *Diary-1758;* MS owned by M. B. Farrar, So. Lincoln, Mass.
Booth, Captain Joseph: *Journal-1760;* in C. E. Booth's: One Branch of the Booth Family; N.Y., 1910.
Bouquet Collection: in Canadian Archives-Volumes I-III.
Boston Evening Post - 1755-1760.
Boston Gazette & Weekly Republican Journal--1755-1760.
Boston News-Letter--1755-1760.
Bourlamaque Collection: in Canadian Archives; Vols. II-VI.
Bowen, Ashley: *Journal; 1759*, Quebec; Essex Inst. Hist. Coll., LXX, 227-66.
Boyle, John: *Journal* 1759-1778, Boston; N.E. Hist. Gen. Reg. Apr. 1930, 145-56.
Bradbury, Deacon John: *Diary*-L.Champlain, 1760. Maine Hist. Soc. Coll, II, 330
Bradbury, Lt. John: *Military Journal, Apr. 1760-Aug. 1762,* L. Champlain, in "Bradbury Memorial," by J. M. Bradbury, Portland 1890.
Brehm, Lt. Diederick: *Travel Journal--Rogers' Detroit Expedition, 11/1760-Feb. 1761.*N. Eng. Hist. Gen. Reg. XXXVII 1883 pp 22-26.
Brehm, Lt. D.: *Journal to Detroit - 1760*-W.O. 34/49
Briggs, David: *Diary-L. George-1758,*Mass.Arch.
Broom, J.:*The Penobscot Loyalists;* Acadiensis, July, 1903-v.3, pp 172-182.
Brown, J.P.: *Old Frontiers-The Story of the Cherokees;* Kingsport, Tenn., 1938.
Brown, Capt. Silas: *Orderly Book-L. Champlain 1760;* MS in Mass. Hist. Soc. Unpublished
Brown, W. Howard: *Colonel John Goffe,* Manchester, N.H., 1950.
Browne, G. Waldo: *Scout Journals 1757.* (Narrative of James Johnson, a captive during French & Indian War) Manchester, 1902.
Browne, G. Waldo: *With Rogers Rangers;*Chapter XXVII, 278-86--Bits of Biography.
Buchanon (Master's thesis, Univ. of Tenn.1927) "The Relations of the Cherokee Indians with the English in America prior to 1763."

Budd, Surgeon Gilbert of H.MS. Kingston--*Diary Louisbourg 1758*--MS Lib. of Congress.
Bull, Capt. J.: *Orderly Book--Niagara-1759*.
Burr, A.: *Diary-1758--Roxbury to Schenectady*.
Burr, S.: *Diary-1760--Hingham to L.Champlain;* N.Y. State Library. Unpublished.
Burr, Lt. T.: *Diary-1758--Ft. Frontenac;* N.Y. S. Library
Burrill, Sergt. John: *Diary-1759-60--Ft. Frederick;* in Acadiensis, V, p. 187.
Canadian Archives Report, 1905, I, 45.
Canavan, M.J.: *Ben Comee.* A Ranger novel. 1899.
Carter, C.E.: *Gage Corr. with Secy's of State -1763-1775;* 2 vols. Yale Univ.Press,1931.
Carver, Captain Jonathan,Jr.: *The New Hampshire Ranger;* poem in the Knickerbocker Magazine, XXVI, 1845.
Catlin, Ranger: *Recollection* (to Gen. Hoyt) in M. Wade's *Francis Parkman,* p. 191.
Chamberlin (1), Arthur N. III: *A New England Outpost* (No. 4, N.H.) in Tradition Mag. #19, Newton Publ. London.
Ibid (2): *Militia & Provincial Troops in America, 1745-1763*--Some Notes on Organization, Uniforms & Equipment, In Ibid.
Chambers, R.: *War Paint & Rouge* -A Ranger Novel.
Champion, Col. H.: *Diary-1758*--in Champion Gen., 417-350.
Chandler, Rev. S.: *Diary-1755-6*--N.E. Hist. Gen. Reg. 10/630
Charland (1), Pere Thomas: *C'est arrive le 4 Octobre 1759;* in Revue d'histoire de l' Amerique Francaise, Dec. 1959.
Ibid (2): *Histoire des Abenakis D'Odanak,1875-1937.* Les Editions du Levrier, 1964, Montreal.'
Chatham Papers, Vol. 96, Misc. Papers, 1758-63.
Claus, Daniel: *Narrative;* in Soc Colonial Wars.
Cleaveland, Rev. John: *Diary-1758-59;* Essex Inst-XII, 130
Clements, W.L.: *Transcripts:* In his Library are many notes that were not published with Rogers' Michilimackinac Journal, edited by Mr. Clements. The notes, "In a very chaotic condition," are lodged with the transcript of Rogers' Michilimackinac Journal. Considerable Biographical material relative to Rogers; also the history of Michilimackinac and neighboring tribes of Indians.
Clough, G.: *Diary-1759-60--Louisbourg*--Essex It-18610
Cobb, E.: *Diary-1758*--Goreham Hist., McLellan, 66
Cobb, Capt. S.: *Orderly-Book--L.George-1758.*
C.O.: Colonial Office Papers, 5/54.
Coleman, Emma Lewis: *New England Captives Carried to Canada between 1677-1760,* 2 vols. Portland, Me., 1925.
Comstock, Clerk C.:*Diary-1758-9-L.George*-- Conn. Hist. Soc.

Connecticut Gazette 1755-61
Corkran, David H.: *The Cherokee Frontier*;Univ. Oklahoma Press, 1962.
Corse, Trader James: *Travel Diary, April 1730* (Ft. Dummer to L. Champlain on old Crown Pt. Road) Vt. Hist. Soc. Proc. II, 1931, 165-7.
Cresswell, Nicholas: *Journal 1774-77*;Lon.1925.
Crockett, W.H.: *A History of L. Champlain-1946.*
Croghan, George: *Detroit Expedition Journal;* in Pa. Mag. of Hist., Oct., 1947.
Cruikshank, E.A.: *The Garrisons of Toronto & York-1750-1815* (French occupation,Queen's Rangers, etc.) Can. Mil. Inst.--Selected Papers--Toronto 1934-5, pp. 17-65.
Cuneo (2) John R.: *The Location of the First French Fort of 1755 at Ticonderoga;* MS typescript deposited with Ft. Ticonderoga Museum Library.
Ibid (3): *Mysterious Ft. Wentworth.* MS typescript dep. N.H. Historical Soc.
Ibid (4): *The Early Days of the Queen's Rangers, Aug. 1776-Feb. 1777;*in Journal Military Institute, Summer, 1958,pp.65-74.
Ibid (5): *Factors Behind the Raising of the 80th Foot in America;*in Military Collector & Historian Jrn., Winter, 1959 pp 97-104.
Curtiss, Frederick: *Narrative of St. Francis Raid,* related Oct. 4, 1760. MS in Connecticut State Library.
Cutter, A.R.Jr., Dr.: *Diary-1756-8;* Cutter Geneology.
Darling, J.Jr.: *Diary-Louisbourg Demolition 1759;* in Bangor Hist. Mag. II, 76; Dodge, ed.
Davidson, J.N.: *History of the Stockbridge Indians.*
Day, R.E.: *Robert Rogers;* Quart. Jrn. of N.Y. State Hist. Asso., Oct. 1928, 395-97.
Day, Gordon M.: *Rogers' Raid in Indian Tradition,* in Historical New Hampshire, June, 1962.
Day, Mrs. C.M.: *History of the Eastern Townships,* Montreal, 1869.
Demers, P.: *Le General Hazen, Seigneur de Bleury Sud: Essaie de monographie regionale;* Montreal: Librarie Beauchemin 1927, p. 18.
DeVoe, T.F.: *Geneology of DeVoe Family.*
Dibble, E.: *Diary-1759;*Starr, Hist. of Cornwall.
Dorr, M.: *Diary-1758-Ft. Standwix & Frontenac* -N.Y. Hist., XVI-Oct. 1935, 452-64.
Doughty, A. & Burpee, L.J.: *The Makers of Canada, Index & Dictionary of Canadian History.*
Douglass, Capt. Wm.: *Orderly Book-1759-*Conn. State L.

Downey, Fairfax: *Louisbourg: Key to a Continent*, 1965, Prentice-Hall.
Drake, S.A.: *Heart of the White Mountains;* London.
Drake, S.G.: *Biog. & Hist. of N. American Indians*.
Durkee, J.: *Orderly Book-1759;* N.Y.Hist. Soc.
Edwards, T.J.: *Origin of British Light Infantry Regiments;* Brit. Army Quar. - July, Oct., 1936.
Eliot, Rev.J.:*Diary*;Cambridge,Mass.1944,83 pp
Elliott, T.C.: *Origin of the Name Oregon;* Oregon Hist. Soc.
Embleton, R.S.: English painter of "Major Rogers' Campaign" (original owned by the author.
Embleton, G.A.: *The Black Watch at Ticonderoga,* Tradition Mag., No. 19.
Ibid,: *Color Plates of French & British Infantry at Ticonderoga, 1758;* Ibid.
Farrow, E.S.:*Military Encyclopedia;*N.Y.,1885.
Fisher, Dorothy Canfield: *Vermont Tradition,* Boston, 1953.
Fisher, S.: *Diary-1758;* Photostat in Library of Congress.
Fitch, Col. E.: *Orderly Book-1759;* Mass. Hist. Soc.
Foote, (1), Wm. A.: *The American Independent Companies of the British Army,1664-1764;* M.A. Thesis.
Ibid (2): *The 80th Regiment of Light Armed Foot, 1757-1764,*being plate #230 in Military Collectors & Historians Journal pp 81-82.
Ford, W.C.: *British Officers Serving in America, 1754-74;* Compiled from the Army Lists.
Fort Ticonderoga Museum Bulletins: Vol. II, No 5, Jan. 1932; III-IV, 1933-38; VI, Jan. 1941; Jan. 1942; July 1942; VII, Jan. 1946; July, 1946; July, 1947.
Fortescue, J.W.: *Hist. of British Army--II & III;* London.
Foster, A.: *Diary-1758;* N.E. Hist. Gen. Reg, Apr. 1900.
Foster, J.: *Orderly Book-1758;* Unpublished.
Franquet, L.:*Voyages et Memoires le Canada;* Quebec, 1899.
Fraser, Col. M.: *Journal-1759-60;* Jour. Soc. Army. Hist. Res., XVIII, 1939, 135-168, ill. map.
French, Capt. Christopher; *22nd Regiment;* 3 Vol. MSS in Lib. of Congress.
Frizzel, J.: *Diary-1756-9;* Unpublished.
Frost, J.Jr.:*Diary-1760;* Old Eliot, IV, VIII.
Fuller, A.: *Diary-1758;* Essex Inst. Hist. Coll. 1910.
Fuser, Lt. L.F.: *Journal-1759-60-Military Affairs in N. America,* Pargellis, ed., p. 439-446.

Gage, Gen. T.:*Orderly Book-1759-77*;Brit. Mus.
Gaine, Hugh: N.Y. printer. *Diary-War News 1757-58*, in The Journals of Hugh Gaine by Paul Ford, N.Y., 1902, II, 3-15, 16-163.
Gallup, B.A.: Minute Book-1759-Conn. His.Soc. Unpublished.
George III:Correspondence-1760-83-II-III,Fortescue.
Germaine Papers-Clements Library-for Queen's Rangers.
Gilroy, M.: Loyalists & Land Settlement in Nova Scotia-N.S. Pub. Arch. Publ. no 4, 1937.
Glazier, B.: *Journal-1758-60*; Topsfield Lib.-Unpublished.
Goodrich, J.: *Diary-1758-L.George*;Unpublished
Gordon, H. (Royal Engineers): *Journal-1755-64* -In Military Affairs N.America;Pargellis -ed.
Gordon, James: *Recollections*.
Gordon, Wm. Augustus: *Highland Infantry, Louisbourg April-Aug. 1758.* in Royal United Services Inst. Jrn. LX-1915, 117-52.
Grant, Lt. Alex: *Journal-May 8-15, 1760*; W.O. 34, Vol 51, ff 24-5.
Grant, Lt.-Col. James: *1761 Cherokee War Journal*; W.O.34, Vol 40, ff 95-8.
Grant, Lt.-Col. James: *Military Journal Cherokee War*, June-July 1961. Report to Amherst. In Florida Hist. Soc. Quar. XII, 25-36.
Guild, Ensign A.: *Diary-1758*; published by G. A. Plimpton.
Hadaway, W.S.: *Battle of Heathcote's Hill*; in McDonald Papers, part I, 20-26; 62 (publication of Westchester Co. Hist.Soc,IV.
Haldimand, F.: *Diary-1756-78*; Can. Arch. Rep. 1889.
Haldimand Papers: Pioneer Hist. Coll. (Michigan).
Hale, R.Jr.: *Diary-1755-62*;Amer. Antiq. Soc. Unpublished.
Hamilton, (1) Edward P.: *The French & Indian Wars - The Story of Battles & Forts in the Wilderness*; N.Y., 1962. Doubleday.
Ibid, (2): *Fort Ticonderoga--Key to a Continnet.* 1964.
Hannay, J.D.C.L.: *History of the Queen's Rangers*; Royal Soc. of Canada Proc. II, 1908-123-86
Hardy, C.: *Diary-1759*;N.E.Hist. Gen.Reg.-LX Ju 1906.
Harris, O.: *Diary-1758*;Huntington Lib.-HM 591.
Harvey, D.C.: *The French Regime in Prince Edward Island*; Chapter 13, pp 188-201.
Haskins, J.: *Diary-1759-60--Louisbourg*;in Ancestry of Katharine Choate Paul-Milw., 1914.
Haviland, Col. Wm.: *Journal-Aug.11-Sept. 3, 1760*;W.O.34, Vol 77, ff 130-131.

Hawks, Maj. J.: *Orderly Book-1759-60;* Soc. Col. Wars.
Hay, Lt. Jehu: *Journal-Siege of Detroit;* Hough, ed., Albany 1860.
Hayden, A.: *Diary-1758-9--Records of the Conn Line of the Hayden Family;* H. Hayden, 1888.
Hayward, B.: *Journal-1757-8-Ft.Ed.;* Conn Hist Soc.
Heath, Maj-Gen. Wm: *Memoirs.*
Heath, Maj-Gen. Wm.: Papers; Mass. Hist. Soc. Col-IV
Hemenway, A.M.: *Vermont Historical Magazine, II;* Burlington, Vt., 1871.
Henderson, J.: *Diary-1758-9;* N.E.Hist.Gen.Soc.
Henshaw, W.: *Diary-1759;* Am. Antq. Soc. Trans. XI, 185.
Hilbert, Christopher: *Wolfe at Quebec;* N.Y., 1959.
Historical MSS Commission; Report on Dartmouth MSS.
Hobart, Adj. S.: *Orderly Book-1760;* Lib. Cong. Unpublished.
Hodge, Capt. Samuel, Jr.: *Orderly Book-1760;* in Vineland Hist Mag, Vol 18, nos 3, pp 300-05; 4, 353-56; Vol 19, no 1, 28030.
Holden, D.: *Diary-1760;* Mass Hist Soc Pro-June 1889.
Holman, J.: *Diary-1759;* Unpublished.
Holt, J.: *Diary-1758;* N.E.Hist.Gen.Reg-Oct 1856
Hough, F.B.: *Detroit Siege-Diary-1763;* N.Y.1860
Hough, F.B.: Transcripts-In N.Y.State Library.
Hough, F.O.: *The Neutral Ground*-Part II, Chapters 2,8 & 9-A Queen's Ranger Novel.
Howe, Sir Wm.: *Diary-1777*-Harvard College Lib.
Hoyt, E.: Antiquarian Researches comprising a *History of the Indian Wars;* Mass., 1824.
Hudleston, F.J.: *Warriors in Undress.*
Hufeland, O.: *Westchester County During the American Revolution;* 129; 186-7; 191.
Hurlburt, J.Jr.: *Diary-1759;* Mag. Amer. Hist.- V. 29.
Ilsley, Lt. J.: *Diary-1758;* Unpublished.
James, A.P.: *The Writings of General John Forbes;* Menasha, 1938.
Jarvis, S.: *Diary-1777-83*-Queen's Rangers-Champlain Society, Vol 27.
Jenks, S.: *Diary-1760;* Mass Hist Proc-March, 1890.
Johnson, Capt. Noah: *Journal-Feb. 16-Marh.10, 1759;* in Gage Papers--Haldimand to Gage 3/16/59
Johnson, T.: *Journal-1781;* Wells, Hist. of Newbury.
Johnstone, Chevalier de: *Memoire of the Chevalier de Johnstone;* 3 Vols, trans. from the original French by C. Winchester, 1871.
Jones, E.A.: *Loyalists of Massachusetts.*
Jones, E.A.: ed: A Letter Regarding the Queen's Rangers; In Va. Mag. Hist.- Oct. 1922-Vol 30.

Jones, J.E.: *The Armed Loyalists*.
Judd, Rev. J.: *Diary-1742-1801*; Unpublished.
Kellog, L.P.: *The French Regime in Wisconsin; Early Narratives of the Northwest: The Mission of Jonathan Carver*;Wis.Mag.Hist.
Kemble Papers; 2 Vols-N.Y.Hist Soc Coll-1883.
Kent, J.:*Diary-1760*;Wells-Hist of Newbury Vt.
Kerrallain, Rene de: *La Jeunesse de Bougainville*.
King, C.: *Andia-ta-roc-te*; 1935.
King, T.: *Narrative...Prisoner of the Indians 1755-8*; Bull Conn Hist Soc 1938-21 pp.
Kingsford, W.: *History of Canada-1755-60*.
Knapp, N.: *Diary-1758-9*; Soc. Col. Wars of Mass-1895.
Knowlton, L.: *Diary-1759*; Unpublished.
Lake George & Ft. Wm. Henry Hotel (History). 1891.
Lake George Mirror.
Lamb, W.E.: *L.George-Facts & Anecdotes-1938*.
Lamb, W.E.: *L.Champlain & L.George Valleys*-- 3 vols.
Lane, Ranger Daniel: *Diary-1759*; N.E. Hist. & Gen. Reg-Vol 26, pp 236-41.
Lane, Farmer Samuel: Stratham, N.H. *Diary 1739-1803*. C. Hanson ed. Concord, 1937.
Light Infantry Regiments--dates on which certain Regiments were constituted--Jour Soc Hist Res, Oct., 1932, pp 239-43.
Lists of Forts constructed in N. America & Canada 1700-60-Jour Soc Army Hist Res- Oct 1926 pp 215-16, map.
Locke, Deacon John: Sea Journal-1762- *Attack on Martinique*-Book of the Lockes, p. 59.
Loescher, (1) Burt G.: *The History of Rogers Rangers--The Beginnings, Jan. 1755-April 6, 1758*, with colored Uniform Plates by Helene Loescher, Illus, Maps (including 3-page map of The Battles of Rogers Rangers), 442 pp. Limited autographed and numbered edition.

Loescher (2), Burt G.: *Officers and Non-Commissioned Officers of Rogers Rangers, 1755-1763*. Burlingame, 1957. Rare biographical data. Limited Edition. Copies available unbound at $6.25 including postage from same address as above.
Loescher, (3) Burt G.: *Ranger Goodwin's Rum*, Historical Factual Novel, 50,000 word MS with Appendix (unpublished).
Loescher (4), Burt G.: *Shirley's Dirty Half Hundred*, The British 65th (50th) Foot 1746-1758. Colonial American unit series, part 3, in The Dispatch Case of The Guild of Miniature Figure Designers & Collectors, I, no. 5, September-October, 1954, illustrated.

Loescher (5), Burt G.: *Gorham's Rangers, 1744-1763*, with Uniform plate, in Ibid, I, no 2, pp 10-11 and front plate.

Loescher (6), Burt G.: *Abenaki Aphrodite-Rogers St. Francis Raid-Fact, Legend & Lost Treasure*. A definitive study of the Raid based on much new evidence. Illustrated by the Author. Documented Maps, Limited signed and numbered edition. Send subscription to same address as *Loescher* (1).

Lonergan, T.F.: *Historic Crown Pt., Ft. St. Frederic, Ft. Amherst;* Troy, N.Y., 29 pp illus.

Long, J.C.: *Lord Jeffery Amherst;* N.Y., 1933.

Loture, R.: *Journal-Louisbourg-1758;* Revue Maritime-Nova Scotia-no 175, pp 52-70.

Lyon, L.: *Diary-1758-A.* Tomlinson, ed.-N.Y. 1885.

MacClintock, Rev. S.: *Diary - 1760--*N.H. Hist Soc., unpublished.

MacDonald, O.: *Last Siege of Louisbourg.*

MacKenzie, Lt. F.: *Diary -* Vol I, Oct 23, 26, 1776.

Mahon, R.H.: *James Murray;* London, 1921.

Malone, D.-ed: *Dictionary of Amer. Biog;* Vol 16, pp 108-09. N.Y., 1932.

Marquis, T.G.: *War Chief of the Ottawas;* Tor, 1921.

Mass Postcript: June 23, 1768-Articles of Intelligence respecting Major Rogers, etc.

Maurault, Abbe: *History of the St. Francis Indians.*

Maxwell, H.: *Diary - The Christian Patriot-*1933, N.Y.

Maxwell, Maj. T.: *Diary-1757-1813;* Essex Inst Hist Coll-Vol 7, p 97. A Rogers Ranger.

Mayer, J.J.: *Major Robert Rogers, Trader-*N.Y. State Historical Asso-XV-Oct. 1934-388-97

Mayo, L.S.: *Jeffery Amherst;* 1916.

McCormick, Lt. Caesar: *Letter-Diary 1758-9;* See Knox Journal, Jan 20, 1759 entry.

McCrady, E.: *The History of S.C. under the Royal Government-1719-76.*

McDonald, Lt. J.: *Journal-May 6-Oct. 3, 1763-* W.O.34, Vol 49, ff !-11. (Siege of Detroit).

Meloizes, Renaud d'Avenue: *Journal,* in Rapport de l'Archivte de la Province de Quebec, 1928-1929 edition.

Merriam, Sergt. S.: *Diary-1759;* Sheldon, G.: Hist. of Deerfield, Mass.

Monckton, Col.: *Report of the Proceedings of the Troops on the Expedition up St. John's River in the Bay of Fundy under the command of Col. Monckton;* Coll N.B. Hist. Soc.-5-1904.

Montcalm, Marquis de: *Lettres du Marquis de Montcalm,* trans. in Report of the Public Archives 1929. His corr. for 1756-58.

Montressor, Lt. J.: *Journal-1757-78*;N.E. Hist Gen. Reg., Jan, 1882; N.Y. Hist. Soc. Colls, 1881.
Monypenny, Capt.-55th: *Orderly Book-1759*; Ft. Tic. Mus Bull, II, pp 219-52.
Moore, H.P.: *Life of General John Stark*-N.Y.- 1949.
Moore, Sergt. Wm.: *Recollection;* in J.Farmer & J. B. Moore: Coll Hist & Miss & Monthly Lit Jour; Vol III, pp 87-88. A Rogers Ranger.
Morris, Samuel: *Journal;* MSS of 1758 Ticonderoga campaign in Clements Lib.
Morrison, M.: *Wm. Pitt, Earl of Chatham;* 3 vols.
Motion Picture of K. Roberts' *Northwest Passage;* 1940.
Mowat, Capt. H.: *Diary-1759;* Me. Hist. Soc. Proc., 1891, p. 345.
Munroe, Ensign Edmund: *Orderly Book-1758*;N.E. Hist. Gen. Reg., July, 1862, pp 217-20.
N.H. Gazette and Historical Chronicle.
N.H. Historical Society Collections, Vol X.
N.Y. Gazette.
N.Y. Mercury.
Nicola: *Journal up Kennebec R.-1759*-W.O.34, Vol 25, March 11, 1759. Unpublished.
Nichols, T.: *Diary-1759;* Dr. A.H. Nichols, Boston; Unpublished.
North, J.W.: History of Augusta, Me.
Northcliffe Collection-Pub. Arch. of Canada-1926 Rep.
Noyes, Capt. J.: *Diary-1758;* Essex Inst Coll-V. 45.
O'Dwyer, G.F.: *Irish Soldiers at the Siege of Louisbourg*, N.S.-Jour. Amer. Irish Soc; Vol 27, pp 278-84 (1928).
Occom, Samson: *Diary-1743-89;* Dartmouth Coll.
Oxley, J.M.: *With Rogers on the Frontier; A Story of 1756;* F.J. Devitt-A Ranger Novel.
Pargellis, S.M.: *The Four Independent Companies of N.Y.* - in Essays in Colonial History, p. 96.
Parkman, Rev. E.: *Diary-1756-61;* Amer. Antiq. Society.
Parkman, F.: *Conspiracy of Pontiac;* 2 vols. 1899.
Parkman, F.: Short Stories in Knickerbocker Mag: March 1845: The Rangers' Adventure-XXV, Apr. 1845: The Scalp Hunter-XXV-297 -303. Aug 1845: The N.H. Ranger-XXVI-146-8.
Parkman, W.: *Diary-1758;*Mass Hist Soc Proc-XVII.
Patten, Judge M.: *Diary-1754-99;* Pub. by Concord N.H.
Payson, Lt. Col. N.: *Orderly Book-1758 and 60* Conn. Hist. Soc; Hoadley Coll., Box 9.
Perry, D.: *Recollections French & Indian War.*
Philopatrios, *A Letter from Philopatrios.*Some

Observations on the Two Campaigns Against the Cherokee Indians in 1760-61. Sold by P. Timothy, MDCCLXII. (Charlestown, S.C.)
Pichon, *Memoirs du Cap Breton;* p. 284.
Pike, Robert E.: *Fighting Yankee,* (John Stark) Schuman, N.Y., 1955.
Plant, S.: *Diary-1760* (With Amherst)-Unpub.
Poor, E.: *Diary-1759-60;* Ft. Frederick-Unpub.
Porter, S.: *Diary-1751-70;* Unpublished.
Price, E.: *Diary-Letter-1758;* Boston. Athenaeum.
Proctor, J.: *Diary-1758-60;*Essex Inst Coll-LXX
Putnam, R.: *Diary-1758-60;* Pub: Munsell & Sons, 1886.
Quaife, M.M.: *Wisconsin, Its History & Its People, 1634-1924;* See Vol I, pp 225-42.
Quaife, M.M.: *Robert Rogers;* A Leaflet of Burton Hist Series of Detroit Biographies-1928.
Raymond, W.O.: *Loyalists in Arms;* N.B. Hist. Coll 1904.
Ray, Frederick E. & John R. Elting: *The 55th Regiment of Foot, 1758,* being Plate No. 226 in M.C. & Historian Jrn., XV, N.2, Summer, 1963, pp 44-45.
Rea, Dr. C.: *Diary-1758;*Essex Inst Col-IV & VII.
Relations de ce que s'est passes en la Nouv. France.
Remington, Frederic: *Ranger Goodenough's Old Letter,* in Harper's Monthly, November, 1897, Illustrated by Remington.
Revue Canadienne, Moses Hazen-IV, p 865.
Roberts, K.: *Northwest Passage;* Special Edition; 2 Vol.
Robertson, J.: *Journal-1758;* Mil. Affairs in N. America
Roby, Dr. E.: *Diary-1758;* Unpublished.
Rolfe, S.: *Diary-1758;* Unpublished.
Rogers, Mary Cochrane: *The Mary Cochrane Rogers Collection* in Fort Ticonderoga, has many photostats of value relating to Rogers Rangers.
Rogers (2), Robert: *Journals of Major Robert Rogers.* Reprinted from the 1765 edition. Corinth Books, N.Y., 1961, 171 pp.
Rogers, R.: *Journals-1755-61;* London, 1765.
Rogers, R.: *Concise Account of N. America;* London, 1765.
Rogers, R.: *Journal for Receiving the Capitulation of Western French Forts;* V.Paltsits, ed.; Bul N.Y. Pub Lib, XXXVII, pp 261-76.
Rogers, R.: *Michilimackinac Journal;* Amer.Antiq. Soc. Proc.; W.L. Clements, ed.
Rogers, R.: *Petitions of Major Robert Rogers to the King, his ministers, and council, offering to seek a Northwest Passge;* by T.C. Elliott; Ore Hist Soc Quart-June 1921.

Rogers, R.: *Ponteach;* London.
Rogers, R.: Michigan Hist Mag, XIII,p 278.
Rogers, W.: *Rogers, Ranger and Loyalist;*Royal Soc Can Proc-2nd Ser-VI-1900 pp 49-58.
Roy, R.: *Au Siege de Louisbourg-1758;* Bul.Recherches Hist-XLI-Corps names & wounded.
Russell, N.V.: *Battle of Bloody Run;* Can Hist Rev-120
Russell, P.: *Early Life & Letters (1755-92)* Ont. Hist Soc Papers, XXIX, 121-140.
Sabine, L.: *Biog. Sketches of Loyalists-Amer Rev.*
Sartell, N.: *Orderly Book-1760;* Mass Hist Soc -Unpublished.
Scharf: *Westchester County;* p 676.
Schultz, John A.: *William Shirley, King's Governor of Mass.,* Chapel Hill, 1961.
Scott, J.A.: *Forts Stanwix & Oriskany;* 1927.
Serafini, Enzo: *Fort Wentworth,* MSS in possession of Serafini.
Sewall, D.: *Diary-1759-60;* Unpublished.
Seelye, E.E.: *L.George in History;* 1896.
Seymour, G.D.: *Doc Life of Nathan Hale;* New Haven, 1941.
Shafroth, J.F.: *The Capture of Louisbourg-1758; A Joint Military & Naval Operation* -U.S. Naval Inst., Jan., 1938, ill, pp 78-96.
Shafroth, J.F.: *The Capture of Quebec-1759; A Joint Military & Naval Operation;* Ibid-Feb. 1938.
Shepherd, Samuel & George: Recollections of Burbank's Massacre; Hist of Canterbury-N.H.
Sherwood, J.: *Diary-1783;* Stevens Papers-Montpelier.
Shute, D.: *Diary-1758;* Unpublished.
Shy, John W.: *James Abercrombie & the Campaign of 1758,* a thesis for the Graduate College of University of Vermont, June,1957.
Siebert, W.H.: *Exodus of Penobscot-Loyalists to Passamaquoddy;* N.B. Hist Soc Col-1914 -III
Siebert, W.H.: *Loyalist Refugees of N.H.;*Ohio State Univ Bull-XXI, no 2-1916.
Siebert, W.H.: *Loyalists in Prince Edward Island(*Simcoe, J.G.: *Military Journal...)*
Simcoe, J.G.: *Military Journal;* Queen's Rangers.
Smith, J.: *Diary-1758;* Conn Col Wars Proc-I-1896.
Smith, R.: *Diary-1759;* Farmington Papers-J. Gay, ed.
Smith, Bradford: *Rogers Rangers & The French & Indian War,* Juvenile, 1956.
Smyth, Captain John Ferdinand Dalzie:*Journal, 1777.* Queen's Ranger. Extracts in Pa. Mag. Hist. Biog. XXXIX, 1915.
Smith, W.J.: *Grenville Papers*
S.C. Gazette-1755-61.

Spaulding, Lt.: *Diary - 1758* - Photostat in Lib. of Cong.
Spicer, A.: *Diary-1758*-Bost, 1911; pp 388-408.
Sprague's *Journal of Me Hist.*; V & IX-Black Jones.
Stacey, Charles P.: *Quebec, 1759: The Siege & The Battle*, N.Y., 1959.
Stark (1), Caleb: *Reminiscences of the French War*, Concord, N.H., 1831.
Stark (2) Caleb: *Memoir & Correspondence of General John Stark*, Ibid, 1860.
Stark, Capt. J.: *Diary-1757-88;* Unpublished.
Steele, Capt. R.V.: *The Rangers & Light Infantry in N. America-Their Leaders, Uniform and Equipment-1755-78*-Ft. Tic. Bul-VII-Jul-'47.
Stevens, Lt. Simon: *Journal-1758-9*-Bost-April 28-1760.
Stobo, R.: *Memoirs*-Pittsburgh, 1854.
Strang, H.: *Rob the Ranger*-A Ranger Novel-NY-1907.
Stryker, R.: *The N.J. Volunteers.*
Susane, L.: *Histoire De La Ancienne Infanteri Francaise*-8 vols-1848-53.
Sweat, Capt. W.: *Diary-1758*-MS Essex Institute.
Taylor, L.: *Diary-1759*-in *Colonial & Revolutionary Homes of Wilton, Norwalk, Westport & Darien & Vicinity*-1901-Norwalk D.A.R.
Thompson, Sergt. J.: *Diary-1758-1830*-Lit. & Hist. Soc. of Quebec Transactions, No.22.
Thompson, Lt. S.: *Diary-1755-8*-Woburn Pub Lib.
Tinkham, Sergt S.: *Diary-1758*-D. Hurd-*Hist Plymouth County*-1884.
Townshend, C.: *Military Life of Townshend*--London, 1901.
Treasury Minutes-Pub Rec Office London-Dec. 21, 1769; July 13, 1770; Feb. 1772; Mar 7, 1773.
Trent, Captain William: *Indian Trader. Journal-Ft. Pitt 1763*, in M.C. Darlington: Ft. Pitt & Letters from the Frontier, 84-110.
True, Rev. H.: *Diary-1759*-Pub Marion, Ohio, 1900.
Vail, H.: *Diary-1760*-Amer. Antiquarian Soc.
Van DeWater, F.: *L. Champlain & L. George*-1947.
Vetromile, E.: *The Abenakis & Their History*-NY-1866.
Vogt, Karl: *Der Mohawk Scout*-A monthly historical Publication giving location, Histories, etc., of Corps in French and Indian War. (14a) Ulm-Donau, Schillerstr. 4, U.S. Zone, Germany.
Volunteer Impartial Account of Bradstreet's [Ft. Frontenac] Expedition-Lond., 1759.
Wade, M.: *Francis Parkman, Heroic Historian*-1942.

Wade, M.: *Journals of Francis Parkman*-1949.
Waite, Capt. J.: *Sea Journal-1759*-Me Hist Soc.
Wallace, W.S.: *On Fraser's Highlanders*-Can. Hist. Rev.
Walker, J.: *Diary-1760*-Hist of Bedford-Bost-1851.
Walker, J.B.: *Life & Exploits of Robert Rogers the Ranger*-A paper read before the N.E. Hist. Gen. Soc., Nov. 5, !884-Bost, 1884.
Walker, Rev. T.: *Diary*-N.H. Hist. Soc. Coll-IX-p 123.
Wallace, W.S.: *Dictionary of Canadian Biography*.
Wallace, W.S.: *The United Empire Loyalists*.
War Office 1, Vol II, pp 871-75. Vol I, p 339.
Ward, A.: *Diary-1758*-Unpublished.
Ward, C.L.: *The Delaware Continentals*-Chapter 8: Heathcote's Hill, pp 78-82 & 559-60.
Warner, S.: *Diary-1759*-Peck: *Hist of Wilbraham*
Washington, G.: *Writings of*..J.C. Fitzpatrick -ed. Vol III, IV and V.
Waterman, A.: *Diary-1760*-Pub. by W.P.Eddy-Brooklyn.
Webster, B.: *Diary-1760*-Owned by E. Webster-Tic.
Webster, R.: *Journal-1759*-Ft. Tic. Mus. Bul-Jan-1931.
Weekly Post-Boy (N.Y.) 1755-59.
Wells, *History of Newbury, Vermont*--pp 13-14.
Wesson, E.: *Orderly Book-1758-9*-Vt Hist. Gazeteer
Wheeler, J.: *Diary-1758-98*-Pierce-*Hist of Grafton*.
Wheelock, S.: *Orderly Book-1760*-Uxbridge Wheelocks.
Whitcomb, J.: *Orderly Book-1760*-Pub. Lib.-Lancaster.
Whiting, N.: *Orderly Book-1758*-Litchfield Hist. Soc.
Whitier's Ballad-The Ranger-(Reputed to be a ballad of Rogers' courtship of Elizabeth Browne.
Willard, A.: *Orderly Book & Narrative-1755-9*-- Owned by Huntington Library-San Marino-Cal.
Williams, J.: *Diary-1758*-Harvard College Lib.
Wilson, Commissary: *Orderly Book-1759*-No 1-Munsell's Hist. Series, Albany, 1857.
Winslow, J.: *Diary-1758-Louisbourg*-Unpub.
Witherspoon, J.: *Diary-1757-9*;N.S. Hist. Soc. Col, II, p 31.
Wolfe, J.: Unpub Louisbourg Letters to Duke of Richmond-L. Carver-ed., Univ. Toronto, Quart VIII, 1938, 11-40 Letters from 1755-8.

Woodhull, Col. N.: *Journal-1760*-Hist-Mag-V-Sept-1861.
Woods, J.: *Diary-1759*-Genealogical Mag-Feb.-1906.
Wolfe, J.: *Journal-1759*-Copy in McGill Univ. Tor.
Wood, L.: *Diary-1759-60*-Essex Inst. Col-v-19-21.
Wood, W.: *Logs of Conquest of Canada*-Champlain Society, 1909.
Wood, W.: *The Great Fortress*-Toronto, 1921.
Woolsey, M.T.: *Letter-Diary*-
Wooster, D.: *Orderly Book-1759*-Lib of Cong.
Wright, J.: *A Compleat Hist. of Late War*-Dublin, 1763. Contains Abercrombie's Letters.
Wrong, G.M.: *Rise & Fall of New France*-1928-2 vol.
Wrong, G.M.: *Fall of Canada-1759-60;* Oxford Univ.

INDEX

With emphasis on names and activities of Rogers Rangers. 'R.R.' designates 'in Rogers Rangers'; R.Q.R.: Rogers Queens Rangers; 'R.K.R.': Rogers Kings Rangers. This definitive guide will enable one to trace the activities of a particular individual Ranger. The correct spelling is given first, cited mispellings in parenthesis, so the reader may identify. This Index also covers Volume 1-THE HISTORY OF ROGERS RANGERS-The Beginnings, Loescher (1.). Any references for Volume 1* will be after those for this book ('Genesis').

Abercrombie, General James, English Commander, Lake George from 1; Rangers-Abercrombie's Eyes, 1; rebukes Rogers, 5; compliments Rogers, 20.*I: opinion of Rangers, 214, 261, 431; reluctance to promote Rogers, 262, note 259; Rogers' commission, 437.
Abercrombie, Captain James, report responsible for defeat at Tic., 11-12. I: on-party with Rogers, 94
Abraham, ——, Stockbridge R.R. Captured in St. Francis peace mission, 355; exchanged, 355.
Actions, I: Stark's March 21st Sortie, 350-2; Rum Sortie, 350-2; Rich Rogers' attack on Coutre Coeur, 352; the hunting scout, 355; Misbehaviour Scout, 355-6; Xmas Eve Tic. attack, 356-60; Arnoux's Defeat, 361; Morning Patrol, 363.
Adams, Edward, R.R. I: killed at Rogers' Rock, 369 (J.Stark's Co.)
Adams, John, R.R., captured, 351;
Akin, Wm., acting Sergt R.R. I: 72
Amesbury, William, R.K.R. (Rogers' Kings Rangers), attempt to destroy John Paul Jones warship, 196
Andersen (Anderson), Peter, Ensign R.K.R. Niagara rendezvous, 181; Prince Edward post, 197, 283.
Andrews, Ashel, R.R. at Miamis 245
Anonymous, Rogers Ranger Officer Diary references: Actions, 222, 218, 216, 235, 236, 240; Ranger Uniforms, Appendice IV, 248-250.
Anson, Wm., R.R. at Miamis, 245.
Aphrodite, Abenaki, references to: dance, 59; iii, 222, 224, 225.
Appy, John, Amherst's Sec'y, 45.

Arms, Rangers, I: 115-116.
Arnoux, Defeat by R.R., I: 361
Askin, John, Sutler, RR 127;Askin & Rogers partner, 164.
Aspinwell, Richard, R.R., Pontiacs War, 148, 272.
Atherton (Ethorington), Phineas, Lieutenant, R.R. valour at Frontenac, 26; rewarded, 26; commands, 123; Detroit Expedition, 229.
Atwood, Joshua, R.R. chops down Whipping Post, I: 205.
Avery, Elias, Ensign, St. Francis Raid, 59; party captured, 61.

Babington, ——, Capt. R.K.R., 181
Bacon, Jacob, R.R. Captured at Rogers' Rock, I: 369.
Baker, Robert, Vol. 44th, wounded-captured La Barbue Crk I: 112, 329
Banck, Josiah, Lieutenant RR, 124; accompanies Amherst, 124-125.
Banyar, Goldsbrow, doubts Rogers' veracity, I: 43-44.
Barbue Creek (Putnam's Creek) 120; battle losses (Names), I: 329-330.
Barlow, Abner, Corporal, R.K.R. noted spy, 190, 191.
Battles of Rogers Rangers: See Appendice II, 203, I: 312-388.
Battles: I: Isle of Mutton, 313-19 Barbue Creek, 112, 324-45; 1st Defense Ft.Wm.Henry, 350-2; Siege-Massacre Wm.Henry, 354-5; Rogers' Rock, 364-388.
Beale, ——, Ensign, R.K.R., 181.
Bellfore, ——, Ensign, Rogers' Rock Volunteer, I: 243.
Bennet, Elisha, R.R., Death, I: 70
Beard, Frank, RR, Miamis, 135, 245.
Beers, Joseph, Ens. RKR, 197, 283.
Beatie, ——, Ens. RKR, Hanged, 196.
Beaubien, Sergt. RR:
W.Stark's Wolf-dog 31; Louisbougg bloodhound scouts, 31; geneology, 253. I: 90-1; on muster-roll, 91.
Beverly, David, RR, Pontiac W, 154
Beverly, Thomas, Sergt, R.R. Escapes, 70, 89; Held-up, 89; capture 225; perilous trek, 94-5, 242, 103
Bills, Juda, RR, captured, 44, 237.
Blake, Timothy, RR, capture 24, 234
Blanchard, Col. Recommends Rogers to General Johnson, I: 26.
Bloodhound Scouts for deserters, I: 172, 239.
Boishebert, Sieurde Charles Desechamps, French partisan, 33, 207.

303

Bolton, John, Sergt. R.R., 209
Bowing, Timothy, RR, captured, 217
Boyd, John, R.R. captured, 44, 237
Boyd, Samuel, RR, rum confinement, I: 202; flogged, 203; cupidity, 204.
Bradford, Benjamin, R.K.R., pilot in Royal Navy, 200.
Bradley, Benjamin, Sergt, RR, 60.
Brady, Joseph, RR, captured, 217.
Breckenridge, David, Ens., RKR, 192
Breckenridge, James, Capt-Lt., R.K.R., 181; Liason for Rogers, 192; espionage, 193; temper, 192, 193; diplomatic scouts, 193.
Brewer, David, Capt., RR, 60 Guineas Scout, 21; in Three Battles, 38; near Captaincy, 44; Captain, 87; rescues escaped Rangers, 106.
Brewer, Jonathan, Capt. R.R., at Louisbourg, 27, 35, 72, 233; captures pirates ships, 34; L.George front: 87; Pointe au Fer, 95; Richelieu Raid, 100; Spruce Beer Scout, 106, 243; Point Rogers action wound, 107; Detroit, 128, 229 I: Ensign, 103; N.S. daring, 103; La Barbue Crk, 113; superceded for Captaincy, 143-4; rage, 144, 150; confines J. Stark, 169-70; courtmartial & acquital, 170, 425-6
Brewer, Moses, Capt. R.R. Mohegan Indian Co., 5; skill at Tic. Siege, 47, 48, 219, 239; discovers Rogers' whaleboats, 63, 241.
Brown, Thomas, Sergt. R.R. I: Narrative, 331-40, 418; 115; 157.
Budd, English Surgeon on H.M.S. at Rangers' Louisbourg Landing, 30.
Bulkeley, Charles, Capt., R.R., I: Indian Fighter, 102; able recruiter, 148, 421; Captain, 148; killed at Rogers Rock, 242, 246, 249
Bradbury, Sanders, Sergt R.R., Miamis vigil, 135, 245.
Brheme, Diederick, Lt.R. Engineers Three Battles, 37-8; Detroit, 128-34
Brown, Nicholas, RR, captured, 217
Burbank, Jonathan, Capt., R.R., 5; scouts, 2, 233; La Corne fiasco, 14-15; defeat, 42-3; killed, 216. I: Ensigncy, 81; personality, 162
Burbank, Nathaniel, Sergt. R.R., shipwrecker's fight, 65-66.
Burbeen, Paul, Clerk, R.R., 69, 92.
Burgin, Philip, Capt, N.J. I: 173, 426
Burnside, Thomas, R.R., I: 114.
Burton, Isaac, RR, captured, 217.
Bush, Zebulon, RR, I: defense, 154.
Butler, John, Lt., RR, wounded, 80, 219; St Paul Raid, 81; deadly dispatch duty, 112-13, 241; services, 114, skill at: Pt. Platon, 119, Varennes, 120, Last Battle, 120, Detroit, 128, Fts. Miamis & Quatanon, 132, 135, 245; holds Miamis, 136-7; accounts, 138, 270.
Butler, John, RR, captured, 351.
Butler, Capt Tom, Frontenac, 26.
Butterfield, Isaac, RR capture, 217

Cadet Co. I: names: 297-303, 186, 187-8, 429 note 202, 430 note 206
Cahill, John, RR, I: wounded, 149.
Cahon, Frederic, RR, 148, 272.
Camp Women, Sutlers employ, 106; droll incident, 266; I: 169, 188.
Campbell, Capt 80th, manouver, 45-6
Campbell, Archibald, Lt. R.R. 297 Cadet, 297; killed, 241, 249.
Campbell, Archibald Jr, Ensign RR, 1758 services: 14, 209g. I: 435.
Campbell, James, RR, 135, 245.
Cargill (Cargyll), Abernathan, Lt. RR, Rogers ' recommends, 107.
Carruthers, Francis, Ensign, R.R. Freshwater Cove hero, 29, 30, 31.
Castleman, John, Sergt. RR, 26.
Catlin, ___, RR close escape, 209.
Catto, James, RR deserted, I: 410.
Chalmers, Ronald, RR English Cadet, I: 298; on Rogers' scout, 93.
Chamberlin, Ebil, RR capture, 107; Montreal escape, 106, 244.
Chandler, Joseph, R.R. (kin to Abenaki Aphrodite), 148, 272.
Chase, Abner, R.R., capture, 217.
Cheeksaunkun, Jacob, The Elder, RR Capt. Mohegan Co., 44; men's rum, 44; defeat & capture, 45, 218; I: 68; inertia, 410; scalp scout, 93 Wood Crk, 92; disbanded, 96, 415.
Clark, James, Lt RR Ty Battle, 12. I: Sergt, 243; Ltcy award, 243.
Clark, John, Ensign RR, I: 243.
Clark, Nathaniel, RR killed, 369. I
Clark, Robt, RR I: Whip P.M, 203.
Clark, William, Sergt R.R. amazing escape, 44, Rogers intercedes, 43 I: captured at Rogers' Rock, 243.
Clay, Jonathan, R.R., captured, 217
Clish, Thomas, RR, S.C., 148, 272
Coburn, Pat, RR Miamis, 135, 245.
Collingwood, __, RR Cadet, 124.
Columbiere, French Capt, foray, I:83
Colson, Isaac, RR I: 70-1, 16-22.
Commando, defined, I: 235, note 247
Conky, Joshua, Sergt R.R., escape from English navy, 44; I: 369.
Cooper, Billy, RR, S.C., 148, 272.
'Coos', defined, I: note 3, p 400.

Counterfeiting, I: Rbt. Rogers, 264
Coutre Coeur, I: defined, 37; 41, 45
Craig, John, RR, Miamis: 135, 245.
Crain, Cloud, RR, I: killed, 369.
Creed, Francis, Vol. 27th, Lt., R.R.
I: awarded Lieutenantcy RR, 243.
Crofton, Edward, Lt. RR., Louisbourg, 32, 206; engages Montcalms dragoons, 81; I: Rogers Rock, 242 254, 255, 260; sketch, 298-299.
Croghan, George, Johnson agent, 132
Crow, Zach, RR, bravery, I: 154.
Crown Point: description, I: 403-5 'Cumberland', Rangers' flagship, 90.
Cummings, Elias, RR, I: capture, 181
Cunningham, Thomas, Sergt R.R., I: 161, 422.
Curtin, Capt John of ESSEX, attempt to impress Rogers Rangers, 44.
Cutter, Ammi Ruhamah, Surgeon, RR, I: 167-8; n. 169; 428, 169.

Dalyell, Capt James, Marins Defeat 17; Detroit, 155.
Darby, John, Col. 17th. Champion of RR berth for Lt. Cargill, 107
Darcy (D'Arcy), Robert, Lt. R.R.: maps Wood Crk-S.Bay, 65, 241; Indian escort, 66; 67; 1st Ltcy 104
David, Joseph, RR, captured, 217.
Davis, Lt., Royal Artillery, 128.
Dawson, Henry, RR, I: flogged, 202.
Day, Isaac, RR, I: Harvard Stdt. 182
Denbo, Elijah, RR, escape, 74.
Dewey, John, RR, captured, 217.
Dickey, James, RR, Miamis, 135, 245.
Dorey, James, RR, I: bravery, 154.
Downing, Ensign 55th, captured, 3-4
Dunbar, James William, Lt. 80th: death, 61; I: a Rogers Cadet, 95.
Duquipe, Joseph, Stockbridge Lt. R.R., 93; Detroit Expedition, 128.
Durantaye, Canadian Ensign, I: repulse at Rogers' Rock, 247, 249.
Dutton, Joshua, RR, I: hero, 154.

Eagles, John, Capt. R.Q.R., ruse at battle Heathcote's Hill, 174.
Eastman, Joseph, RR, Quebec feat, 95
Eastman, Samuel, RR, I: lost, 74-75.
Eastman, Stilson, R.R., finds cow for General Amherst, 49; I: 340-1
Edmonds, John, Corp. R.R., I: 114, killed at La Barbue Creek, 329.
Edmunds, Jonathan, R.R., I: 155 wd.
Edwards, Adonijah, R.R., 135, 245.
Elder, Charles, RR, I: W.P.Mty, 203.
Ethorington, (See: Atherton, P.).
Etowaukaum, Ensign Jonas, R.R., defeat, 2; killed, 48.

Evans, John, Sergt R.R. cannibal in St. Francis Raid, 61, 222.

Fall, James, R.R. Pontiac War, 154
Farnham, Timothy, Sergt RR, 245.
Farrington, Jacob, Lt. R.R. Pointe au Fer fame, 95-8; Richelieu Raid 100; 2nd Ltcy, 104; Cherokee War, 147-52, 272; Regular Vol., 152.
Farrington, John, RR capture, 217.
Farris, Wm., RR capture-exch, 217.
Faulkner, James, Lt RR, I: 243.
Ferguson, Israel, Lt RKR, 191-5.
Fish, Joseph, R.R., enlists 27th Regiment, 139; deserts, 139.
Fish, John, RR, I: furlough, 149.
Fisk, Joseph, RR capture-exc, 237.
Fisk, Sam, Corp RR I: killed, 114.
Flagg, Gershom, RR, captured, 24.
Flanders, Philip, Sergt RR I: 243.
Fleming, Samson, R.R. Detroit merchant, 155; joins Rogers, 274.
Fletcher, John, Lt. RR Takes Crown Pt., 48, 219; La Prairie, 52; Fight and capture, 53, 221; 67; 85.
Fontenay, French officer captured by Rogers, I: 73.
Fossit, Benj., Lt RR, death, 43.
Fowler, Abraham, RR, 148, 272.

Gage, Gen. Thomas: Frustrates Rogers, 36; despairigment, 37, 40-41
Gardiner, Andrew, R.R. Cadet I: 113; K. at Barbue Crk, 127, 329.
Gardner, George, R.R. enlists into 27th Regt. against Cuba, 145.
Gauph, Oliver, RR, captured, 217.
Gear, Rangers, I: snowshoes, 112-13
Gill, Marie-Jeanne, War Chief's wife captured by Rogers, 59.
Gilman, Garty, R.R. I: Counterfeiting, 20-1; R.R., 65; service, 409
Goodenough, Joshua, R.R. Tic., 207 Pointe au Fer, 227; I: Gruesome Scout, 190-2; saved from wolf, 197 close escape, 228; sketch R., 410
Goodwin, Luxford, Sergt R.R. Novel about cited, ii; perilous Que. mission, 95, 242, 111; 267.
Gordon, James, Sutler R.R., 127; in Rogers & Co. as Clerk, 164-5.
Gorham, Capt Joseph: Comdt Gorhams Rangers-N.S., 27; See Loescher (5) I: Rogers' seniority dispute, 171-2
Gray, John, RR capture-exch, 217.
Gray, Levi, RR, bravery, I: 154.
Great Warrior, Cherokee Chief, 146
Grant, James, Commodore, 1759-60, 91
Green Berets, similarity to R.R., introduction.

Green, Caleb, Ensign R.K.R., Secret Service, 191; Poughkinsie Sct, 195

Hackett, James, Sergt R.R., harrowing escape, 16, 209; builds warships, 91; Pointe au Fer, 95.
Hair, Wm., Lt. RR, Frontenac Exp., 26
Haldimand, Frederick, Gen., Command Ft. Ed., 36; Rangers' Mutiny, 41; ill-advised winter scouts, 42; fleeced by Rogers, 182-84; 1 battalion RKR under him, 185, 200.
Hale, Josiah, Sergt RR, I: kill,243
Hall, Samuel, RR, capture-exchnge 217; Re-capture, 70.
Hallowell, Jacob, RR, wd.-dies, 107.
Hamilton, Partridge, Sergt RR, I:- 182, recruiting, 428.
Hanns, Charles, RR, Ft.H.hero, 154.
Hartwell, Sergt R.R., accidentaly killed by English sentry, 7, 233.
Hatfield, Capt RKR, 181, 183.
Haviland, Wm., English Col. & Brig. constant disparigment of RR, 70, 227; would disolve corps, 103; I: predudice, 207-9, 216; snubs Rogers, 226; baits Rogers, 227, 237; treacherous act, 237, 436 n. 254.
Hazen, Ensign RR, 82; 122, 268.
Hazen, Moses, Capt R.R., 43; St. Anne's Raid, 72-3; captaincy, 73; commended, 78; cowboy, 78; Quebec scouts: 354; L'Ange Gardien, 79; defeats Langlade, 79; Montmorenci 80; takes prisoners, 80; Boon-qua rter scout, 219; Will-o-the-wisp, 81; disarms Canadians, 112; twarts cattle rustlers, 114, 226; takes Pt. Levi, 114; Old Lorette, 114-15, 226; morale strategy, 115 Battle Ste Foy, 114-18; marksmanship, 118; bravery, 117; wd., 117 Co. strength, 119, 267; Land venture with Robert Rogers, 165.
Headquarters Base Camps of R.R.: Rogers' Is., 1; near Ft.Wm.H., 5; Half-Way-Brook, 21; Castle Is., Dartmouth, N.S., 28; Louisbourg, 31; Chimney Pt., 99; 1760-Summer, Rogers' Pt., 103; 1758-9 Winter, 35, 254, 1759-60 Winter, 123, 268 1760-61 Winter, 141, 270; I: 169.
Henry, James, Sergt R.R. Original R.R., I: 114; Isle of Mutton, 114 Barbue Creek acc't, 331, capture, 330; Paul Bunyan yarn confuses French re: Rogers' Secret Water passage, 411; escape, 331; color illustration of, 104.
Herwood, Vol. Royals, death, 235.

Hewitt, Robert, R.R. captured, 42 false info to French, 42, 215.
Higgins, Paul, RR, Miamis, 135, 245
Hill, Ensign RKR Recruiting, 181.
Hobbs, Humphrey, Capt RR, Origin of Co., I: 98-102; famous Deacon Indian Fighter, 101; RR., 106 112; smallpox death, 103, 112.
Hodge, Sam, Jr., Capt Pioneer Co in RR, 108; service, 109.
Hodgkins, Jonathan, RR, I: 164
Hogg, Wm., RR, Miamis M, 135, 245.
Hoit (Hoyt), Stephen, Sergt RR, dies in St. Francis Raid, 60-61.
Holland, Stephen, Lt. R.R., 43; I: Sergt at La Barbue Creek, 114.
Holmes, Sergt RR, Recruiter, 85.
Holmes, Robert, Lt. RR, Scouts, 8 canoe ambuscade, 22-3, 213; Three Battles, 38; scouts, 47, 236, 238 explores Hudson R., 51, 240; Wigwam Martinique, 95, 243, 102-3 265; Detroit Exp., 128, 131; Ensigncy in Royal Am., 137; Commandant of Fort Miamis, 137.
Hooper, Jacob, RR, capture, 217.
Hopkins, Joseph, Capt of own Q.R. 155, 274; action, 158.
Hopkins, Joseph, Sergt-Major R.R. incredible fish exploit, 52-3; attempt to burn L'Esturgeon, 54, 240
Hopkinson, Tim, RR, cpt-exch, 222
Howard, John (Jonathan) Sergt RR, I: killed at Barbue Crk, 114, 329.
Howe, George Augustus, Viscount, 3 untimely death, 11; designs badge (button) for RR, 248.
Howgill, Francis, R.R., escape, 89
Hughson, Lt. RQR, killed, 175.
Humphreys, Sergt 27th, I: 244. vol
Hunter, John, jr. RR I: cptr, 369
Hurlburt, Daniel, Sergt RR, grim-action, 42; capture-feeds French misleading data, 42, 215.
Hutchings, Benjamin, Ensign, R.R. Dispatches to Wolf, 50, 81; capture by pirates, 50; winter resignation, 105; Capt, Mass province, 105; re-Ensigned R.R., 105, 107; rescues Rangers, 106.

Insley, Ensign RKR, 181.
Irwin, Wm., Ensign 80th, wager, 17

Jacob, Duke, RR, survivor SFR, 60
Jacobs, John, Stockbridge RR, 355
Jameson, James, English Surgeon, 98 lacks medicine for wd. RR, 226.
Jellison, Derry, RR, Miamis, 135, 245
Jewell, Sam, RR, Miamis, 135, 245.

Johns, Soloman, Lt. RKR, spy, 191
Johnson, Nathaniel,Corp, RR, I: 47
Johnson, Noah, Capt R.R., service: 37, 235; 65; 51, 239; 68; Pointe au Fer-wd.-dies on ship, 95, 98; I: Isle of Mutton, 36, 40; Ensign 47; commands, 61, 65; 1st Ltcy, 80 411; commands at Wm.Henry, 175-81 paroled, 181; petitions, 181, 427-8
Johnson, Sir Wm., Approves Rogers, I: 26; defends Rogers, 32-3, 44.
Jonas, Stockbridge Ensign, RR, 48.
Jonathan, escaped captive joins R. R., 93.
Jones, John, Capt R.K.R. Reknown, 197; daring, 198-199.

Kelsey, Moses, Sergt R.R. I: 182; killed at Rogers' Rock, 243.
Kenedy, Sergt R.R., wounded, 215.
Kennedy, Samuel, Lt. RR., Noted-Surveyor, I: 103; Barbue Crk, 113 127; gruesome death, 156.
Kennedy, Quinton, Capt 17thMessage to Wolfe, 50; capture, 56, 220; Cherokee War, 147; I: Scout race with Rogers, 85-86.
Kent, Michael, Vol 27th, I: 243.
Kerr, David, Sergt R.R. tragic end by English sentry, 7, 233.
Kimble, David, RR, I: informs, 156.
Kisensik, Nipissing Chief, 203.
Knowlton, Charles, RR, I: 154.

La Force, French partisan defeated by Rogers, 96; mortal wound, 98.
Lake George, I: description, 406.
Lakin, Oliver, RR, Quebec escape, 74
Lane, Daniel, R.R. Hazen's Post, 218; fierce ambush, 219; 220; Quebec service, 219-220.
Langy-Montegron, Ensign, French foe of R.R., 8; Rogers' Rock victory, 8; avoids clash, 8; defeat by Rogers, 9-11; Ranger Payroll Massacre, 83-4; Captures Tute and drowns in St. Lawrence R., 85; I: thorn in Rangers side, 83; 229-31 Rogers' Rock, 248-260.
Latterly, Wm., RR, Miamis, 245.
Leech, Sam, RR, I: first RR flogged, at Whipping Post, 199, 201.
Leighton, John, RR, I: 48.
Lindsay, John, R.K.R., gains confidence J. P. Jones to burn ship, 196
Lock, Joshua, Lt. RR, recruits, 257
Longstreet, John, Capt RKR, 181.
Longville, French partisan defeated at Pointe au Fer, 96, 98.
Lopos, Solomon, RR, I: 154.

Lotridge, Capt, leads Mohawks in Three Battles, 38-40; praised, 40.
Loudoun, Earl of, English Commander, plans for Rangers, I: 146, 420; Ranger bodyguard, 108, 419; proposes RR officers, 221, 432-433.
Lounsberry (Lounsbury), Wm. R.Q.R. grim death battle, 171, 229.

Macomb, John, Albany merchant associate of Rogers, 127.
McCormick, Caesar, Lt., RR., capture, 34; duress letters, 35, 214 exchange by Rogers, 43, 257; takes scalps, 79; recruiter, 85; 89 leads L Inf. Richelieu Raid, 99-100 key to Trojan Horse plan on St. Johns, 101; Detroit Exp., 128, 134 Michilimackinac, 133; Trader, 155 Pontiacs War, 155; Askin & Rogers partner trading venture, 164-165; Cadet in RR, I: 192.
McCoy, P., Corp RKR, Spy, 191.
McCurdy, John, Capt R.R., Louisbourg, 27; Jemseg Raid, 34; rescue scout, 34; accidental death, 43, 72 I: Isle of Mutton, 40; Sergt, 47; 2nd Ltcy, 81, 144, 425; scout, 166 prerequisite food & rum, 183-184; captures frenchman, 190.
McDaniel, Ranal, Sergt R.R., 25-26
McDaniel, John, alias Sullivan of-Boston, counterfeiter, I: 17-19.
McDonald, Gregory, Ensign, R.R. I: Cadet, 192; RRk, 241, 247, 249-51
McDugle, James, RR, killed, 369.
McKane (McKeen), Wm., Sergt R.R., captured-La Gallete-exchanged, 221
McKeen, John, R.R. Captured-burned at stake, I: 180-181.
McKay, Isaac, RR Capture-exch, 217
McLauchlan, James, R.R. I: prisoner to France- exchanged, 181.
McLean (McLane), Benj. R.R. accused of desertion-acquited, 125; West Indies, 142-4; Cuba, 145.
McMullen, Andrew, Lt. R.R. Service 14, 209; feud with Rogers overpromotion, 40, 260, 86; loses Cap taincy, 86-7, 104; heroism, 58.
McNeal, James, Corp. R.R. I: 70-1.
McSterling, RR I: stops Mutiny,205
Mainwairing, Ed., Capt RKR, 197.
Mamenash, Sam, RR Cher. W, 148, 272
Maps: I: R.R. Battles (end pp); La Barbue Crk, 125; Rogers Rock, 250
Marin, Canadian Col. defeat by Rogers, 17-18; I: thorn to RR, 83.
Martin, Joshua, Ensign R.R. 44; I: Counterfeit suspect, 17-18; Barbue

Crk, 114; wd-amazing escape, 135;
Sergeantcy & Ensigncy, 136.
Maxwell, Thompson, R.R. draftee.
 deadly race, 9; Marins Defeat, 211
Meloise, French Ensign. Forays, 183
Merchant Marine Academy-site of Rogers' most successful battle, 96.
Micmac Indians, fight with RR, 74.
Miller, John, RR, wounded, 80.
Miller, Jonathan, R.K.R. espionage
 191; Ballstown Mission, 195.
Miller, Wm., RR, P.War, 148, 272.
Misbehaviour Scout, I: 214, 431.
Mitchel, John, R.R. I: survivor, 70
Mohawks, beaten up by R.R., 21; 3
 Battles bravery, 39-40; praise, 40
 I: false alarm given, 45.
Montcalm's Cavalry, Rangers engage
 at Pointe-aux-Trembles, 81.
Moor, Hugh, R.R. Pontiacs War, 154
Moor, Increase, Lt. R.R. I: Sergt,
 wd-Barbue Crk, 114, 329; killed at
 Rogers' Rock, 243, 249, 243.
Moore, Sam, R.R., capture-exch, 217
Moore, Wm., R.R., harrowing captivity-escape by ruse, 343-344.
Morris, Wm., Lt. R.R., 23; 209; I:
 demoted, 114; Barbue Crk capture-escape, 114, 330-331.
Morrison, Hugh, R.R. I: wd-captured Barbue Creek, 329; dies, 330.
Munroe, Edmund, Sergt-Major R.R.,
 21; almost Ensign, 105.
Mutiny, Second Ranger, 40-42; I:W
 Post Mutiny, causes, 202-3, 201-210; Courtmartial, 304-11; English, dim view of, 213-219.
Myers, John, Capt R.K.R., Ballstown
 Raid, 188; spy, 192; detatched,
 191; Blake-Schuyler house capers,
 192; Ludlow's Regt. service, 191.

Nae, Robert, RR, capture, I: 369.
Napier, English Surgeon General:
 Negligence in furnishing Medicine
 chest to Rangers' Surgeon, 98.
Napkin, Wonk, RR, Crke War, 148, 272
Nash, Littlefield, RR, cptre-exc, 206
Naunauphtaunk, Jacob, Capt RR., 21,
 scouts, 2, 203; avoids fight, 3-4;
 Tic, 14; 1759 re-entry, 40; grief
 45; Message to Wolfe, captured, 50
 220; St.F.peace envoy, 125-6, 244
 I: Ltcy, 68; ambuscades, 324, 85,
 414; dictates journal, 85.
Neale, James, Capt R.R., presides
 at RR courtmartial, 21; leaves, 37
Nelson, Moses, RR, Pontiac War, 154
Nepash, Daniel, RR, Ibid, 148, 272.
Ninhem, Aaron, RR, cptr-escape, 252

O'Brian, Morris, R.R. captured-Tic
 9, 206, escapes impressment, 44.
O'Brian, Sam, R.R. C.War, 148, 272
Ogden, Amos, Capt RR, St. F. Raid,
 59, 63; Captaincy, 123-6; with Amherst, 123-6; rebuilds C.Pt, 138;
 West Indies service, 142-144.
Ogden, Nathaniel, Ensign, RR, 123.
On Party, defined: I: 415.
Outetat, French partisan, defeats-RR at Wood Creek, 2.

Page, Caleb, Ensign R.R., I: 81,
 411; killed-Barbue Crk, 112, 113.
Paige, Sergt RR, saves comrade, 9.
Parker Mt. I: 56.
Parnell, Robert, Sergt RR, I: 243.
Parrot, Abraham, R.R. I: Leader-Whipping Post Mutiny, 204-5.
Patten, John, Lt. RR Quebec fight,
 80, 219; discovers fleet, 118; commands Hazen's Co., 119; Pt. Platon,
 119, 227; at Varennes, 120, 228.
Pay, Rangers, I: 107-8; privates
 sold out by Rogers, 141-143.
Perry, Abraham, Ensign RR, I: 24.
Perry, D., RR Recollections, 354-5
Perry, Ebenezer, Corp RR, I: 114.
Phillip, Sergt RR, Indian King, 62
 first into Louisbourg, 254; St. F.
 Raid, 62, 63.
Phillips, John, RR, I: 148.
Phillips, Wm. Hendrick, Lieut R.R.,
 St. F. Rd, 62; Ensigncy, 94, 105; W.
 Martinique, 94; I: Sergt, 114; La-Barbue Crk, 129-30; Ensign, 148;
 148, 159, 422, 228; Rogers' Rock-capture, 242, 245, 254-5; 162.
Pollard, John, RR, I: escape, 179
Pontiac, Ottawa Chief, 129-30, 153-9
Porter, Noah, Lt. RR, scouts, 3, 4,
 I: priv leads W. Post Mutiny, 204
Portuga, Emanuel, RR, I: 115, 249
Pottinger, James, Lt. R.R. I: indescretions, 187-8; Cadet, 192;
 generosity, 242; R.Rock death, 249
Pringle, Henry, Capt-Lt 27th, I:
 volunt-R. Rk-surrenders, 243, 254-9
Pritchard, Azariah, Capt RKR, 189;
 noted spy, 189; captures, 190;
 black market operations, 191.
Prologue-Birth of RR, I: 17-22.
Promotions in RR, I: 160-2, 163.
Proudfoot, Chris, RR cptr, 106-7
Punishment, Method to RR, 53-4
Putnam, Major Israel, co-command
 under Rogers, 16; captured, 17, I
 scouts with Rogers, 34, 36-8, 45.

Ranger Prisoners, French held, 2-3

308

Ranger School, I: Rogers' formation, 184-9; disbandment, 192$29.
Rations, Ranger landing fare at Louisbourg, 29; I: daily, 54, 183 401; on party, 116, 117.
Red Head, Onondago Chief, Fort E, 26
Reynolds, Samuel, RR, capture, 70.
Rice, Isaac, RR, capture-exch, 206
Richards, Mitchel (Ben), R.R., I: saves boys life, 179.
Richerville, French Ensign, I: 383
Robertson, Sam, RR, captre-exc, 217
Robins, John, Ensign RKR 181,197,283
Roche, Boyle, Lt. 27th, I: 243, 259
Rogers' Island, Ranger base at Ft. Ed., 1; Rogers Island Historical Association, contemporary inhabitants; poeticly described, I: 91-3 414; flooded, 225-6, 434.
Rogers, James, Capt & Major R.R.-RKR, Louisbourg, 27; L. Labrador-Raid, 73-4; senior Capt Quebec, 78 lauded by Wolfe, 78; 82; L.George 87, 104, 106, 138-9; Pontiac War, 154-9, 245; rescues Rogers from F. prison, 167; Major-R.K.R., 181; assumes Rt.Rogers' debts, 184; St. John's Hdqt, 184, 186; espionage, 195, 247; corresspondence, 281; I: Ensign, 102; Barbue Crk, 112; defense Ft. W.H., 152; Halifax, 182
Rogers King's Rangers: organized, 179-81; Actions, 181, 186, 187, 188, 198-9; secret service, 188; Hdqrt, 189; posts, 181, 184, 197, note 356; Uniforms, 185, 278, note 337, drawing, 6, Appendix IV disbandment, 200-201, 283.
Rogers Queen's Rangers: organized, 170; recruits captured, 171; Hdqr 170; 1776-7 campaign, 172-77; Heathcote's Hill, 172-6; colours taken, 175; corps' composition, 177 lack of complete uniform-1776, 174 Uniform drawing, 6, text, 249-250
Rogers' Rangers: fame deserving of History, introduction; Battle losses, 118, 16, 23, 24, 31, 37, 43, 45, 48, 61, 79-80, 84, 98, 144; snowshoe skill, 114; Death: freezing, 113, 69; drowning, 134, 108, 267; accidental, 7, 72, 254; grim 60, 84, 42, 140; frostbitten, 70, 88, 141; taken prisoners, 2, 24, 35, 44, 53, 56, 85; exchanged, 67, 68, 107; amazing escapes, 3, 9, & 16, 23, 44, 52, 74-7, 89, 90, 106 107, 105, 91, 93; desertion, 53-4 125, 140, 73, 141, 270; courtmartials, 21; audacity of scouts, 2,

21, 22, 23-4, 28, 48, 49, 54-5, 58; ruses of, 49, 42, 115, 119; punishment of, 53-4; recruitment, 5, 7, 25), 25, 27-8, 253, 68, 87, 123, 44, 257, 85-7, 186, 281, 265 124, 268; bravery, 13, 29-30, 50, 74, 78, 79, 80, 110, 113, 118,157 158; marksmanship, 17, 18, 47 , 107, 118, 254; tactic reviews, 21 Gage's opinion of, 41, 254; rewar -ded, 26, 111, 113; Returns, 253, 25, 73, 263, 144, 145, 18), 184, 278; postal service, 124, 138-41; appearance alarms West Indians, 143; Drafts from Provincials, 108 258; Daily Orders, 46, 258-9; dis -chargments, 69, 263, 77, 82; revived: Pontiac's War, 154, 159, 274; American Rev., 170, 179-81; Officers & Non-Coms (See Loescher (2)); droll tales (Loescher (3)); I: value of, 164; character, 197, 201, 410; losses, 290-1; pay establishments, 304, 412, 420, 421; as N.H. Co., 23-4; Engineers, 24; build: Ft.Wentworth, 25; Ft. Ed.127 1755 Winter, 31, 47, strategy,110 English reliance on, 109; augmented, 412, 219-22; build snowshoes 233-4; Rogers' Own Co., 287, 400; six establishments, 63-4, 287-90; Rogers' Ranging Rules, 291-7; Cadet Co., 297-304; Pay establishments, 304; early Actions, 312-88 early Scouts, 389-94; Genesis to World War II, 407; cost of huts, 415; strengths, 417; recruiting officers contract, 428; pre-enlist ments, 219, 432; snowshoe road, 234; See Books by Author, i-ii.
Rogers, Richard, Capt R.R. I: 24, 32, 47, 411; 36, 40; 46-7; 61; 65 66; 72; 73; Capt, 80, 413; 139, 146; last action, 173; death, 175
Rogers, Robert, Major-Col, R.R., R Q.R., R.K.R. majority, 1; 1758 service: 1; wd., 4; Abercrombie's indictment, 5; drawing pwr for recruits, 6-7; strategy-Tic, 12-14; 14; 15; defeats Marin, 16-20; duel, 18; Easter boats, 25; recruit strategy, 25; last winter exp, 37 -40; Williams rank dispute, 37; squelches mutiny, 41, 255; foils disbandment, 43; frostbitten, 40, 255; presents bearskin, 45; defeats Bournie, 47; cuts Ty boom, 47 secret road, 49, 239; 49; St.F.Rd 56-65; Payroll Massacre, 83-4; near capture, 91; Richelieu Raid,

100-102; Haviland feud over command, 103; captures French fleet 109-10; pursues Bougainville, 110 comments on French Canadian women 110-1; corps reunited, 111; forms Trading Co., 128; Pontiac Pow-Wow 129-30; hung in effigy, 131; Capt. in Regulars, 134; trades commands 153; Pontiac War, 153-9; peculations, 160-6; Askin & Rogers Co., 164; Major Rogers & Associates, 165-6; loses to Gorham, 167; Americans prisoner, 167-8, 169-70; captures Nathan Hale, 171, 245; Howe's support, 175-6; Heathcotes Hill, 172-6; Bedford Raid, 176; White Plains, 176; 177; British envy, 177-8; boastfulness, 179-81 at Castine, 181; erroneousness, 182-4; divorce, 183, 279; dossier of Rogers' twilight, 184, 421. I: 1755-58: counterfeiting, 264-70, 17-22; Inquiry on Mutiny, 206 establishes reputation, 50; full-color plate by H. Loescher, frontispiece; humour, 227, 434; obedience-method, 75-6; offered Provincial Colonelcy, 216, 220; TROJAN HORSE plan, 222-3, frustrated, 239 has smallpox, 141; secret water passage, 79, 411, 437; wound, 127 140; awarded Majority, 262, 411; commission verbatim, 437; battles ix-x; scouts-expeditions, xi-xii.
Rogers' Rock: reference to, 1; RR bloody defeat, 3; survivors, 48, 252; battle illus by Ferris, I: 252; casualties-names, 369-370.
Rose, Samuel, RR, Miamis vigil, 135
Ross, Andrew, Ensign RR, I: 241.
Rossier, John, Sergt RR, 65, 241.
Ruiter, Henry, Capt RKR, 192.
Rum, Rangers' fondness for; 105-6; death, 140, 141; Stockbridges, 93 99, 147; Mohawks, 21, 252; I: Laced Rum, 111, 151; save from fire, 155; ration, 401; potency, 111, 419
Ryan, John, RR, I: killed R.Rk, 369

St Francis Raid: Individual participants, 223; Silver Madonna Legend, 222, Ranger accounts, 222, English accounts, 223, Provincial accounts, 224; French, 224; losses, 64, 223; survivors, 67, 224, 69, 223; Reference to Loescher's definitive study-ABENAKI APHRODITE Rogers' St Francis Raid, 222, 224 225; I: Rogers' early plans for stymied, 96-8, 111, 165, 416; 167

Samadagwis, Stockbridge R.R. betrays RR at St Fr.-killed, 59.
Scott, Capt. George, 40th, provissional command Louisbourg Rangers 28; landing, 29-ep; siege, 31-2.
Seat, Dematres, RR, I: 154.
Secret Service, by R.K.R., 189, 281-282.
Secret Water Passage, Rogers', confounds French, 238; location revealed, 49, 239; I: map, end pp.
Sever, Jacob, Sergt RR Ft.Ed., 26.
Severance, Martin, Sergt R.R., escape from Man-o-War, 44; I: courier, 83; Hudson R. scout, 189.
Shamburn, Christian, RR, Burbank's Defeat-capture-unique freedom, 217
Shankland, 'Shanks', R.R. Gruesome scout, I: 190-1; close escape, 228 illustration, 105; ambuscade, 361
Sharks, attack Rangers, I: 169.
Shepherd, George, RR, grim captre 42; exchanged, 217.
Shepherd, John, Capt R.R., Scouts-1758: 2, 22, 233, 234, 237, 260,; resigns, 46; R.Q.R., 175; I:sketch 423; Co. forms, 166, 423; stops W. Post Mutiny, 204-206.
Shepherd, Sam, RR cap-exch, 42, 217
Shepherd, Samuel, Ensign, R.R. I: recruiting, 182, 428.
Sherwood, Justus, Haldimand's British espionage co-chief, 188-89; RKR officers chief agents, 189-91.
Shirley, Wm, Governor, Mass., Plans for Rangers, I: 100-101, 416-418.
Shute, John, RR Quebec dispatches, 95; Reminiscences, 242; I: 114; account of Barbue Crk, 340-341.
Sillaway, Jonathan, RR I: cptr, 70
Sleater, Peter, RR hero, I: 154.
Smyth, Doctor George, British Espionage co-chief, 188, 189, 191.
Snell, Jacob, Ens. RR., Resigns, 26
Solomon (See Uhhaunwaumot, Solomon)
Speakman, Thomas, Capt R.R. I: 100 101; Boishebert action, 102; in R R., 112; Barbue Crk, 112-13; scalped alive, 103; grim death, 136-7
Spear, John, RR Miamis, 135, 245.
Spencer, Matthew, RR I: cptr, 369.
Spruce Beer, I: RR fond of, 111.
Stark, Archibald, L+ R.R. 3 Battle 38; naval duty, 91; W. Martque, 95
Stark, John, Capt R.R. 1758: 2, 11 12, 233; senior under Rogers, 5; Capt Abercrombie feud, 11-12; rescue, 236; decoy, 44-5; builds Crn Pt. Road, 51, 239; reviews RR, 68 declines Co. command, 68; seeks

Captaincy, 85-6; backs Rogers in 1775-6, 168-9; I: 1755-8: Lt, 24; home, 32; 2nd Lt, 65; ill, 66; importance at Barbue Crk, 112, 119-20, 121-2, 129, 340; 1st Lt, 81; Canada Scout, 86; Ft.Wm.H.command 149-50; saves Fort, 151-2; sortie 350-2; wd, 155; personality, 162; smallpox, 167; locked-up, 169-70; misses ship, 170; Misbehaviour Scout, 193-7, 355-6; 229; 407; relieves Rogers Rock survivors, 259.
Stark, Samuel, Lt. R.R. Falls from horse-cannot serve, 1760, 94.
Stark, Wm., Capt R.R. Louisbourg-27; seeks re-Capt, 85-6; I: Cadet 90; Wolf-dog companion, 90-91.
Steel, John, RR, Pontiacs War, 154
Sterling, Hugh, RR Clerk, I: 24, 32.
Sterling, James, RR, Pont.War, 274
Stevens, Nicholas, partner in Askin & Rogers trading firm, 164-5
Stephens, Roger, Ensign R.K.R. Spy disguise, 191, 194; Doc Smyth spy pay dispute, 195; espionage, 194.
Stevens (Stephens), Samuel, Lt. RR tragic omissions-St Francis Raid, 58, 61-2, 64, 401-403; Amherst's censor, 63; Rogers' wrath, 64; courtmartialed, 65; I: RR Cadet, 192.
Stevens (Stephens), Simon, Capt R. R. Negotiates exchange, 2; capture, 8, 205; escape odyssey, 74-77; Quebec Siege, 77; news-reporter RR, 95, 266; re-joins Rogers, 104; Pointe au Fer, 95; Richelieu Raid, 98; Captaincy, 104.
Stevens, Lt. RR, Ambushed, 215.
Stewart, John, RR, I: capture, 369
Stinson, John, Capt RKR, 181, 200.
Stockbridge, Mass., I: described ; 409; warrior strength, 409-410.
Stockbridge (Mohegan) Rangers: Recruitment, 5, 251, 44, 258; Amherst's criticism, 40, 254, 44, 45, 257, 262; Dischargment, 24, 252; Cherokee War service, 147-52; refuse to don British uniforms, 152
Stone, Nathan, Lt. R.R., 342; capture, 8; exch, 67; at Que, 74; 87 241; wd, 110; Regular Ensign, 273
Strang, Daniel, Capt R.Q.R. Hanged as spy, 171, 246.
Sutlers to R.R.: John Askin, James Gordon, 127, I: Levi, 151, Best, 238

Taylor, Peter, Sergt RKR, Spy, 191.
Tecomans, Job, RR, I: 427.
Tervin, Richard, R.R. West Indies, 142-5; in 17th against Cuba, 145.

Thompson, Wm. R.R. Miamis dty, 245
Three Battles, Rogers' last, most successful winter action, 36-39.
Throckmorton, John, Lt., RKR, 197 Prince Edward Is. station, 283.
Ticonderoga ('Ty'), described, I: 405-406.
Tincomb, Ebenezer, RR cpt-exc, 217.
Titcomb, Capt John, N.H. Prov. Rangers. I: temp-assigned to RR, 168 424; biographical sketch, 424.
Torry, John, R.R. cpt-exchange, 209
Townsend, Jacob, Sergt RR I: Corp, 151; Sergt, 243; k. at R. Rock, 243
Trepezac, French Capt, defeat, 9-11
Tribout (Tiebout) Lt R.R. Reported killed, 215; recruiting, 215.
Trojan Horse attack on Crown Point Rogers' plan, I: 222, 433; stolen by Abercrombie & Loudoun, 223-225
Trumball, Vol. 42d. Stark saves, 44
Turner, George, Lt. R.R. Observesdance of Ab'enaki Aphrodite, 59; escapes Dunbar's Massacre, 61.
Tute, James, Capt RR Biscuit scout 15; Hunting exploit, 24, 213; Ty map guide, 38; relief mission, 39 Capt, 46; harrowing scout, 51-52, 221; captured-La Gallete, 55-56, 221; loans to captive RR, 222, army adopts his 'blanket-sails', 65 exch, 67; leads Rogers' Co., 68; 2nd capture, 84-5, 241; exch, 107 La Gallete route utilized, 108; I Sergeant at Rogers' Rock, 243.
Tyler, Wm., Lt., R.K.R., Spy, 191; Squire Palmer seizer attempt, 195

Uhhaunwaumot, Solomon, Capt R.R. commands Stockbridge Mohegan Cos, 66; Capt, 89; rum slows march, 93 Richelieu Raid, 100; I: Ensign, 68
Uniforms of RR: Rogers advances money for, 43; officer loses uniform 50; uniform made-up, 66-7; advance, 82; blanket coats-Detroit Exp 131; deserters, 139; QR lack of endangers lives, 174; R.K.R., 185 note 337, p 423; Rifle frock, 381; See Appendice IV, 248-50, also, plate, 6; I: 1755-58: nondescript uniform, 271-86, 26, 48, 106; at-Barbue Crk, 115; blanket-coats, p 116; officers sword, 205; Loudouns proposal, 219-20; new uniforms, 236; Rogers' jacket, 256; Shirleys plan, 417; Stockbridges, 236, 435 Appendice B, 271-86; Color Plates Major Rogers, frontispiece, Sergt and Private, xiii, 104-105.

Vander Heyden, David, jr, R.R. capture at R.Rock, 20; escape, 252.
Van Tyne, Richard, Lt., R.R., 123; with Amherst, 123-6; ardous mail service, 139-41, 270; rejoins Ogden, 141; W. Indies death, 142, 144
Vaudreuil, Marquis de, Governor of Canada, exagerated accounts of: St F. Raid, 64; Pointe au Fer, 226
Venays, Peleg, RR I: deserted, 410
Vesteroot, Lowris, RR, 148, 272.

Wait (Waite), Benjamin, Ensign RR: Freshwater Cove bravery, 204; recruiter, 123; Detroit, 128; holds Ft. Miamis, 133, 135, 245; ardous march, 136, ingenuity, 269.
Wait (Waite), Joseph, Capt RR: 43; Ft. Brewerton post, 68, 123; Detroit, 126, 129, 132-3, 229; West Indies duty, 142-5; I: 1755-8: 242
Wall-Pieces, artillery used by Rogers, I: 35-6, 40-41.
Walker, Isaac, RR, cpt-exch, 217.
Walker, Wm, RR, capture-exch, 217.
Walsh, Capt RKR, Rogers abuse, 183.
Wallace, Hugh, Vol. Inniskillings, cited for St F. Raid service, 64.
Walter, Charles Joseph, Sergt R.R. I: Barbue Crk, 114, grim order to 123-4; recruiting, 151.
Watson, Jonathan, RR I: dead, 369.
Wauwaumpequvnaunt, Stockbridge Co. Clerk, I: delinquency, 96.
Way, David, RR, Crke War, 148, 272.
Webster, Daniel, RR Miamis, 135, 245
Wellesley, Sergt RR, action, 209.
Wells, Aggrippa, R.R., captured at Burbank's Massacre, 44; rescued from English navy by Rogers, 43.
Wells, Phillip, Sergt R.R. veteran in Rogers Own Co. Convoy, 46, 238
Wendell, Henry Isaac, Capt R.R. At Ft. Stanwix, 25; resigns, 43; desserter problems, 256; Co. hist, 257
Wentworth, Benning, Governor, N.H. I: peculations, 400
Whipping Post Mutiny of RR, I: 304 311; Mutiny defined, 409.
White, James, Ensign R.R., Loudoun sponsored, I: 242; killed at Rogers' Rock, 242, 245, 246, 249.
Whiteham, Daniel, R.R: in Cherokee War platoon, 148, 272.
Whitworth, John Dean, Lt. R.K.R.: Old Lorette post, 181; Loses sight of eye in harrowing winter scout, 200; obtains England leave, 200.
Williams, Moses, Corporal R.K.R.: secret service, 191.

Wilson, John, Ensign R.R.: Isle au Noix Scout, 51; explores La Barbue Creek, 65, 241; re-builds Crown Point bastion, 138.
Wind-Mill-Point, landmark of RR, I: 87.
Wobi-Madaondo (White Devil) Title bestowed on Robert Rogers by enemy French Indians, 4.
Wolf, General James, commands landing at Louisbourg, 29.
Wolf, French partisan, defeats Rogers at Ticonderoga River, 3-5.
Wonton, James, R.R. Pontiac W., 154
Wood, Elijah, RR Miamis, 135, 245.
Wood, John, Ensign, 17th, on party with Rogers, 94; killed at Point au Fer, 98.
Woodall, Benjamin, R.R. I: captured at Barbue Crk, 329; collaborator with French, 156.
Wright, Corporal, R.R. draftee, killed, 9.
Wrightson, Rogers Rock Vol. It 243

****

Self-portrait of author Burt. G. Loescher

"Ranger Goodwin's Rum Rescue Sortie, Fort William Henry, 22 March 1757." Oil painting by Burt Loescher. Rangers moving rum to safety of fort.

"Falcons of the Lakes." Robert Rogers and John Stark
on the summit of Black Mountain, 1756.
(Sunset over Lake George.) Oil painting by Burt Loescher.

"Major Robert Rogers receives surrender of Detroit from French."
(Note effigy of Rogers atop fort wall.) Oil painting by Burt Loescher.

www.ingramcontent.com/pod-product-compliance
Lightning Source LLC
Chambersburg PA
CBHW060942230426
43665CB00015B/2029